Behavior Modification
in Applied Settings

The Dorsey Series in Psychology

Editor HOWARD F. HUNT *Columbia University*

Behavior Modification in Applied Settings

ALAN E. KAZDIN
Associate Professor of Psychology
The Pennsylvania State University

 1975

THE DORSEY PRESS   Homewood, Illinois   60430
Irwin-Dorsey International   London, England   WC2H 9NJ
Irwin-Dorsey Limited   Georgetown, Ontario   L7G 4B3

First Printing, January 1975

ISBN 0-256-01681-X
Library of Congress Catalog Card No. 74–12928

Printed in the United States of America

To Eve, Joann, and Nicole—
past, present, and future
sources of inspiration

Preface

The purpose of this book is to provide an introduction to behavior modification techniques in applied settings. The major focus is placed upon the application of operant principles, implementation of behavior modification techniques, and measurement and evaluation of program effectiveness. The applications include a variety of settings such as hospitals and institutions, schools, day-care centers, and the home, as well as "outpatient" applications. By emphasizing the application of operant procedures, details can be provided that ordinarily would be sacrificed in a cursory review of the entire domain of behavior modification.

A number of books on behavior modification have appeared, including introductory manuals designed for specific audiences such as teachers, parents, or mental health workers, and scholarly texts which present theoretical disputes and review the general field. The hiatus between "how-to-do-it" manuals and extensive scholarly reviews which deemphasize applied research in behavior modification is obvious. This is further reflected in the lack of resources available for undergraduate audiences of diverse disciplines who wish to learn about research and practice in behavior modification. In this book I attempt to emphasize applied research and clinical intervention techniques and achieve a balance not usually found in behavioral texts.

Various features of the content and emphasis should contribute to the unique coverage of behavior modification in applied settings. First, a number of topics are detailed which are infrequently discussed in other texts. These include an elaboration of the methodology of assessment and experimentation in applied operant work, techniques to develop response maintenance and transfer of training, applications and problems of self-control procedures, and ethical issues. Second, a number of populations in treatment, rehabilitation, and education, as well as other settings, are included throughout the text. Variations of techniques are illustrated with a wide range of target behaviors, clients (e.g., patients, residents, delinquents, children, students, spouses), and staff or agents of behavior change (e.g., attendants, teachers, parents, peers). Third, I have tried to point out complexities of applications and nuances of research which pertain to effective treatment. Applied research is quickly subject to oversimplification by practitioners who seize one or a few principles and techniques. Yet, the failure of a number of treatment interventions may well be due to the failure to profit from the existing empirical findings in their full bloom, ambiguity, and (perhaps) confusion.

Early chapters (1, 2, and 3) place the behavioral approach, broadly conceived, in the context of traditional conceptualizations of behavior. These chapters detail assumptions and learning principles, and discuss popular misconceptions of and objections to the application of operant procedures. Perhaps the most distinguishing characteristic of behavior modification in applied settings is the stance taken toward objectification of behavior change and program evaluation. Thus, a detailed discussion of methodology of behavioral interventions in terms of assessment, evaluation, and experimental design is provided (Chapter 4). A major portion of the text elaborates positive reinforcement, punishment and negative reinforcement, and extinction (Chapters 5, 6, and 7). For each principle, diverse technique options, dimensions which dictate program effectiveness, limitations, and salient issues are reviewed. As noted earlier, detailed consideration is provided for applications of self-control (Chapter 8) and issues and techniques pertaining to response maintenance and transfer of training after a behavior modification program is withdrawn (Chapter 9). The final chapter (10) discusses ethical issues implicit in the use of a behavior change technology in general and with respect to controversial treatment procedures. In addition, future directions of applied operant work are discussed in this chapter. At the end of the book is a glossary which provides brief definitions of technical terms employed in the text. While the glossary is useful for review or simple clarification, it does not provide sufficient information to fairly represent the phenomena or principles elucidated in the text.

It is with great pleasure that I acknowledge the assistance of Howard F. Hunt, Consulting Psychology Editor for Dorsey Press, and Jeanne P. Phillips both of whom extensively reviewed the entire manuscript and provided thoughtful, constructive, and incisive comments. The book was also guided by Hal Arkowitz and A. Robert Sherman who critically reviewed select sections. Johanna Zeman and Sandy Ranio provided essential secretarial aid. I am grateful for research support by a grant from the National Institute of Mental Health (Grant No. MH 23399) which facilitated completion of the book.

December 1974   ALAN E. KAZDIN

Contents

1
Introduction

The procedures one employs for psychological treatment, rehabilitation, education, or counseling depend to a large extent upon the view of "human nature" to which one adheres. Treatment strategies follow directly from presuppositions and conceptions of normal and abnormal behavior, personality development, and human motivation. Given the behavior of a particular individual who has been referred for treatment or who is residing in an institutional setting, vastly different interpretations, inferences, and assumptions can be made about events in the past or present which account for behavior and about what needs to be done to effect therapeutic change. Behavior modification can be fully understood only by presenting the differences which exist between traditional and behavioral conceptions of man.

APPROACHES TOWARD PERSONALITY AND BEHAVIOR

Although there are a myriad of conceptions of personality and behavior (Hall & Lindzey, 1970), they can be grouped according to whether behavior is viewed primarily as a product or personality attributes which inhere in the individual or of external environmental determinants. Of course, such a dichotomy is not completely accurate, but it does represent the different emphases of intrapsychic and behavioral positions (cf. Mischel, 1971).

1

Intrapsychic Approach

Traditionally, personality has been viewed by many theorists as an assortment of psychic forces inside the individual, including drives, impulses, needs, motives, and personality traits. "Normal" behavior represents a socially acceptable expression of intrapsychic forces or the development of socially appropriate traits. On the other hand, abnormal behavior reflects a dysfunction or "disease" process in personality or the development of maladaptive traits. Maladaptive psychological processes are considered to account for abnormal behavior.

The traditional view can be referred to as an intrapsychic approach because of the role accorded psychological forces in the individual which propel behavior. Variations within the intrapsychic model result from an emphasis on different psychological forces or motives as determinants of behavior. Two major versions of the approach will be described briefly. These two views are referred to as the medical or disease model and trait theory.

Medical Model. A major version of the intrapsychic approach is referred to as a *medical* or *disease model* because it is analogous to the view of disease adhered to in the practice of medicine. In medicine, internal conditions of the individual (e.g., bacteria, virus, lesions, disease, organ dysfunction) account for symptoms (e.g., fever, infection, discomfort). However distressing the symptoms may be, they are not the "real" problem, that is, the disease or abnormal condition which interferes with normal functioning. Treating the symptom alone is insufficient because the underlying condition which is causing the problem has to be remedied.

Extending the analogy from medicine to psychology has led to a concern with supposed internal motivational causes of behaviors rather than with the behavior itself. Behavior is considered to reflect basic underlying motives which form personality. An individual's behavior is peculiar or diseased because of some underlying defect in personality. Although it is obvious that the medical model has been useful for physical ailments, its extension to the treatment of problems in psychotherapy, education, counseling, and behavioral rehabilitation has been disappointing.

Sigmund Freud's (1856–1939) psychoanalytic theory of personality contributed greatly to adherence to the medical model by emphasizing that behaviors can be traced to underlying psychological drives. He explained virtually all behaviors by referring to manifestations of unconscious personality processes. Understanding behavior required a careful scrutiny of personality to determine the meaning of behavior, that is, what motives behavior represents. The psychological processes and motives behind behavior were regarded as existing in the individual. The Freudian view frequently is referred to as a *psychodynamic* view. Dynamics refers to a branch of mechanics in which phenomena are explained by referring to energy forces and their relation to motion, growth, and change in physical matter. Freud's dynamic view of personality describes behavior in terms of psychological energies or motivating forces, drives, and impulses, and their interrelation. Growth and psychological development are traced to the psychological impulses and their expression at various stages early in the child's development. Diverse behaviors can be traced to the expression of a few psychological forces to which they owe their origin.

Freud posed three structures of personality: The id, which houses instincts and provides the source of psychic energy (libido) for all psychological processes and behavior; the ego, which interacts with the demands of reality in fulfilling instinctual wishes; and, the superego, which represents the internalization of social and parental standards and ideals of behavior. These structures operate in constant conflict. Each personality structure contributes in determining whether an impulse will be expressed, and precisely when and in what form it will be expressed. The expression of psychic energy can be traced to different sources of instinctual gratification as the child develops. Freud delineated stages of psychosexual development through which everyone passes. At each stage, the source of pleasure or instinctual gratification is associated with different areas and functions of the body. As the child develops, the expression of psychic energy invariably leads to conflicts with reality and within the structures of personality. Anxiety reactions, defense mechanisms, and alternate modes of behaving result from instincts not obtaining direct and immediate expression. Impulses, such as attraction toward the opposite-sexed parent, may not be resolved and result in a breakdown of normal personality development. Normal behavior develops from the expression of impulses, wishes, and desires in socially appropriate ways. Abnormal behavior, according to the psychoanalytic view, is attributed to maldevelopment of personality, and the disruption of the normal unfolding and expression of drives and needs, and their gratification. Psychological drives can become blocked or fail to find expression in socially appropriate ways. Drives and unresolved conflicts may, however, find expression in psychological symptoms or aberrant behaviors.

Criticisms have been levied against the Freudian position including the difficulty in verifying many of its propositions scientifically, inconsistencies within the theory itself and the therapeutic procedures derived from the theory, and lack of empirical support in many areas (e.g., aspects of child development) in which relevant research has been conducted (cf. Stuart, 1970). There have been revisions and additional contributions to Freudian theory which give a greater role to environmental determinants (Hall & Lindzey, 1970). However, for our purposes it is only important to note the traditional orientation toward behavior which has not been radically altered by followers who have supplanted Freud's views.

Trait Theory. The Freudian view is not the only intrapsychic position.

Trait theory also posits underlying personality structures which account for behavior (Mischel, 1971). Traits refer to consistent relatively enduring ways of behaving which distinguish one individual from another. Traits are inferred from behaviors which seem to persist over time and across various situations. Although different trait theorists disagree on the traits which best explain behavior, they all adhere to the notion that there are behavioral patterns which are consistent and these patterns are expressions or signs of underlying traits. A trait position is familiar to virtually everyone. In everyday life, people frequently allude to traits as aggressiveness, kindness, carelessness, dominance, submissiveness, honesty, laziness, and others to explain behavior.

When traits are employed as summary labels to characterize apparent patterns of behavior, they may be quite useful. For example, if a person is referred to as being very kind (having the trait of kindness), this may be useful in describing that this individual, in fact, behaves or has behaved in a particular fashion. However, frequently traits are used to *explain* behavior. Traits are inadequate as explanations of behavior for at least three reasons.

First, traits are inferred from behavior. A person who behaves in an aggressive fashion is considered to have the trait "aggressiveness." The trait which has been inferred from behavior is used to account for behavior. For instance, the reason a person behaves aggressively is attributed to his trait "aggressiveness." Yet, how does one know there is a trait of aggressiveness without inferring it from behavior? The account of traits and behavior is circular. To be meaningful, the existence of traits would have to be determined independently of the behaviors they are supposed to explain. One possible rebuttal to this objection is that traits are not inferred from a single behavior performed in one situation but from different behaviors performed in a variety of situations. The behavior of individuals with various traits or a great amount of a given trait is consistent across situations and over time. This view brings us to the second criticism of traits as an explanation of behavior.

As a second point, evidence suggests that individuals do not always perform consistently across a variety of situations and over time, as would be predicted from a trait position (Mischel, 1968). Also, different behaviors which are considered to make up a general trait often are not highly correlated. For example, an individual might be labeled as honest or as having the trait of honesty. Yet evidence reveals that various behaviors which might make up such a personality trait are not performed consistently. An individual who performs honestly in one situation may not perform honestly in another situation. Similarly, a person may perform one behavior thought to reflect the trait of dependency but not perform other behaviors considered to comprise the same trait. Much of behavior is situation specific. As situations change, a person's responses change as well.

For example, children display different patterns of aggressive behavior (Bandura & Walters, 1959) and social behavior (Redd, 1969) depending upon the person with whom they are interacting. Apparently, the consistency in behavior required to support a trait theory of personality is lacking. The consistency that an individual *perceives* in the behavior of someone appears to come from conceptions of the perceiver rather than the person he is observing (e.g., Dornbusch, Hastorf, Richardson, Muzzy, & Vreeland, 1965).

A third criticism of a trait explanation of behavior is that the antecedent conditions which explain traits are not explained. If traits account for behavior, what accounts for traits? How do traits originate? Skinner (1953) has noted that a behavior is not explained by relating it to an underlying trait or mental state until the trait or state has been accounted for. He refers to underlying concepts which are used to explain behavior in this way as "explanatory fictions" or "mental way stations." Instead of giving a complete account of behavior, the trait explanation only goes partially back in the causal chain of behavior. Very often, attributing behavior to a trait *appears* to provide an explanation of behavior. Yet, because the traits themselves are not explained, no actual explanation is provided.

Despite the criticisms of the psychoanalytic and trait theories—two popular versions of the intrapsychic model, the model has persisted in some form as the guiding view in mental health and education. The model pervades virtually all aspects of clinical lore including psychological assessment, diagnosis, and treatment of "psychological" problems.

Assessment and Diagnosis.   The intrapsychic model has strongly influenced psychological assessment and diagnosis of behavioral disorders. Because people are assumed to have underlying psychological motives or traits which account for their behavior, emphasis is placed upon assessing underlying personality rather than observing behavior directly. Assessment, then, focuses upon underlying motives which are assumed to explain behavior. The overt behavior which may have caused the client to seek treatment or to be institutionalized is not of direct interest. For example, an individual may seek therapy to overcome anxiety which arises in social situations. The specific situations which appear to precipitate anxiety are not focused upon. Assessment is concerned with the client's psychodynamics or traits. Through psychodynamic assessment, the psychologist attempts to provide global descriptions of personality, to reconstruct the individual's psychological development, and to determine how the person reacted to important psychological impulses (e.g., sex and aggression) in his or her past, what defense mechanisms have developed, and what basic characteristic traits or psychic defects account for behavior. It is believed that once these psychological processes are revealed, the source of the behavioral problem will be evident.

Projective tests exemplify diagnostic tools of traditional personality assessment. These tests attempt to assess personality indirectly through behaviors such as reactions to inkblots, creative stories in response to ambiguous stimuli, free associations, or other unstructured tasks. Projective tests provide the client with an ambiguous situation on which he or she must impose meaning and structure. The responses are considered as signs which reveal personality structure, psychodynamics, and unconscious motivation. Conclusions are made by interpreting the meaning of the behavioral signs and inferring underlying processes. Interpretation of projective tests requires clinical judgment to extract meaning from the responses. There has been serious criticism of the reliability and validity of these interpretations in predicting behavior (Lanyon & Goodstein, 1971). Individuals who interpret the tests often disagree on the psychological processes or disorders to which test responses are attributed. On the basis of these and other reasons, the overall utility of projective tests has been questioned (Mischel, 1968, 1971; Peterson, 1968).

In addition to projective tests, there is a plethora of psychological tests and inventories which assess aspects of the client's personality, character traits, and psychological needs, deficits, or defects (e.g., tests of anxiety, paranoid tendencies, extraversion, impulsiveness, brain damage, and intelligence).

An important characteristic of traditional assessment is that the client who is tested is temporarily removed from the situation in which his or her maladaptive behavior occurs. Thus, the tester may never observe the client's characteristic "real-life" behaviors in the test situation. In addition, the testing situation itself or the individual who administers the test may influence behavior (Masling, 1960). Of course, since traditional assessment is concerned with personality patterns, rather than behaviors which follow from them, it is assumed that personality dictates the pattern of responding across all situations. As mentioned earlier, there is little evidence for the existence of personality traits to which consistent performance across situations can be attributed (Mischel, 1968). In any case, the tests administered attempt to provide a profile of traits or a diagnosis of problem areas in personality or psychological development. In clinical use, the purpose of such tests is to understand behavior and describe or diagnose personality.

A major task of diagnosis is to assign a label to an individual which implies the underlying condition or defect responsible for the behavioral problem. The labels include "schizophrenia," "neurosis," "mental retardation," "learning disability," "brain damage," "hyperactivity," "emotional disturbance," and numerous others which depict the motivational problem, or inherent deficit, defect, or disease. The major focus has been on identifying disorders and symptom patterns which go together. Once the disorders are clearly delineated, it is hoped that the etiology of the disorder will be more readily discovered. The rationale is that if the cause can be uncovered, knowledge of the treatment and prognosis of the disorder will follow.

The purposes of diagnosis are to describe the presenting problem, identify conditions related to its occurrence, suggest a therapeutic plan to alter the problem, and predict the outcome of treatment (Stuart, 1970). These purposes have been fulfilled with many disorders in medicine. However, there are several problems in extrapolating the traditional diagnostic approach to behavior problems. The use of traditional diagnosis in psychiatry has met with great disillusionment (Kanfer & Saslow, 1969; Zigler & Phillips, 1961). Often there is low agreement between professionals who independently assign patients to diagnostic categories (e.g., Schmidt & Fonda, 1956). Also, there are great differences in the behavior of persons ascribed the same diagnosis as well as similar behaviors in individuals assigned diverse diagnoses. Diagnosis of a person seems to provide little information beyond the "symptomatology" which was already known when the diagnosis was made. Specifically, little information is given about the etiology, treatment of choice, and prognosis, which should be major advantages of using diagnosis and classification (Kanfer & Saslow, 1969; Zigler & Phillips, 1961).

Treatment. One would expect that once assessment and diagnosis are completed, the information gained would be useful in treating the client. However, this is not the case. Traditional assessment is used minimally or is neglected entirely by practicing clinicians conducting therapy (e.g., Meehl, 1960; Rogers, 1951). Assessment of underlying personality provides little information which can be used for treatment (Peterson, 1968) or educational purposes (Blanco, 1970; Hewett, 1968). The failure of assessment and diagnosis to be related to treatment has been a great concern of psychologists (Arthur, 1969; Goldfried & Pomeranz, 1968; Kanfer & Phillips, 1969).

The medical model has had relatively little to recommend in the way of treatment for individuals whose behavior is labeled abnormal in some way. Psychological treatments based upon the medical model have not advanced as well as have medical treatments for physical disorders. Yet the promise for effective treatment is implicit in the development of psychiatric hospitals, residential settings, outpatient clinics, and other facilities modeled after medical treatment. The efficacy of treatment for psychotics, neurotics, sociopaths, retardates, delinquents, emotionally disturbed children, and others has been seriously questioned in recent years (Dunn, 1971; Eysenck, 1966; Fairweather & Simon, 1963; Levitt, 1971; Paul, 1969a). There is little actual treatment with demonstrated efficacy that can be provided. Individual or group psychotherapy or counseling, which is carried out in an outpatient and inpatient setting, is regarded as a general treatment strategy for patients independent of the "personality problems" or diagnosis (London, 1964; Stuart, 1970). In actual practice,

depending upon the orientation of the therapist, a client receiving psychotherapy is required to relate aspects of his or her experiences to the
therapist to uncover underlying personality. Therapy can progress only
when underlying aspects of personality are revealed and altered.

For many individuals, treatment even may be associated with deleterious effects. For example, psychotherapy with different types of patients
(Bergin, 1971) and institutional care for psychiatric patients (Goffman,
1961; Scheff, 1966) and the retarded (Kaufman, 1967) sometimes are associated with decrements in adaptive behaviors. Treatment based upon the
medical model requires that psychiatric patients and institutional residents
give up many of their personal responsibilities and lose certain rights
which make the break with society even greater than the presence of
deviant behaviors alone. The institution fosters dependency and lack of
self-sufficiency which may detract from the individual's subsequent adjustment to the community. The stigma resulting from institutionalization
ensures that posthospitalization adjustment will be difficult at school, home,
or in the community.

The psychodynamic model assumes that problematic behaviors cannot themselves be treated since they are only symptoms of the underlying
problem. If treatment focused upon the actual behaviors, the individual
would not be "cured." Even if the behavior were changed without treating
the underlying disorder, another symptom might substitute for the problem behavior. This notion is referred to as *symptom substitution.* Symptom
substitution is predicted by the dynamic model because the impulse, drive,
psychological conflict, or deficit which was expressed in the symptom,
may still seek expression and produce new symptoms. Cure can only
result from removal or reduction of the impulse, drive, or conflict which led
to the behavior. There has been a great deal of dispute about whether
symptom substitution occurs, whether it can be assessed empirically,
whether substitute symptoms can be predicted in advance, and whether
their occurrence necessarily supports the dynamic model (Bandura, 1969;
Cahoon, 1968; Stuart, 1970; Ullmann & Krasner, 1965, 1969). At present,
there is little evidence which demonstrates that deleterious effects follow
treatment of specific behavior problems. In fact, as discussed later, beneficial side effects frequently follow behavioral treatment.

Role of the Professional. Since traditional approaches focus on the
underlying personality problem or character disorder (e.g., neuroses and
psychoses), defect (e.g., retardation), or emotional disturbance (e.g., hyperactivity), it is no surprise that professional training in assessment, diagnosis, and treatment is extensive. The complexity of the psychological
problem or deficit warrants treatment from highly trained professionals.
Yet, there are many undesirable consequences of this approach. First,
professionals provide treatment or rehabilitation in situations which often
remove the client from the environment in which the problem behaviors

were performed. For example, often psychiatric patients, retardates, and emotionally disturbed children are withdrawn from the community in which their behavior has been deficient to a noncommunity situation where a special treatment or training service is provided. Analogously, children who show severe problem behaviors in the home or classroom are treated by counselors, social workers, and therapists in an office away from the situation in which the problem behaviors are performed. The resemblance of this approach to medical treatment is obvious. In medicine, patients frequently are taken out of their everyday life and placed in a special setting for treatment by someone who is trained to administer special procedures. Only when the patient is cured can he or she return to community life. In any case, psychological treatment, as dictated by the intrapsychic model, usually takes place in a situation (e.g., office or institution) different from that in which the problem was evident (e.g., the home). This is undesirable because behavior in the special situation is not likely to resemble the problematic behavior in the original situation. Moreover, the environmental conditions which contribute to the problem behavior may be present only in the original situation.

A second undesirable consequence is that there are too few professionals for the number of clients who need treatment and therapy, special training and education, and rehabilitation (e.g., Sobey, 1970). The manpower shortage necessitates that numerous individuals with behavioral problems or psychological impairment go untreated and that others are treated en masse. Reliance upon professionals alone cannot resolve the "mental health crisis." A large reservoir of potential personnel which could be employed for treatment and rehabilitation purposes, namely, nonprofessionals (parents, teachers, peers, spouses, and friends) has not been utilized. Nonprofessionals can be used directly to provide treatment and to serve training functions. However, according to traditional views of therapy and training, there is little that nonprofessionals can do in the way of treatment because they cannot be easily trained to alter the underlying problems or basic defects in the individuals with whom they interact.

The main role of nonprofessionals has been to identify behavior problems and refer the clients to professionals rather than to do something directly to alter the problem. When recommendations are made to nonprofessionals, often they are nonspecific and provide little insight on how to alter problem behavior. For example, teachers of emotionally disturbed children are instructed to accept the child and convey understanding or to satisfy the child's demands so that a relationship can be established (cf. Hewett, 1968). These recommendations, however, do not lead directly to actions resolving the problems for which the child was identified and labeled "emotionally disturbed." By not actively employing nonprofessionals as therapeutic agents, a large source of manpower is neglected.

A few investigators have responded to the manpower problem by determining whether nonprofessionals can conduct tasks traditionally considered to require extensive training. In fact, nonprofessionals are often as effective as professionals, and in some cases more effective. For example, in one investigation (Rioch, Elkes, Flint, Usdansky, Newman, & Silber, 1963), married women with two years of part-time training were adequate as psychotherapists in treating clients with varied problems. Poser (1966) evaluated the relative impact of psychiatrists, social workers, and undergraduates in altering the behavior of psychotic patients. The undergraduates were not trained in psychotherapy nor informed how to conduct the therapy sessions. They conducted group discussions whereas psychiatrists and social workers conducted group psychotherapy. The patients who were seen by the undergraduates showed greater gains than patients who received no treatment or who were treated by psychiatrists or social workers. Similarly, in a rehabilitation setting, Truax (1967) compared counselors working in a traditional manner, counselors assisted by aides (trained nonprofessionals), and counselor aides functioning as counselors. On measures of client progress, the best results were obtained by the counselor aides functioning as counselors. In other reports, parents have been trained to perform therapy with their children. Also, college student volunteers have had therapeutic impact on various client populations (cf. Guerney, 1969). Other functions aside from treatment or therapy have been accomplished by nonprofessionals. For example, Allerhand (1967) showed that after three training sessions, parents administered intelligence tests as effectively as did psychology graduate students.

In spite of the favorable results obtained with the use of nonprofessionals, this resource has not made substantial impact in traditional psychological treatment, education, and rehabilitation. It is usually assumed that little impact can be made by individuals who are not thoroughly trained to deal with psychological problems.

Impact of the Medical Model

There has been a major beneficial effect of adopting the medical model of deviant behavior that should not be ignored. Prior to the medical model, ancient and medieval conceptions attributed deviant behavior to possession by demons, evil spirits, or supernatural powers. Individuals were thought to be inhabited by spirits as retribution for their wickedness and sins. Exorcism was required to treat abnormal behaviors. Often, harsh and inhumane procedures were used (e.g., flogging and starvation) to make the body uninhabitable by the spirits. Recasting the deviant individual as mentally ill or diseased has contributed to increased sympathy and humane treatment. Although the public currently still rejects and negatively evaluates individuals who have been labeled mentally ill or who have associated with psychiatric treatment (e.g., E. Cumming & J. Cumming, 1957;

Nunnally, 1961), the attitudes probably are more favorable and treatment is more humane than would be the case if demonology were widely practiced. Of course, there are still differences between being physically and mentally ill, such as in the social stigma and ostracism which results from psychological abnormalities (Scheff, 1966).

A possible disadvantage of adopting the medical model has been that pessimism may result from diagnosis and traditional formulation of the problem (Stuart, 1970). The problems clients have are described in terms which suggest that they are not readily amenable to change. Terms are used which implicitly or explicitly state that there is a defect, deficit, inability, or deeply rooted cause. The labels imply a permanent state which is not alterable. For example, "hyperactive" behavior is frequently used to imply brain damage or cerebral dysfunction. Even though brain damage is applied as a diagnosis, very often with little or no substantive basis (Werry, 1967), it suggests that there is little hope in altering the problem. Brain damage does not have a readily available cure. Other deficits, including psychiatric disorders, provide little optimism. When defects of personality development are considered responsible for the person's problem, there is little that can be accomplished in the way of treatment. Thus, an unfortunate consequence of applying the medical model to deviant behavior is that the problem is inferred as being in the person and, therefore, is less amenable to treatment than if the problem could be altered by factors in the person's environment. Pessimism stems from assuming that the problem is severe, deeply rooted, caused by trauma in one's past, and cannot be readily altered. Of course, in any given instance such pessimism may be warranted. Yet this cannot be determined *a priori* but only after available treatment alternatives have been systematically applied and evaluated.

Behavioral Approach

The behavioral approach departs from the traditional conception of behavior by rejecting inferred motives, hypothesized needs, impulses, and drives which supposedly explain behavior. Rather, emphasis is placed upon environmental, situational, and social determinants which influence behavior. The behavioral approach considers the majority of behaviors to be learned or alterable through learning procedures. The focus is placed upon behaviors which have been learned or need to be learned. Explicit attempts are made to train behaviors rather than to alter aspects in the person which, according to the medical model, underlie behavior.

Abnormal behavior is not regarded as distinct from normal behavior in terms of how it develops or is maintained. Abnormal behavior does not represent a dysfunction or disease process which has overtaken normal personality development. Rather, certain learning experiences or a failure to receive or profit from various learning experiences can account for behavior. Principles of learning explain how behavior develops, whether or not the behavior is labeled as abnormal.

Labeling behavior as abnormal is based upon subjective judgments rather than objective criteria (Bandura, 1969; Szasz, 1960; Ullmann & Krasner, 1969). A given behavior may be viewed by different people as abnormal or normal. For example, fighting among male children may be regarded as an expression of masculinity by peers and parents but regarded as a sign of emotional disturbance by teachers and school counselors. The individual who evaluates behavior plays a major role in deciding whether it is normal or deviant.

The social context is also important in determining whether a given behavior is regarded as deviant. For example, staring out into space with a fixed gaze is acceptable when one is traveling on a bus and looking out a window. Yet, staring into space while standing on a street corner may be taken as a sign of abnormal behavior. Behaviors which seem similar are differentially interpreted depending upon the social context. Abnormal behavior is inferred from the degree to which behavior deviates from social norms (Scheff, 1966). Since social norms vary across cultures and across groups within a given culture, it is difficult to objectively define criteria for abnormal behavior. For example, aggressive behaviors labeled as antisocial reflect patterns of behavior which are socially condoned and strongly supported in many peer groups where street fighting and crime are commonly accepted activities. Labeling the behavior as antisocial and indicative of psychological disturbance is based on value judgments rather than evidence of "diseased" psychological processes. The differences in behavior across individuals reflect differences on a continuum rather than differences in illness and health.

Of course, where there is an objective basis for making a diagnosis, such as cases of brain damage, organic psychoses, and other physiological aberrations, there may be clear qualitative bases for distinguishing normal from abnormal individuals. Yet even with individuals who have organic impairment, the problem is in the behavior that is deviant rather than the impairment. Lindsley (1964) expressed this point in the case of retarded children by noting that: "Children are not retarded. Only their behavior in average environments is sometimes retarded. In fact, it is modern science's ability to design suitable environments for these children that is retarded [p. 62]." With careful design of the environment, retarded children can be trained to engage in a variety of responses. Individuals considered abnormal perform in ways which distinguish them from their peers. However, the differences are in behavior rather than psychological illness or defect. A goal of behavior modification is to provide learning experiences which promote adaptive and prosocial behaviors in the individual.

Types of Learning

Three types of learning are considered important in developing and altering behavior: classical or respondent conditioning, operant conditioning, and observational learning.

Classical Conditioning. Classical conditioning, investigated by Pavlov (1849–1936), is concerned with stimuli which automatically evoke responses. Certain stimuli in one's environment such as noise, shock, light, and the taste of food *elicit* reflex responses. These stimuli are referred to as unconditioned stimuli. The reflex responses elicited by these stimuli are referred to as respondents or unconditioned responses. Respondents frequently are considered involuntary or automatic responses which are not under control of the individual. Examples of respondents include salivation in response to the presence of food in one's mouth, pupil constriction in response to bright light, flexion of a muscle in response to pain, or a startle reaction in response to loud noise. The connection between the unconditioned stimulus and the response is automatic, i.e., not learned. However, reflex behavior sometimes occurs in response to a stimulus which does not automatically elicit the response. Through classical conditioning, a stimulus which is neutral, that is, does not automatically elicit a particular reflex, is made to elicit a reflex response. To achieve this, the neutral stimulus (referred to as a conditioned stimulus) is paired with an unconditioned stimulus. Pairing a conditioned stimulus with an unconditioned stimulus eventually results in the conditioned stimulus alone eliciting the response (referred to as a conditioned response). The process whereby new stimuli gain the power to elicit respondent behavior is classical or respondent conditioning. In respondent conditioning, events or stimuli which *precede* behavior control the response.

A dramatic example was provided by Watson and Raynor (1920) who demonstrated that fears could be learned through respondent conditioning. An 11-month-old boy named Albert served as a subject. Albert freely played with a white rat without any adverse reaction. Prior to the study, the investigators noted that a loud noise (unconditioned stimulus) produced a startle and fear reaction (unconditioned response) in Albert. In contrast, a white rat given to Albert to play with did not elicit any adverse reaction. The investigators wished to determine whether the startle reaction could be conditioned to the presence of the white rat. To condition the startle reaction, the presence of the white rat (neutral or conditioned stimulus) was immediately followed by the noise. Whenever Albert reached out and touched the rat, the noise sounded, and Albert was startled. Over a period of one week, the presence of the rat and the noise were paired only seven times. Finally, the rat was presented without the noise, and Albert fell over and cried. The conditioned stimulus elicited the fear response (conditioned response). Moreover, the fear generalized so that other objects he was not afraid of previously (e.g., a rabbit, dog, Santa Claus mask, seal-skin coat, and wool) also resulted in the fear reaction. This demonstrated that fears can be acquired through respondent conditioning. Of course, whether fears evident in everyday experience in fact *are* acquired through respondent conditioning is difficult to say, since one rarely has access to an individual at the time fears develop. Other evidence suggests that fears may be acquired for objects with which the individual has had no direct personal contact (Bandura, 1971; Rachman, 1972). Independently of how fears are actually learned, respondent conditioning may be useful in ameliorating fears because the power of conditioned stimuli which elicit fear reactions can be altered.

Some behavior therapy techniques are derived from a respondent conditioning framework. A widely used treatment of enuresis (bed wetting) is based upon classical conditioning. Enuresis can be conceptualized as a failure of certain stimuli (bladder cues) to elicit a response (waking) so the individual can get up and urinate appropriately. To condition waking to the bladder cues (distension), a stimulus which elicits waking is required. O. H. Mowrer and W. A. Mowrer (1938) devised an apparatus to classically condition waking to the cues which precede urination while the child is asleep. The apparatus includes a liquid-sensitive pad which is placed in the child's bed. As soon as the child urinates, a circuit is closed and an alarm is activated. The alarm serves as an unconditioned stimulus for waking. Bladder distension which precedes the unconditioned stimulus eventually elicits waking prior to urination and sounding of the alarm. The procedure results in control of urination and permits the individual to sleep through the night without urinating (Ross, 1972). Although the procedure was originally derived from classical conditioning, its precise interpretation is a matter of dispute (Lovibond, 1964; Ross, 1972).

Another procedure derived from a classical conditioning framework is called *systematic desensitization* (Wolpe, 1958) and is used primarily for the treatment of anxiety responses. Certain cues or stimuli in the environment elicit anxiety or fear reactions. The fear can be altered by conditioning an alternative response to those cues which is incompatible with fear responses. The procedure employs a nonanxiety response, usually deep muscle relaxation, which is considered to be incompatible with fear. The fear-eliciting cues, placed in an ascending order on the basis of their arousal value, are paired with the relaxation response. The client relaxes and imagines a scene which includes mildly anxiety-provoking cues. While being relaxed, the mild anxiety which might arise is inhibited by the deep relaxation. Gradually, as relaxation is paired with the mild anxiety cues, scenes with greater anxiety-eliciting cues can be imagined with little or no arousal. Relaxation becomes associated with each scene in the hierarchy of items which is imagined. Finally, the capacity of the stimuli to elicit anxiety is eliminated. Altering the valence of stimuli closely adheres to the respondent paradigm. Other behavior therapy techniques derived from respondent conditioning have been used to alter a variety of behaviors, including excessive eating, drinking, cigarette smoking, and deviant sexual behavior (see Bandura, 1969; Kanfer & Phillips, 1970; Yates, 1970).

Operant Conditioning. A major portion of human behavior is not involuntary nor *elicited* by stimuli in the sense of reflexive reactions. Rather, many behaviors are *emitted* spontaneously and are controlled primarily by their consequences.[1] Behaviors amenable to control by altering consequences which follow them are referred to as *operants* because they are responses which operate (have some influence) on the environment, and generate consequences (Skinner, 1953). Operants are strengthened (increased) or weakened (decreased) as a function of the events which follow them. Most behaviors which are performed in everyday life are operants. They are not reflex responses controlled by eliciting stimuli. Examples of operant behaviors include reading, walking, working, talking, nodding one's head, smiling, or any response freely emitted. Operants are distinguished by virtue of being controlled by their consequences. The types of consequences which control behavior will be elaborated in the next chapter.

Most of the behaviors altered in applied settings are operants. Clients engage or fail to engage in responses which could be controlled by altering consequences. Speech in mute individuals, academic, self-care, or social skills in retardates, aberrant behavior in psychotics, aggressive acts in delinquents, and similar responses are operants which can be modified by altering the consequences which follow behavior. It is for this reason, in part, that the book will be devoted to operant conditioning techniques.

It should be pointed out that the distinction between respondent and operant conditioning becomes blurred in many situations (Kimble, 1961). A response may be elicited (respondent conditioning), yet be controlled by consequences which follow it (operant conditioning). For example, crying may be elicited in a child in response to an aversive event (a look of anger from a parent which may have been associated previously with physical punishment). Once the crying begins, it may be maintained by its consequences (e.g., sympathy or cuddling). This may exemplify how crying episodes can develop into frequent tantrums. Independently of how the tantrums begin, they can be maintained or eliminated by altering their consequences (Hall, Alexrod, Tyler, Grief, Jones, & Robertson, 1972; Nordquist, 1971; Williams, 1959).

---

[1] There is evidence that some responses previously considered involuntary such as heart rate, blood pressure, intestinal contractions, vasomotor reflexes, and galvanic skin responses can be altered by the consequences which follow them (Kimmel, 1967; Miller, 1969).

Another reason that the distinction between respondent and operant conditioning seems vague is that operant behaviors can be controlled by antecedent stimuli. Operant behaviors are performed in certain situations with various cues present. When the consequences which follow behavior consistently occur in the presence of a particular set of cues (a certain person or place), the cues alone increase the probability that the behavior is emitted. The stimuli which have preceded the response set the *occasion* for the response to be performed. For example, the sound of music may serve as a stimulus for singing or dancing. This is not an example of respondent conditioning because the antecedent stimulus (music) does not force the response (singing) to occur. In operant conditioning, the stimulus does not produce a response; it only occasions the response or increases the probability that the response will be performed (Reynolds, 1968). (The control that stimuli exert over operant behavior is detailed in Chapter 2.)

The major difference between respondent and operant conditioning should be kept in mind. In respondent conditioning, the primary result is a change in the power of a stimulus to elicit a reflex response. In operant conditioning, the primary result is a change in the frequency of the response emitted or a change in some other aspect of the response such as intensity, speed, or magnitude.

Observational Learning.   Observational or vicarious learning, or modeling (Bandura & Walters, 1963) includes both types of responses discussed above (respondents and operants). Observational learning occurs when an individual observes a model's behavior but performs no overt responses nor receives direct consequences himself. The behavior is learned by the observer from merely watching a model. By observing a model, a response may be learned without actually being performed. Modeling can train new responses as well as alter the frequency of previously learned responses.

To clarify modeling effects, it is important to distinguish *learning* from *performance*. The only requirement for learning via modeling is the observation of a model. The modeled response is assumed to be acquired by the observer through a cognitive or covert coding of the events observed (Bandura, 1969). However, whether a learned response is performed may depend upon response consequences or incentives associated with that response. The importance of response consequences in dictating performance has been demonstrated by Bandura (1965). Children observed a film where an adult modeled aggressive responses (hitting and kicking a large doll). For some children, the model's aggression was rewarded, for others, aggression was punished, and for others, no consequences followed the model's behavior. When children had the opportunity to perform the aggressive responses, those who had observed the model punished displayed less aggression than those who observed aggression rewarded or ignored. To determine whether all children had *learned* the responses, an attractive incentive was given to children for performing aggressive responses. There were no differences in aggressive responses between the three groups. Apparently, all groups learned the aggressive responses, but consequences to the model and observer determined whether they would be performed.

The extent to which modeling stimuli influence performance also depends upon similarity of the model to the observer; prestige, status, and expertise of the model; the number of models observed; among other variables (Bandura, 1971; Rachman, 1972). As a general rule, imitation of a model by an observer is greater when the model is similar to the observer, is more prestigious, is higher in status and expertise, and when there are several models performing the same behavior.

Modeling procedures have been used to alter arousal and fear responses (Kazdin, 1973a, 1974a; Meichenbaum, 1971) which might be considered respondents, and aggressive responses (Bandura, 1965) and verbalizations (Schwartz & Hawkins, 1965) which might be considered operants. A classic application of modeling to alter behavior was reported by Jones (1924). A young boy, Peter, was afraid of a rabbit and several other furry objects (e.g., fur coat, feather, cotton, and wool). Peter was placed in a play situation where three other children and a rabbit were present. The other children, selected because they were unafraid of rabbits, interacted with the rabbit in a nonanxious fashion. Peter touched the rabbit immediately after observing others touch it. Other procedures were employed with Peter to overcome his fear, such as associating the rabbit with the presence of food, so it is unclear what the precise contribution of modeling was in reducing his fear.

Recent studies have been reviewed which attest to the efficacy of modeling as a therapy technique (Bandura, 1971; Rachman, 1972). Observational learning has had an increasingly important role in altering behaviors in applied settings, such as speech in Head Start children (Lahey, 1971) and predelinquents (Bailey, Timbers, Phillips, & Wolf, 1971), social skills in withdrawn children (O'Conner, 1969), and interpersonal skills in juvenile delinquents (Sarason & Ganzer, 1969) and adults (Kazdin, 1974b). For individuals who do not readily perform responses which are modeled, imitative behavior can be trained by reinforcing it directly (e.g., Baer & Sherman, 1964).

Types of Learning: Summary. Each of the three types of learning has been used extensively for treating a variety of problems traditionally seen in clinical settings. However, in applied settings where groups of clients receive training or treatment, operant conditioning procedures have dominated. Nonetheless, knowledge of the other types of learning is essential for two reasons. First, respondent conditioning and modeling are valuable as behavior change techniques in their own right. Second, operant conditioning procedures as ordinarily practiced include aspects of other types of learning. For example, an operant program in a classroom setting may increase desirable student behavior (e.g., working on assignments) of one student by following it with a favorable consequence or event (e.g., praise from the teacher). Yet, modeling and respondent conditioning may be operative in the situation in addition to operant conditioning. Students other than the one who is praised may increase in desirable behavior because of modeling influences, i.e., observing peers (Kazdin, 1973c). Classical conditioning might also be involved in control of classroom behavior. For example, the teacher may shout (unconditioned stimulus) at a student which leads to a startle reaction (unconditioned response). The presence of the teacher within close proximity of the child (conditioned stimulus) may, through repeated association with shouting, eventually elicit anxiety and arousal (conditioned response). Of course, if proximity of the teacher to the child elicits anxiety, this might detract from the teacher's reinforcing properties. As is obvious by this point, the behavioral approach draws heavily on the psychology of learning to explain how behavior develops, is maintained, and is altered. The behavioral view, just as the traditional view of personality, has far-reaching implications for the assessment and treatment of behavior problems.

Assessment.   The behavioral approach toward assessment of behaviors departs radically from traditional diagnostic assessment (Arthur, 1969; Mischel, 1968; Peterson, 1968). The focus is on the behaviors which are to be altered rather than on the underlying personality considered to cause behavior. Although a problem may be described in vague or general terms (e.g., hyperactivity), the behavior modifier seeks to clarify these terms by observing the behavior that requires change and the events which precede and follow the behavior. For example, if an attendant claims an institutionalized retarded child has a "bad temper," the behavior modifier would want to measure the behaviors which prompted the attendant to make the statement, the frequency of these behaviors, and the antecedent and consequent events which are associated with any outbursts.

Two components of assessment are usually used by behavior modifiers: (1) assessment of behavior itself and (2) assessment of the events which precede and follow the behavior. In short, assessment focuses on the behavior of the client as well as environmental events. Assessment of the behavior to be changed (referred to as the *target behavior*) is essential to ascertain the extent of the "problem" or the extent of change that is required. Observed behaviors are of direct interest in their own right, rather than as reflections of underlying psychological problems. Assessment also is made of the factors which precede and follow behavior. These factors may be useful in altering the target behavior. Events which precede behavior may include the presence of a particular person, instructions, and other cues in the environments that affect the frequency with which a response is performed. Events which follow behavior include favorable events such as attention, praise, candy, prizes, or other "rewards" which may be useful in increasing behavior; undesirable events such as reprimands, isolation, and loss of privileges, which may be useful in reducing behavior. Assessment of such environmental events which go on outside of the person is unlike traditional assessment which measures processes inside the person. (A detailed description of behavioral assessment in applied settings is provided in Chapter 4.)

Treatment. Behavior modifiers place a great deal of emphasis upon external events in the environment which can be used to alter behavior. This is not to say that events within the individual do not influence behavior. However, the emphasis on overt behaviors and on external situational determinants permits the behavior modifier to readily alter specific determinants which influence behaviors. The behaviors shown by a number of individuals in treatment, rehabilitation, and educational settings may result from internal factors such as physiological deficiencies or anatomical anomalies. Yet, adaptive behaviors can be learned which minimize the limitations imposed by actual physical aberrations. Even if a person's behavior is thought to have an organic basis, principles of learning may still make dramatic changes in behavior, as shown with mentally retarded clients and autistic or hyperactive children with known organic problems. Most behaviors for which treatment and rehabilitation are sought can be altered through direct manipulation of environmental events.

Behavior modifiers are concerned with isolating the events which maintain deviant behavior or develop adaptive behaviors where deficiencies exist. To this extent, the behavioral approach is concerned with those events which determine or cause behavior (Bandura, 1969). Yet the determinants sought are not intrapsychic factors or underlying motives. Moreover, instead of considering early childhood events as responsible for present behavior, behavior modifiers focus on current environmental events which affect and maintain behavior.

Behavior modifiers do not adhere to the notion of symptom substitution, for which there is a paucity of support. Behaviors are not regarded as symptoms of some problem but the problem itself (Eysenck, 1959). Thus, altering a problematic behavior is not considered likely to result in a replacement by another problem behavior, primarily because behaviorists do not consider such behavior as reflecting supposed psychic impulses which seek expression. In fact, behaviorists predict that once a particular problem behavior is altered for an individual, other aspects of his or her life and behaviors may improve as well. The beneficial effects of treating one behavior may spread or *generalize* to other behaviors. For example, if the behavior of a "hyperactive" child is altered so that he or she can sit in class and pay attention to lessons, it is likely that other behaviors (such as academic performance), may improve, since the child can now learn his or her lessons. Moreover, socially desirable behavior on the part of a deviant student increases the probability that peers will develop greater interest in him or her and promote social interaction. Similarly, if a stutterer is trained to speak more fluently, additional positive changes might be expected to result. He or she may be more "confident" and "extraverted" and less "shy" in his or her everyday life. Changing one problem may begin a series of changes in the person's life.

Diverse behavioral techniques have noted the generalization of beneficial effects to behaviors not originally included in treatment for anxieties and fears, speech disfluencies, self-destructive behaviors, social responses, "psychotic" behaviors, and appropriate classroom behaviors (Kazdin, 1973g; Mahoney, Kazdin, & Lesswing, 1974). Thus, altering one behavior can inadvertently improve other behaviors not directly focused upon. Of course, it is possible that a person who has one behavior altered will still have additional problems. However, this is far removed from the notion of symptom substitution. Similarly, it is possible that once deviant behavior is reduced, the person has no socially appropriate response in his or her repertoire to take its place (Cahoon, 1968). However, this deficit can be alleviated by developing appropriate behaviors while eliminating inappropriate ones.

An important aspect of behavior modification is that treatment usually is carried out in the settings in which the behavior requiring change is evident, such as the home and school. This is distinguished from traditional treatment where inpatient or outpatient services are provided similar to medical treatment. Numerous advantages accrue to treating problems in the situations in which they arise. First, since behavior is situation specific, isolating the individual from the situation in which a problem behavior arose may hide the behavior which needs to be changed. For example, if a hyperactive child is given individual counseling, it is unlikely that the behaviors which are a problem at home or at school will be evident in the counseling situation; it is the problem behaviors at home and at school which require alteration and not the behaviors in the counseling situation. Second, alteration of a response in a situation removed from the "real world" may not alter behavior in the situation in which behavior was originally a problem. Even if behavior is altered in the counseling setting, it is unlikely to carry over or generalize to other situations. A third advantage of altering behavior in the actual environment rather than isolating the individual from others is that the deleterious effects of institutionalization, mentioned earlier, will not add to the client's problems. Moreover, there may be less stigma if the person is treated in the natural environment than if mental health professionals are sought for treatment (cf. Phillips, 1963).

Role of Professionals and Nonprofessional "Natural Agents" in Every-

day Life. The behavioral approach requires the use of natural agents who normally are in contact with the clients in everyday life. Individuals who have the greatest contact with the client include teachers, relatives, spouses, peers, supervisors, and colleagues. Individuals who are in contact with the client play the major role in altering behavior because they have the greatest opportunity to regulate the consequences which control behavior. Moreover, individuals in contact with the client observe the behaviors in the actual situations in which they are performed so they are in the best position to focus on the behavior as it is actually occurring.

Utilizing individuals who are with the client is especially important since they often contribute to deviant behavior. Indeed, staff, teachers, and parents often contribute to or support those behaviors they wish to eliminate (Patterson & Reid, 1970; Wahler, 1972). To alter the behavior of the client requires that behavior of the agent responsible for the client is altered first. Thus, working with nonprofessionals is often the best way to guarantee change in the clients.

Professionals have a role in training and consulting with nonprofessionally trained individuals to carry out procedures which are likely to alter behavior. Ideally, training includes instruction in identifying problems, selecting treatment goals, and evaluating program efficacy. Lectures, demonstrations, and feedback for actual performance are used to accomplish training of nonprofessionals (Kazdin & Moyer, 1975). Nonprofessionals have included parents, teachers, attendants in institutions and day-care centers, peers, college students, and spouses (cf. Ayllon & Wright, 1972; Guerney, 1969). The principles of operant conditioning are readily amenable to implementation in applied settings by nonprofessionals who can control antecedent and consequent events which can be used to alter behavior.

Major Characteristics of the Behavioral Approach

There are major characteristics which distinguish behavior modification from traditional approaches. These include a focus on observable behavior, careful assessment of the behavior which is to be altered, evaluation of the effect of the program in altering behavior, and concern for socially significant changes in behavior.

A major characteristic of the behavioral approach is a direct focus on observable *behavior*. The behaviors which serve as "symptoms" for the traditional intrapsychic approach are the focus of the behavioral approach. Behavioral treatment should not be viewed as altering symptoms because this implies that there *are* underlying emotional concomitants which are responsible for behavior. Evidence for underlying psychological causal agents is unavailable for those operant behaviors ordinarily focused upon in applied settings. For individuals who are diagnosed as psychotic, the focus usually is on observable maladaptive behaviors which interfere with living in the community, such as expressing delusions or hallucinations or withdrawing from others (Kazdin, 1975). For "hyperactive" children the obstreperous behaviors which led to applying that label will be focused upon (Hewett, 1968).

It should be pointed out that behavioral techniques have been used with "behaviors" which are not publicly observable. For example, private events (Skinner, 1953) such as thoughts, ideas, and images which are not "observable" to anyone other than the person for whom they are occurring, have been altered (Jacobs & Sachs, 1971). Private events, however, have been considered to be *covert operants* (or *coverants*) which respond to the laws of operant conditioning as do overt behaviors (Homme, 1965). For example, Mahoney (1971) reported treating a young male adult with uncontrolled obsessional thoughts about being brain damaged, persecuted, and "odd." Punishment was used to suppress these covert responses. Whenever the individual obsessed, he snapped a heavy-gauge rubber band which was around his wrist. This self-punishment procedure effectively eliminated obsessions in a matter of a few weeks. Subsequently, positive self-thoughts were developed by having the person read a positive statement about himself whenever he smoked. Since smoking was a frequent response, this ensured that positive statements occurred frequently. Eventually, the statements were made spontaneously without being associated with smoking. The frequency of positive self-reference statements increased. Whether the focus is on covert or overt events, behavior modification focuses directly on the behaviors which are creating problems for the patient, client, or resident, rather than on constructs which have to be inferred from those responses.

A second characteristic of behavior modification, related to the emphasis on observable behavior, is *assessment* of the behavior that is to be altered, i.e., the target behavior. Rather than attempting to assess the client's responses to psychological tests or to reveal underlying personality organization, assessment is made of the behavior itself. The number of times a response occurs or the duration of a response may be assessed. For example, learning "problems" may be assessed by measuring the responses performed on academic tasks. Apathy of psychotic patients may be defined by the number of activities that are performed on the ward. Social interaction can be assessed by counting the amount of social contacts made with peers. Similarly, anxiety or fear responses may be assessed by confronting the individual with an anxiety-provoking situation and objectively recording how close the individual can approach the stimulus.

A third characteristic of behavior modification is a careful *evaluation* of the effect of the program which is designed to change behavior. Emphasis is placed on demonstrating the effect of the program empirically. Traditional therapy, as practiced in most clinical settings, is rarely evaluated. When therapy is evaluated, the effect is assessed at the *end* of treatment to determine whether there is any change in personality. With behavior modification procedures, particularly in applied settings, the effect of the program on behavior usually is assessed *while* the program is going on as well as after the program is terminated. Data are gathered constantly to ensure the program is having its intended effect. If the program is not working, it can be altered rapidly in response to the client's behavior. Assessment and treatment are interwoven. There is constant feedback to the professionals and nonprofessionals working in the program.

A fourth characteristic, related to the above, is a concern for effecting behavior change that is *socially significant.* The behavior change resulting from the program should make a difference which is noticeable to the individuals in the person's environment. The change should move the individual appreciably closer toward the level of performance necessary for functioning in society (Risley, 1970). This is not to say that normality or conformity is a goal toward which all should strive. However, the populations for which behavioral techniques are often used engage in behaviors which make them deviant when evaluated by social standards held by the public. A socially significant change may be evident when the procedures markedly alter the target behavior so it is aligned with normative standards. For example, in a school setting, a "hyperactive" child may run around the room 90% of the time during class, whereas most students engage in this behavior less than 10% of the time. If a behavior modification program reduced the student's inappropriate behavior to 60%, there would be grounds for not regarding the program as successful or making a socially significant change in the student's behavior. A much larger reduction of running around the room is required to make the child less distinguishable from his or her peers. The example conveys that the behavioral approach often seeks large behavior changes. In most instances, normative data are not gathered to determine the degree to which one's peers perform or fail to perform a behavior. In these cases, the extent of change and its social significance is evaluated in part by comparing preprogram rates of the behavior with rates obtained during the program. (See Chapter 4.) Yet, the magnitude of change should be substantial so that it is evident in the person's social environment that improvement was made.

Behavioral interventions attempt to effect changes in behaviors which are socially important. Numerous examples attest to the marked changes in behaviors of social and therapeutic import. Self-destructive behavior has been eliminated in autistic children, social behaviors have been developed in withdrawn adult retardates, activity has been increased in "apathetic" chronic psychiatric patients, stuttering has been eliminated, levels of academic achievement and intelligence quotients have been increased (Bandura, 1969; Kazdin, 1975; Kazdin & Craighead, 1973; Ullmann & Krasner, 1969), as well as changes in several other socially significant behaviors which will be evident throughout subsequent chapters.

Remaining chapters will be devoted to explaining the principles of operant conditioning and a variety of behavior modification programs which have been derived from them. The emphasis throughout will be on operant procedures because their application in applied settings has been extensive and because the training required for their use by nonprofessionals usually is less than is required of other behavioral techniques.

2

Principles of Operant Conditioning

In the previous chapter, three kinds of learning—classical conditioning, operant conditioning, and observational learning—were discussed. Behavior modification programs in applied settings rely primarily upon the principles of operant conditioning. In this chapter, a brief explanation of these principles will be provided. Later chapters will elaborate major principles and the various procedures through which they are implemented.

The *principles of operant conditioning* describe the relationship between behavior and environmental events (antecedents and consequences) which influence behavior. In developing behavior modification programs, it is important to understand the types of antecedent events and consequences which influence behavior. In most applications of the principles of operant conditioning, emphasis is placed on the *consequences* which follow behavior. For a consequence to alter a particular behavior it must be dependent or contingent upon the occurrence of that behavior. Behavior change occurs when certain consequences are *contingent* upon performance. A consequence is contingent when it is delivered only after the target behavior is performed and is otherwise not available. When a consequence is not contingent upon behavior, this means it is delivered independently of what the individual is doing. The noncontingent delivery of consequences ordinarily does not result in systematic changes in a preselected target behavior because the consequences do not consistently follow that behavior. For example, if a psychiatric patient receives attention (the consequence) from an attendant on the ward each time he or she speaks, attention is considered to be contingent upon speech. On the other hand, the patient may receive attention every so often from an attendant independently of what the patient is doing. Attention would be delivered noncontingently. To systematically increase speaking, attention should be delivered contingent upon instances of speaking.

In everyday life, many consequences are contingent upon our behavior. For example, wages are contingent upon working, grades are contingent upon studying for exams, and health is contingent, to some extent, upon the care with which we treat ourselves. A *contingency* refers to the relationship between a behavior and the events which follow the behavior. The notion of a contingency is important because behavior modification techniques alter behavior by altering the contingencies which control (or fail to control) behavior. The principles outlined below refer to different kinds of contingent relationships between behavior and the events which follow behavior. Four major principles to be discussed include positive and negative reinforcement, punishment, and extinction.

Reinforcement

The *principle of reinforcement* refers to an increase in the frequency of a response when it is immediately followed by certain consequences. The consequence which follows behavior must be contingent upon behavior. A contingent event which increases the frequency of behavior is referred to as a *reinforcer*. Positive and negative reinforcers constitute the two kinds of events which can be used to increase the frequency of a response (Skinner, 1953). *Positive reinforcers* are events which are presented after a response is performed and increase the frequency of the behavior they follow. *Negative reinforcers* (which will also be referred to as aversive events or aversive stimuli) are events which are *removed* after a response is performed and increase the behavior that preceded their removal.

Positive Reinforcement. *Positive reinforcement refers to an increase in the frequency of a response which is followed by a favorable event (positive reinforcer).* The positive or favorable events in everyday language frequently are referred to as rewards. However, it is desirable to distinguish the term "positive reinforcer" from "reward." A positive reinforcer is defined by its effect on behavior. If an event follows behavior and the frequency of behavior increases, the event is a positive reinforcer. Conversely, any event which does not increase the behavior it follows is not a positive reinforcer. An increase in the frequency or probability of the preceding behavior is the defining characteristic of a positive reinforcer. In contrast, rewards are defined as something given or received in return for service, merit, or achievement (*Random House Dictionary*, 1968). Although rewards are highly valued, at least subjectively, they do not necessarily increase the probability of the behavior they follow (Skinner, 1974).

Many rewards or events that are evaluated favorably when a person is queried serve as reinforcers. However, this cannot be known on the basis of verbal statements alone. An individual may be unaware of, or not consider as rewards, many events which are reinforcers. For example, in some situations verbal reprimands (e.g., "Stop that!") inadvertently serve as positive reinforcers, presumably because they provide attention for a response. Therefore, behaviors followed by reprimands may increase (cf. Madsen, Becker, Thomas, Koser, & Plager, 1970; O'Leary, Kaufman, Kass, & Drabman, 1970). It may be that a number of disruptive child behaviors in everyday life are *increased* rather than decreased by reprimands. Even though certain kinds of reprimands may serve as positive reinforcers, it is unlikely that anyone would refer to them as rewards. Hence, a reward is not synonymous with a positive reinforcer. Whether an event is a positive reinforcer has to be determined empirically. Does the frequency of a particular behavior increase when the event immediately follows behavior? Only if the behavior does increase, is the event a positive reinforcer.

Examples of positive reinforcement in everyday life would seem to be abundant. However, rarely does anyone actually measure whether a favorable event which followed behavior increases the frequency of that behavior. Nevertheless, it is useful to provide some examples of situations which probably depict positive reinforcement. A student who studies for an examination and receives an "A" probably is reinforced. Studying is likely to increase in the future because it was reinforced by an excellent grade. Alternatively, if an infant cries before going to sleep and is picked up by his parents, the frequency of crying before sleeping may increase. Picking up a child provides attention and physical contact which are likely to be positive reinforcers. (Of course, the risk involved in increasing crying in the future must be weighed against the possibility of the child crying because of pain or discomfort.) Winning money at a slot machine usually increases the frequency of putting money into the machine and pulling the lever. Money is a powerful reinforcer which increases performance of a variety of behaviors.

Positive reinforcers include any events which, when presented, increase the frequency of the behavior they follow. There are two categories of positive reinforcers, namely, *primary,* or unconditioned, and *secondary,* or conditioned, reinforcers. Events which serve as primary reinforcers do not depend upon special training to have acquired their reinforcing value. For example, food to a hungry person and water to a thirsty person serve as primary reinforcers. Primary reinforcers may not be reinforcing all of the time. For example, food will not reinforce someone who has just finished a large meal. However, when food does serve as a reinforcer, its value is automatic (unlearned) and does not depend upon a previous association with any other reinforcers.

Many of the events which control behavior are not primary reinforcers.

Conditioned reinforcers which include events such as praise, grades, money, and completion of a goal, have acquired reinforcing value through learning. Conditioned reinforcers are not automatically reinforcing. Stimuli or events which once were neutral in value may acquire reinforcing properties as a result of being paired with events that are already reinforcing (either primary or other conditioned reinforcers). By repeatedly presenting a neutral stimulus prior to or along with a reinforcing stimulus, the neutral stimulus becomes a reinforcer. For example, praise may not be reinforcing for some individuals. It is a neutral stimulus rather than a positive reinforcer. To establish praise as a reinforcer, it must be paired with an event that is reinforcing, such as food or money. When a behavior is performed, the individual is praised and reinforced with food. After several pairings of the food with praise, the praise alone serves as a reinforcer and can be used to increase the frequency of other responses. When praise is a neutral stimulus, it can be developed as a conditioned reinforcer by pairing it with another event which is a reinforcer (Miller & Drennen, 1970).

Some conditioned reinforcers are paired with more than one other primary or conditioned reinforcer. When a conditioned reinforcer is paired with *many* other reinforcers, it is referred to as a *generalized conditioned reinforcer*. Generalized conditioned reinforcers are extremely effective in altering behaviors because they have been paired with a variety of events rather than just one. Money and trading stamps are good examples of generalized conditioned reinforcers. They are *conditioned* reinforcers because their reinforcing value is acquired through learning. They are *generalized* reinforcers because a variety of reinforcing events contribute to their value. Additional examples of generalized conditioned reinforcers include attention, approval, and affection from others (Skinner, 1953). These are generalized reinforcers because their occurrence often is associated with a variety of other events which are themselves reinforcing. For example, attention from someone may be followed by physical contact, praise, smiles, affection, or delivery of tangible rewards such as food and other events. In behavior modification programs, generalized reinforcers in the form of *tokens* are used frequently. The tokens may consist of poker chips, coins, tickets, stars, points, or checkmarks. Tokens serve as generalized reinforcers because they can be exchanged for a variety of other events which are reinforcing. For example, in a psychiatric hospital tokens may be delivered to patients for attending group activities, grooming and bathing, and other behaviors. The tokens may be exchanged for snacks, cigarettes, and privileges such as watching television and attending social events. The potency of tokens derives from the reinforcers which "back up" their value. The events which tokens can purchase are referred to as *back-up reinforcers*. Generalized conditioned reinforcers, such as money or tokens, usually are more powerful than any single reinforcer because they can purchase a variety of back-up reinforcers. (Generalized conditioned reinforcers will be discussed at length in Chapter 5.)

In identifying positive reinforcers, it is important to keep two considerations in mind. First, an event (e.g., praise, candy, or pat on the back) may be a positive reinforcer for one person but not for another. Although some events have wide generality in serving as reinforcers (e.g., food or money), others may not (e.g., sour candy). Second, an event may be a reinforcer for one person under some circumstances or at some time, but not under other circumstances or at other times. These considerations require careful evaluation of what is reinforcing for a given individual. Because of cultural norms and common experiences of many people, some suggestions may be given as to events which probably serve as reinforcers. However, at any given time there is little guarantee in advance that a particular event will be reinforcing.

Reinforcing events referred to above include *stimuli* or specific events such as praise, smiles, food, or money which are delivered or presented to an individual after a response. However, reinforcers are not limited to stimuli presented to an individual. Allowing an individual to engage in certain *responses* can be used as a reinforcer. Certain responses can be used to reinforce other responses. Premack (1959, 1965) noted that behaviors an individual performs with a relatively high frequency when given the opportunity to select among various responses can reinforce behaviors performed with a relatively low frequency. If the opportunity to perform a more probable response is made contingent upon performance of a less probable response, the frequency of the latter response will increase. Hence, behaviors of a relatively higher probability in an individual's repertory of behaviors are reinforcers of lower probability behaviors. In various ingenious laboratory experiments, Premack altered the probability that rats drank water and engaged in activity (running) by depriving them of either access to water or to an activity wheel. When rats were deprived of water (thus making drinking a higher probability behavior), drinking reinforced running (a low probability response). When the animals were deprived of activity (making running a high probability behavior), running reinforced drinking. In each case, a lower probability behavior was increased (reinforced) by following it with a higher probability behavior. At different times, eating was the higher probability response and running was the lower probability response, and vice versa.

On the basis of the laboratory work outlined above, the _Premack Principle_ has been formulated as follows: *Of any pair of responses or activities in which an individual engages, the more frequent one will reinforce the less frequent one.* Stated another way, a higher probability behavior can be used to reinforce a lower probability behavior. To determine what behaviors are high or low frequency requires observing the behaviors an individual engages in when he or she is left to perform behaviors *freely.*

The behavior observed to occur more frequently can be used to follow and reinforce a lower frequency behavior. For example, for many children, playing with friends is performed at a higher frequency than is practicing a musical instrument. If the higher frequency behavior (playing with friends) is made contingent upon the lower frequency behavior (playing the instrument), the lower probability behavior will increase.

A dramatic example of the Premack Principle was reported by Homme, deBaca, Devine, Steinhorst, and Rickert (1963). In a nursery school classroom, three children spent a great deal of time running around the room, screaming, pushing chairs, or playing games. These behaviors were of a higher frequency than sitting quietly. When the children were instructed to sit in their chairs, they would continue to engage in the undesirable high probability behaviors. To increase the target response, sitting quietly, the higher probability behaviors were made to follow the lower probability behavior. When the children sat quietly for a short period of time (lower probability behavior), they were told they could "run and scream" (higher probability behavior). Repeatedly, the opportunity to run and scream was made contingent upon sitting quietly. In a few days, the children, when instructed, sat quietly for longer periods of time than they had before. Sitting quietly increased in frequency which demonstrates that access to the high probability behavior, running and screaming, was a positive reinforcer.

Numerous behaviors that an individual performs, such as engaging in certain activities, hobbies, or privileges, going on trips, being with friends, and other relatively frequent responses, can serve as reinforcers for other behaviors. The requirement of the Premack Principle is that the target response to be altered is of a lower probability than the behavior which will reinforce that response. Of course, in everyday life, high probability behaviors often *precede* rather than follow low probability behaviors. For example, students may study (low probability behavior for many students) after going out with their friends (high probability behavior). Spouses may complete yard work (low probability behavior) after watching a football game (high probability behavior). In such cases, the low probability behavior is not likely to increase in frequency unless the sequence of behaviors is reversed. Performing the high probability behavior before performing the low probability behavior amounts to the noncontingent delivery of reinforcers.

Negative Reinforcement. *Negative reinforcement refers to an increase in the frequency of a response by removing an aversive event immediately after the response is performed.* Removal of an aversive event or negative reinforcer is contingent upon a response. An event is a *negative reinforcer* only if its removal after a response increases performance of that response (Skinner, 1953). Events which appear to be annoying, undesirable, or unpleasant are not necessarily negatively reinforcing. The qualifications made in the discussion of positive reinforcers hold for negative reinforcers. An undesirable event may serve as an aversive event for one individual but not for another. Also, an event may be a negative reinforcer for an individual at one time but not at another time. A negative reinforcer, just as a positive reinforcer, is defined solely by the effect it has on behavior.

It is important to note that reinforcement (positive or negative) always refers to an increase in behavior. Negative reinforcement requires an ongoing aversive event which can be removed or terminated after a specific response is performed. Examples of negative reinforcement are evident in everyday experience, such as putting on a coat while standing outside on a cold day. Putting on a coat (the behavior) usually removes an aversive state, namely, being cold. The probability of wearing a coat in cold weather is increased. Taking medicine to relieve a headache may be negatively reinforced by the termination of pain. Similarly, a loud noise (aversive event) may be terminated by putting one's finger in one's ears or leaving the situation. Termination of the noise reinforces the responses used to escape the noise. Strictly, whether negative reinforcement occurs in the above examples depends upon whether the behavior which terminates the undesirable state increases.

Interesting combinations of positive and negative reinforcement occur in social interaction and may foster socially undesirable behavior (Patterson & Reid, 1970). In social interactions, the response of one individual sometimes is negatively reinforced because it terminates an aversive behavior initiated by another individual. Yet, the aversive behavior of the other individual is positively reinforced. For example, parents may pick up a child who is whining. Whining is an aversive event for the parents which is terminated after they respond. Picking up the child is negatively reinforced by a cessation of whining. However, the child may be positively reinforced for whining since he or she receives parental attention contingent upon this behavior. As another example of positive and negative reinforcement in social interaction, someone who is the victim of an aggressive act (e.g., physical assault) may respond in a particular way (e.g., comply with the wishes of the aggressor) to terminate an aversive situation. Unfortunately, the act of compliance positively reinforces the aggressor. The probability of future aggression by the aggressor is increased. It should be evident from these examples that the principles of operant conditioning can explain how behavioral problems develop and are maintained as well as how they can be altered.

A frequently cited example of negative reinforcement was reported by Lovaas, Schaeffer, and Simmons (1965). These investigators developed social behaviors in a pair of autistic twins. A painful aversive stimulus (shock) was used because the children showed no improvement with conventional treatment methods. Moreover, the children were unresponsive to adults. Adults could not interact, express affection, or make requests effectively because the children either did not respond or actually resisted. A major goal with autistic children is to develop responsiveness to adults. Once the children are responsive, the relationship between the children and adults can serve as a basis of subsequent treatment and training. To begin the negative reinforcement procedure, the children were placed in a room which had an electrified floor. Electric shock could be given to individuals standing barefoot on the floor. Two adults stood at different sides of the room. One adult said, "Come here," and held out his hands. The shock (aversive stimulus) was turned on. As soon as the child moved toward an adult, the ongoing shock was terminated. Thus, movement toward an adult (the behavior) was negatively reinforced. This procedure dramatically increased the number of times the children responded to the instructions to come to the adults. A similar procedure was used to train the children to hug and kiss adults. A shock delivered to the buttocks was terminated when the children hugged or kissed the experimenter. Kissing and hugging were negatively reinforced because the aversive event was terminated when the responses were performed. These demonstrations of negative reinforcement are particularly impressive since many procedures often employed to alter the behavior of autistic children have little or no success (Lovaas et al., 1965).

Negative reinforcement requires some aversive event that is presented to the individual before he or she responds, such as shock, noise, isolation, and other events which can be removed or reduced immediately after a response. As with positive reinforcers, there are two types of negative reinforcers, primary and secondary. Intense stimuli, such as shock or loud noise, which impinge on sensory receptors of an organism serve as primary negative reinforcers. Their aversive properties are not learned. However, secondary or *conditioned aversive events* have become aversive by being paired with events which are already aversive. For example, disapproving facial expressions or saying the word "no" can serve as aversive events after being paired with events which are already aversive (Lovaas et al., 1965).

Negative reinforcement occurs whenever an individual *escapes* from an aversive event. Escape from aversive events is negatively reinforcing. However, *avoidance* of aversive events is negatively reinforcing, too. For example, one avoids eating rancid food, walking through an intersection with oncoming cars, and leaving the house without an umbrella on a rainy day. Avoidance occurs before the aversive event takes place (e.g., becoming sick from rancid food, being injured by a car, getting wet from rain). How are avoidance behaviors maintained since no aversive events seem to have occurred?

Avoidance learning is an area where classical and operant conditioning are operative. Avoidance behavior is sometimes learned by pairing a neutral stimulus (conditioned stimulus) with an unconditioned aversive event (unconditioned stimulus). For example, a frown (conditioned stimulus) from a parent may precede corporal punishment (unconditioned stimulus) of the child. Corporal punishment may elicit crying and escape from the situation (unconditioned response). The child learns to *escape* from the situation when the adult frowns and thereby *avoids* corporal punishment. The sight of the frowning parent elicits crying and escape. Avoidance of unconditioned aversive events is actually escape from the conditioned aversive event. Thus, classical conditioning may initiate avoidance behavior. Operant conditioning is also involved in avoidance behavior. Behaviors which reduce or terminate an aversive event, conditioned or unconditioned, are negatively reinforced. The escape from the conditioned aversive event (e.g., frown) is negatively reinforced since it terminates the event. To reiterate, the conditioned aversive event elicits an escape response (classical conditioning) which is negatively reinforced (operant conditioning).

Operant conditioning is involved in yet another way in avoidance learning. A conditioned aversive event serves as a cue signaling that particular consequences will follow. The presence of the conditioned aversive stimulus signals that a certain response (escape) will be reinforced (Reynolds, 1968). A variety of cues control avoidance behavior in everyday life. Indeed, most avoidance behavior appears to be learned from verbal cues (warnings) by others rather than from direct experience with unconditioned aversive stimuli. For example, a sign saying, "Danger" or "Beware of Dog," signals that certain consequences (e.g., physical harm) are likely to occur if a particular response is performed (e.g., trespassing). The escape response made after reading the sign is not *elicited* in the sense discussed above with classical conditioning. The sign merely acts as a cue that consequences of a particular sort are likely to follow alternate courses of action. An individual does not have to experience physical harm to learn to avoid particular situations. In examples from everyday experience, avoidance behavior is under the control of antecedent stimuli (e.g., air raid sirens, screeching car brakes, threats, and traffic signals) which signal that a particular event is likely to follow.

The distinction between classical and operant conditioning is difficult to maintain. Indeed, they are both operative in avoidance. Although both types of conditioning play a role in the development of avoidance behavior, the processes by which avoidance behaviors are developed and eliminated are not completely understood (Bandura, 1969; Kanfer & Phillips, 1970; Rachman & Teasdale, 1969).

Punishment

Punishment is the presentation of an aversive event or the removal of a positive event following a response which decreases the frequency of that response. This definition is somewhat different from the everyday use of the term. Punishment, as ordinarily defined, refers to a penalty imposed for performing a particular act. The technical definition includes an additional requirement, namely, that the frequency of the response is decreased (Azrin & Holz, 1966). Because of the negative connotations frequently associated with punishment, it is important to dispel some stereotypic notions that do not apply to the technical definition of punishment. Punishment does not necessarily entail pain or physical coercion.[1] In addition, punishment is not a means of retribution or payment for misbehaving. Sometimes punishment is employed in everyday life independently of its effects on subsequent behavior. For example, children are "taught a lesson" for misbehaving by undergoing a sacrifice of some kind. Similarly, criminals may receive penalties which do not necessarily decrease the frequency of their criminal acts. *Punishment in the technical sense is an empirical matter; it is defined solely by the effect on behavior*. Only if the frequency of a response is reduced can punishment be operative. Similarly, a punishing event is defined by its suppressive effect on the behavior which it follows. As is evident in later chapters, a variety of events which suppress behavior depart from ordinary practices which are termed punishment in everyday life.

There are two different types of punishment. In the first kind of punishment, an aversive event is *presented* after a response. Numerous examples of this pervade everyday life, such as being reprimanded or slapped after engaging in some behavior. Similarly, being burned after touching a hot stove involves the presentation of an aversive stimulus after a response. Of course, whether these examples in everyday life qualify as punishment depends, in part, upon whether there is a reduction in the responses.

A second type of punishment is the *removal of a positive reinforcer* after a response. Examples include losing privileges after staying out late, losing money for misbehaving, being isolated from others, and having one's driver's license revoked. In this form of punishment, some positive event is taken away after a response is performed. For example, in one report, loss of television time was used to train a child to dress herself each morning (Hall et al., 1972). The child spent a large amount of time dressing herself each morning. If the child spent over 30 minutes to dress herself after waking, she lost time from watching television that day. When the withdrawal of television privileges was contingent upon the response (taking over 30 minutes to dress), dressing time decreased considerably. From this example alone, it should be clear that punishment is not necessarily physically painful. However, in both types of punishment some consequence occurs which an individual is likely to label as undesirable.

---

[1] As Skinner (1974) has noted, the word "pain" etymologically traces back to Latin and Greek. The Latin word from which it was derived refers to punishment which explains, in part, why the two notions are inextricably bound in language and thought.

It is important to keep punishment distinct from negative reinforcement with which it is sometimes confused. *Reinforcement,* of course, refers to procedures which *increase* a response whereas *punishment* refers to procedures which *decrease* a response. In negative reinforcement an aversive event is *removed* after a response is performed. In punishment, an aversive event is *presented* after a response is performed.[2] Figure 2–1 further clarifies the operations involved in the different principles discussed to this point. It depicts the two operations which can occur after a response is performed. Something can be *presented* to the individual or *removed* from him after he performs a response. The left side of the figure shows that events may be presented or removed after a response. The top of the figure shows the two types of events which can be presented or removed, positive and aversive events. Each cell in the figure depicts a procedure discussed to this point. Positive reinforcement occupies cell I; negative reinforcement occupies cell IV; punishment occupies both cells II and III.

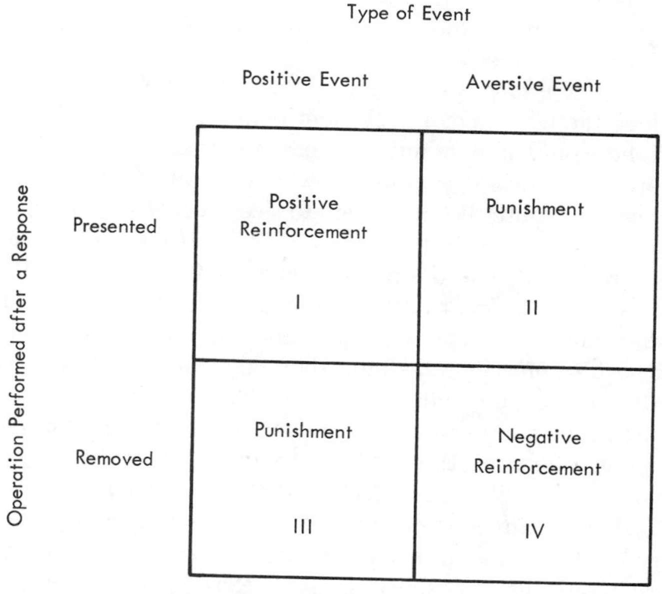

Type of Event

	Positive Event	Aversive Event
Presented	Positive Reinforcement I	Punishment II
Removed	Punishment III	Negative Reinforcement IV

Operation Performed after a Response

FIGURE 2–1 Illustration of principles of operant conditioning based upon whether positive or aversive events are presented or removed after a response is performed.

---

[2] As a general rule, an event which can negatively reinforce behavior usually also can be used to suppress (punish) some other response it follows. However, it is not necessarily the case that a given event which has been shown to negatively reinforce behavior will suppress a response it follows or that a stimulus which effectively suppresses a response is negatively reinforcing (See Azrin & Holz, 1966; Church, 1963). In the present text, the term "aversive stimulus" (or "aversive event") will be used to include any event which may be negatively reinforcing and/or punishing.

Extinction

Behaviors that are reinforced increase in frequency. However, a behavior which is no longer reinforced decreases in frequency. During extinction, a response which was previously reinforced is no longer reinforced. *Extinction refers to the cessation of reinforcement of a response.* Nonreinforcement of a response results in the eventual reduction or elimination of the behavior. It is important to keep this procedure distinct from punishment. In extinction, no consequence follows the response, that is, an event is not taken away nor is one presented. In punishment, some aversive event follows a response or some positive event is taken away. In everyday life, the usual use of extinction is in the form of ignoring a behavior that may have been reinforced previously with attention. A mother may ignore her child when the child whines. A physician may ignore the physical complaints of a hypochondriac. A teacher may ignore children who talk without raising their hands. A therapist or counselor may ignore certain self-defeating statements made by the client. In each of these examples, the reinforcer (e.g., attention, approval, or sympathy) usually available for the response is no longer presented.

A dramatic example was reported by Williams (1959) who used extinction to reduce the tantrums of a 21-month-old child. When the child was put to bed, he would scream until the parents or an aunt returned to the room. In order to prevent a tantrum, whoever put the child to bed remained in the room until the child went to sleep, which was about one-half hour to two hours after the initial bedtime. To remove social reinforcement (attention) for the tantrum, the parents were told to put the child to bed and leave the room. When the tantrum began, it was ignored. The child cried for 45 minutes the first night of extinction. However, the next day there was no tantrum. In remaining days, tantrums were less than ten minutes. After a week, the child had a severe tantrum. The aunt reinforced this by going in the child's room and staying with him until he fell asleep. Thus, the aunt reinforced the tantrum. Extinction was carried out again on subsequent nights. By the nineth session there were no tantrums. Moreover, no further tantrums were reported over the next two years.

In everyday life, extinction may contribute to behavior problems as well as ameliorate them. Often desirable behavior is accidentally extinguished. For example, parents sometimes ignore their children when they are playing quietly and provide abundant attention when the children are noisy. Essentially, quiet play may be extinguished while noisy play is positively reinforced. Merely altering parental attention so it follows appropriate play is often sufficient to develop appropriate behavior and to extinguish inappropriate behavior.

Cessation of attention is not the only example of extinction. For example, putting money into vending machines (a response) will cease if the reinforcer (e.g., cigarettes, food, or drink) is not forthcoming; turning on a radio will cease, if the radio no longer functions; and attempting to start a car will extinguish, if the car does not start. In each of these examples, the consequences which maintain the behavior are no longer forthcoming. The absence of reinforcing consequences reduces the behavior. Extinction can be used to reduce or eliminate behavior. However, the events which reinforce behavior must be identified so they can be prevented from occurring after the response.

Shaping and Chaining

Frequently, the development of new behavior cannot be achieved by reinforcing the response when it occurs. In many cases, the response may never occur. The desired behavior may be so complex that the elements which make up the response are not in the repertoire of the individual. For example, developing the use of words requires, among other things, the use of sounds, syllables, and their combinations. *In shaping, the terminal behavior is achieved by reinforcing small steps or approximations toward the final response rather than reinforcing the final response itself.* Responses are reinforced which either resemble the final response or which include components of that response. By reinforcing *successive approximations* of the terminal response, the final response is achieved gradually. Responses which are increasingly similar to the final goal are reinforced and they increase, while those responses dissimilar to the final goal are not reinforced and they extinguish. Shaping, along with other procedures, is used to develop talking in children. Responses which approach the final goal (e.g., sounds and syllables) are reinforced. Responses which are emitted which do not approach the goal (e.g., screaming and whining) are extinguished along the way toward the final goal.

An obvious example of shaping is training animals to perform various "tricks." If the animal trainer waited until the tricks were performed (e.g., jumping through a burning hoop) to administer a reinforcer, it is unlikely that reinforcement would ever occur. However, by shaping the response, the trainer can readily achieve the terminal goal. First, food (positive reinforcer) might be delivered for running toward the trainer. As that response becomes stable, the trainer may reinforce running up to the trainer when he is holding the hoop. Other steps closer to the final goal would be reinforced in sequence, including walking through the hoop on the ground, jumping through the hoop when it is slightly off the ground, and then high off the ground, jumping through it when it is partially on fire and finally, jumping through it when the hoop is completely on fire. Eventually, the terminal response will be performed with a high frequency, whereas the responses or steps developed along the way are extinguished.

In one study, shaping was used to reinstate verbal behavior in two psychotic patients (Isaacs, Thomas, & Goldiamond, 1960). One patient had been mute for 19 years. The terminal response (talking) was developed by reinforcing approximations toward vocalizations. In several sessions, the experimenter held out gum (the reinforcer) in front of the patient. Gum was given for different responses which came increasingly closer to the terminal goal. Initially, gum was given for eye movements toward the gum, then movements of the lips, then spontaneous vocal noises, and finally use of words. By the end of the sixth week of training (after a total of 18 sessions), the patient said, "Gum, please" when the experimenter said, "Say gum, gum." The patient then answered questions about his name and age. In this example, shaping was required to reinstate speech because the terminal response could not be reinforced at the beginning of training. Since talking never occurred early in the program, it could not be followed with gum.

Shaping requires reinforcing behaviors already in the repertoire of the individual which resemble the terminal response or approximate the goal. As the initial approximation is performed consistently, the criterion for reinforcement is altered slightly so that the response which is to be reinforced resembles the final goal more closely than the previous response. Through reinforcement of responses which approach the terminal goal and extinction of responses which do not, the terminal response is developed. In the above example, shaping was used to develop behavior that was previously in the individual's repertoire of responses. Speech had been absent for many years although it had been performed at one point in the patient's life. Reinforcing successive approximations is used in an identical fashion to develop new behaviors that have never been performed by the individual, such as feeding, walking, and dressing.

Most behaviors consist of a sequence of several responses. A sequence of responses is referred to as a *chain.* The component parts of a chain usually represent individual responses already in the repertoire of the individual. Yet the chain represents a combination of the individual responses ordered in a particular sequence. For example, one behavioral chain which illustrates the ordering of component responses is going to eat at a restaurant (Reynolds, 1968). Going out to eat may be initiated by a phone call from someone, hunger, or some other event. Having been initiated, several behaviors follow in a sequence, including leaving the house, entering the restaurant, being seated, looking at a menu, ordering a meal, and eating. Each response proceeds in a relatively fixed order until the chain is completed and the last response is reinforced (e.g., eating). Later responses in the chain (such as sitting at the table) are preceded by a series of responses (traveling in the car and so on). The order is fixed so that early responses must precede later ones. Interestingly, each response in the chain does not appear to be reinforced. Rather, only the last response (the response immediately preceding eating) is followed by the reinforcer (food). Because a reinforcer alters or maintains only the behavior that immediately precedes it, it is not obvious what maintains the entire chain of behaviors leading to the final response. However, there are many chains of responses which are maintained in everyday experience. For example, dieting, mastering a musical instrument, preparing for athletic competition, studying for an advanced degree, and writing a book all require a series of intermediate responses before the final reinforcing event is achieved. The major question is what maintains all of the intermediate responses which precede attaining the final goal. The answer requires explanation of the factors which link response components of a chain.

Initially, it is important to note that an event which immediately precedes reinforcement becomes a signal for reinforcement. An event which signals that behavior will be reinforced is referred to as a *discriminative stimulus* (S^D). An S^D sets the *occasion* for behavior, i.e., increases the probability that a previously reinforced behavior will occur. However, an S^D not only signals reinforcement but eventually becomes a reinforcer itself. The frequent pairing of an S^D and the reinforcer gives the S^D reinforcing properties of its own. This procedure was mentioned earlier in the discussion of conditioned reinforcement. The discriminative stimulus properties of events which precede reinforcement and the reinforcing properties of these events when they are frequently paired with reinforcers are important in explaining how chains of response are maintained.

Consider the chain of responses involved in going out to eat, described above. (The chain could be divided into several smaller components than those listed above.) A phone call may have signaled the first response to go to a restaurant to eat. All of the behaviors in the chain of responses are performed ending in positive reinforcement (eating). The final response in the chain before reinforcement was ordering a meal. This response is directly reinforced with food. Recall that any event which precedes reinforcement becomes an S^D for reinforcement. In this chain of responses, the last response performed (ordering a meal) becomes an S^D for reinforcement, since the response signals that reinforcement will follow. Yet the constant pairing of an S^D with the reinforcer (food) eventually results in the S^D becoming a reinforcer as well as a discriminative stimulus. Hence, the response that preceded direct reinforcement has become an S^D for subsequent reinforcement and a reinforcer in its own right. The response serves as a reinforcer for the previous link in the chain of responses. The response (ordering food) becomes a reinforcer for the previous behavior (looking at a menu). Since looking at a menu now precedes reinforcement, it too becomes an S^D. As with other responses, the pairing of the S^D with reinforcement results in the S^D becoming a reinforcer. The process continues in a *backward* direction so that each response in the chain becomes an S^D and a reinforcer. (The very first response becomes an S^D but does not reinforce a prior response.) Each component response is both an S^D for the next response in the chain and serves as a reinforcer for the prior response in the chain. Although the sequence appears to be maintained by a single reinforcer at the end of the chain of responses (food in the above example), the links in the chain are assumed to take on conditioned reinforcement value. To accomplish this, building response chains requires training from the last response in the sequence which precedes direct reinforcement back to the first response. Since the last response in the sequence is paired immediately and directly with the reinforcer, it is most easily established as a conditioned reinforcer which can maintain other responses. Also (as will be discussed at length in Chapter 5), the shorter the delay between a response and reinforcement, the greater the effect of reinforcement. The last response in the chain is immediately reinforced and is more likely to be performed frequently.

Shaping versus Chaining. It may be unclear what the differences are between shaping and chaining and the different conditions which dictate choosing between these techniques. Generally, shaping is used to develop new behaviors. Cues such as instructions and gestures may be used as discriminative stimuli combined with direct reinforcement (e.g., praise) for responses that approach the terminal goal. Chaining usually is used to develop a sequence of behaviors using responses that are already present in the individual's repertoire. To obtain a chain of responses consisting of discrete behaviors, shaping may be used first to develop component behaviors. Certainly, the major difference is that chaining proceeds in a backward direction beginning with the last response and building prior behaviors, whereas shaping works in a forward direction. Moreover, in shaping, the goal is to develop a terminal response. The behaviors along the way toward the goal usually are not evident when shaping is completed. In chaining, behaviors developed early in training are still evident when training is completed.

In spite of the differences in shaping and chaining, the relative utility of the procedures in applied settings has not been evaluated empirically. Sequences of behaviors (chains) can be developed by shaping and using cues and reinforcement for the performance of behaviors in a particular sequence. Thus, in many situations either chaining or shaping may be used. For example, toilet training of children consists of a series of responses which follow in sequence, including walking to a bathroom, lowering pants, positioning oneself in front of or on the toilet, and so on. Reinforcement for appropriate toileting following completion of the entire chain can be praise for proper elimination. Although chaining can be used to develop this sequence of responses, shaping is also effective (Azrin & Foxx, 1971; Mahoney, Van Wagenen, & Meyerson, 1971).

In light of current research, it is not clear when chaining or shaping should be selected. However, for some individuals cues normally used in shaping (e.g., instructions) may exert little influence on behavior so that the behaviors in a sequence of responses are not consistently performed. Chaining might be particularly useful in this situation because each behavior in the chain becomes a cue for the next response to be performed. Moreover, the conditioned reinforcement provided by each response in the chain facilitates performance of the correct order of responses. Shaping is particularly well suited to developing a single terminal behavior. However, it may work effectively in developing a chain of several responses, particularly when cues such as instructions are effective in initiating the early behaviors in the chain.

Prompting and Fading

Developing behavior is facilitated by using cues, instructions, gestures, directions, examples, and models to initiate a response. *Events which help initiate a response are prompts.* Prompts precede a response. When the prompt results in the response, the response can be followed by reinforcement. When a prompt initiates behaviors that are reinforced, the prompt becomes an S^D for reinforcement. For example, if a parent tells a child to return from school early and the child is reinforced when he does this, the instruction (prompt) becomes an S^D. Instructions signal that reinforcement is likely when certain behaviors are performed. Eventually, instructions alone are likely to be followed by the behavior. As a general rule, when a prompt consistently precedes reinforcement of a response, the prompt becomes an S^D and can effectively control behavior.

Developing behavior can be facilitated in different ways, such as *guiding* the behavior physically (e.g., holding a child's arm to assist him in placing a spoon in his mouth); *instructing* the child to do something; *pointing* to the child to come inside the house; and *observing* another person (a model) perform a behavior (e.g., watching someone else play a game). Prompts play a major role in shaping and chaining. Developing a terminal response using reinforcement alone may be tedious and time consuming. By assisting the person in beginning the response, more rapid approximations to the final response can be made.

Mahoney et al. (1971) used a variety of prompts to train normal and retarded children to walk to the lavatory as a part of toileting skills. For example, toys were placed near the entrance to the lavatory to increase the likelihood of approach responses (visual prompt), the experimenter led the child by the hand to the lavatory (physical prompt), and instructions ("Let's go potty.") were used (verbal prompt) to initiate walking. An additional prompt consisted of an auditory signal (transmitted through an earphone in the child's ear) which sounded when the experimenter gave instructions, "Go potty." Pairing the auditory signal with instructions resulted in the signal alone initiating walking toward the lavatory.

The use of prompts increases the likelihood of response performance. For example, walking to the lavatory was much more likely to occur when the experimenter actually guided the child than when the child was left to respond on his or her own. While a response is being shaped, prompts may be used frequently to facilitate performance of the terminal goal. As soon as a prompted response is performed, it can be reinforced. Further, the more frequently the response is reinforced, the more rapidly it will be learned. A final goal usually is to obtain the terminal response in the absence of prompts. Although prompts may be required early in training, they can be withdrawn gradually or faded as training progresses.

Fading refers to the gradual removal of a prompt. If a prompt is removed abruptly early in training, the response may no longer be performed. But if the response is performed consistently with a prompt, the prompt can be progressively reduced and finally omitted, thus faded. For example, in the toilet training project mentioned earlier (Mahoney et al., 1971), several prompts helped train walking to the lavatory. As the children began to perform the behavior with physical guidance and verbal prompts, the experimenter began to fade the prompts. Instead of holding the child's hand to guide walking, the experimenter walked in front of the child, further away from the child, and eventually behind the child, so the child led the way to the lavatory. Also, verbal prompts (instructions) were reduced. To achieve behavior without prompts requires fading and reinforcing the responses in the absence of cues or signals. It is not always necessary to remove all prompts or cues. For example, it is important to train individuals to respond in the presence of certain prompts such as instructions which exert control over a variety of behaviors in everyday life.

Discrimination and Stimulus Control

Operant behavior is influenced by the consequences which follow behavior. However, antecedent events also control behavior. Prompts, discussed earlier, represent a group of controlling events (e.g., instructions, physical guidance, models, and cues) which precede and facilitate response performance. Yet, other antecedent stimuli come to exert control over behavior. In some situations (or in the presence of certain stimuli), a response may be reinforced, while in other situations (in the presence of other stimuli) the same response is not reinforced. *Differential reinforcement* refers to reinforcing a response in the presence of one stimulus and not reinforcing the same response in the presence of another stimulus. When a response is consistently reinforced in the presence of a particular stimulus and consistently not reinforced in the presence of another stimulus, each stimulus signals the consequences which are likely to follow. The stimulus present when the response is reinforced signals that performance is likely to be reinforced. Conversely, the stimulus present during nonreinforcement signals that the response is not likely to be reinforced. As mentioned earlier, a stimulus whose presence has been associated with reinforcement is referred to as an S^D. A stimulus whose presence has been associated with nonreinforcement is referred to as an S^Δ (S delta). The effect of differential reinforcement is that eventually the reinforced response is likely to occur in the presence of the S^D but unlikely to occur in the presence of the S^Δ. The probability of a response can be altered (increased or decreased) by presenting or removing the S^D (Skinner, 1953). The S^D occasions the previously reinforced response or increases the likelihood that the response is performed. When the individual responds differently in the presence of different stimuli, he has made a *discrimination*. When responses are differentially controlled by antecedent stimuli, behavior is considered to be under *stimulus control*.

Instances of stimulus control pervade everyday life. For example, the sound of a door bell signals that a certain behavior (opening the door) is likely to be reinforced (by seeing someone). Specifically, the sound of the bell frequently has been associated with the presence of visitors at the door (the reinforcer). The ring of the bell (S^D) increases the likelihood that the door will be opened. In the absence of the bell (S^Δ), the probability of opening the door for a visitor is very low. The ring of a door bell, telephone, alarm, and kitchen timer, all serve as discriminative stimuli and signal that certain responses are likely to be reinforced. Hence, the probability of the responses is increased. Stimulus control is also evident in the selection and consumption of food. For example, a ripe fruit (e.g., a red apple) is associated with a sweet taste, whereas a green apple (of the variety that is not ripe when green) is associated with a sour taste. The sweet taste of a ripe apple reinforces selection and consumption of a red apple. The color of the fruit is a stimulus which controls the future probability of eating certain fruit. In social interaction, stimulus control also is important. For example, a smile or wink from someone is likely to occasion a social response on our part (e.g., initiation of conversation). Whereas a smile serves as an S^D (signals that reinforcement is likely to follow our social response), a frown serves as an S^Δ (signals that reinforcement is not likely to follow a social response).

The notion of stimulus control is exceedingly important in behavior modification. In many behavior modification programs, the goal is to alter the relation between behavior and the stimulus conditions in which the behavior occurs. Some behavior problems stem from a failure of certain stimuli to control behavior although such control would be desirable. For example, children who do not follow instructions given by their parents illustrate a lack of stimulus control. The instructions do not exert influence over the children's behavior. The goal of a behavior modification program is to increase responsiveness to instructions. Other behavioral problems occur when certain behaviors *are* under control of antecedent stimuli when such control is undesirable. For example, the eating behavior of obese individuals is controlled by the mere sight of food (among other stimuli), rather than hunger. Treatment of overeating focuses on eliminating the control that the sight of food has on eating. (Treatments based upon stimulus control will be discussed further in Chapter 8.)

Stimulus control is always operative in behavior modification programs. Programs are conducted in particular settings (e.g., the home) and are administered by particular individuals (e.g., parents). Insofar as certain client behaviors are reinforced or punished in the presence of certain environmental cues or of particular individuals and not in the presence of other stimuli, the behaviors will be under stimulus control. In the presence of those cues associated with the behavior modification program, the client will behave in a particular fashion. In the absence of those cues, behavior is likely to change because the contingencies in new situations are altered.

The control that different stimuli exert over behavior explains why behavior often is situation specific. (Mischel, 1968). Individuals may behave one way in a given situation or in the presence of a particular person and differently in another situation or in the presence of another person. Since different reinforcement contingencies operate in different circumstances, individuals can discriminate among those stimuli which are likely to be followed by reinforcement.

A dramatic example of discriminative responding and stimulus control was reported by Redd and Birnbrauer (1969). In this study, two adults working at different times reinforced retarded children with food (candy, ice cream, or sips of coke) and praise for performing a specified response (e.g., playing cooperatively with another child). When the first adult was with one child, reinforcement was administered for the cooperative response (contingent delivery of praise). When the second adult was present, the same child was reinforced independently of his actual behavior (noncontingent delivery of praise). Overall, each adult administered the same amount of the available reinforcers. In a short period, the adults exerted stimulus control over the behavior of the children. The presence of the adult who was associated with the contingent delivery of praise led to performance of cooperative play, whereas the presence of the adult who was associated with the noncontingent delivery of praise did not. The children discriminated the different contingencies associated with the adults. Thus, adults can serve as discriminative stimuli for reinforcement. Children respond differentially to adults depending upon the behaviors that are differentially reinforced in each adult's presence.

Individuals make discriminations across a variety of situations for most behaviors. For example, eating habits probably are slightly different depending upon whether one is at home or in a restaurant. Discriminations are made which are even more subtle. Eating behavior may be different depending upon whether one is in an "expensive" restaurant or in a roadside cafe. Individuals behave differently in the presence of their co-workers compared with their boss. Numerous other differences in behavior are evident because of differences in situations and the contingencies associated with them.

Generalization

The effect of reinforcement on behavior may generalize across either the stimuli conditions beyond which training has taken place or across the responses that were included in the contingency. These two types of generalization are referred to as stimulus generalization and response generalization, respectively.

Stimulus Generalization. Behavior occurs in specific situations. A response which is repeatedly reinforced in the presence of a particular situation is likely to be repeated in that situation. However, situations and stimuli often share common properties. Control exerted by a given stimulus is shared by other stimuli which are similar or share common properties (Skinner, 1953). A behavior may be performed in new situations similar to the original situation in which reinforcement occurred. If a response reinforced in one situation or setting also increases in other settings (even though it is not reinforced in these other settings), this is referred to as stimulus generalization. *Stimulus generalization refers to the generalization or transfer of a response to situations other than those in which training takes place.* Generalization is the opposite of discrimination. When an individual discriminates in his performance of a response, this means that the response fails to generalize across situations. Alternatively, when a response generalizes across situations, the individual fails to discriminate in his performance of that response.

Figure 2–2 illustrates stimulus generalization. The term S_1 refers to the stimulus condition or situation in which the response is reinforced. R_1 refers to the behavior or response which is reinforced. The figure shows that the trained response (R_1) is performed across a variety of stimuli or situations (S_2, S_3, S_4, S_5). The degree of stimulus generalization is a function of the similarity of new stimuli (or situations) to the stimulus under which the response was trained (Kimble, 1961). Of course, over a long period of time, a response may not generalize across situations because the individual discriminates that the response is reinforced in one situation but not in others.

Examples of stimulus generalization are frequent in everyday experience. For example, a child may say certain things in the presence of his family. Discussion of certain topics is reinforced (or not punished) among family members. However, the child may also discuss these same topics in the presence of company. Behavior of the child (talking about certain

Stimulus Conditions   Response
(situations)

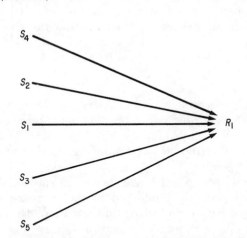

FIGURE 2–2 Stimulus generalization: A response
(R_1) reinforced in one situation (S_1) generalizes to
other situations (S_2, S_3, S_4, S_5) which are similar to
the original situation.

topics) has generalized across situations. Parents may show considerable
embarrassment when children freely discuss "family secrets." Generalization also is readily apparent when a child responds to a teacher in a fashion
similar to that of a parent (e.g., in the expression of affection). To the
extent that parents and teachers are similar to a child, the stimulus control
exerted by parents will be shared by the teacher.

An example of generalization across situations in a psychiatric hospital
was reported by Bennett and Maley (1973). Psychiatric patients were reinforced for conversing with each other in daily 30-minute sessions. The
sessions were conducted in a special room where conversation could be
carefully monitored. The amount of talking between patients increased
markedly in the sessions when they were reinforced. In addition, communication in the experimental sessions generalized to the ward. Although
talking was not reinforced on the ward as part of the program, this behavior generalized from one situation (experimental sessions) to another
(the ward).

Stimulus generalization represents an important issue in behavior modification. Although training takes place in a restricted setting (e.g., institution, special classroom, hospital, day-care center, home), it is desirable
that the behaviors developed in these settings generalize or transfer to
other settings (Kazdin & Bootzin, 1972).

Response Generalization. An additional type of generalization involves responses rather than stimulus conditions. Altering one response can inadvertently influence other responses. For example, if a person is reinforced for smiling, the frequency of laughing and talking might also increase. *The reinforcement of a response increases the probability of other responses which are similar* (Skinner, 1953). This is referred to as response generalization. To the extent that a nonreinforced response is similar to one that is reinforced, the similar response too is increased in probability. Figure 2–3 depicts response generalization, where S_1 refers to the stimulus condition in which training of a response takes place, and R_1 refers to the response which is reinforced. Although only one response is trained in the situation, a variety of other responses (R_2, R_3, R_4, R_5) which are similar may also be performed.

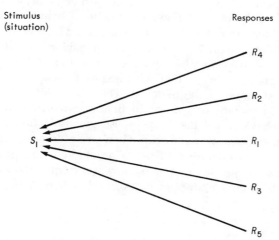

FIGURE 2–3 Response generalization: Reinforcement of one response (*R*) in a given situation (*S*) may result in an increase of other responses (R_2, R_3, R_4, R_5) which are similar to the reinforced response.

Alteration of one behavior is sometimes associated with alteration of related behaviors. For example, one study reported response generalization in a preschool child (Buell, Stoddard, Harris, & Baer, 1968). Teacher attention reinforced the child's use of outdoor play equipment. Not only did the reinforced response increase, but related behaviors, such as touching and talking with other children, increased as well. Generalization across responses has also been reported in programs using punishment. Lovaas and Simmons (1969) punished self-injurious behaviors in retarded children by administering electric shock. A decrease in crying, whining, and avoiding adults also occurred even though these were not punished.

Response generalization demonstrates that a behavior modification program can lead to a variety of changes in behavior beyond those resulting from direct reinforcement, punishment, or extinction (cf., Sajwaj, Twardosz, & Burke, 1972).

The notion of response generalization often is used to explain changes in responses which are not included as the target response in a given behavior modification program. For example, a child who is reinforced for studying in class may improve in reading (even though reading per se was not the reinforced response). Although one may speak of this as generalization, it may be the *direct* operation of reinforcement. When a child is reinforced for paying attention, he or she is probably reading at least on some of the occasions when reinforcement is delivered. So reading may be reinforced directly although inadvertently on a few occasions. Thus, it is difficult to speak of response generalization merely because reading was not specified as the target behavior. Sometimes behaviors are performed along with other responses that are reinforced which increase as a direct result of reinforcement. Moreover, once behaviors are increased (e.g., reading in the above example), new reinforcers in the situation may maintain them. For example, a child who begins to read may be reinforced by the interest value of the material. The main point of this discussion is to note that sometimes change in behavior which is associated with the target behavior may not be response generalization per se because a variety of responses are reinforced when a reinforcer is delivered. In any case, the main consideration in behavior modification programs is that improvements in one area of behavior are frequently associated with improvements or concomitant changes in other behaviors (Kazdin, 1975).

Conclusion

The principles outlined in this chapter provide the basis for the majority of operant conditioning programs in applied settings. However, the complexity of the programs used in behavior modification cannot be conveyed by perusal of the principles. Each principle requires elaboration because of the several factors which determine its effective application. In later chapters, principles which have been widely employed in a variety of settings will receive detailed attention. Prior to discussing the techniques derived from the principles, it is important to consider some objections which are frequently voiced in using behavior modification principles.

Misconceptions of Behavior Modification

Various misconceptions and objections are frequently voiced about the application of operant principles. Individuals concerned about behavior change have often discussed the possible misuse of behavioral techniques and the potentially adverse side effects which may result even when the techniques are used appropriately. As is often the case with objections and misconceptions, they embody threads of truth. However, it is important to isolate those points where objections are valid and those where they are not. Several of the more common objections and misconceptions will be discussed. Most of the objections and misconceptions to be discussed stem from the use of positive reinforcers. Although objections pertaining to the use of aversive events (in punishment and negative reinforcement) will be discussed briefly, many issues regarding aversive stimuli are based upon ethical considerations. Since ethical issues pervade the practice of virtually all forms of treatment and behavior change, they will be treated separately later in the book. (See Chapter 10.)

Reinforcement is "Bribery"

A frequent concern with using reinforcers, especially tangible reinforcers such as candy, toys, stars, and others, is that there is no "real" change in behavior of the person who is reinforced. The person is just being "bought" or "bribed" to perform a particular behavior. The bribery objection includes many points (O'Leary, Poulos, & Devine, 1972).

At the outset, the definition of "bribery" should be made explicit so it can be compared to the definition of reinforcement given earlier. Bribery refers to the illicit use of rewards, gifts, or favors to pervert judgment or corrupt the conduct of someone. With bribery, reward is used for the purpose of changing behavior, but the behavior is corrupt, illegal, or immoral in some way. The definition of bribery includes immoral, illegal, or dishonest behavior for which the reward is delivered or promised. Although bribery and reinforcement both involve the delivery of favorable events, their purposes are different. With reinforcement, as typically employed, events are delivered for behaviors which are generally agreed upon to benefit the client, society, or both. Behaviors which are altered with reinforcement include social and academic skills, grooming behaviors, appropriate speech, or psychotic behavior. These behaviors are rarely considered corrupt, illegal, or counter to society. Thus, the intent of the individual who provides the incentive and the purpose for which the incentive is delivered dictate whether bribery or reinforcement is at issue. Reinforcement is clearly distinguished from bribery when the precise meaning of bribery is made explicit.

Bribery, in a less strict sense, is considered a general way to influence others by giving them something. However, this general definition applies to reinforcement as well. Both are techniques to influence behavior with the major distinction stemming from the kinds of behaviors which are influenced and the purposes toward which each is directed. So there is a broad similarity between bribery and reinforcement. Yet, when discussing reinforcement it may be difficult to convey that bribery and reinforcement are similar only in that they can both influence behavior. The word "bribery" is so emotionally loaded that rarely can its superficial similarity to reinforcement be conveyed independently of the negative connotations.

Although reinforcement is *not* bribery, there are related concerns that bribery may be learned by those individuals who are influenced by rewards. First, if reinforcement is used to alter the behavior of a child, this serves as a model for the child of how one person should go about influencing others. Perhaps, reinforcement may train bribery. Although there is little direct evidence, investigators have suggested that means of behavior control employed by parents may be adopted by their children. For example, parents who use punitive methods of discipline have children who are aggressive in their interactions with peers (Bandura & Walters, 1959). Thus, children may learn to use reinforcement and punishment in the way their parents do. Yet, teaching a child to influence others with reinforcers (e.g., smiles, approval, money, and others) is not inherently bad, but the child might use these techniques to entice others into performing dishonest acts, i.e., bribery.

A second and related objection is that individuals who are exposed to reinforcement will perform desirable behaviors only when a reward is offered. Individuals will learn that some behaviors are reinforced and that they should only perform certain behaviors when they are reinforced. A person may withhold desirable behavior unless a reinforcer is given. Other individuals in the person's environment will be "manipulated" into providing the reinforcer. Manipulation of others can be inadvertently reinforced in an attempt to control behavior. For example, when a child has a tantrum, parents may try to control it with a variety of procedures (e.g., reprimands and physical control). If the tantrum does not end, a reinforcer may be offered to the child for "being nice." It is possible that the child may even have learned to say, "I will not stop unless you give me a reward." When the child stops the tantrum (or even before he stops), he receives a reinforcer. The parents may have thought that if cessation of the tantrum were reinforced, tantrums would be likely to decrease. Yet the tantrum may become a discriminative stimulus for reinforcement. Tantrum behavior eventually was followed by reinforcement. A chain of responses culminating in termination of a full-blown tantrum was reinforced. From the child's standpoint, reinforcement in the future may depend upon performing tantrum behaviors. If a child deliberately engages in tantrums or makes "deals" to behave appropriately, these may be direct attempts to control others for his or her own advantage. If these manipulative responses are successful in controlling parent behavior, they are likely to be more frequent in the future. Increased manipulation does not necessarily result from the use of reinforcers, but only from their delivery after manipulative responses.

A dramatic instance of manipulation was reported by Meichenbaum, Bowers, and Ross (1968). These investigators implemented a program with a class of institutionalized adolescent females who were described as aggressive, manipulative, and uncontrollable. At one point in the program, the girls received money for appropriate behavior during afternoon classroom sessions. Although appropriate behavior improved in the afternoons, behavior became much worse in the mornings when no money was given. One girl reported, "If you don't pay us, we won't shape up [p. 349]." The girls were trying to manipulate the psychologists by offering appropriate behavior as a reward for the money! Of course, it might be undesirable if individuals consistently became manipulative after participating in a program and required reinforcers to perform desirable behaviors in new situations. Although an instance of clients becoming manipulative to gain reinforcers is dramatic, evidence suggests that this is *not* widely found in behavior modification programs. When individuals receive reinforcers for performing behaviors in one situation, they sometimes show improvements in other situations even though no reinforcer is given (e.g., Bennett & Maley, 1973; Kazdin, 1973h). Even when behavior fails to change in the situations in which reinforcement is absent, behavior typically does not become worse in those situations (c.f., Wahler, 1969).

Hence, the concern expressed in the objection does not appear to be well justified. Reinforcing individuals for particular behaviors in a given situation rarely leads to a deterioration of those behaviors in other situations.

Many individuals object that extrinsic and tangible "rewards" are used in behavior modification. A frequent claim is that individuals should work for the intrinsic rewards associated with the activity rather than have to be "bribed." However, this claim fails to consider pervasive use of extrinsic and tangible reinforcers in everyday life. Few individuals would remain at their jobs, if wages were not provided. In fact, sometimes when individuals do not obtain high enough wages, they stop working and strike. Similarly, grades in school are used, in part, to provide incentives for academic performance. Although working and learning are implicitly regarded as worthwhile tasks in their own right, extrinsic reinforcers are used to enhance their performance. Other sources of tangible reinforcers for behavior include awards, prizes, medals, scholarships, pensions, advanced educational degrees, and trophies. Any objection levied against the use of extrinsic reinforcers in behavior modification programs applies as well to a variety of other behaviors in everyday life. Extrinsic reinforcers are present everywhere. Any objection can only be based on the behaviors for which extrinsic reinforcers are used.

It is important to mention briefly here that reinforcers used to change behavior often are events which *are* ordinarily present in the situation (i.e., "naturally occurring" reinforcers). For example, praise, smiles, approving gestures, or privileges are not extrinsic events introduced by a psychologist. They are reinforcers ordinarily available which are merely presented systematically and consistently when incorporated into a behavior modification program. (Chapter 5 will elaborate different kinds of reinforcers used in behavior modification programs.)

Individuals Become "Dependent" upon Extrinsic Reinforcers

The notion of bribes has contributed to a related objection about the use of reinforcement. Implicitly bribes are considered to be restricted to effecting short-term changes in behavior. One usually thinks of bribes to change a particular behavior or influence a decision at some moment in time. This suggests that bribes (and by association, positive reinforcement) may not lead to long-term changes in performance. Thus, concern frequently is expressed about developing a "dependency" on reinforcers.

There are two ways in which "dependency" may be manifest: (1) clients may require special reinforcers (candy, extra privileges) in order to perform any desirable behavior, and (2) behaviors will not be maintained after reinforcers are withdrawn. The objection is that reinforcement leads to dependence upon reinforcers. If this means that extrinsic reinforcers will be required for the person to perform desirable behavior in any situation, the claim presently has no well established basis, as mentioned in the discussion of bribery. On the other hand, if this means that behavior change is limited to those situations or periods of time during which reinforcement is delivered, this is a different matter.

When reinforcement is no longer provided for behavior, the behavior usually extinguishes. In this sense, individuals *do* become dependent upon the delivery of reinforcers. Discontinuing reinforcement for appropriate behavior may be expected to result in a decrease in that behavior. Obviously, one might wonder why reinforcement or other techniques should be used at all since behavior which is no longer reinforced may extinguish. First, although reinforcement may need to be continued to maintain behavior, the form or type of reinforcement may change. Initially, candy may be used, but eventually praise, attention, and privileges can be substituted (Hopkins, 1968; Kale, Kaye, Whelan & Hopkins, 1968). Second, in the beginning of a program a client may be dependent upon immediate reinforcement (e.g., candy for speaking), but eventually the reinforcement can be delayed considerably without loss of effectiveness. Finally, the frequency of reinforcement may be reduced by the end of a program. Thus, the type of reinforcement and various aspects regarding its delivery may change so that a person's behavior need not be reinforced each time by some extrinsic event. After behavior change has been achieved, the individual can be weaned systematically from the contingencies. Specific techniques can ensure that behavior is maintained once the contingencies are withdrawn. (The issue of response maintenance and the techniques useful in achieving long-term behavior change are considered in Chapter 9.)

The concern that behavior changes will not last beyond the program's duration is not always justified. When a program is terminated, extinction of behavior does not always occur (e.g., Ayllon, 1963; Hewett, Taylor, & Artuso, 1969; Kazdin, 1971a, 1973b; Kazdin & Polster, 1973; Surratt, Ulrich, & Hawkins, 1969). Changing an individual's behavior sometimes produces noticeable changes in how others in the person's environment respond to him. Even when extrinsic reinforcers are withdrawn, the reactions of others to the person whose behavior was changed may maintain the recently acquired behavior.

Behavior Modification Is "Coercive"

Another objection is that behavior modification is coercive. The concern with "coercion" includes diverse but related issues each of which has its own implications for designing treatment programs. The first and major objection pertaining to "coercion" is that *aversive means* may be used in behavior modification to compel or force individuals to perform various behaviors. The objection is to the means employed to modify behavior. The use of forceful techniques including aversive methods in general, threats, and perhaps even physical abuse to overcome client resistance is a possible concern of those who fear "coercion." A second and related aspect of coercion is that an individual may be compelled to perform behavior *against his or her own volition.* The individual may not agree to the goals of the program or personally select as desirable those behaviors which the program attempts to develop. This aspect of coercion emphasizes the *consent* of the client rather than merely the specific techniques that are used to alter behavior. Even if nonaversive techniques are used (e.g., positive reinforcement), the question is whether the client wishes to change at all and change along the lines specified by the program. A third aspect of the coercion objection is that *influencing behaviors* of other individuals, however benign, should be avoided. The concern here is better expressed as exerting any influence or control techniques over the behavior of others. The control procedures may not necessarily rely on aversive means or be against the volition of the individual client. Rather, alteration of other people's behavior as a legitimate endeavor is objectionable to many individuals. Of course, behavior modification is inherently controlling and by design attempts to influence behavior, although it does not necessarily rely on aversive means or act against an individual's volition.

The different aspects which are included or implied in the objection that behavior modification is coercive are complex and multifaceted. The present discussion will focus on the issues pertaining to the use of force or aversive means to alter behavior and actions against the volition of the clients. Ethical and treatment considerations which arise by the use of aversive techniques and the ethics of behavior control, in general, will be reserved for a separate discussion. (See Chapter 10.)

The use of force is a legitimate concern because there is always the possibility that even when the goals of a program seem beneficial to the client, the means used to achieve these goals may be harsh, unfair, and even cruel. Clients may be given little alternative but to respond in a particular way or be treated severely. Also, in most treatment and rehabilitation settings (e.g., psychiatric hospitals and prisons), the volition of clients, by design of the setting, is not considered. Rather, the facilities are viewed as institutions for inculcating the volition and values of "society." The use of force and actions against the volition of the clients are related. Forceful techniques may be resorted to when the goals are against the volition of the clients (as in the case of torture to compel individuals to divulge military secrets). In behavior modification programs, the major concern of the use of force is that individuals will be compelled to perform some response to avoid deprivation of reinforcers such as food, sleeping quarters, and privileges which are regarded as essential to everyday living, or when they are subjected to aversive procedures such as shock or physical restraint.

An example of a program which relied on force and utilized unnecessarily harsh techniques was reported by Cotter (1967) who employed electric shock to alter the behavior of psychiatric patients in a Vietnamese hospital. One-hundred-thirty male patients were given a "choice" between receiving electric shock three times a week and working for their living in the hospital. Justification of the procedure was that escape from shock would serve as negative reinforcement for the response of working. Individuals who worked would avoid shock. The procedure motivated most of the patients. However, it was then tried with a group of female patients with little success. Only 15 of 130 female patients were working by the end of 20 shock treatments. The procedures were made more severe for the females. Meals were made contingent upon working. The majority of patients missed three days of meals before finally giving in and working. The program is objectionable for at least two reasons related to the issue of coercion. First, extremely aversive means were employed. Second, the program goals certainly conflicted with the volition of the patients. Although some of the goals of the program may have been desirable (e.g., to augment activity and the level of functioning of the patients), the means employed were cruel and against the patients' volition.

Various precautions are available to ensure that a behavior modification program does not employ harsh means to force the performance of certain behaviors and act counter to the client's goals. First, in many instances, the client can participate in the development of his or her individual program. *Contingency contracting* (Homme, Csanyi, Gonzales, & Rechs, 1969) may be used where an agreement or contract is devised between the attendant, parents, teacher, or therapist and the client. The agreement specifies the behaviors which are required and the consequences which follow behaviors when they are or when they are not performed. The contract is negotiated with the parties involved (e.g., parents and child). The contract specifies the reinforcers and penalties. Privileges and reinforcers (e.g., allowance, privacy, and car privileges) are made contingent upon performance of certain behaviors (e.g., completing chores, coming home at certain times, obtaining certain grades at school). The contract system actually involves an exchange of reinforcers between two parties (Stuart & Lott, 1972). Each party "gives" something (a reinforcer or performance of a target response) and "receives" something in exchange (the desired behavior or the desired reinforcer). There may be a clause in the contract which says that the contract can be changed at any time, if both parties agree. This ensures that any program can be altered and adjustments can be readily made. Contracts have been used in programs with children in classroom settings (Homme et al., 1969), psychiatric patients (Liberman, 1971), delinquents (Stuart & Lott, 1972), adolescent behavioral problems (Tharp & Wetzel, 1969), and school dropouts (MacDonald, Gallimore, & MacDonald, 1970). A related method of permitting clients to contribute to the program is to give them administrative authority in determining the contingencies (Kazdin, 1975).

It may not always be possible to use contingency contracting or group participation in planning the program with all populations. For example, with severely and profoundly retarded or autistic children, and some psychiatric patients, the terms of the contract might not be understood. Nevertheless, in those instances where contracts can be used, it is unlikely that the clients will be forced to perform behaviors with aversive or harsh methods. Of course, the contract is designed to ensure that the contingencies are consistent with the client's own goals. The contracts provide a viable check in developing a fair and "noncoercive" program. (Contingency contracts will be detailed further in Chapter 5.)

Sometimes harsh and unfair methods may be viewed as necessary alternatives because individuals are not responding to less compelling procedures. Thus, force may be exerted to achieve effects that appear to be unobtainable with less severe techniques. Aversive means sometimes are seen as a necessary alternative (as seen in military invasion as an alternative to negotiations). Yet, in behavior modification programs there are ways to maximize responsiveness of a client to the program without relying on aversive techniques. The use of force and harsh methods can be avoided by making response requirements for positive reinforcement relatively lenient at the initial stages of a program so that it is extremely likely that the person will be able to perform them. If a client does not have the response well developed, it is unreasonable to devise a stringent contingency specifying that the response must be performed proficiently. In many programs, the requirements for reinforcement are individualized so that the client only has to make some improvement rather than meet a rigidly specified criterion to earn reinforcers. As improvements are made, the criterion for reinforcement may be altered gradually. *A client's response to the contingencies is a function of how well the contingencies are devised.* If a client fails to respond, the criteria for reinforcement should be lowered until the behavior can be performed. Shaping and modeling can be useful in developing higher levels of performance. Thus, a second way that harsh or unfair treatment can be avoided is by making demands that can be met by the client. This can be determined by beginning with low performance demands and gradually increasing them as they are met. If the client does not respond, the program should be altered. (Additional procedures to maximize responsiveness of a client to a program without relying on aversive techniques are discussed in Chapter 5.)

A third precaution against forcing clients to perform various behaviors against their volition or treating them unfairly and harshly is to allow them to leave the program when they wish. For example, Ayllon and Azrin (1968b) devised a program for psychiatric patients. A variety of reinforcers were available for performance of adaptive behaviors such as grooming, attending activities, and working at jobs on the ward. Clients were told explicitly that they could transfer to wards where there was no "reward" system. Other investigators have allowed clients to leave the program when they wish or by earning their way off the contingencies. In these latter types of programs, clients who perform the target behaviors for prolonged periods are no longer required to perform specific behaviors for access to reinforcers. In effect, control by external contingencies is faded.

A final procedure often employed to reduce aversive means is the reliance upon positive reinforcement rather than negative reinforcement or punishment. Presumably, programs exert less force if the individual is not deprived of essential reinforcers. Of course, it is possible to completely withhold powerful positive reinforcers (e.g., food) and dispense them for particular behaviors, as described in an example given earlier (Cotter, 1967). However, an obligation on the part of the program's designers is to provide incentives above and beyond essential everyday events which are normally granted and to which individuals are entitled. For example, psychiatric patients may be given extra privileges such as leaving the ward to attend a special activity, living in nicely decorated quarters, attending a canteen, and similar privileges. The reinforcers should be sufficiently attractive to entice the client rather than force him to perform in a certain way (Ayllon & Azrin, 1968b). Of course, the distinction between enticing and forcing an individual can be difficult to make. Reliance upon positive reinforcement may eliminate aversive means to achieve behavior change but it does not eliminate all aspects of "coercion," as defined earlier. With positive reinforcement, it is possible to seek treatment goals which are counter to a client's volition. Thus, reliance upon positive reinforcement does not completely ensure a "noncoercive" program.

Perhaps, the best check on the degree to which a client may be "forced" to engage in various behaviors is to provide the option of leaving the program without penalty. Further, use of a contract arrangement can ensure that the client is committed to specific goals which he views in his best interest.

The possibility of coercion in a behavior modification program should be recognized. However, in actual practice there are different ways in which the potential for unfair treatment, harsh methods, and forced compliance to arbitrary standards against the client's volition can be reduced. Increasingly, clients are encouraged to participate in the development and execution of the contingencies (Kazdin, 1975).

Negative Effects of Behavior Modification on Others

Behavior modification programs often are implemented in group settings (institutions for psychiatric patients, retardates, delinquents, prisons, day-care centers, and classrooms) where the behavior of only one or two individuals may warrant particular attention. Frequently, programs are implemented for these individuals who are considered to warrant attention because of behavior problems, while the behaviors of other clients are regarded as adequate without such a program. A concern which arises is that reinforcing one or a few clients for behaving in a desirable fashion and not others who are already behaving appropriately may have deleterious effects on the latter. When the clients who already behave appropriately see that only the disruptive person earns rewards, will they too become disruptive to increase their opportunity for reinforcement? O'Leary et al. (1972) referred to an instance in which reinforcers delivered to one student resulted in negative reactions on the part of other children. Hence, the possibility exists that excluding individuals from a reinforcement program has undesirable effects.

Several points need to be made in response to this objection. First, programs in group settings need not be limited to the performance of one individual. Often the reason that a few individuals come to mind when considering programs is that their behavioral "problems" may involve dramatic or intense behaviors such as psychotic verbalizations, tantrums, or fighting. However, in most settings, the behavior of all clients can be improved in some fashion. For example, the excellent, well-behaved elementary school pupil may profit from some form of an incentive program to increase gains made in academic performance. Although one or a few individuals in a given setting may appear to require special programs, it may well be that most or all of the individuals in the setting could profit from programs in which some behaviors were systematically reinforced. The behaviors reinforced need not be the same for each individual. Yet, the available reinforcers can be the same.

A second response to the objection is that programs for only one or a few individuals can be structured to include the group for whom no special program seems necessary. Programs can be devised so that the performance of one individual (or a few) earns extra reinforcers for the group as a whole including the individual himself or herself. The group shares in the reinforcing consequences which increases their involvement in the program. A number of investigations have shown that programs in which one individual earns reinforcers for the group is very effective for children in classrooms (Jones & Kazdin, 1975; Wolf, Hanley, King, Lachowicz, & Giles, 1970), psychiatric patients (Olson & Greenberg, 1972), and delinquents (Phillips, 1968). There are advantages to this kind of group program aside from merely including peers who might otherwise be excluded from the positive reinforcers. Peers give praise for appropriate behavior because they earn reinforcers whenever the individual is reinforced. The praise itself may contribute greatly to behavior change in the individual for whom the contingency was designed. The major point is that even when a program seems to be required for one or a few individuals, others can be included. The main reason investigators plan individual programs to include the peer group is not necessarily to avoid negative effects on others but rather to provide peer reinforcement (e.g., praise) and group pressure to help the individual perform appropriately. If peers profit from an individual's performance, they are likely to increase praise for that individual and socialize more with him. These beneficial effects alone warrant using group programs to change the behavior of one individual. (Group contingencies will be discussed in Chapter 5.)

A third reply to the objection is that it is not well established that there are negative side effects to giving one person reinforcers while excluding others. In fact, there is evidence for positive side effects of reinforcing one individual on the behavior of other individuals. There are *vicarious* effects of reinforcement so that reinforcing one individual improves the behavior of individuals who are nearby as shown in rehabilitation settings for the retarded (Kazdin, 1973d) and classrooms (Bolstad & Johnson, 1972; Broden, Bruce, Mitchell, Carter, & Hall, 1970; Kazdin, 1973c). (Vicarious effects of reinforcement will be discussed in Chapter 5.)

Behavior Modification Is Nothing New—Everyone Does It All of the Time

When behavior modification is described, individuals often are impressed with the simplicity of the principles and their familiarity with the use of the techniques. The claim is made that the principles are not new, and the techniques are widely practiced all of the time to deal with pets, children, spouses, roomates, students, adults, and others.

As with other objections or misconceptions, there certainly is truth to this for at least two reasons. First, principles and techniques of behavior modification are deeply woven into the fabric of major social institutions and human existence, in general, as evidenced by child rearing, education, business, government and law, and religion (Skinner, 1953). In child rearing, parents rely on reinforcement and punishment to control behavior. Reinforcement in the form of privileges and praise, and punishment in the form of verbal reprimands and physical discipline are commonly used in the home. In education, teachers attempt to increase the performance of academic skills in students by using grades and point systems. In business and industry, performance on the job is reinforced with bonuses, commissions, and promotions. These applications are deliberate attempts to alter behavior with positive reinforcement. Punishment also is widely practiced as evident in law. Sentences and penalties are invoked for a variety of behaviors that society wishes to suppress, ranging from acts of violence to infractions of local traffic ordinances. Of course, the deliberate use of behavior modification principles is evident in many religions where delayed (in some cases posthumous) positive or negative events are held to be contingent upon performance during one's life. Since reinforcement and punishment are embedded in major aspects of social living, it would be false to claim that the principles or their application are new.

In another sense, behavior modification is used all of the time by virtually everyone. The principles of operant conditioning suggest that behavior is always controlled even when they are not deliberately applied. Everyone reinforces, punishes, and extinguishes behaviors of others with whom they are in contact each day even though no explicit attempts may be made to control behavior. In conversation with others we may smile, show interest, or agree with the person who is talking. These events are likely to increase the frequency that the other person converses with us. On the other hand, we may also look disinterested, disagree, or yawn which may punish the behavior of someone with whom we are conversing. It is likely that both favorable and unfavorable consequences are administered at different points in conversation so that certain topics and opinions expressed are reinforced, while others are punished. Certainly, extinction sometimes is used in a very deliberate fashion. Leaving the room or ignoring someone talking is frequently used to stop someone from saying something we do not wish to hear. Nagging is treated in this fashion. The point is that even without realizing it, everyone in contact with others is applying consequences for behavior and thereby modifying that behavior. Whether we provide consequences for a response (reinforcement or punishment) or ignore it altogether (extinction), we are modifying someone's behavior. So it would seem fair to claim that behavior modification is not new and that everyone is using the techniques all of the time.

In an important sense, however, the claim is untrue. Behavior modification is characterized by the *systematic* and *consistent* application of various techniques. If reinforcement is employed in a behavior modification program, the behavior it follows is carefully defined and the reinforcer is applied regularly, in a similar fashion each time, and with a particular goal in mind. Reinforcement, punishment, or extinction, as typically used in everyday life, are not carried out systematically. To continue the above example, in conversation with a particular individual, rarely does our attention and the attention of others (smiles or expressions of interest) consistently follow certain responses with a goal of altering these responses. The consequences which follow behavior will probably not be consistent across time and across the individuals who provide consequences. On some days, certain responses will be reinforced but the contingency will not be continued over time, so that no systematic change in behavior is evident. Similarly, across all the individuals with whom someone comes into contact, the reinforcement and punishment is delivered inconsistently. Some individuals reinforce certain responses while other people ignore them.

An example of the inconsistent application of consequences can be seen in students trying to alter the behavior of their instructor in a large college class. Students have at their disposal a very potent reinforcer, namely, paying close attention to the instructor while he or she is lecturing. However, this reinforcer is usually dispensed in an unsystematic fashion. Some students in class pay attention most of the time, others only when humor is introduced to make a point, and others when the instructor is discussing some socially relevant issue. Paying attention is somewhat idiosyncratic. Although the professor's behavior may change in response to some of the reinforcement, reinforcement and punishment usually are applied consistently enough for there to be too much impact. Moreo reinforcement is probably administered for incompatible responses (giving well-planned lectures versus talking informally as in discussions). Reinforcement is being applied but in a haphazard fashion. If students united to systematically reinforce a particular behavior, a change could be made. An example of this frequently referred to is shaping professors into standing on one side of the room. Students could pay attention to the instructor when he or she approached one side of the room (positive reinforcement) and look disinterested or bored when he or she approached the other side of the room (extinction). Eventually, through reinforcement of successive approximations (shaping), the instructor would stand on one side of the room. However, for this to be achieved, consistent application of reinforcement would be required. Other elements would also be essential before referring to this as a behavior modification program, such as collection of data and precise evaluation of the contingency.

Principles of behavior modification frequently are applied inconsistently in the home. Parents often try to employ reinforcement and punishment for specific behaviors in their children. For cleaning one's room, a child may earn privileges such as going out with friends. Yet, the definition of room cleaning may change from day to day so that sometimes the privilege is earned for thoroughly cleaning the room, while at other times only a few tasks are required. In addition, each parent may define the room-cleaning response differently so that the criteria are not consistently enforced. Similarly, the privilege used for a reinforcer may be given "free" because an opportune occasion arises for the child to go out with peers. Hence, the reinforcer is delivered without requiring room cleaning at all. When reinforcement is not contingent upon the response and the behaviors are reinforced inconsistently, behavior is not likely to improve.

Various characteristics of behavior modification differentiate it clearly from the accidental use of reinforcement and other principles in everyday life. First, the response to be changed in behavior modification is carefully defined so that observers agree as to what constitutes occurrences of the response. Second, data are collected to ascertain the frequency that the behavior is performed. Observers who may be parents, teachers, attendants, therapists, or the clients themselves, record the behavior over a period of time to determine the extent of the problem. Third, when the program is implemented to alter behavior, the collection of data continues so that any behavior change will be evident. Finally, an attempt is made to determine whether the program and not some extraneous events caused the behavior change. The explicit use of behavioral techniques requires careful and precise evaluation of behavior change. This is rarely approximated when the principles of behavior modification are applied inadvertently in everyday life.

With regard to the notion that everyone does behavior modification all of the time, it should be clear that this is only partially true. The defining characteristics of behavior modification are methodical implementation of the principles and evaluation of the effects of the contingencies. Although people apply the principles in everyday life, in most cases they do not apply them systematically. The technological advances which have been made in the application of behavioral principles, discussed throughout remaining chapters, will clearly show the distinction between systematic and nonsystematic effects of the procedures.

GOALS OF BEHAVIOR MODIFICATION

In discussing objections to and misconceptions of behavior modification it is important to make the goals of behavior-change programs explicit. Since the objections include some valid points, the reasons for undertaking behavior modification programs need to be clear.

In most settings where behavior modification is conducted, the goal is to make long-term changes in behavior of the clients. The goal is not a transitory change. Yet, the techniques used in some circumstances may require an artificial arrangement of the situation on a temporary basis so that behavior is systematically changed. For example, an adult retardate working in a sheltered workshop setting may be reinforced with privileges and money for promptness in coming to work. In light of the objections discussed earlier, one might be concerned with the individual becoming dependent upon the reinforcers. Because the world outside a sheltered workshop will offer no special privileges for promptness, will the behavior be maintained? This concern is important but somewhat premature. The initial goal is to develop the behavior so it is performed consistently. After the behavior is well established, procedures need to be used to ensure its maintenance. At the early stage of a program, performance is likely to depend upon the delivery of reinforcement or punishment. If the adult retardate no longer received reinforcement for his behavior, promptness might quickly extinguish. Yet, the goals of behavior modification are to change behavior and to have the change maintained after the program is terminated, that is, remove dependence upon the contingencies that existed during the program. General long-range goals of behavior modification require sustained performance of socially appropriate behaviors.

For any individual participating in a therapeutic environment, a major objective is to maximize the reinforcement (praise, accomplishment, esteem from others, self-esteem, social interaction) and minimize the punishment (stigma, social censure, self-depreciation, repeated failure) in one's life. To maximize reinforcement and minimize punishment in a social milieu requires that the individual perform social and personal skills and effectively control his environment. To achieve the latter may require temporary artificial programming of the situation to develop basic social and per sonal skills. Individuals in a therapeutic environment have not responded to the somewhat irregular contingencies operative in the "real world." If reinforcement were frequent enough for these individuals or delivered in a systematic fashion in ordinary social interaction, the use of behavior modification techniques might not be required. Where specific techniques are required, the interim goal is to develop specific target behaviors to enhance social and personal competence. However, the long-term goal is to provide the individual with the greatest opportunity possible for rein forcement in everyday life. An artificially programmed environment at tempts to develop behavior so that it may be responsive to reinforcement and punishment contingencies which normally occur in the "natural" social environment.

The behavior modification program to which some individuals are exposed may not be temporary. For example, for clients whose behavioral deficits are so great as to require institutional care, it is not readily feasible to develop behavior to a point at which the reinforcement contingencies in the natural environment will control behavior. The alternatives for treatment consist of whether or not the environment in which such in dividuals live should be programmed to maximize the degree of behavior change, skill acquisition, and the amount of reinforcement available. In any case, in some settings behavior modification programs may constitute a semipermanent environment. Of course, it is the goal of such programs to increase skills in various areas (e.g., personal hygiene) so that gradually fewer behaviors need to be regulated by external control.

An ultimate goal of operant techniques, and indeed most treatment techniques, is to give an individual the means of controlling his own behavior. Control over behavior may be transferred from external agents to the individual himself. With many individuals, it is feasible to train them to analyze their own responses and to apply consequences to them selves for their own behavior. (Fox, 1962; Goldiamond, 1965). Self-control training is a goal of behavior modification. Of course, with several popula tions for whom behavior modification techniques are implemented (e.g., severely and profoundly retarded and autistic children, and psychiatric pa tients), it may not be feasible to achieve this goal. In cases where individ uals can be trained to control their own behaviors, some objections to behavior modification subside. For example, there is less need to be con cerned with the transience of behavior change if the individual has self control skills. Presumably, the individual's behavior can achieve or sustain a certain level of performance at any time he or she chooses to arrange the environment in such a way as to increase or to decrease that behavior. (Self-control will be discussed in Chapter 8.)

How to Begin and Evaluate a Behavior Modification Program

There is a variety of decisions to be made and practical steps to be executed when implementing a behavior modification program. The decisions and steps apply to almost all settings, populations, and behaviors. Major steps include identifying the specific target behavior to be focused upon, assessing the target behavior and antecedent or consequent events associated with the behavior, and evaluating the efficacy of the program. Included in these steps are several obstacles which may be a function of the setting in which one is working, the behavior focused upon, the resources available to implement and evaluate the program, and the control one has over the environment. This chapter will consider the requirements for initiating and evaluating a behavior modification program in virtually any setting.

Identifying the Goal of the Program

Implementation of a behavior modification program requires a clear statement of the goal(s) of the program and a careful description of the target behavior. Although the goal of the program is to change some behavior, the change is not made by simply focusing on the behavior alone. It is important to specify the environmental conditions associated with the behavior and the conditions which will be used to achieve behavior change. Environmental conditions include those antecedent and consequent events which bear relation to and influence behavior.

Many behavioral problems stem from a failure of behavior to be performed in the presence of particular antecedent events. These behaviors are considered to reflect a lack of appropriate stimulus control. For example, a child may complete his schoolwork when he should be looking at the board, reciting, or playing at recess. The teacher may constantly remind the child to put his materials away or pay attention. Yet the child's behavior is not controlled by these instructions (antecedent events). Training may focus on instructing the child to engage in some behavior and reinforcing compliance. Similarly, parents often cajole, coax, and command their children to engage in a variety of behaviors. Yet these verbalizations frequently do not markedly influence the behavior of their children. Thus, it is important to develop behaviors in the presence of certain antecedent events.

Other situations clearly involve consideration of antecedent conditions. For example, in developing talking in a mute psychiatric patient, it is important to reinforce verbalizations only in relation to specific conditions. A patient might be reinforced for talking to other individuals (antecedent stimuli) rather than to himself. Verbalization is only appropriate under a limited number of stimulus conditions. A program must associate verbalizations with reinforcement in these "appropriate" situations so that the situations provide a cue (S^D) for talking. From the above examples, it should be evident that development of behavioral objectives requires consideration of antecedent events. Under what circumstances or in the presence of what cues should the target behavior be performed? The program ultimately will focus upon developing specific behaviors in the presence of certain cues and not in the absence of these cues.

The goal for most clients is to develop behaviors in presence of certain stimulus conditions. For some individuals, an initial goal is to train responsiveness to certain consequent events. These individuals normally do not respond to events which play a major role in social interaction, such as attention, physical contact, praise, or mild disapproval. Autistic children have been described as unresponsive to events which are reinforcing for most children (Ferster, 1961). Similarly, delinquents and conduct-problem children in the home are often unresponsive to praise (Wahler, 1972). In such cases, contingencies are devised to alter the value of stimuli such as physical contact or praise from an adult (Lovaas et al., 1965; Wahler, 1968). In these programs, neutral stimuli (e.g., statements of approval) are paired with events which are reinforcing (e.g., food and termination of an aversive event). Eventually, the previously neutral stimuli serve as positive reinforcers. Once the events are established as reinforcers, the program focuses on developing specific target behaviors. Thus, establishing effective consequences is usually a preliminary goal. Once achieved, other programs are begun. For example, once autistic children are trained to be responsive to adults (i.e., adults serve as reinforcers), various skills are trained, including language and interpersonal communication (Lovaas, 1968).

The main goal of a program is to alter a particular target behavior. A target behavior may not be performed at all or infrequently, or it is performed too frequently and should be decreased or eliminated. Again, the above statement applies to a particular stimulus condition (e.g., home, classroom, certain times of the day, or presence of particular individuals). Nevertheless, the main question is what *behavior* is to be changed in the stimulus conditions specified.

Identification of the behavior to be changed may appear to be a relatively simple task. In almost all settings there is general agreement among staff members as to the behavioral "problems" of the clients, which individuals need to be changed, and the general goals to be achieved. Agreement is often expressed in complaints about individual clients which suggest that certain problem areas require therapeutic intervention. However, the general or global statements of behavior problems which are usually provided are insufficient for actually beginning a program. For example, it is insufficient to select as the goal alteration of aggressiveness, learning deficits, speech, social skills, depression, psychotic symptoms, self-esteem, and similar notions. Traits, general summary labels, and personality characteristics are too general to be of much use. Moreover, definitions of the behaviors which make up these general labels may be idiosyncratic across different staff members, parents, and teachers. The target behaviors have to be defined explicitly so that they can actually be observed, measured, and agreed upon by individuals administering the program. Behaviors need to be defined very carefully so it is clear when they occur.

Behavior should be *described* in such a fashion that few or no inferences are required to detect the response. Before developing the precise definition of behavior, it may be useful to casually observe the person who is to be included in the program. Descriptive notes of what behaviors occur and which events are associated with their occurrence may be useful in generating specific response definitions. For example, if a psychiatric patient is labeled as being "withdrawn," it is essential to observe the patient's behavior on the ward and to isolate those specific behaviors that have led to the use of the label. From these notes, behaviors can be derived which define global concepts such as aggressiveness, negativism, hyperactivity, and similar terms. The specific behaviors become the object of change rather than the global concept.

Behavior modification programs have reported clear behavioral definitions which were developed from global terms. For example, Phillips (1968) noted that "aggressiveness" exhibited by predelinquent boys usually was inferred from their frequent use of comments which threatened others. Aggressive comments including threats of destruction to an object, person, or animal were denoted as target behaviors. As another example, Milby (1970) increased the social interaction of two socially isolated schizophrenic patients. The definition of interaction included talking to and working or playing with another patient at any time during the period in which data were gathered. In one program, bickering among children in the home was the target behavior (Christophersen, Arnold, Hill, & Quilitch, 1972). Bickering was defined as verbal arguments between any two or all three children which were louder than the normal speaking voice. These examples show that clear behavioral definitions can be derived from general terms (e.g., aggressiveness, social interaction, and bickering) which ordinarily have diverse meanings to different individuals.

A useful preliminary exercise before embarking on a behavior modification program is to select various concepts and trait labels used in everyday language and to provide alternative behavioral definitions for each one. Although the definition of the target response may be different across behavior modification programs, even for two individuals who are referred to as "aggressive," practice in specifying target behaviors is valuable.

Assessment

Target Behaviors. When behavior has been defined in precise terms, assessment can begin. Assessment and specific response definitions are closely related. A response is carefully defined, in part, so it can be measured. Alternatively, when a response is measured, it is carefully defined.

Assessment of behavior is essential for at least two reasons. First, assessment determines the extent to which the target behavior is performed. Assessment reflects the frequency of occurrence of behavior prior to the program. The rate of preprogram behavior is referred to as the *baseline* or *operant rate.* Reliance on human judgment in the absence of objective assessment may distort the extent to which the behavior is actually performed. For example, tantrums in a child are often so intense that parents or teachers recall them as occurring very often. Because tantrums are so noticeable, they may seem more frequent than they actually are. In contrast, some children may have so many tantrums and episodes of whining that parents become somewhat accustomed to a high rate. Thus, tantrums may be perceived as frequent but not nearly as frequent as they actually are. Human judgment sometimes does not correspond to actual data obtained from observing behavior (Kazdin, 1973h; Schnelle, 1974). Only careful assessment reveals the extent to which behavior is performed and the degree of behavior change required.

Second, assessment is required to reflect behavior change after the program is begun. Since the major purpose of the behavior modification program is to alter behavior, behavior during the program must be compared with behavior during baseline. Careful assessment throughout the program is essential. It is unwise to rely upon human judgment and informal impressions to determine whether behavior has changed because the relation of these criteria to actual behavior may be very low. Even when there is no actual change in the behavior of a client, some staff members may report improvement (Loeber, 1971). Accurate assessment reduces bias which often pervades human judgment.

Stimulus Events.   Recording the occurrence of the target behavior excludes a great deal of important information which may be useful in designing a behavior modification program. Various antecedent and consequent events are likely to be systematically associated with the performance of the target behavior. In most applied settings, social stimuli or interactions with others constitute a major category of events which influences behavior of clients. For example, attendants, parents, and teachers may provide verbal statements (e.g., instructions or praise), gestures (e.g., physical contact, motions, or nonverbal directives), and expressions (e.g., smiles or frowns) which exert control over behavior. These stimuli may precede (e.g., instructions) or follow (e.g., praise) the behavior focused upon in a behavior change program. In any given setting, it is useful to obtain descriptive notes to record the events which immediately precede or follow behavior (Bijou, Peterson, & Ault, 1968). Antecedent and consequent events associated with the target behavior may lead to hypotheses of which events control behavior and thereby can be used to alter behavior. These hypotheses can be tested directly by altering the events to determine their influence on behavior. For example, informal observation may indicate that the target behavior is performed at some particular time during the day, prior to a specific event, in the presence of some other person, and so on. These clues, if born out by careful assessment, may provide insights about stimulus conditions which exert control over the target behavior.

Observing consequences which ordinarily follow behavior is exceedingly important. If an undesirable behavior is performed consistently, it is likely that some environmental event is maintaining it. Conversely, if a desirable behavior is not performed consistently, it may be that certain environmental events (i.e., positive reinforcers) fail to follow it. In a behavior modification program it is important to systematically assess consequences which follow behavior. In the majority of programs, consequences which follow the target response are altered in some way. To ensure that the consequences are delivered in a particular fashion (e.g., contingently and with a high frequency), they must be assessed. If they are not assessed, there is no systematic way to determine whether the consequences were altered as intended. Antecedent or consequent events can be assessed while the target response is being recorded. Investigators frequently record (and alter) events in the environment to demonstrate their influence on target behaviors. For example, altering the frequency of parent or teacher behavior (e.g., attention and praise, disapproval and reprimands) influences behavior of children (e.g., Hall et al., 1968; Kazdin & Klock, 1973; Wahler, 1969; Zeilberger, Sampen, & Sloane, 1968). Antecedent or consequent events which exert control over target behaviors in clients often are the *behaviors* of the staff who supervises them. Hence, the behaviors of staff need to be assessed as well as the behaviors which are controlled or developed in the clients.

Strategies of Assessment

Assessment of behavior of the client and the individuals who may influence the client's behavior can be accomplished in different ways. Behavior can be assessed by recording the *frequency* with which a response is performed, the *amount of time* (duration) it occurs, the *intensity* of magnitude of the response, or its *latency* (i.e., the amount of time until a response is performed). In most behavior modification programs, either a frequency count or measure based on the amount of time the target response occurs is used.

Frequency Measures.   Frequency counts require simply tallying the number of times the behavior occurs in a given period of time. This measure is referred to as *response rate* (frequency of the response divided by time). Measures of response rate are particularly useful when the target response is *discrete* and when the response takes a *relatively constant amount of time* each time it is performed. A discrete response has a clearly delineated beginning and end so that separate instances of the response can be counted (Skinner, 1966b). The performance of the behavior should take a relatively constant amount of time so that the units which are counted are approximately equal. Ongoing behaviors, such as smiling, sitting in one's seat, lying down, and talking, are difficult to record simply by counting because each response may occur for different amounts of time. For example, if a person talks to a peer for 15 seconds and to another peer for 30 minutes, these might be counted as two instances of talking. However, a great deal of information is lost by simply counting instances of talking because they differ in duration. Similarly, in a classroom setting, recording the frequency of sitting in one's seat would be difficult because a student might be in his seat for 20 minutes and this would count as one response. Also a student may change positions drastically so that it is not readily apparent when sitting is ending and beginning, that is, it may not be discrete. On the other hand, the number of times a person performs a discrete behavior is amenable to frequency recording.

Frequency measures have been used for a variety of behaviors. In experiments with predelinquent boys living in a home-style treatment cottage, frequency measures were used to assess the number of academic assignments the boys completed, the number of specific bathroom cleaning tasks that were completed, the number of aggressive phrases used, and the number of times the word "ain't" was used (Phillips, 1968). In an investigation designed to train social responses in psychotic patients, the frequency that patients greeted staff was counted daily (Kale et al., 1968). Staff members on the ward approached the patients several times each day to ensure that there were opportunities for social greetings by the patients. In another report, tantrums of a retarded child were recorded by simply counting them (Sailor, Guess, Rutherford, & Baer, 1968). A frequency tally could be employed because the tantrums were discrete and of a consistent duration (10 to 15 seconds). Finally, Lovaas et al. (1965) recorded the frequency that autistic children responded to commands to come toward the experimenter. There are additional examples of discrete behaviors that can be easily assessed with frequency counts, including the number of cigarettes smoked, number of times a person attends an activity or that one person hits another person, number of objects thrown, number of vocabulary words used, number of errors in speech, and so on.

Frequency measures require merely noting instances in which behavior occurs. Usually there is an additional requirement that behavior be observed for a constant amount of time. Of course, if behavior is observed for 20 minutes on one day and 30 minutes on another day, the frequencies are not directly comparable. However, the rate of response each day can be achieved by dividing the frequency of responses by the number of minutes observed each day. This measure will yield frequency per minute or rate of response which is comparable for different durations of observation.

A frequency measure has several desirable features for use in applied settings. First, frequency of a response is relatively simple to score for individuals working in natural settings. Keeping a tally of behavior usually is all that is required. Moreover, counting devices are available, such as golf counters worn as a wristwatch, which facilitate recording. Second, frequency measures readily reflect changes over time. The number of times a response occurs is sensitive to change resulting from alterations in contingencies. Since the principles of operant conditioning refer to changes in the frequency of a response, it is desirable to observe the response frequency or rate directly (Skinner, 1966b). Third, and related to the above, frequency expresses the *amount* of behavior performed, which usually is of concern to individuals in applied settings. In many cases, the goal of the program is to increase or decrease the number of times a certain behavior occurs. Frequency provides a direct measure of the amount of behavior. There are additional advantages of response frequency as a measure which have been discussed elsewhere (Bijou, Peterson, Harris, Allen, & Johnston, 1969; Kazdin, 1973g; Skinner, 1966a, 1966b).

Another measure related to frequency is the *number of individuals* who perform a given behavior. Of course, this number does not refer to the rate of responding, as discussed above. Yet the number of individuals is a discrete measure that usually can be easily recorded. It has been used in situations where it is desirable to alter the number of individuals in a group who perform a response such as the number of psychiatric patients who use eating utensils at meals (Ayllon & Azrin, 1964), the number of individuals who brush their teeth (Lattal, 1969), the number of hospitalized delinquent soldiers who participate in various activities on the ward (Colman & Boren, 1969), or the number of welfare recipients who attend community meetings (Miller & Miller, 1970).

Although the number of individuals who perform the behaviors is easily recorded, this measure might be less sensitive than the frequency of response measure for individual subjects. As mentioned earlier, since operant procedures act directly on the frequency of responses, response rate is the most direct measure of change. Using the number of individuals who engage in a behavior as a measurement strategy depends upon the goal of a program. In many programs, the goal is to alter the behavior of one or a few individuals so rate of response of *each* individual rather than number of individuals who perform the response more closely follows this goal.

Interval Recording. A frequent strategy of measuring behavior in an applied setting is based on units of time rather than discrete response units. Behavior is recorded during short periods of time for the total time that it is performed. The two methods of time-based measurement are interval recording (sometimes referred to as time sampling) and response duration.

With interval recording, behavior is observed for certain intervals of time. Typically, interval recording samples behavior for a *single block of time* such as 30 or 60 minutes once per day. A block of time is divided into a series of short intervals (e.g., each interval equaling 10 or 15 seconds). The behavior of the client is observed during each interval. The target behavior is scored as having occurred or not occurred during *each* interval. If a discrete behavior, such as hitting someone, occurs one or more times in a single interval, the response is scored as having occurred. Several response occurrences within an interval are not counted separately. If the behavior is ongoing with an unclear beginning or end, such as talking, playing, and sitting, or occurs for a long period of time, it is scored during each interval in which it is occurring.

Behavior modification programs in classroom settings frequently use interval recording to score whether students are paying attention, sitting in their seats, and working quietly. Behavior of an individual student may be observed for 10-second intervals over a 20-minute observational period. For each interval, an observer records whether the child is in his or her seat working quietly. If the child remains in his seat and works for a long period of time, many intervals will be scored for attentive behavior. If the child leaves his seat (without permission) or stops working, inattentive behavior will be scored. During some intervals, a child may be in his seat for half of the time and out of seat for the remaining time. Since the interval has to be scored for *either* attentive or inattentive behavior, a rule has to be devised how to score behavior in this instance. Often, getting out of the seat will be counted as inattentive behavior and will nullify the remaining period of attentive behavior within the interval. Interval recording for a single block of time has been used for several responses including appropriate mealtime behaviors of retardates (Barton, Guess, Garcia, & Baer, 1970), social responses of psychiatric patients (Milby, 1970) and withdrawn children (O'Connor, 1969), and uncooperative child behavior in the home (Wahler, 1969).

Interval scoring of behavior is facilitated by a scoring sheet where intervals are represented across time. (See Figure 4–1.) In Figure 4–1, each number across the top denotes a time interval. During each interval a

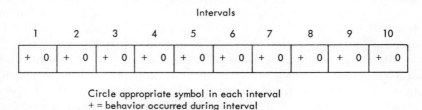

Circle appropriate symbol in each interval
+ = behavior occurred during interval
0 = behavior did not occur during interval

FIGURE 4–1 Example of interval scoring sheet for one individual.

"+" or "0" is circled or checked to denote whether the behavior has occurred for the subject. The basic sheet can be expanded to include many individuals and intervals as shown in Figure 4–2. For example, each individual in a classroom or on a ward can be observed for a large number of intervals. The first subject would be observed for the first interval (e.g., 15 seconds). After behavior was recorded, the second subject would be observed. This would be continued until each subject has been observed for one interval (down the left column in Figure 4–2). The order would then be repeated until each subject was observed for another interval, and so on for remaining intervals. Often more than one behavior is scored in an interval so that the presence of several behaviors will be judged during each interval. To accomplish this, a data sheet may include many symbols in each interval block so various behaviors can be coded. A letter or symbol is checked or circled for different categories of behavior which occur during the interval. Developing detailed codes and scoring sheets has been discussed in other sources (e.g., Bijou et al., 1968).

In using an interval scoring method, an observer looks at the client during the interval. When one interval is over, the observer records whether

Intervals

Individuals	1	2	3	4	5	6	7	8	9	10
1	+ 0	+ 0	+ 0	+ 0	+ 0	+ 0	+ 0	+ 0	+ 0	+ 0
2	+ 0	+ 0	+ 0	+ 0	+ 0	+ 0	+ 0	+ 0	+ 0	+ 0
3	+ 0	+ 0	+ 0	+ 0	+ 0	+ 0	+ 0	+ 0	+ 0	+ 0
4	+ 0	+ 0	+ 0	+ 0	+ 0	+ 0	+ 0	+ 0	+ 0	+ 0
5	+ 0	+ 0	+ 0	+ 0	+ 0	+ 0	+ 0	+ 0	+ 0	+ 0
6	+ 0	+ 0	+ 0	+ 0	+ 0	+ 0	+ 0	+ 0	+ 0	+ 0
7	+ 0	+ 0	+ 0	+ 0	+ 0	+ 0	+ 0	+ 0	+ 0	+ 0
8	+ 0	+ 0	+ 0	+ 0	+ 0	+ 0	+ 0	+ 0	+ 0	+ 0
9	+ 0	+ 0	+ 0	+ 0	+ 0	+ 0	+ 0	+ 0	+ 0	+ 0
10	+ 0	+ 0	+ 0	+ 0	+ 0	+ 0	+ 0	+ 0	+ 0	+ 0

FIGURE 4–2 Example of interval scoring sheet for many individuals.

the behavior occurred. If an observer is recording several behaviors in an interval, a few seconds may be needed to record all the behaviors that were observed in that interval. If the observer recorded a behavior as soon as it occurred (before the interval was over), he or she might miss other behaviors which occurred while the first behavior was being scored. Hence, many investigators use interval scoring procedures which allow time to record after each interval of observation. Intervals for observing behavior might be ten seconds, with five seconds after the interval for recording these observations. If a single behavior is scored in an interval, no time may be required for recording. Each interval might be ten seconds. As soon as a behavior occurred, it would be scored immediately. If behavior did not occur, a quick mark could indicate this at the end of the interval. Of course, it is desirable to use short recording times, when possible, because when behavior is being recorded, it is not being observed. Recording consumes time that might be used for observing behavior.

There are significant features of interval recording which make it one of the most widely adopted strategies in applied settings. First, interval assessment is very flexible because virtually any behavior can be recorded. The presence or absence of a response during a time interval applies to any measurable response. Whether a response is discrete and does not vary in duration, is continuous, or sporadic, it can be classified as occurring or not occurring during any time period. Second, the observations resulting from interval recording can be easily converted into a percentage. The number of intervals during which the response is scored as occurring can be divided by the total number of intervals observed. This ratio multiplied by 100 yields a percentage of intervals that the response is performed. For example, if social responses are scored as occurring in 20 or 40 intervals that were observed, the percentage of intervals of social behavior is 50% (20/40 x 100). A percentage is easily communicated to others by noting that a certain behavior occurs a specific percentage of time (intervals). (In some cases, frequency measures can provide a percentage of responses. For example, correct responses on an examination are readily converted into a percentage by forming a ratio of correct responses to total responses and multiplying by 100.) Whenever there is doubt as to what assessment strategy should be adopted, an interval approach is always applicable and can be readily employed. Yet, as discussed below, some practical considerations make interval recording more cumbersome than a simple frequency measure.

Duration. A second time-based method of observation is duration of the response. This method of assessment is useful in programs where the goal is to increase or decrease the length of time a response is performed. Duration measures have been used for a variety of behaviors including the length of time a claustrophobic patient spent sitting voluntarily in a small room (Leitenberg, Agras, Thompson, & Wright, 1968), the time predelinquent boys spent returning from school and errands (Phillips, 1968), the time children spent working on classroom assignments (Surratt et al., 1969), and the time retarded children spent engaging in cooperative play (Redd, 1969) and social responses (Whitman, Mercurio, & Caponigri, 1970).

Duration may be useful as a response strategy even when one wishes to eliminate a behavior entirely. For example, in a psychiatric hospital a patient may come to the nurse for medication late each day. To measure tardiness for medication, the nurse can simply record the amount of time between the scheduled time for medication and the patient's arrival to the nurse's station. Tardiness would be defined by the total number of minutes and seconds late each day. A program can be implemented to decrease tardiness. The effect of the program would be reflected in the length of time the patient takes to come for medication. Ultimately, if the program is successful, the patient will not be late (i.e., "0" seconds beyond the designated time).

Assessment of response duration is a fairly simple matter requiring that one starts and stops a stopwatch or notes the time when the response begins and ends. However, the onset and termination of the response must be carefully defined. If these conditions have not been met, duration is extremely difficult to employ. For example, in recording the duration of a tantrum, a child may cry continuously for several minutes, whimper for short periods, stop all noise for a few seconds, and begin intense crying again. In recording duration, a decision is required to handle changes in the intensity of the behavior (e.g., crying to whimpering) and pauses (e.g., periods of silence) so they are consistently recorded as part of the response or as a different (e.g., nontantrum) response.

Use of response duration is generally restricted to situations where the length of time a behavior is performed is a major concern. In most behavior modification programs, the goal is to increase or decrease the frequency of a response rather than its duration. There are notable exceptions, of course. For example, it is desirable to increase the length of time that students study. However, because interval measures are so widely used and readily adaptable to virtually all responses, they are often selected as a measure over duration. The number or proportion of intervals in which study behavior occurs reflects changes in study time since interval recording is based on time.

Selection of an Assessment Strategy. Selecting the assessment strategy either based upon frequency counts, interval recording, or duration need not be difficult. Some behaviors lend themselves well to frequency counts because they are discrete (such as the number of profane words used, or number of appropriate toileting or eating responses) and others to interval recording (such as reading, working, or sitting), or duration because they are ongoing behaviors (such as time spent crying, studying, or getting dressed). However, in most cases the target behavior can be assessed in more than one way so there is no single strategy that must be adopted. For example, an investigator working in an institution for delinquents may be interested in recording the aggressive behavior of a particular individual. Hitting other individuals (e.g., making physical contact with another individual with a closed fist) may be the specific response of interest. What assessment strategy should be used?

Aggressive behavior (hitting other individuals) could be assessed using the various strategies discussed earlier. A frequency measure of aggressive responses may be employed by having an observer record the number of times the individual hits others during a certain period of time each day. Each hit is counted as one response. The behavior could also be observed using interval recording. A block of time such as 30 minutes could be set aside for observing the child. The 30 minutes could be divided into 10-second intervals. During each interval, the observer records whether an aggressive behavior (hit) occurs. The proportion of intervals in which hitting occurs would be the measure of aggressive behavior. The aggressive behavior might also be observed with the response duration measure. An observer could begin a stopwatch whenever the individual begins to perform aggressive responses. This might be somewhat difficult to do unless a burst of aggressive responses (e.g., a fight) occurred, rather than a single instance alone. If a series of aggressive acts occurs, the stopwatch could be started during each series of responses and terminated when the episode ends. The accumulated time within a given observation period would provide the duration of aggressive responses. For example, in an observation period of 30 minutes, the aggressive response may have occurred for a total of 15 accumulated minutes. An alternative duration measure which would be more easily recorded is the length of time from the beginning of each day until the first aggressive response. This measure yields the amount of continuous time without an aggressive response.

Issues and Problems in Sampling Behavior

The purpose of assessment is to provide a sample of the extent to which behavior is performed over the total period of time that behavior change is desired. Performance fluctuates over time on a given day and across days and weeks. It is important to determine the level of behavior without allowing the fluctuations to misrepresent the overall rate. If behavior were unvarying in its level over each hour and each day, any sample of that behavior (e.g., one hour) would be representative of behavior at all other times. For example, if behavior were performed once every 10 minutes of a client's waking hours, establishing the baseline rate of behavior would require one single 10-minute period. This assessment would accurately reflect performance. However, behavior is rarely performed at a consistent rate. (The only time there is virtually complete consistency is when the behavior is never performed and the rate is zero.) Thus, to obtain a representative sample, assessment must be carried out over an extended period of time.

Three decisions need to be made regarding the observations that are required. First, the number of times that data will be collected must be decided. When possible, it is desirable to observe behavior each day or during each session (e.g., in a classroom) that the target behavior may occur. The frequency of observation depends upon various factors including the variation of behavior over time, the availability of observers, and scheduling exigencies in the treatment setting. If the target behavior is very stable from one day to the next, daily assessment becomes less essential than if behavior fluctuates radically. Investigators have shown that observation of behavior every other day closely approximates the average rate obtained from daily observations (Bijou et al., 1969). As a general rule, behavior should be observed on as many occasions as possible. However, convenience and practical exigencies necessarily dictate the actual schedule. In many settings, there may not always be individuals who can devote time to recording behavior.

A second decision to be made prior to beginning assessment is the length of time set aside for a given observation period. As with the previous decision, demands of the setting (e.g., schedule of activities), observer availability, difficulty in recording behavior, and the frequency of the behavior determine this decision. However, the guiding general rule is that behavior should be observed for a period of time that will yield data representative of typical performance. The information should represent performance over the entire time of interest. For example, if it is desirable to alter behavior in the classroom, observational data should reflect performance over a relatively long period (e.g., one hour) rather than just a few minutes. For some behavioral problems or in some settings, the target behavior occurs for a specific period during the day. An observation period should be a period of time which provides a representative sample of performance. If a response has a low rate of occurrence, it might be possible simply to tally the behavior for an entire day. Observation of a low frequency behavior for a total of only five minutes per day may be too short to obtain a representative sample of behavior. Large periods of observation are not always required to reflect behavior change. For example, in studies in classroom settings, students may be observed for as little as 15 minutes each per observation period. However, it is unclear that performance during a short observation period represents performance over the entire school day.

A third decision related to the length of time behavior is observed is when the observations are conducted. Observations using frequency, interval, or duration methods can record behavior in a block of time in a single day or at different times throughout the day. The advantage of sampling behavior at various times over the entire day is that the observed behavior is more likely to be representative of behavior over the entire day. If behavior is observed during the mornings only, for example, this may not represent performance during afternoons. If behavior is sampled at various times, a period of time is set aside throughout the day. For example, in one project with psychiatric patients (Schaefer & Martin, 1966), observers recorded the frequency of various patient behaviors every half hour for a large portion of the day. The observations could have been made by an observer for one block of time, yet they may have been less representative of behavior throughout the day.

Whether a sample of behavior represents behavior over the entire period of interest cannot be determined in advance. Assessment conducted at different times can be used to determine whether performance varies throughout the day. For practical reasons, often it is unfeasible to observe behavior over several periods throughout the day. In these instances, behavior might be observed for a single block of time during that period in which behavior change is most obviously required. An initial assessment over a few days at different times can determine those periods which in fact require the greatest attention. Subsequently, assessment can focus on those periods.

In addition to the above decisions, if interval assessment is used, the duration of the interval has to be decided. Although observations may be made for 30 minutes or one hour each day, the length of intervals within that period must be decided. If behavior occurs at a high rate or is an ongoing response, relatively short intervals might be used (e.g., 10 or 15 seconds). Longer intervals (such as 60 seconds) would exclude much of the responding because the interval is recorded for the presence or absence of only one response. If the behavior occurs 20 times during one 60-second interval, the interval is scored upon the occurrence of the first response. The behavior cannot be scored again until the next interval. However, a great deal of behavior has gone unrecorded. As a result of a behavior modification program, behavior may change from 20 to 10 times per 60-second interval. However, this change will not be reflected in the data because the interval will continue to be scored for the presence of the response. Thus, there are several points to consider which dictate the duration of intervals.

First, interval duration should be relatively short (e.g., 10 or 15 seconds) for discrete behaviors which occur frequently. Second, very short intervals (e.g., 5 or fewer seconds) sometimes are difficult to score reliably because observers have difficulty in synchronizing observations. The interval is so short that it is not clear in which interval the behavior was performed. Third, if behavior is continuous (e.g., reading or watching television), the length of the interval may not be as important as when behavior is discrete because shorter or longer intervals are not likely to exclude "instances" of behavior. Many studies have used 10-second intervals, whereas others have reported intervals of one or a few minutes. Since there are no fixed rules for interval length, a wide range of durations has been employed.

Reliability of Assessment

Need for Reliability. It is important that individuals who observe the target behavior agree upon the occurrence of the response independently of the assessment strategy employed. Agreement is important for three major reasons. First, assessment will be useful only when it can be achieved with some consistency. For example, if frequency counts differ greatly depending upon who is counting, it will be difficult to know what the client's actual performance is. The client may be scored as performing a response frequently on some days and infrequently on other days as a function of observers who score behavior rather than differences in actual client performance. Inconsistent measurement introduces variation in the data which adds to the variation stemming from "normal" fluctuations in client performance. If measurement variation is large, there may *appear* to be no systematic pattern to the behavior. If a behavior modification program were implemented, it might be difficult to determine whether behavior is changing because the data are highly variable as a function of inconsistent recording. Stable patterns of behavior are required to reflect behavior change. Hence, reliable recording is essential.

Even if there is a systematic pattern to behavior, there is a second reason for obtaining reliability. If a single observer is used to recording the target behavior, any recorded change in behavior may result from a change in the observer's definition of the target behavior rather than in the actual behavior of the client. The observer might become lenient or stringent over time. For example, after a behavior modification program is introduced, the observer may perceive improvement in the target behavior even though no improvement actually occurs. If the program is withdrawn, the observer may expect behavior to become worse and reflect this expectation in inaccurate recording. Thus, an observer may unintentionally introduce systematic error which presents biased observation of behavior. Using separate observers to observe the target behavior at the same time may help determine whether the definition of the target behavior has changed by one of the observers. Yet, observers working together may change in the definition in a similar direction (O'Leary & Kent, 1973). Of course, it is important that when two observers are observing the behavior of a client, at least one does not know whether a particular behavior modification program is in effect or what the experimenter is investigating. If both observers are familiar with the program, they both might show bias (cf. Lipinski & Nelson, 1974).

A final reason that agreement between observers is important is that it reflects whether the target behavior is well defined. If observers readily agree on the occurrence of the behavior, it will be easier for individuals carrying out the program (administering reinforcement or punishment) to agree on the occurrence of a response. If a response can be observed consistently, it is more likely to be reinforced or punished consistently.

Estimating Reliability. Reliability provides an estimate of how consistently the behavior is observed and scored. The procedures for estimating reliability differ somewhat depending upon whether frequency or interval methods of assessment are used. In all procedures, at least two observers are required. Ideally, one of the observers should be relatively unfamiliar with details of the program. This ensures that the observer who assists with reliability is not "biased" to perceive improvements during the program, as the observer who carries out assessment every day may be. Obtaining observers who are unfamiliar with the program, while desirable, is not always possible.

Reliability of frequency measurement requires that two observers simultaneously, but independently, count the target response during the time set aside for observation. At the end of the observation period, the frequencies obtained by the observers are compared. The major interest is whether each observer records the target behavior with equal frequency. A percentage of agreement can be formed to measure the degree to which two observers agree in their final counts.

For any two observers, it is likely that they do not agree perfectly in their recorded frequency. That is, one observer will obtain a lower frequency count than the other. To determine the percentage of agreement, a fraction is formed from the frequency obtained by each observer. *Reliability is determined by dividing the smaller frequency by the larger frequency and multiplying by 100.* For example, in the home, parents may count the number of times a child spills food on the floor during a meal. During a reliability check, both parents independently count food spills. By the end of the meal, one parent has counted 20 instances of spilling, whereas the other parent has counted 18 instances. To form a percentage of agreement, the smaller number (18) is divided by the larger number (20) and multiplied by 100. Agreement for this observation period was 90% (18/20 x 100).

Interpretation of this percentage must be made cautiously. The figure indicates that observers agree on the total frequency of the behavior with a 10% (100% minus 90%) margin of error. It does not mean that the observers agree 90% of the time. Although one observer recorded 18 responses and the other recorded 20 responses, there is no way of knowing whether they recorded the *same* responses. For example, if both observers each recorded 18 responses, the percent of agreement would be 100%. Yet one observer may have seen 18 responses that were different from the 18 responses seen by the other observer. Although this is unlikely, it is possible that at least some of the responses recorded may not have been for the *same* behaviors. Thus, reliability reflects agreement on the total number of responses rather than agreement in any specific instance. A potential disadvantage in using a frequency measure is that when the behavior is not carefully defined, a high percentage of agreement for frequency data may still conceal a substantial amount of disagreement.

When response duration is used as the measure of behavior, calculation of reliability is similar to the above formula. Two observers independently record the duration of the behavior in a given session. Agreement is calculated by forming a fraction with the time each observer records the target behavior. The smaller duration is divided by the larger duration and multiplied by 100. With a duration measure, observers usually disagree on the response time only if one observer begins or finishes timing the response before or after the other observer.

Calculation of reliability is somewhat different when an interval-recording assessment strategy is used. Reliability is computed on the basis of the proportion of intervals two observers agree on the occurrence of the target response. An agreement is scored if both observers record the occurrence of behavior in the *same* interval. A disagreement is scored when one observer scores a behavior in an interval and the other does not score the behavior in that interval. For example, a reliability check made between two observers independently recording the attending behavior of students in an elementary classroom requires that both observers begin to observe the same child at the same time. Each records what he observes for several intervals. During each interval the observer marks the occurrence or non-occurrence of the behavior. If many children are being observed, it is important that observers always assess the same child at the same time. When the observers finish recording, reliability can be calculated.

Reliability is determined by dividing the number of intervals in which both observers mark the behavior as occurring (agreements) by the number of agreements plus the number of intervals in which one observer scored the behavior and the other did not (disagreements) and multiplying by 100. For example, if observers recorded behavior for 50 10-second intervals and both observers agreed on the occurrence of the behavior in 20 intervals and disagreed in 5 intervals, reliability would be $20/(20 + 5) \times 100$, or 80%.

Although observers recorded behavior for 50 intervals, all intervals were not used to calculate reliability. An interval is counted only if at least one observer recorded the *occurrence* of the target behavior. Excluding intervals in which neither observer records the target behavior is based on the following reasoning. If these intervals were counted, they would be considered as agreements since both observers "agree" that the response did not occur. Yet in observing behavior, many intervals may be marked without the occurrence of the target behavior. If these were included as agreements in the calculation of reliability, the reliability estimate would be inflated beyond the level obtained when occurrences alone were counted as agreements. In the above example, behavior was not scored as occurring by either observer in 25 intervals. By counting these as agreements, reliability would increase to 90% ($45/(45 + 5) \times 100 = 90\%$) rather than 80% obtained originally. To avoid this increase in reliability, most investigators restrict agreements to response occurrence (Bijou et al., 1969).

Conducting Reliability Checks.   Reliability checks need to be made before baseline data are gathered to ensure that the behavior is agreed upon. A few days of prebaseline observation usually are useful to finalize the rules for observing behavior and to handle instances in which it is not clear whether the target behavior has occurred. Once baseline begins, reliability checks need to be continued intermittently throughout the program to ensure that behavior is consistently observed. If checks are made only at the inception of the program, over time observers may become increasingly lax in their scoring. Hence, observations may become less reliable. In addition, systematic biases may influence observers so that they record improvement while a program is in effect, even though there is no actual change in the client's behavior. Also, idiosyncratic patterns of observing and interpreting behavior may change over time, so that there appears to be no systematic pattern in the client's behavior. Typically, reliability should be assessed intermittently (e.g., once a week or every three or four days) over the course of the project. When reliability is consistently high (near or at 100%), fewer checks would be required.

A few requirements should be met during reliability checks to obtain an accurate assessment of agreement between observers. First, observers should work independently without access to each other's scoring sheet. If observers cooperate or communicate while observing, their agreement may be inflated because they are influencing each other. Second, it is useful to have observers supervised during a reliability check to ensure that independence of observing is maintained. Third, the observer employed for reliability checks (i.e., the observer who is not regularly gathering data) should be unaware of the contingencies implemented to alter client behavior and when they are in effect. Finally, it is desirable to conduct reliability checks when observers are unaware that checks are being conducted. Investigations reveal that observers show a higher percentage of agreement when they know a reliability check is being conducted than when they do not (O'Leary & Kent, 1973). Reliability checks can be conducted without the observers being aware, if each observer has a scoring sheet observing the individuals in a different order. To all appearances, observers are observing different individuals at completely different times. However, some of the intervals may coincide so that at some points observers are scoring the same person. A comparison of the intervals in which the same person is recorded by both observers during the same interval will yield reliability information. When only one subject is being observed, it may be difficult to obscure the fact that a reliability check is being made. Recommendations for conducting reliability checks and handling problems that arise have been provided by O'Leary and Kent (1973).

Reliability has to achieve an acceptable level prior to beginning baseline observations and to maintain this level throughout the project. Although no single criterion for acceptable agreement has been set, convention dictates agreement should be between 80 and 100%. Reliability lower than 80% suggests that a moderate amount of error occurs in recording. In many instances, low reliability signals that the response definition should be more carefully specified. Obtaining low reliability is no reason to be discouraged before a program is begun. It is a signal that additional work in specifying behavior is required. It is desirable to find this out early so the response definition can be clarified for those who administer the program as well as for those who observe behavior.

TRAINING INDIVIDUALS TO BE BEHAVIOR MODIFIERS

Before implementing a program, it is important to ensure that the individuals who carry out the procedures are well trained. As mentioned earlier, a characteristic which distinguishes behavior modification from attempts at behavior change in everyday life is the systematic manner in which behavior modification programs are implemented. If a program is to be effective, the contingencies need to be applied to the client in a precise fashion. For example, investigations have shown that when an individual is reinforced contingently on some occasions and noncontingently on the other occasions, behavior is not dramatically altered. In contrast, when an individual is consistently reinforced contingently, behavior markedly changes (Redd, 1969; Redd & Birnbrauer, 1969). Thus, the degree to which the contingencies are administered systematically determines the efficacy of the program. Before a program can be implemented to alter the behavior of a given client, attention has to be given to those agents who will administer the program.

In many cases, it is obvious that the behavior of the person who desires change in a given client needs to be modified. For example, parents often seek consultation to alter the behavior of their children. Frequently, behavior problems in the home are inadvertently maintained by the parents themselves. Parents may contribute to disobedient behavior of their children by providing extra attention to the children when they are obstinate, and by "letting well enough alone" (ignoring the children) when they are cooperative (cf. Wahler, 1972). Similarly, psychiatric aides frequently attend to bizarre behaviors of patients on the ward. When a patient is particularly bizarre, the attendants may give "tender loving care." Although the sympathetic behavior on the part of the staff is well intended, it may reinforce the bizarre behaviors. When attendants are trained to ignore bizarre behavior and reinforce appropriate behavior, patients behave more appropriately on the ward (Ayllon & Michael, 1959). Teachers also can inadvertently reinforce undesirable behavior. Children may repeatedly shout out loud in class without raising their hands. While the teacher may want the children to raise their hands, she often attends to the students who shout, allowing the child who raises his or her hand to go unnoticed. In this way, shouting is frequently reinforced while raising one's hand is extinguished (McNamara, 1971).

The purpose of these examples is not to oversimplify how deviant behavior may develop or be maintained. Rather, the purpose is to illustrate that a client's behavior is performed in a social environment and that many contingencies adhered to by others can contribute to undesirable behavior. In numerous settings, as will be discussed throughout subsequent chapters, dramatic changes have been effected by merely altering the behavior of those individuals in contact with the client.

A major task in initiating a behavior modification program is to train those individuals who will administer the contingencies. Those individuals who control access to the reinforcing consequences of the client must be trained to carefully administer these events. Of course, a major question arises, namely, what is the best way to alter behaviors of the individuals who are to serve as behavior modifiers?

Procedures to Train Staff. The principles of behavior change apply to all of us, not just the clients whose behaviors have been identified as "problematic." Thus, to change staff behavior the same principles which are used to alter the behavior of the clients must be employed. Essentially, altering the behavior of individuals in contact with the client requires a behavior modification program in its own right. Initially, the target behaviors that need to be changed in the individuals who serve as the behavior modifiers have to be identified. In a general sense, of course, these individuals have to effectively use the principles of learning, outlined earlier. Yet, "using the principles" is not a specific target behavior and must be defined more carefully. The specific behaviors to be learned by the behavior modifiers will vary as a function of the clients they supervise. For example, in training teachers, a goal might be to have them provide reinforcement (e.g., praise) to children for achieving high rates of correct responses on academic assignments and studying, and to ignore disruptive behavior. In training parents, the goals might be to ignore (extinguish) excessive talking in a verbose child, but to praise (reinforce) talking in a sibling who appears extremely reticent. Of course, the goal in training behavior modifiers is to develop competence in simultaneously managing a number of contingencies beyond those included in a specific program to alter a single target behavior. However, training usually begins by changing only one or a few behaviors of the behavior modifier.

Many approaches have been used to train parents, teachers, and attendants to implement behavior modification programs. Usually, instructional or didactic procedures are emphasized. For example, workshops or discussion groups may be conducted for individuals who work in a particular setting or are interested in a common set of behaviors in their clients. At the workshops, client behavior problems and the techniques which might be useful in changing behavior are discussed. A well-trained behavior modifier is likely to direct the group and explain the procedures which are useful. Unfortunately, discussion and instructional methods have not proved to be very effective in changing behavior and in training behavior modifiers (Kazdin & Bootzin, 1973; Kazdin & Moyer, 1975). While individuals receiving such training learn about the principles of behavior change, they do not effectively implement them (Gardner, 1972).

Ideally, trainers receive some practice or simulated practice in using the techniques rather than merely instruction. Sometimes individuals who are learning the techniques role-play in order to provide opportunities to simulate the actual situation. One staff member may take the role of a client and the other the role of the staff member who is trying to develop a behavior. Under close supervision, along with feedback and guidance by someone trained in behavior modification, this training is effective (Gardner, 1972).

Because merely instructing individuals in the principles of behavior change has not proven effective, many investigators employ behavior modification programs with the staff. For example, reinforcement, punishment, and modeling have been used to train teachers of "normal" and special education classes, and attendants working in institutions for psychiatric patients and retardates (e.g., Kazdin, 1973f; Kazdin & Moyer, 1975). In these programs, specific target behaviors usually are followed with reinforcing consequences. For example, in one institution for the retarded, staff received green stamps as a reinforcer for interacting appropriately with the residents (Bricker, Morgan, & Grabowski, 1972). In training programs conducted in schools, teachers sometimes receive praise from the psychologist for interacting appropriately with their students. Contingent praise delivered to teachers is effective in altering behavior (Cossairt, Hall, & Hopkins, 1973).

As a general rule, careful training is required of those individuals who will administer the contingencies. However, on occasion only brief training is sufficient. For example, in training parents to modify the behavior of their children, only brief consultation is sometimes required. One therapist consulted with parents on only a few occasions so that they could alter the behavior of their children (Christopherson et al., 1972). The therapist told the parents how to administer reinforcers for specific target behaviors and had them begin a behavior modification program. The therapist visited the home and made phone calls to ensure that the program was running smoothly. The parents effectively increased performance of various chores (e.g., cleaning one's room, feeding the pets, and emptying the trash) in their three children. Parents usually have a major investment in altering the behavior of their children so that special incentives to carry out the procedures may not be required. However, special training in carefully implementing the contingencies is required. With rare exceptions, training requires some contingencies to alter the behaviors of the trainers. Essentially, the reinforcing agents themselves need reinforcement. After individuals have been trained to implement behavior modification techniques, it is important to ensure that the behaviors continue to be performed. Evidence suggests that as soon as extrinsic consequences are withdrawn for staff performance, behavior reverts to pretraining levels (Kazdin & Moyer, 1975). Thus, it cannot be assumed that merely training individuals in behavior modification skills is sufficient to maintain their execution of these skills.

Training individuals to conduct a behavior modification program requires defining the behaviors which are to be changed, assessing these behaviors to determine baseline rates of performance, implementing some techniques to change behavior, and ensuring that behavior will be maintained once training is completed. The steps are identical with those required to alter behavior of the clients who are served by the staff. The basic techniques which are used to change behavior (mentioned briefly in the discussion of operant principles in Chapter 2) and procedures to maintain behavior change will be elaborated in subsequent chapters.

PROGRAM EVALUATION

A distinguishing feature of behavior modification is the careful evaluation of the treatment or training program. Assessment of behavior, program implementation, and evaluation are closely interrelated. Behavior has to be carefully defined so it can be reliably assessed. In addition, when the behavior is carefully defined, certain events can be designated to follow the behavior. The target behavior can be followed with contingent consequences only when the occurrence of the behavior is agreed upon. Moreover, assessment of behavior throughout the program determines whether behavior changes, or whether it is similar to performance prior to implementing specific contingencies.

Assessment of behavior can reflect change. Since the goal of the program is to change some response, assessment has obvious significance. However, assessment does *not* reveal what causes a change in behavior when it occurs. Behavior modifiers are extremely concerned about determining the cause of behavior change. To investigate the procedures and to determine how the principles can be effectively applied require careful evaluation of the program. However, in some cases the individual who conducts the program is interested only in obtaining the change in behavior rather than isolating the cause of the change. For example, a parent may want a child to stop fighting. The priority of determining the cause of behavior change usually is low for individuals conducting the program. Yet usually it is desirable to show what procedure *causes* the change. Once the cause of behavior change is clear, our knowledge about variables which control behavior is increased. Additionally, if the program has been shown to be responsible for behavior change, it may be applied to the same individual in the future, or to other clients and settings with an increased confidence that behavior may change in the new applications as well.

It is possible for behavior to change without the behavior modification program being responsible for that change. For example, a program might be carried out in a home to reduce the frequency of fighting in two children. After a few weeks of recording fighting (baseline), a program is begun (e.g., praising the children for playing cooperatively). Assessment may reveal that behavior changed once praise was delivered for cooperative play. Was the delivery of praise responsible for behavior change? Alternative explanations of the change might be advanced. For example, there may have been changes at school which led to changes in the fighting at home. Further, one of the children may have been physically ill and irritable but improved at the same time the program began (or was healthy and became ill when the program began and had less opportunity to fight). Similarly, changes in behavior of the children's peers or parents (in addition to praising the child) may have contributed to behavior change. All of these explanations need to be ruled out to claim that praise was responsible for behavior change.

There are different ways to demonstrate that the program caused the change in behavior. The individual who designs the program must plan the situation so that the specific contribution of the program to behavior change can be demonstrated. The plan of the program which is used to demonstrate what accounted for behavior change is referred to as the *experimental design*. There are different experimental designs which can be used to show that the program, rather than extraneous events, altered behavior. (Detailed discussions of various designs used in the evaluation of behavior modification programs and the rationale behind their use have been provided in other sources [e.g., Baer, Wolf, & Risley, 1968; Bijou et al., 1969; Kazdin, 1973g; Risley, 1970; Sidman, 1960].)

Reversal or ABAB Design

The reversal design demonstrates the effect of the behavior modification program by alternating presentation and removal of the program over time. The purpose of the design is to demonstrate a *functional relationship* between the target behavior and the experimental condition (program). A functional relationship is demonstrated when alteration of the experimental condition or contingency results in a systematic change in behavior. Behavior is a function of the environmental events which produced change.

In a reversal design, behavior is assessed to obtain the baseline rate of performance prior to implementing specific contingencies. The baseline period or phase (referred to as the A phase) is continued until the rate of the response appears to be stable or until it is evident that the response does not improve over time. A stable rate of behavior during baseline serves as a basis for evaluating subsequent change. Baseline provides an estimate of what behavior would be in the future if the program were not introduced (Risley, 1970). After behavior stabilizes and follows a consistent pattern (several days are usually sufficient), the experimental phase is begun. During the experimental phase, the behavior modification procedure (e.g., reinforcement, punishment, extinction or some combination of procedures) is implemented. The experimental phase (referred to as the B phase) is continued until behavior reaches a stable level or diverges from the level predicted by the baseline rate. Figure 4–3 provides a hypothetical example of observations of some desirable behavior plotted over several days. Although the behavior fluctuates during baseline, there is a reasonably stable pattern or a fairly narrow range within which the frequency occurs. During the experimental phase (e.g., reinforcement of the target behavior), there is an increase in performance. Up to this point in the program, the *change* in behavior is evident. However, the *cause* of the change is unclear.

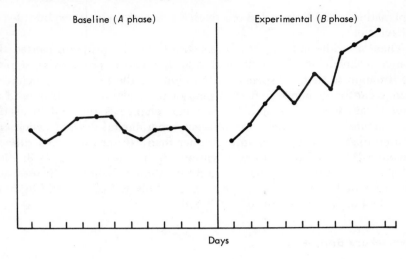

FIGURE 4–3 Hypothetical rate of some behavior plotted over baseline and experimental phases.

Since the change in behavior coincides with implementation of the program, it is likely that the program accounts for the change. However, one cannot be sure.

After behavior attains a stable level, the experimental condition is withdrawn and the baseline condition (A phase) is reinstated. During the baseline condition, of course, no program or intervention is used to control behavior. A return to baseline conditions is called a *reversal* phase because the experimental condition is withdrawn and behavior usually reverses (i.e., returns to or near the level of the original baseline). The purpose of the reversal phase is to determine whether performance would have remained unchanged (relative to baseline) had the program not been introduced. When behavior reverts to baseline, the experimental phase (B phase) is reinstated. Changes in A and B conditions from one phase to another are not made until performance during a given phase is stable or is clearly different from the previous phase.

The design is referred to as a reversal design because phases in the design are reversed to demonstrate the effect of the program. Alternatively, the design is referred to as the ABAB design because A and B phases are alternated. If performance changes in the experimental phase relative to baseline, reverts to baseline or near baseline levels during the second baseline phase, and again changes in the final experimental phase, this provides a clear demonstration of the experimental condition.

Examples of reversal designs are abundant. In one program (Kazdin & Klock, 1973), the effect of teacher praise on the behavior of retarded children was examined in a special education classroom. During baseline, students were observed for nine days to assess study behavior (paying attention to the teacher and working on assignments). Using an interval recording system, teacher approval (verbal and nonverbal) for student behavior and student attentiveness to classwork were observed each day. After baseline, the teacher was instructed to increase her use of nonverbal approval to the students by smiling, physically patting them on the back, and nodding approvingly for paying attention to her. When the teacher did this, study behavior increased. The use of nonverbal teacher approval to control student behavior was discontinued in a reversal phase to demonstrate that the program was responsible for behavior change. Finally, the experimental phase was reinstated and the teacher increased in her use of nonverbal approval. The results for the group of 12 students as a whole are presented in Figure 4–4. The figure shows that performance during each reinforcement phase increased over baseline and reversal phases, respectively. This demonstrated that behavior improved only when nonverbal approval increased. By showing changes in behavior when the experimental condition is presented, withdrawn, and represented, it is unlikely that other influences accounted for the results.

The reversal design requires that the experimental condition is presented and temporarily withdrawn at some point in time. There are variations of this basic design. Sometimes it is undesirable to begin with a

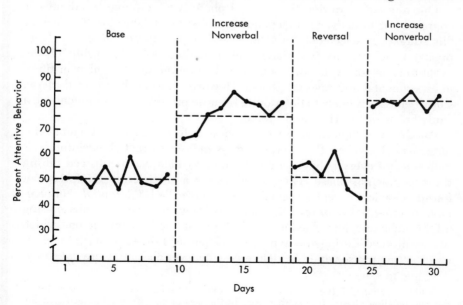

FIGURE 4–4 Mean daily rate of attentive behavior in the class. (Source: Kazdin, A. E. & Klock, J. The effect of nonverbal teacher approval on student attentive behavior. *Journal of Applied Behavior Analysis,* 1973, **6,** 643–54.)

baseline phase because some immediate intervention is urgently required. For example, if fighting among delinquents were frequent and intense in a given setting, it might be undesirable to begin with a baseline period because some immediate therapeutic intervention is needed. In other situations, it also might be reasonable to forego the initial baseline phase. For example, in some cases target behaviors such as social skills or talking have not been performed at all or their rates are exceedingly low (e.g., a mute psychiatric patient) so that baseline might not be the first phase of the program. In these instances where baseline is not employed initially, a BABA design might be used. This is the reversal design beginning with the experimental phase (B) followed by baseline or reversal (A) phases (cf. Kazdin & Polster, 1973).[1]

Reversal Phase. The requirement for the reversal design is that the contingency is altered during the reversal period to determine whether behavior is controlled by the experimental intervention. Removing the contingency (thereby returning to baseline conditions) is frequently employed to achieve a reversal. However, returning to baseline conditions is not the only way to show a relationship between behavior and the environmental events. Alternative operations can be employed in a reversal phase. In demonstrating each of these operations, consider the example of a program where approval is delivered for study behavior as reported by Kazdin and Klock (1973).

One alternative during the reversal phase is to continue to administer approval but to deliver it independently of student behavior. The reason this strategy is selected is to show that it is not the event per se (e.g., praise) which results in behavior change, but the relationship of the event to behavior. Approval could be delivered the same number of times in experimental and reversal phases. However, during the reversal phase, study behavior is likely to deteriorate because praise is not contingent upon study behavior (cf. Hall et al., 1968).

Another variation in the reversal phase is to continue contingent reinforcement. However, the contingency is altered so that the reinforcer is delivered for every behavior *except* the one which was reinforced during the experimental phase. The procedure for administering reinforcement for all behaviors except a specific response is called *differential reinforcement of other behavior* (or DRO schedule). During a reversal phase using a DRO schedule, all behaviors would be reinforced except the one which was reinforced during the experimental phase. For example, in a classroom setting praise would be delivered whenever children were *not* study-

---

[1]Other versions of the reversal design employ several different phases between the two baseline phases. Rather than ABAB, the design may be $AB_1B_2B_3AB_3$. In this version, the basic reversal requirement of the design is met but several different experimental interventions ($B_1B_2B_3$) are evaluated between the baseline phases (e.g., O'Leary, Becker, Evans, & Saudargas, 1969).

ing. The DRO schedule is different from the previous variation of the reversal phase in which reinforcement was delivered independently of behavior. During a DRO phase, reinforcement is contingent on behavior but on behaviors different from the one reinforced during the experimental phase (e.g., study behavior). The reason for using a DRO strategy in a reversal phase is to rapidly show the effect of the contingency. Behavior reverses quickly when "other" behavior is reinforced. Investigators have used a DRO schedule to demonstrate the effect of experimental contingencies in a reversal design (e.g., Bostow & Bailey, 1969; Kale et al., 1968; Kazdin, 1973c; Sherman, 1965, Surratt et al., 1969). Whether a reversal phase employs a return to baseline, noncontingent presentation of an event, or a DRO schedule, the purpose is to show that alteration of the contingency changes behavior.

Problems and Considerations in Using a Reversal Design.   A reversal design requires that behavior reverts to baseline or near baseline rates at some point to demonstrate that behavior change was caused by an alteration of the contingencies. Yet there are problems associated with this design related to the reversibility of behavior.

Sometimes when a program is withdrawn and a reversal phase is implemented, behavior does not return to the baseline rate of performance. When there is no reversal in behavior, it is not clear whether the experimental condition or some other event led to initial behavior change. For example, in one program (Kazdin, 1971a), punishment was used to reduce incoherent statements made by a female retarded adult. In a psychiatric evaluation, the client was described as "prepsychotic" primarily because of talking to herself. The program, conducted in a sheltered workshop, began by obtaining baseline observations on the frequency of incoherent statements (statements made to herself). After baseline, a punishment procedure was invoked whereby a conditioned positive reinforcer (cards which purchased rewards, such as candy, toiletries, lounge privileges) was removed for each incoherent statement. The statements decreased dramatically. However, when baseline conditions were reinstated and positive reinforcers were no longer removed, behavior did not return to baseline levels. It remained at a very low rate. It appears reasonable to attribute the reduction of incoherent statements to the punishment procedure since incoherent statements had a long history. Strictly, however, it is not clear whether the punishment procedure *caused* the change because performance remained low even after the contingency was withdrawn.

In some programs removal of the experimental contingency has not resulted in a reversal of behavior (e.g., Hewett et al., 1969; Medland & Stachnik, 1972; Osborne, 1969). It is possible in these instances that factors (e.g., increased social contact with parents or teachers) other than contingencies programmed during the experimental phase were responsible for behavior change. The same factors might remain operative during a reversal phase and account for the failure of behavior to reverse. Because behavior does not always reverse when the experimental contingency is altered or withdrawn, the reversal design may not always demonstrate a causal relationship between behavior and environmental events even when contingency actually caused the initial change.

In some situations, a reversal design should not be used because behavior would not be expected to reverse in a reversal phase. Once certain behaviors are developed or altered, they may be maintained by favorable consequences which result directly from their performance. For example, if an "aggressive" child is praised by an attendant, improvement in behavior may lead to enduring changes in the child's environment. Peers in the child's environment may be more socially responsive because the previously aggressive child can play nicely with others. Even if there were a reversal phrase (removal of attendant praise), attention from the child's peers may maintain the desirable behavior. A reversal of behavior may be difficult to achieve in situations where the behavior is maintained by naturally occurring events in the environment which are not directly manipulated by the teacher, attendant, therapist, or investigator.

An extremely important practical consideration in using the reversal design is that even if it is possible to demonstrate a reversal of behavior, it may be *undesirable*. For example, autistic and retarded children sometimes severely injure themselves by banging their heads for extended periods of time. If a program decreased this behavior, it would be undesirable to show that headbanging would return in a reversal phase. Extensive physical damage to the child might result. Even when behavior is not dangerous, such as sitting on the floor in a hospital ward, daydreaming in class, or doing poorly on an academic assignment, it is usually undesirable to make behavior worse after gains have been made even if the reversal phase is short. Fortunately, other designs are available to clearly demonstrate the effect of the program without using a reversal of conditions.

Multiple-Baseline Designs

Multiple-baseline designs do *not* rely on a reversal of conditions or phases to show the effect of the program. Rather, the effect of the contingency is demonstrated by showing that behavior change is associated with introduction of the contingency at different points in time. One of three types of multiple-baseline designs is usually used depending upon whether data are collected across behaviors, individuals, or across situations.

Multiple-Baseline across Behaviors.   In this version of the design, baseline data are collected across *two or more behaviors* of a given individual or group of individuals. After each baseline has reached a stable rate, the experimental condition is implemented for only one of the behaviors while baseline conditions are continued for the other behavior(s). The initial behavior subjected to the experimental condition is expected to change while other behaviors remain at baseline levels. When rates are stable for all behaviors, the second behavior is included into the contingency. This procedure is continued until all behaviors for which baseline data were gathered are included into the contingency. Ideally, each behavior changes only as it is included into the experimental contingency and not before. Control of the specific experimental contingency is demonstrated when behavior change is associated in each case with the introduction of the contingency. No reversal is required to demonstrate what caused behavior change. The multiple-baseline design across behaviors is useful when an individual or group has a number of behaviors which are to be changed.

An example of this design was reported by Hall, Cristler, Cranston, and Tucker (1970). A 10-year-old girl had minimally engaged in several activities at home that her mother wished to increase. The girl failed to perform various tasks consistently, including practicing clarinet, working on projects for Campfire girls, and reading her school work. A multiple-baseline design across these three behaviors was used. The amount of time (duration) each behavior was performed was determined each evening. After a few days of baseline across all behaviors, the mother told the child that she would have to go to bed one minute earlier than her regular bedtime for each minute less than 30 that she practiced clarinet. Thus, a punishment program was used, but only for one behavior. Baseline conditions (no contingency) were continued for the other two behaviors. Data were gathered for all three behaviors. After a few days, clarinet practice increased although the other behaviors did not change. At this point, the girl was told that she would lose a minute off her bedtime for each minute less than 30 that she worked on her projects as well as clarinet practice. Each behavior had to be performed for 30 minutes to avoid going to bed early. Baseline conditions continued for the last behavior (reading). After a few days, reading was also included in the contingency so that the girl had to perform 30 minutes on each task to avoid going to bed early. Figure 4–5 shows the results of the program. Each behavior changed as it was included into the bedtime contingency. It is important to note that relatively stable rates of performance were maintained for each behavior during baseline prior to including the behavior into the contingency. If all three behaviors had been changed when only the first one was included into the contingency, it would have been unclear whether the contingency caused the change. In that case, an extraneous event may have influenced all behaviors simultaneously.

Multiple-Baseline across Individuals. In this design, baseline data are collected for a *particular behavior across two or more individuals*. After the behavior of each individual has reached a stable rate, the experimental condition is implemented for only one of the individuals while baseline conditions are continued for the other(s). The behavior of the person ex-

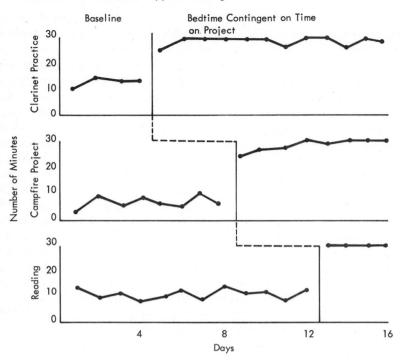

FIGURE 4–5 A record of time spent in clarinet practice, Campfire honors project work, and reading for book reports by a 10-yr-old girl. *Baseline*—before experimental procedures. *Early Bedtime Contingent on Less Than 30 Min of Behavior*—1 min. earlier bedtime for each minute less than 30 engaged in an activity. (Source: Hall, R. V. Cristler, C., Cranston, S. S., & Tucker, B. Teachers and parents as researchers using multiple-baseline designs. *Journal of Applied Behavior Analysis,* 1970, **3,** 247–55.)

posed to the experimental condition should change while the behavior of the other individual(s) should not. When behavior stabilizes for all individuals, the contingency is extended to another person. This procedure is continued until all individuals for whom baseline data were collected are included into the contingency. As with other multiple-baseline designs, no reversal of the experimental condition (e.g., return to baseline or DRO) is required to demonstrate that the contingency was responsible for behavior change. The multiple-baseline design across individuals is useful when a given behavior is to be altered across a number of clients in a group.

Hall et al. (1970) used this design with three tenth-grade students who had been earning D and F grades on class quizzes. Baseline data were gathered on daily grades (A through F) for each student. After several days, the first student was informed that whenever he earned a score of D or F on a quiz, he would be required to stay after school for tutoring. The grades of other students were not included in this contingency, although baseline data continued to be collected on their quiz performance. When the behavior of the first student changed, the contingency was extended to include the second student. For each of the two students, quiz grades of D or F resulted in after-school tutoring. Eventually, the quiz behavior of the last student was included into the same contingency. As can be seen in Figure 4–6, the grades of each student improved only when the contingency (after-school tutoring for low grades) was introduced. This represents a clear demonstration that after-school tutoring was responsible for behavior change. Events occurring in time other than the contingency, such as changes in study habits or difficulty of the quizzes, or general improvements over time due to practice, and similar factors do not explain why the

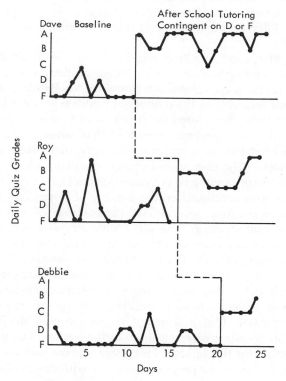

FIGURE 4–6 A record of quiz score grades for three high school French-class students. *Baseline*— before experimental procedures. *After School Tutoring Contingent on D and F Grades*—pupils required to stay after school for tutoring if they score D or F on daily quizzes. (Source: Hall, R. V., Cristler, C., Cranston, S. S. & Tucker, B. Teachers and parents as researchers using multiple-baseline designs. *Journal of Applied Behavior Analysis, 1970, **3**, 247–55).

changes occurred for each student at the precise time the contingency was introduced.

Multiple-Baseline across Situations (or Time).   In this design, baseline data on a given behavior for an individual or group are collected *across two or more situations* (e.g., at home and at school). After behavior has stabilized in each situation, the experimental contingency is implemented in the first situation. The baseline phase is continued for behavior in the other situation(s). Eventually the contingency is extended to behavior in the next situation while baseline data continue to be gathered in the remaining situations. The contingency is extended to each situation until all situations have been included. The specific effect of the contingency is shown, if behavior changes in a particular situation only when the contingency is introduced. The multiple-baseline design across situations is useful when an individual or a group performs or fails to perform a behavior across different situations or at different times within a given situation.

Hall et al. (1970) used a multiple-baseline design across situations in one of their studies. In a fifth-grade class, students tended to be late when returning from noon, morning, and afternoon recess. Baseline data in each of these periods consisted of the number of pupils who were late (entered class after the teacher had closed the door). After baseline data were gathered in each situation, students were told that anyone who was in the room on time after the noon recess would have their name placed on a chart of "patriots." (The class was studying American colonists and patriotic activities and appeared to be enthusiastic about being "patriots.") Baseline conditions were continued on the number of pupils late for morning and afternoon recess. After several days, the contingency was extended to those students who were on time after both morning and noon recess. Eventually, the contingency was extended to include students on time after *all* of the recess periods. The results are presented in Figure 4–7. The contingency (having one's name placed on a list of "patriots" each day when punctual) led to dramatic changes in behavior. However, changes did not occur in a given situation until the contingency was extended to include that situation. It should be noted that the program illustrated in Figure 4–7 also reveals a reversal phase in the design. The program was withdrawn during the third phase. This phase was not necessary to demonstrate the causal effect of the program since the requirements for a multiple-baseline design were met.

Problems and Considerations in Using Multiple-Baseline Designs. Multiple-baseline designs are used for demonstrating the effects of the contingencies without using a reversal phase in the design. There is no need to return to baseline conditions and temporarily lose some of the behavior gains made during the program. Hence, these designs should be used when a reversal in behavior would be undesirable or unexpected. The

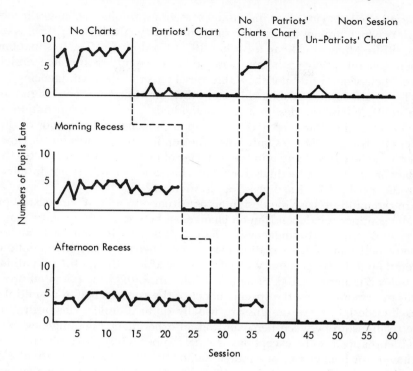

FIGURE 4–7 A record of the number of pupils late in returning to their fifth-grade classroom after noon, morning, and afternoon recess. *No Charts*—baseline, before experimental procedures. *Patriots' Chart*—posting of pupil names on "Today's Patriots" chart contingent on entering class on time after recess. *No Chart*—posting of names discontinued. *Patriots' Chart*—return to Patriots' Chart conditions. *Un-Patriots' Chart*—posting of names on "Un-Patriots' " chart contingent on being late after recess. (Source: Hall, R. V., Cristler, C., Cranston, S. S., & Tucker, B. Teachers and parents as researchers using multiple-baseline designs. *Journal of Applied Behavior Analysis, 1970,* **3,** 247–55.)

designs require that there are either two or more behaviors, individuals, or situations which can be observed.

There are possible problems with multiple-baseline designs which should be mentioned. In the multiple-baseline design across behaviors, a clear demonstration of the effect of the contingency depends upon showing that behavior changes *only* when the contingency is introduced. If behavior changes before the contingency is introduced for that behavior (i.e., during baseline), it is unclear whether the contingency is responsible for change. If changing the first behavior also changes the second behavior before the second behavior is included into the contingency, the specific effect of the contingency on behavior is unclear. Some studies report that altering one behavior of an individual sometimes results in changes in behaviors which are not included in the contingency (Buell et al., 1968; Kazdin, 1973b; Maley, Feldman & Ruskin, 1973; Nordquist, 1971). In situations when generalization across responses occurs, a multiple-baseline design across behaviors would not show the causal effect of the contingencies.

There are similar problems in the other multiple-baseline designs. In the multiple-baseline design across individuals, a clear demonstration of the effect of the contingency depends upon showing that behavior of different individuals changes only when the contingency is introduced. However, in some cases changes in the behavior of one individual may alter the behavior of other individuals for whom baseline conditions are in effect (Broden et al., 1970; Kazdin, 1973c; Kounin, 1970.)

In the multiple-baseline design across situations, a clear demonstration of the contingency depends upon changes in behavior only in those situations in which the contingency is in effect. However, in some cases alteration of behavior in one situation may change behavior in other situations even though the contingency is not introduced into these other situations (Hunt & Zimmerman, 1969; Kazdin, 1973h). In spite of the potential problems in demonstrating the specific effect of the contingency in a multiple-baseline design, these designs are usually quite useful in demonstrating the relationship between behavior and an experimental contingency. The problems appear to be exceptions. Yet, if it appears likely that altering one behavior (or behavior of one individual, or behavior in one situation) can produce generalized effects, a multiple-baseline design might be avoided.

Changing-Criterion Design

The effect of a contingency can be demonstrated in another way using neither reversal nor multiple-baseline designs. A changing-criterion design demonstrates the effect of the contingency by showing that behavior matches a criterion which is set for reinforcement (or punishment). This design has not been used widely. In fact, its name has been coined in print only recently (Axelrod, Hall, Weis, & Rohrer, 1974). After a baseline period of observation, the experimental contingency is introduced so that a certain level of performance is required to earn reinforcement. For example, the behavior has to be performed a certain number of times per day to earn the reinforcer. When performance consistently meets the criterion, the criterion for reinforcement is increased or made more stringent. The criterion is repeatedly changed until the terminal goal of the program is achieved. The effect of the contingency is demonstrated, if the behavior appears to match the criterion as that criterion is changed. When behavior changes in response to the criterion, it suggests that the contingency rather than extraneous influences led to behavior change.

An example of the changing-criterion design was reported in the treatment of cigarette smoking with a 23-year-old female graduate student (Axelrod et al., 1974). The student collected data on the number of cigarettes smoked daily. For a 17-day baseline period, she averaged 16.6 cigarettes per day. The experimental condition consisted of having her tear a dollar bill whenever smoking exceeded 15 cigarettes. A one-dollar bill was to be destroyed for each cigarette over 15 (the daily criterion). After a few days, the criterion for tearing dollar bills was lowered to 14, then to 13, 12, and so on until one cigarette per day was the criterion for tearing a dollar bill. The criterion for punishment (loss of $1.00) changed throughout the study. Figure 4–8 shows the response of the subject to the changing criterion. Smoking appears to have been controlled by changing the criterion for punishment.

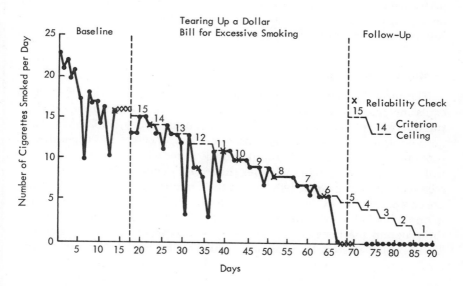

FIGURE 4–8 Record of the number of cigarettes smoked per day. (Source: From *Self-control: Power to the person,* by M. J. Mahoney & C. E. Thoresen. Copyright © 1974 by Wadsworth Publishing Company, Inc. Reprinted by permission of Brooks/Cole Publishing Company, Monterey, California, and Axelrod et al., 1974.)

The changing-criterion design is particularly well suited to behaviors which have to be shaped to reach a terminal goal. In the beginning of the program, after baseline data are collected, the criterion for reinforcement or punishment can be lenient. As the criterion is met, it is altered gradually. Eventually, behavior will be performed at a level very different from the initial criterion.

Problems and Considerations in Using a Changing-Criterion Design. Since this design has not been employed extensively, it is not clear what problems are involved in its use. However, some preliminary considerations may be useful. Initially, the design is suited to those responses which are shaped gradually rather than acquired in one or a few trials. Similarly, to show that changes in the criterion account for changes in behavior, the behavior has to occur relatively frequently so several changes can be made in the criterion before the terminal goal is achieved.

The changing-criterion design is less satisfactory than reversal and multiple-baseline designs in controlling extraneous events which could account for behavior change. Even if behavior matches the criterion, it may be that behavior is changing as a function of some event in the person's life which has led to a directional change (e.g., a decrease or increase) in the behavior over time. Even if an initial baseline suggests that performance of the target response is stable, it remains possible that the beginning of the experimental phase is associated with an event that accounts for behavior change.

Control Group Design

The control group design is another way to demonstrate the effect of an experimental contingency. There are a variety of control group designs suitable for applied settings (e.g., Campbell & Stanley, 1963). The basic design requires at least two groups, one which receives the experimental program (the experimental group) and the other which does not (the control group). To determine whether the experimental contingency was effective, rates of the target behavior in the experimental and control groups are compared. For example, a reinforcement program might be conducted in one school classroom but not in another. Immediately before and after the program the behavior of all students in both classrooms is assessed. To determine whether the program is effective, the averages in performance for the groups are compared at the end of the program. If the group averages are different between the classes, it suggests that the program was responsible for the change. To be sure that any difference between the two groups is due to the program, the groups must be similar to begin with. The best procedure to control for systematic differences between groups before the program is implemented is to *randomly assign* clients to one of the two groups. If subjects are not randomly assigned to groups, the likelihood is greater that the groups may be different in their performance of the target behavior before the program is implemented and differentially change in the target behavior over time for some reason other than the effect of the program.

A control group design was used to compare the effects of contingent and noncontingent delivery of token reinforcement with hospitalized psychiatric patients (Schaefer & Martin, 1966). By flipping a coin, patients were assigned to one of two groups (contingent or noncontingent token reinforcement) so that there were 20 subjects in each group. The behavior observed was considered to reflect the degree of "apathy" each patient exhibited. Patients were observed to determine whether they were engaging in behaviors other than walking, running, standing, sitting, or lying down. Behaviors other than these were considered to reflect activity on the ward. Behaviors indicative of activity included talking, singing, playing music, listening to others, and other responses as well. During the program, the experimental group received tokens (brass coins) for engaging in behaviors such as grooming themselves, interacting socially, and working on jobs. The tokens were earned on the basis of the patients' performance. The tokens could be exchanged for privileges on the ward such as watching television. The control group (noncontingent tokens) simply received the tokens without having to engage in any of the target behaviors. Patients in each group were observed before the program began, one month after it had been in effect, and two months after it had been in effect. The results are presented in Figure 4–9. The apathy ratings of the patients show that the experimental group changed during the program whereas the control group did not. By the third observation period, the groups were different in their performance. The results were evaluated with statistical tests using conventional rules for deciding whether the differences were reliable, that is, were likely to occur by chance. The results of this study revealed statistically significant group differences favoring the experimental group.

Problems and Considerations in Using a Control Group Design. The control group design has not been employed extensively in behavior modification programs in applied settings. One reason is that usually it is not possible to assign subjects randomly to groups in settings such as schools and hospitals. Thus, there is no assurance that the differences obtained between groups after a program are not due to initial differences which the investigator was not able to control through random assignment. Yet, control group designs are still worthwhile even when random assignment is not possible (Campbell & Stanley, 1963).

The major reason that the control group design is not used is that it focuses on the behavior of groups rather than on the behavior of individuals. When the control group study is done, the *average* frequency of behavior of individuals in the control group is compared with the average frequency of behavior of individuals in the experimental group. The focus on averages hides the behavior of individual clients (Sidman, 1960). Thus, the average performance of a group may change although only a few individuals in the group may have actually been affected by the program. Behavior modification programs in applied settings usually are concerned with achieving relatively large changes in the behavior of individuals (Risley, 1970). Changes in group averages are not as important as ensuring the behavior change of the individual.

A final reason why the control group design is used infrequently in ap-

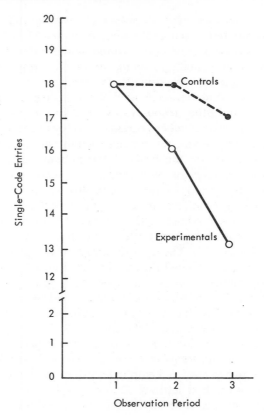

FIGURE 4–9 Number of single-code entries averaged for 20 experimental patients receiving selected reinforcement for certain behaviors and 20 control patients who received no reinforcement. (Source: Schaefer, H. H. & Martin, P. L. Behavioral therapy for "apathy" of hospitalized schizophrenics. *Psychological Reports,* 1966, **19,** 1147–58.)

plied settings is that behavior of groups is not usually measured continuously throughout the program. Behavior may be assessed prior to and immediately after the program. However, in behavior modification programs, it is important to assess behavior continuously so that the investigator knows how well the program is progressing while it is in effect. Programs often are altered after being in effect for only a short period of time. Continuous observation may reveal that the program is not working very well. Because the observations are made while the program is in effect, the program can be changed immediately. If behavior is assessed only at the end of the program, as it is usually in a control group design, it is too late to change the program if it does not work.

In spite of these criticisms, the control group designs are being used increasingly in behavior modification programs. In many situations, a control group can provide valuable information. For example, for comparing the effectiveness of one experimental program with another, separate groups of clients are needed. Both programs cannot be given to one group, because the first program may make some relatively permanent change in behavior. When the second program is administered, there may be a carryover effect from the first program. Thus, it is unclear how to compare the treatments. (See Kazdin [1973g] for a discussion of the use of control groups in behavior modification programs.)

Magnitude of Change

In the reversal, multiple-baseline, and changing-criterion designs, a comparison is made within individuals or groups. The degree of behavior change is reflected by comparing performance during baseline with performance during the experimental phase. A major issue is the degree of change essential to provide a convincing demonstration that behavior has improved. The decision that change has occurred is important in the execution of the design. For example, in the reversal design, the experimental condition is removed or altered, and reinstated on the basis of when behavior changes markedly (Sidman, 1960). In many instances, behavior change is dramatic. Examination of a graph sometimes reveals that performance during baseline does not overlap with performance during the experimental phase. That is, during the program the rate of behavior never approaches baseline. In cases such as these, there would be little disagreement that change has occurred.

In many instances, there may be changes which are less clear and require more subjective evaluation. The main criterion in evaluation of change is whether the difference in behavior is of *applied or practical significance*. Effects produced by the program have to be large enough to be of practical value (Risley, 1970). Individuals who are in constant interaction with the patient, resident, student, or client who was in the program usually evaluate whether this criterion has been achieved (Baer et al., 1968).

When an experimental control group design is used, the results are evaluated statistically. There are various statistical tests to determine whether the differences between groups are likely to be due to chance or to veridical treatment effects. (A discussion of the tests and their rationale is beyond the scope of this chapter.) Most statistical tests compare the averages of the experimental and control groups. As mentioned earlier, behavior modification is primarily concerned with changes in the performance of *individuals* rather than averages across a number of individuals. Thus, statistical tests tend to hide the performance of individual clients. (Sidman, 1960). The criterion for an effective program in behavior modification is whether the individual (or group or many individuals in a group) has made socially important changes in behavior. A statistical test cannot reveal this. Whether the change made in behavior is important requires examining the individual in his or her social context in light of the behavioral goals in that context.

Summary

In this chapter, important issues were discussed related to essential ingredients for the implementation and evaluation of behavior modification programs. The first issue is identification of the behaviors to be changed. Specific and objective behavioral criteria are needed so that the response is clearly defined. In addition, stimulus events in the environment which appear to be associated with the target behavior need to be specified and assessed. Once the target behavior is decided upon, a measurement strategy needs to be selected. The strategies which may be used include frequency, interval recording, and duration. Prior to baseline observations, independent observers should assess the target behavior to determine reliability of observations. When observers agree on the occurrence of the behavior, baseline observations can begin. Reliability checks need to be continued throughout the program to ensure that agreement between observers is maintained. Finally, an experimental design needs to be selected which will be used to demonstrate the causal relation between the contingencies and behavior change. Experimental designs were discussed including the reversal design, multiple-baseline designs, the changing-criterion design, and the control group design.

5

Positive Reinforcement

The problems of various populations in treatment, education ,and rehabilitation settings often include behavioral deficits or lack of appropriate skills. For example, autistic and retarded children often lack a variety of personal, social, and intellectual skills. Problems of other individuals may include deficits but frequently are associated with disruptive and deviant behaviors as well. For example, individuals identified as delinquents may perform deviant behaviors which have to be eliminated. However, elimination of the deviant behavior will not ensure that socially appropriate behavior will be performed. Socially appropriate behaviors need to be developed. For other individuals whose behavior is identified as problematic, there may be no deficit in behavior. Yet the conditions under which certain responses are performed may be different from those in which they should be performed in everyday life. For example, a "hyperactive" child may "know" how to sit down. However, this behavior rarely occurs in a classroom setting.

In the above cases, low frequency behaviors have to be increased, new behaviors have to be established, or behaviors have to be developed in new situations. Positive reinforcement is an appropriate technique to achieve these goals. Even in cases where the primary intent of the program is to eliminate an undesirable behavior, positive reinforcement plays a major role. Developing desirable and socially appropriate behavior can eliminate undesirable behaviors. By reinforcing socially appropriate behavior, the deviant responses frequently are replaced.

Positive reinforcement refers to an increase in the frequency of a response following the presentation of a positive reinforcer. Whether a particular event is a positive reinforcer is determined empirically. A reinforcer is defined by its effects on behavior. If response frequency increases when followed by the event, the event is a positive reinforcer. Defining a reinforcer by the effects on behavior appears to be circular. However, a reinforcer is not limited solely by its capacity to alter a particular behavior in a single situation. The reinforcer effective in altering one response in one situation may alter other responses in other situations as well. In addition, the Premack Principle, discussed earlier, provides a way to assess whether an event is a reinforcer independently of the effects on behavior. Reinforcing consequences are those behaviors in an individual's response repertoire that have a relatively high probability.

Maximizing the Effect of Positive Reinforcement

The effectiveness of reinforcement depends upon several factors. These include the delay between performance of a response and the delivery of reinforcement, the magnitude and quality of the reinforcer, and the schedule of reinforcement.

Delay of Reinforcement. Responses which occur in close proximity of reinforcement are more well learned than responses remote from reinforcement (Kimble, 1961; Skinner, 1953). Thus, a reinforcer should be delivered immediately after the target response to maximize the effect of reinforcement. If reinforcement does not follow the response immediately, another response different from the target response may be performed in the intervening delay period. The intervening responses will be immediately reinforced whereas the target response will be reinforced after a delay period. The target response is less likely to change. For example, children are often praised (or punished) for a behavior long after the behavior is performed. If a child straightens his or her room, a parent would do well to immediately provide praise. If praise is postponed until the end of the day, a variety of intervening responses may occur (including, perhaps, messing up the room). Similarly, in a classroom setting, children are often told how "good" they are when they are on the verge of becoming disruptive or restless. The teacher may mention that the class was well behaved in the morning and she hopes they will remain well behaved. Although praise is delivered, it is delayed and will be minimally effective.

Immediate reinforcement is important in the early stages of a behavior modification program when the target response is developing. After a response is performed consistently, the amount of time between the response and reinforcement can be increased without a decrement in performance. For example, in classroom settings students sometimes receive points or candy daily while high rates of academic behavior develop. However, after behavior has stabilized, the reinforcers can be delivered every other

day or at the end of several days without a deleterious effect on performance (Cotler, Applegate, King & Kristal, 1972). If a program begins with
delayed reinforcement, behavior might not change at all or not as rapidly
as when reinforcement is immediate.

It is desirable to change from immediate to delayed reinforcement after
a behavior is well developed so that behavior is not dependent upon immediate consequences. A great many consequences in everyday life follow
long after behavior is performed. For example, accomplishments, wages,
grades, and fame follow long after a series of responses is completed.

Magnitude or Amount of Reinforcement. The amount of reinforcement
delivered for a response also determines the extent to which a response
will be performed. The greater the amount of a reinforcer delivered for
a response, the more frequent the response (Kimble, 1961). The amount
can usually be specified in terms such as the quantity of food, the number
of points, or the amount of money.

The effects of different amounts of points on academic performance
were compared in a remedial class of retarded children (Wolf, Giles &
Hall, 1968). Students were reinforced for completing assignments in reading, arithmetic, and English workbooks. Points were earned by each child
for correct responses in each of the workbooks. Points were redeemable for
candy, snacks, toiletries, novelties, field trips, and a variety of other rewards. To evaluate the effect of different point magnitudes, the number of
points earned for correct responses in two areas (e.g., reading and arithmetic) was held constant while the number of points earned for correct
responses in the other area (e.g., English) was increased. An increase in
the number of points for correct responses in one area increased the amount
of work completed for that response area. However, other responses with
point values maintained at the initial level of reinforcement did not increase. Each response increased in frequency when the number of points
given for that response was increased.

Although the magnitude of reinforcement is directly related to performance, there are limits to this relationship. An unlimited amount of reinforcement does not necessarily maintain a high rate of performance of the
response. A reinforcer loses its effect when given in excessive amounts.
This is referred to as *satiation.* Hence, the effect of magnitude of reinforcement is limited by the point at which the individual becomes satiated.
Satiation is especially evident with primary reinforcers such as food, water,
and sex. In a short time, each of these reinforcers in excessive amounts loses
its reinforcing properties and may even become aversive. Of course, satiation of primary reinforcers is temporary because the events regain reinforcing value as deprivation increases. Secondary or conditioned reinforcers such as praise, attention, and tokens are also subject to satiation
(Gewirtz & Baer, 1958; Winkler, 1971b). However, they are less suscepti-
ble to satiation than are primary reinforcers. Generalized conditioned rein-

forcers in particular, such as money, are virtually insatiable because they have been associated with a variety of other reinforcers. Satiation of generalized reinforcers is not likely to occur until the individual satiates on the other reinforcers with which they have been associated. The more reinforcers for which the generalized conditioned reinforcer such as money can be exchanged, the less likelihood that satiation will occur. It is no surprise that few people complain or cease to work because of too much money!

Satiation has been used to reduce the value of stimuli that appear to be reinforcers (Ayllon, 1963). In one case, a psychiatric patient hoarded towels in her room. Even though ward attendants repeatedly removed towels, the patient kept between 19 and 29 towels in her room. Satiation was used to reduce hoarding with the rationale that towels served as a reinforcer. After several weeks of baseline observations of the number of towels in the patient's room, nurses discontinued removing towels and began bringing the patient a large number of towels. During the first week, 7 towels were brought each day. By the third week 60 towels were brought in daily. At the end of three weeks towels were no longer taken to the patient. The patient, however, was removing towels from her room (when they had accumulated to 625). The number of towels in her room readily declined until they averaged 1.5 per week. In the 12 months after the program was terminated the patient no longer collected towels. This example illustrates how a favorable event can lose its effect (and perhaps even become aversive) by being used excessively.

The effect of the amount of the reinforcer on behavior depends upon satiation and deprivation states of the individual with respect to that reinforcer. If the individual has unlimited access to the event (e.g., money), that event is not likely to be very effective as a reinforcer. The amount of a reinforcer needed to change behavior is not as great when the individual is partially deprived of the event. For example, individuals who are temporarily deprived of adult attention are more responsive to attention than are individuals who are not deprived of attention (Gewirtz & Baer, 1958). Of course, intentional deprivation of reinforcers in a behavior modification program is not essential for behavior change. In most everyday situations, individuals do not have unlimited access to events which are reinforcing (e.g., free time in a classroom situation or time with friends for children at home) and thereby normally undergo a mild form of deprivation. Thus, a variety of events are effective as reinforcers without introducing deprivation.

Quality or Type of Reinforcer.   The quality of a reinforcer is not usually specificable in physical terms as is the amount of the reinforcer (Kimble, 1961). Quality of a reinforcer is determined by the preference of the client. Reinforcers that are highly preferred lead to greater performance.

Preference can be altered by taking a reinforcer such as food and changing its taste. For example, animals show greater performance when a food is sweet than when it is sour or neutral in taste (Hutt, 1954).

For a given client, it usually is not difficult to specify activities which are highly preferred. Behaviors engaged in frequently provide a helpful indication of highly preferred reinforcers. However, preference for a particular reinforcer depends upon satiation. At one point in time a reinforcer may be more effective in changing behavior than another because the client is satiated with one and deprived of another (Premack, 1965). However, as will be discussed below, certain reinforcers tend to result in higher performance than others. Hence, the type of reinforcer alone can determine the extent of behavior change.

Schedule of Reinforcement.   Schedule of reinforcement refers to the rule denoting how many responses or which specific responses will be reinforced. Reinforcers are always administered according to some schedule. In the simplest schedule a response is reinforced each time it occurs. This schedule is referred to as *continuous reinforcement*. For example, to train mentally retarded children to follow instructions, reinforcement can be given each time the child responds appropriately. On the other hand, reinforcement may be delivered after some of the responses rather than all of them. This is referred to as *intermittent reinforcement*.

There are important differences between continuous and intermittent reinforcement while the behaviors are reinforced and after reinforcement is withdrawn. A behavior developed with continuous reinforcement is performed at a higher rate during the acquisition or reinforcement phase than if it is developed with intermittent reinforcement. Thus, while a behavior is developing, a continuous or "generous" schedule of reinforcement should be used. However, the advantage of continuous reinforcement is compensated after the reinforcement ceases. In extinction, behaviors previously reinforced continuously diminish at a much more rapid rate than do behaviors previously reinforced intermittently.

The difference between responses developed with continuous and intermittent reinforcement is apparent in examples from everyday experience. One common response which is reinforced virtually every time is putting coins into a cigarette, candy, or soda machine and pressing the appropriate lever. The product almost always is delivered. (Technically this is not a continuous reinforcement schedule because of mechanical failures. However, vending machines are designed to provide continuous reinforcement and will be used as an example of this schedule.) The response (depositing coins) follows a pattern identical to that of continuous reinforcement once reinforcement no longer occurs. As soon as the reinforcer (i.e., the product) is no longer delivered, extinction is almost immediate. Under these circumstances, few individuals repeatedly place more and more coins into that particular machine until there is some evidence that it has been repaired. Extinction of behaviors previously reinforced continuously (or almost continuously) is rapid.

A similar response, putting coins into a machine and pressing a lever, might be maintained by intermittent reinforcement as in the case of slot machines. Sometimes putting money into a slot machine is reinforced (with money) and many other times it is not. If money were no longer delivered (i.e., extinction), the response would continue to be performed at a high rate before extinguishing. It is difficult to discriminate when extinction begins on a highly intermittent schedule of reinforcement. The resistance of a response to extinction depends upon how intermittent or *thin* the reinforcement schedule is. If very few responses are reinforced, resistance to extinction is greater than if many responses are reinforced.

The advantage of continuous reinforcement is that performance occurs at a high level while behavior is reinforced. The advantage of intermittent reinforcement is that resistance to extinction is greater when reinforcement is discontinued. The advantages of both schedules can be obtained by developing behavior with continuous reinforcement until a high rate of behavior is well established. At that point, the schedule can be changed to intermittent reinforcement. The schedule can be made increasingly intermittent to ensure response maintenance (e.g., Kazdin & Polster, 1973).

Another advantage of intermittent reinforcement is its efficient use of available reinforcers. Intermittent reinforcement allows delivery of a few reinforcers for a large number of responses. In addition, by administering reinforcers only a few times, satiation is less likely to occur. For example, with intermittent food reinforcement the client is not likely to become full quickly and to become temporarily unresponsive to food. To sustain high levels of responding, it is important to avoid satiation by providing fewer reinforcers for an equivalent number of responses. A practical advantage in using intermittent reinforcement is that less time is required administering reinforcers than if continuous reinforcement is used.

Intermittent reinforcement can be scheduled many different ways (Ferster & Skinner, 1957), only a few of which will be considered here. Two simple types of reinforcement schedules can be distinguished. Reinforcement can be contingent upon the emission of a certain *number of responses*. This is referred to as a *ratio* schedule because the ratio of the total number of responses to the one which is reinforced is specified by the schedule. Alternatively, reinforcement can be given on the basis of the *amount of time* that passes before a response can be reinforced. This is referred to as an *interval* schedule. With a ratio schedule, the interval of time which passes for the subject to perform the response is irrelevant. The behavior of the subject controls the frequency of reinforcement. With interval schedules, the number of responses performed is irrelevant as long as one response is performed after the prescribed interval of time has elapsed. The frequency of reinforcement is partially determined by the clock (Reynolds, 1968; Skinner, 1953).

In both ratio and interval schedules of reinforcement, the requirement for reinforcement can be *fixed* so that it is the same specified requirement each time. On the other hand, the requirement can be *variable* so that it is different from time to time. Four simple schedules of reinforcement will be discussed: fixed ratio (FR), variable ratio (VR), fixed interval (FI), and variable interval (VI).

A *fixed-ratio schedule* requires that an unvarying number of responses is performed before a response is reinforced. The number following "FR" specifies which response will be reinforced. For example, FR:1 specifies that only one response is required for the reinforcer to be delivered. (FR:1 is also called continuous reinforcement because every response is reinforced.) FR:10 denotes that every tenth response is reinforced.

Performance under fixed-ratio schedules differs to some extent depending upon whether the ratios are small or large. Characteristically there is a temporary pause in responding after reinforcement is delivered and then a rapid rise in response rate until the ratio is completed and reinforcement is delivered. The pause after responding is a function of the ratio with large ratios prodocing larger pauses. Once the responses resume, reinforcement is maximized by performing all of the responses as quickly as possible. Examples of an FR schedule include any instance in which the reinforcer is delivered for a certain number of responses. For example, factory workers who are paid according to how much they produce are reinforced on an FR schedule (commonly referred to as piecework). For every certain number of responses (product produced), the reinforcer (money) is earned. If there are several responses required for reinforcement, there may be a temporary pause (no production) immediately after reinforcement.

A *variable-ratio schedule* specifies that reinforcement occurs after a certain number of responses. However, that number *varies* unpredictably from occasion to occasion. On the average, a certain number of responses are performed before reinforcement is delivered. The number following "VR" specifies the average number of responses required for reinforcement. For example, VR:5 indicates that on the average 5 responses are performed before the reinforcer is delivered. On some occasions, the second response may be reinforced, whereas on other occasions the eighth response may be reinforced. A different number of responses may be required each time. However, across all occasions reinforcement is delivered on the average of the number specified (e.g., 5 in the VR:5 schedule). Of course, any number except 1 can be used in a VR schedule because that would be equivalent to reinforcing every response which is a continuous reinforcement or FR:1 schedule.

Performance under VR schedules is consistently high. The pauses which may be apparent with FR schedules can be virtually eliminated with a VR schedule, unless the average ratio is very long. Immediately after a response is reinforced, the subject begins to respond because the next reinforcer may follow only a few responses. Performance continues at a high rate until reinforcement is delivered and immediately resumes again. Behavior previously maintained under a VR schedule extinguishes more slowly than under a FR schedule, particularly if the variable schedule requires many responses for reinforcement. Performance is relatively persistent and consistent following a VR schedule. Thus, VR schedules are highly suited to forestalling extinction. Prior to withdrawing reinforcement, the ratio gradually can be made very *thin.* To make a schedule thin is to increase the number of responses required for reinforcement. Resistance to extinction can be very great when reinforcement is administered on a relatively thin schedule.

Examples of VR schedules are abundant in everyday experience. The behavior of a fisherman is controlled, in part, by VR reinforcement. Each time a line is tossed into the water (response), a fish (reinforcer) is not caught. Rather, the response is reinforced only some of the time. Yet the variable nature of the schedule ensures that extinction will not take place rapidly. Slot machines, mentioned earlier, represent a dramatic application of VR schedules. Since any response can be reinforced, the person playing the machine usually performs at a consistently high rate. Performance is unlikely to extinguish for long periods of time.

A *fixed-interval schedule* requires that an interval of time (usually expressed in minutes) passes before the reinforcer is available. The first response which occurs after the interval passes is reinforced. In a fixed schedule, of course, the interval is unvarying. For example, an FI:1 schedule denotes that the first response after one minute passes is reinforced. An *interval schedule* requires that only one response be performed after the prescribed interval has elapsed. While this efficiency in responding rarely occurs, the characteristic of FI schedule responding is distinct. Following reinforcement there is usually a pronounced pause where no responses are performed. This does not interfere with receiving reinforcement since a response before the appropriate time elapses is never reinforced. Only if the pause is longer than the fixed interval will the subject postpone reinforcement. FI schedules lead to less consistent rates of responding than do FR schedules because nonresponding immediately after reinforcement during an FI schedule does not postpone reinforcement as it does with an FR schedule.

An excellent example of an FI response pattern in everyday experience is looking to see whether one's mail has arrived (Logan, 1969). For most individuals, mail delivery is once a day with (fairly) fixed periods of time between deliveries. The response (looking for mail in the mail box) is reinforced (finding mail) daily. Immediately after reinforcement there is no longer a response. One does not resume looking for mail again until the interval is almost complete, the next day. At that point, looking for mail increases until reinforcement is obtained.

Behaviors which are controlled by time follow interval schedules. For example, a recent study of the United States Congress showed that passing bills followed a characteristic pattern of FI responding (Weisberg & Waldrop, 1972). For both sessions of each Congress from 1947 to 1968, the number of bills passed was very low immediately after a session began. However, an increasing number of bills was passed as the session came to a close. Thus, a great number of responses was performed immediately before the interval ended. After the interval ended (one session) and a new interval began (second session), there was a pause in performance (few bills passed). Although interval schedule characteristics are apparent in the performance of Congress, one can only speculate as to the reinforcer at the end of the session (Weisberg & Waldrop, 1972).

A *variable-interval schedule* specifies the *average length* of the intervals required for reinforcement. For example, a VI:10 schedule denotes that on the average, ten minutes must pass before a response is reinforced. On any given occasion the interval may be more or less than ten minutes. The reinforcer is delivered for the first response *after* the interval passes. Studying behavior of students follows a pattern characteristic of a VI schedule, if the instructor gives "pop quizzes." The interval between quizzes is unpredictable and varies from quiz to quiz. Studying tends to be relatively consistent under such a schedule.

Responding tends to be more rapid under VI than FI schedules. However, high rates of responding do not necessarily speed up reinforcement in an interval schedule as they do on a ratio schedule. Consequently, the rate of performance under interval schedules is usually lower. As with ratio schedules, extinction is prolonged with a thin variable schedule.

Schedules of reinforcement have important implications for behavior modification programs in applied settings. The implications will be particularly evident in the discussion of maintenance of behaviors. (See Chapter 9.) As mentioned earlier, in the beginning of a behavior change program, it is desirable to reinforce continuously. In practice, it is virtually impossible to constantly survey behavior to ensure that each performance of the target behavior is reinforced. However, a rich schedule can be used initially before changing to increasingly intermittent schedules. The type of intermittent schedule used needs to be determined by considering the characteristic response pattern of the schedule as well as practical exigencies. Although fixed schedules may be convenient to administer, characteristic performance includes pauses or lapses in performance of the reinforced behavior. For example, in an institutional setting, ward attendants may reinforce residents on an FI schedule. At the end of the time periods (e.g., 30 minutes), staff may administer reinforcers to residents behaving "appropriately." However, it is very likely that performance of the residents will be high near the end of the interval with pauses immediately after reinforcement. Variable schedules can alleviate the inconsistency in resident performance.

To summarize the above discussion, the effect of reinforcement can be maximized by reinforcing the target behavior *immediately* with a *potent reinforcer* which is delivered on a *continuous* or near continuous (rich) *schedule* of reinforcement. The extent to which these conditions are met will determine the efficacy of the program. As behavior develops, reinforcement should be increasingly intermittent and increasingly delayed. By providing less reinforcement on a less immediate schedule, behavior can be maintained. In many cases, the ideal conditions for reinforcement delivery cannot be met. Also potent reinforcers (e.g., food and money) sometimes are not available or are objected to on ethical grounds. Moreover, exigencies of the setting may interfere with immediate reinforcement. Finally, reinforcers differ in the ease with which they are administered. In spite of these difficulties, several reinforcement procedures are available. Usually the resources and demands of a particular setting are readily incorporated into a reinforcement program.

Types of Reinforcers

A major task in using reinforcement effectively is selecting powerful reinforcers. Reinforcers differ in their potency as well as the ease with which they are administered in a treatment or educational setting. Behavior modification programs employing different types of reinforcers will be discussed.

Food and Other Consumables. Food qualifies as a primary reinforcer because its reinforcing value is unlearned. Of course, food preferences are learned which make some foods more reinforcing than others and some foods not reinforcing at all unless the individual has been deprived of all food. Because food is a primary reinforcer, it is very powerful. Studies have used food as a reinforcer, including entire meals, bits of cereal, candy, crackers, cookies, soft drinks, ice cream, and other foods.

There are other events which have been used which are nonfood consumables. For example, cigarettes and gum may be strong reinforcers for some individuals. However, since they are not primary reinforcers their appeal does not extend to as many individuals as does food. Although the reinforcing properties of nonfood consumables are learned, eventually the reinforcing power of these consumables resembles that of primary reinforcers. Deprivation may build up in a fashion analogous to that of food. In any case, when nonfood consumables are reinforcers, they tend to be very effective. Food and consumables will be discussed together because they share characteristic advantages and disadvantages.

Food has been used frequently. Hopkins (1968) used candy to increase the frequency of smiling of a retarded boy who constantly appeared sad and dejected. The author decided to increase the frequency of smiling during walks the child took in school. One or two walks were conducted daily to determine how the child responded when someone greeted him. After obtaining the baseline rate of smiling, the child was given a piece of candy each time he smiled when he met another person during a walk. The number of smiles substantially increased. In later phases, candy reinforcement was withdrawn and social reinforcement (attention from others) was substituted. Eventually, no consequences were delivered and a high rate of smiling was maintained.

Whitman et al. (1970) used candy and praise to train social interaction between two severely retarded and withdrawn children. Reinforcers were delivered to the children for playing with each other (e.g., rolling a ball back and forth or coloring together). Social interaction increased and generalized to a situation in which reinforcement was not delivered. Moreover, although the children were reinforced for interacting only with each other, their interactions with other children also increased.

Sherman (1965) used candy, cigarettes, and praise to develop speech in a 63-year-old psychotic patient who had been mute for 45 years. Shaping was used to develop eye contact with the experimenter, grunts, and vocalizations. After a plateau had been reached in training, portions of the patient's lunch and subsequently entire meals were used as reinforcers. (Food at mealtime is usually more reinforcing than food delivered between meals because deprivation is greater at mealtime.) At the end of training, an active vocabulary had been trained. The gains were maintained after six months. Gum has also been used to develop speech in a mute psychotic patient (Isaacs et al., 1960).

Risley and Wolf (1968) used food (such as ice cream, candy, and coke) along with praise to develop functional speech in autistic children who were echolalic (i.e., inappropriately mimicked conversation of others and excessively repeated songs and TV commercials). Children were trained to answer questions, initiate requests and comments, name objects with an increased vocabulary, and use grammatically correct sentences.

Kale et al. (1968) used cigarettes to reinforce social responses of psychotic patients. A cigarette was administered for greetings either made spontaneously or in response to greetings from staff. Over the training sessions, cigarettes were administered on an increasingly intermittent schedule so that fewer and fewer social responses were reinforced. Greeting responses remained at a high level even though reinforcement was eliminated.

Important Considerations in Using Food and Consumables. Since the effect of reinforcement depends upon the strength of the reinforcer, it is no surprise that food has been used frequently. It has been used effectively for severe behavioral problems with autistic children, the severely retarded, and chronic psychotics. In spite of the utility of food and consumables, they have distinct limitations in many applied settings.

The effectiveness of food and other consumables depends heavily upon the deprivation state of the individual. The strength of food or another consumable as a reinforcer is maximized by depriving the individual. If the individual is not at least partially deprived, it may only serve as a weak reinforcer. As mentioned before, investigators sometimes use food reinforcement prior to mealtime or during mealtime itself (Barton et al., 1970). In addition, light meals may be given throughout the day so that slight deprivation is maintained and food will be reinforcing continuously (O'Brien, Bugle, & Azrin, 1972). Even if the individual is deprived of food before training, as training proceeds on a given day the reinforcing value of food may be reduced. The number of times food can be delivered and the quantity delivered after a response are limited because of the possibility of satiation. To forestall satiation, some investigators have delivered small portions of the consumable item such as a bite of food, a few pieces of popcorn, or half a cigarette (Ayllon & Azrin, 1968b; Risley & Wolf, 1968). Nevertheless, food and consumables are still readily subject to satiation.

The effectiveness of food reinforcement depends upon the type of food used. Although food per se is a primary reinforcer, specific foods used in a given program may not be reinforcing for particular individuals. For example, although ice cream may reinforce most children, for many individuals the flavor is a relevant dimension which will determine the reinforcing properties. When a single food or consumable is relied upon, the possibility exists that the event will not be effective with a number of clients. Moreover, preferences within a given individual change from time to time so a single food or consumable item may have short-lived reinforcing properties.

There are potential problems in the administration of food reinforcers. The delivery and consumption of food after a response sometimes interrupts ongoing behavior. For example, if a special education classroom teacher distributed candy to her students while they were working attentively on an assignment, each individual might be distracted momentarily from the task. Although the purpose of reinforcement is to augment attentiveness to classwork, the consumption of the reinforcer may temporarily distract the students. Similar problems occur in the consumption of consumables such as cigarettes or gum.

Another feature related to administration of food and other consumables is that they may be difficult to dispense immediately because they are cumbersome. Although staff can carry pockets full of candy, other foods such as beverages and ice cream generally are not readily carried. Of course, the setting in which food is used dictates the ease with which a particular type of food can be administered. In the home, virtually any food can be administered. However, institutional life usually requires stringent guidelines and rigidly adhered to routines for food delivery.

A related problem is that food is not easily administered to several individuals in a group immediately after behavior is performed. Since the administration of food to several individuals takes some time (e.g., selecting the quantity of food, putting spoon or fork into individual's mouth, or passing a piece to each individual), it is not particularly well suited to group situations where everyone is to be reinforced. Many programs using food have been conducted on an individual basis rather than in groups (Ayllon, 1963; Isaacs et al., 1960; Risley & Wolf, 1968; Sherman, 1965).

Despite the possible disadvantages of food and consumables, they are potent reinforcers. Food and consumables are particularly suited to those individuals who initially fail to respond to events such as approval. Indeed, food is useful in establishing the reinforcing properties of other events such as praise, feedback, attention, smiles, and physical contact. Programs using food and consumables invariably pair the delivery of the reinforcer with praise and other social events so that these latter events can be used to effectively control behavior.

Social Reinforcers. Social reinforcers such as verbal praise, attention, physical contact (including affectionate or approving touches, pats, and hand holding), and facial expressions (including smiles, eye contact, nods of approval, and winks) are conditioned reinforcers. Numerous studies have shown that attention from a parent, teacher, or attendant exerts considerable control over behavior. Praise has been used to increase cooperative behavior of obstreperous children both in the home and at school (e.g., Hart, Reynolds, Baer, Brawley, & Harris, 1968; Wahler, 1969). Social reinforcement has been used extensively in classroom settings where praise is delivered for study behavior while disruptive or inattentive behaviors are ignored (e.g., Hall et al., 1968; Kazdin, 1973c; Madsen, Becker, & Thomas, 1968).

Madsen et al. (1968) used praise to improve attentive behavior in two elementary classrooms. Using a reversal design, different phases were evaluated including classroom rules (telling students the rules for behaving in class), ignoring inappropriate behavior (not attending to those disruptive behaviors which interfere with learning), and praising appropriate behavior (e.g., praising children who worked on assignments, answered questions, listened, and raised their hands to speak). Throughout the program, data were collected on teacher behavior to ensure that her praise increased when it was supposed to. Figure 5–1 shows the behavior of one problem child. Providing rules to the class and ignoring disruptive behavior did not have a noticeable effect on performance. Disruptive behavior decreased only in the last phase when appropriate behavior was praised.

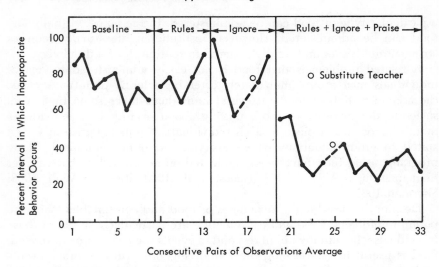

FIGURE 5-1 Inappropriate behavior of one problem child as a function of experimental conditions. (Source: Madsen, C. H., Becker, W. C., & Thomas, D. R. Rules, praise, and ignoring: Elements of elementary classroom control. *Journal of Applied Behavior Analysis*, 1968, **1**, 139–50.)

In most classroom studies, teacher attention consists primarily of verbal praise supplemented with facial expressions and physical contact. However, as noted earlier, nonverbal teacher attention alone, consisting of smiles, physical contact, and approving nods contingent upon appropriate behavior, also improves classroom deportment (Kazdin & Klock, 1973).

Praise has been used in settings other than classrooms. In a psychiatric hospital (Milby, 1970), two psychotic patients received attention for socially interacting (talking, working, or playing with another patient). Social interaction increased when the nursing staff attended to patients, looked at them, or talked approvingly to them when the patients interacted.

Rickard, Dignam, and Horner (1960) used social reinforcement (smiles, nods, and exclamations expressing interest) to increase rational verbalizations of a chronic psychotic patient during individual therapy sessions. Delusional verbalizations were ignored whereas all rational verbalizations were reinforced by the therapist. This resulted in an increase in rational talk which was maintained after two years (Rickard & Dinoff, 1962).

In a study mentioned earlier (Hopkins, 1968), social reinforcement was used (following a phase using candy reinforcement) to maintain smiling of retarded boys. One of the boys wore a sign which said, "If I smile—talk to me. If I look sad—ignore me." Someone walking ahead of the child prompted others to read the sign and follow the instructions. The frequency of smiling increased. When the sign was altered ("If I smile—ignore me"), smiling decreased substantially. Thus, smiling was under control of social reinforcers.

Social reinforcement has also been used in counseling directed toward educational and vocational planning (Ryan & Krumboltz, 1964). As college students talked freely about their educational and vocational ideas, they were verbally reinforced by the counselor with statements such as "That's a good idea," "Good," and "Fine." Some students were reinforced for making decisions (i.e., selecting courses of action or goals) and others were reinforced for deliberating (i.e., considering alternatives and weighing courses of action). Whenever a statement was made reflecting these responses, the counselor responded with verbal praise. Another group of students did not receive reinforcement for either decision making or deliberating. The two groups which received praise increased in the responses that were praised. However, nonreinforced subjects did not change in either of these behaviors over the course of the interview. This study suggests that the effects of praise delivered systematically are not restricted to children or specific treatment settings.

Important Considerations in Using Social Reinforcers.   Social consequences have a variety of advantages as reinforcers. First, they are easily administered by attendants, parents, and teachers. A verbal statement or smile can be given quickly. The complications of delivering food reinforcement are not present with praise and attention. Obviously, little preparation is involved before delivering praise. Providing praise takes little time so there is no delay in reinforcing a number of individuals almost immediately. Indeed, praise can be delivered to a group as a whole as in a classroom.

A second consideration is that praise need not disrupt the behavior which is reinforced. A person can be praised or receive a pat on the back while engaging in appropriate behavior. Performance of the target behavior can continue. Third, praise is a generalized conditioned reinforcer because it has been paired with many reinforcing events. As mentioned earlier, conditioned reinforcers are less subject to satiation than are food and consumable items. Fourth, attention and praise are "naturally occurring" reinforcers employed in everyday life. Some reinforcers (such as food and consumables) do not normally follow desirable behavior such as paying attention in a classroom, interacting socially with others, talking rationally with peers, or working on a job. In contrast, social reinforcers such as attention from others follow socially adaptive behaviors. Behaviors developed with social reinforcement in a treatment or training program may be more readily maintained outside of the setting than behaviors developed with other reinforcers. Social reinforcers in everyday life may continue to provide consequences for newly acquired behavior. In short, a desirable feature of using social reinforcement is that there is an increased likelihood that behaviors will be maintained outside of the specific training setting.

Before embarking on a program employing social reinforcement, it is important to keep a few considerations in mind. Praise, approval, and physical contact are not reinforcing for everyone. Because the reinforcement value of praise and attention has to be learned, one can expect to find individuals who do not respond to events which are normally socially reinforcing (cf. Locke, 1969; Wahler, 1968). Indeed, for some individuals praise may be aversive (Levin & Simmons, 1962). Because social events (praise, approval, and physical contact) are employed in everyday life, it is important to establish them as reinforcers by pairing them with events that are already reinforcers.

High Probability Behaviors.   When provided with the opportunity to engage in a variety of behaviors, an individual selects certain activities with a relatively higher frequency than others. As mentioned earlier, the Premack Principle denotes that behaviors of a relatively higher probability in an individual's repertoire of responses can reinforce behaviors of a lower probability. Engaging in preferred activities and earning various privileges serve as reinforcers because they have a relatively higher probability than other behaviors which are to be increased. To determine whether a particular activity is high in probability, the frequency with which an individual engages in the activity when given the opportunity must be observed. For example, for many adults attending athletic contests, concerts, or operas, and camping or relaxing are high probability behaviors and could reinforce a variety of lower probability behaviors.

Programs in applied settings have used the Premack Principle effectively. Lattal (1969) used swimming (high probability behavior) to reinforce toothbrushing of boys in a summer camp. After baseline observations were made of the number of boys who brushed their teeth, only those boys who brushed were permitted to go swimming. Virtually everyone brushed their teeth during this phase.

Osborne (1969) trained a class of deaf girls to stay in their seats. Children earned 5 minutes of free time for each 15 minutes they remained seated. Only those children who were in their seats earned the 5 minutes of free time in the afternoon. Those who did not, continued to work. For each child the number of out-of-seat responses dropped substantially when the program was in effect. Contingent access to free time has also been used to improve spelling performance in the classroom (Ross & O'Driscoll, 1972).

Access to play has been used to reinforce accuracy of printing of kindergarten children (Salzberg, Wheeler, Devar, & Hopkins, 1971). When predetermined individualized levels of correct printing responses were achieved, the children could play. An interesting feature of this report is that each day, only some of the children were checked. The children who were checked were predetermined daily on a random basis. All nonchecked children automatically received access to play. Nevertheless, the quality of printing for *everyone* increased. Since a child never knew whether his or her performance was to be checked on a given day, the only way to guarantee receiving the reinforcer was to always perform the target behavior. In another program, Hart and Risley (1968) trained children from lower socioeconomic families to use adjectives in spontaneous speech. Access to recreational materials depended upon appropriate speech. Large increases in reinforced language responses were noted.

Keutzer (1967) used a highly reinforcing activity to alter the behavior of a 38-year-old woman. The woman expressed an inability to concentrate or to perform duties and appeared to lack motivation and energy. She was especially concerned with her inability to study and complete her last year of university work. The client was instructed by her therapist to keep a record of her study time. The high probability behavior used as a reinforcer was time in therapy with her therapist. At the end of each week the client earned time in therapy on the basis of how much she studied. An upper limit was set so that the client could earn a maximum of two hours of therapy per week. After 16 weeks, studying behavior increased from approximately 2 hours to a high of 16 hours per week.

In a program with hospitalized drug addicts (O'Brien, Raynes & Patch, 1971), patients earned the opportunity to engage in high probability behaviors (recreation, access to television and radio, pass privileges away from the hospital, and the opportunity to wear street clothes rather than institutional clothes in the hospital). To earn these privileges, patients were required to awaken and groom themselves on time, to attend meetings, and to carry out various routine behaviors on the ward. The percentage of patients who actively engaged in all of the low frequency target behaviors increased from 20% during baseline to 80% during the program.

Important Considerations in Using High Probability Behaviors. High probability behaviors offer distinct advantages as reinforcers. In most settings, activities and privileges are readily available. For example, in the home, access to television, peers, or the family automobile are likely to be high probability behaviors depending upon the age level of the person. At school, access to recess, free-time, games, and entertaining reading materials may serve a similar function. In hospital and rehabilitation facilities, engaging in recreation, leaving the ward, access to desirable living quarters or personal possessions, and sitting with friends at meals can also be used. In short, activities and privileges which can be made contingent upon performance usually are available in any setting. Hence, extra reinforcers (e.g., candy or money) need not be introduced into the setting.

There are limitations in using high probability behaviors as reinforcing events. First, access to an activity cannot always immediately follow low probability behavior. For example, in a classroom setting, activities such as recess or games cannot readily be used to immediately reinforce behavior. Usually, activities and privileges have some scheduling limitations. Hence, in some cases there will be a delay of reinforcement. In cases where access to an activity is frequent such as every 15 minutes (Osborne, 1969), the routine of the setting is interrupted. However, after performance of the lower probability behavior is established, access to the high probability activity can be delayed without loss of behavior gains (Cotler et al., 1972).

A second consideration is that providing an activity is sometimes an all or none enterprise, so that it is either earned or not earned. This can limit the flexibility in administering the reinforcer. For example, in institutions for psychiatric patients or delinquents, access to overnight passes and trips to a nearby town are sometimes used as reinforcing activities. These activities cannot be parceled out so that "portions" of them are earned. They have to be given in their entirety or not given at all. If a client's behavior comes very near the performance criterion for reinforcement but does not quite meet the criterion, a decision has to be made whether to provide the reinforcer. A solution is to shape behavior by initially setting low criteria to earn the activity. Gradually the criteria for earning the reinforcer are increased. Another alternative is to incorporate many privileges and activities into the contingency system (O'Brien et al., 1971). Different behaviors or varying degrees of a given behavior can be reinforced with different privileges.

A third consideration in using high probability behaviors as reinforcers is that relying on one or two activities as reinforcers runs the risk that some individuals may not find them reinforcing. Preferences for activities may be idiosyncratic so that different activities need to be available. Providing free time (Osborne, 1969) is desirable, if individuals can choose from a variety of activities.

A final consideration in using activities and privileges is that in many institutions, activities must be freely available to the clients. Activities which might be made contingent upon performance are delivered independently of the client's performance. The ideology of presenting activities and other potentially reinforcing events (e.g., meals and sleeping quarters) noncontingently was developed to ensure that individuals would not be deprived of basic human rights. Institutionalized clients are usually deprived of many amenities of living simply by virtue of their institutionalization. Withholding or depriving individuals of the already limited number of available reinforcers is viewed as unethical. (The issue of deprivation will be discussed in Chapter 10 along with other ethical considerations.) In any case, in some settings certain activities already given to the clients as part of the setting simply cannot be given contingently.

Informative Feedback. Providing information about performance can serve as powerful reinforcement. Feedback is a conditioned reinforcer because it usually is associated with the delivery of other events which are reinforcing. Feedback is implicit in the delivery of any reinforcer because it indicates which responses are appropriate or desirable from the standpoint of those who provide reinforcement. Thus, when reinforcers such as food, praise, activities, or points are provided, a client receives feedback or knowledge of how well he or she is doing. Perhaps, feedback may include implicit social approval or disapproval. However, feedback can be employed independently of explicit approval or other reinforcers. Individuals can be informed of their behavior or of the extent to which their behavior has changed. Feedback refers to *knowledge of results* of one's performance without necessarily including additional events which may be reinforcing in their own right. Of course, feedback may implicitly include social approval.

Feedback was used with a psychiatric patient who had a severe knife phobia (Leitenberg et al., 1968). She had obsessive thoughts about killing others when using a kitchen knife and became unable to look at or come into contact with sharp knives. The patient was told that practice in looking at the knife would help reduce her fear. The patient was told to look at a sharp knife displayed in a small compartment until she became uncomfortable. Feedback indicated how many seconds the patient kept the compartment open, thereby exposing herself to the knife. Feedback steadily increased the time of self-exposure to the knife. Figure 5–2 shows an increase in seconds of looking at the knife. Adding praise (e.g., "That was great!") to the feedback (second phase) did not appear to augment the effect of feedback alone. Throughout the project, except for the reversal (fourth) phase, feedback continued to improve performance. It is unclear whether praise during the sixth phase was responsible for behavior change. In any case, by the end of the study, the patient was able to use a knife to slice vegetables for use in the ward.

Simply providing verbal feedback is not always sufficient to increase behavior. For example, in a training school setting, retardates were told how many work units of an assembly task they completed each day (Jens & Shores, 1969). Behavior did not improve with verbal feedback. However, when the daily work rates were charted individually for the clients, performance improved markedly. A removal and reintroduction of charting work performance demonstrated the specific control of the graphic display on behavior. In a classroom setting, Salzberg et al. (1971) provided grades to kindergarten children on the basis of accuracy of handwriting (printing). Feedback in the form of grades was ineffective in improving writing. Only when access to play was contingent upon accuracy did writing improve.

Points have been used to provide feedback. Of course, when points are exchangeable for other rewards they serve more than a feedback function. (See discussion of points in the next section.) However, sometimes points

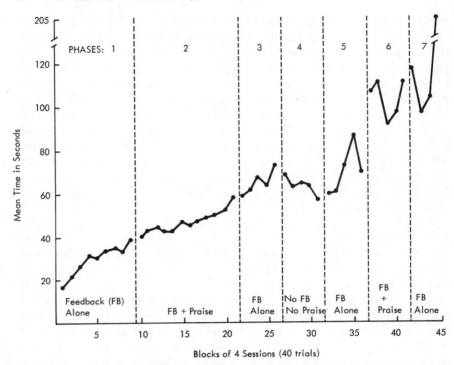

FIGURE 5–2 Time in which a knife was kept exposed by a phobic patient as a function of feedback, feedback plus praise, and no feedback or praise conditions. (Source: Leitenberg, H., Agras, W. S., Thompson, L. E., & Wright, D. E. Feedback in behavior modification: An experimental analysis in two phobic cases. *Journal of Applied Behavior Analysis,* 1968, **1,** 131–37.)

are not exchangeable for other events. The points are delivered to provide feedback as to how well the client is doing. For example, points were used to provide feedback to a child for the performance of household chores (Hall et al., 1972). The child received points depending upon the number of tasks completed. The points were recorded each night. Initially, the points had no value and could not be used to obtain any other reinforcers. Yet points provided feedback to the child and performance improved. Performance of chores increased even further when the points could be traded for pennies.

In a sheltered workshop with multiply handicapped clients, the effect of feedback was evaluated in altering production on an assembly job (Zimmerman, Stuckey, Garlick, & Miller, 1969). A feedback phase preceded a period in which clients received points exchangeable for back-up rewards. During the feedback phase, clients were told how many assembly units they completed at the end of each day. In addition, they were told how many points they would have earned, if points were being delivered. In fact, points were not delivered. Performance increased during this phase relative to baseline. When points (exchangeable for reinforcers) were finally given, performance increased even further.

Important Considerations in Using Feedback.   Feedback can be readily employed in most settings particularly when some performance criterion is explicit, such as academic achievement or productivity on the job. In other situations, performance criteria can be set (e.g., number of hallucinatory statements of a psychotic patient or number of cigarettes smoked), and daily feedback can be delivered to provide information comparing performance with the criterion. When feedback is used, a criterion for performance is essential (Locke, Cartledge, & Koeppel, 1968). By using feedback, extrinsic reinforcers which are not delivered as part of the routine need not be introduced.

The effectiveness of feedback alone has been equivocal. In some studies, providing information about performance has not altered behavior (Kazdin, 1973b; Salzberg et al., 1971). Since feedback is implicit in the delivery of other reinforcers, those other reinforcers should be used along with explicit feedback.

The importance of supplementing feedback with additional reinforcers was demonstrated in a study by Page (1958). In a large number of classrooms across grades 7 through 12, students received feedback for their performance on an objective examination. Each class was divided into three groups. One group received test grades only, with no additional comments on their papers. Another group received individualized comments on the exam along with the grades. A final group received their grades along with a specific short standardized comment depending on the grade. For example, all "A" papers had written on them "Excellent, keep it up!" Of course, receiving a grade on a test serves as feedback. However, the additional comment provides praise and attention for high grades (or punishment for low grades). On the next classroom exam the groups which received written comments in addition to grades, performed better than the group which received grades alone.

Tokens.   Tokens are conditioned reinforcers such as poker chips, coins, tickets, stars, points, or checkmarks. As discussed earlier, tokens are generalized reinforcers because they can be exchanged for a variety of reinforcing events referred to as back-up reinforcers. A reinforcement system based upon tokens is referred to as a *token economy*. In a token economy, tokens function the same way that money does in national economic systems (Winkler, 1971b). The tokens are earned and used to purchase back-up reinforcers including various goods and services. Back-up reinforcers usually include food, consumables, activities, and privileges. The rate of exchange of tokens for back-up reinforcers must be specified so that it is clear how many tokens are required to purchase various reinforcers. The target behavior or behaviors are made explicit, as in most programs, along with the number of tokens which are administered for their performance.

The tokens need to be established as conditioned reinforcers because they have no reinforcing properties in their own right. For some populations it is sufficient to explain that tokens can be exchanged for various goods. After the explanation, the tokens take on immediate value which is maintained by the actual exchange of tokens for other reinforcers. For individuals whose behavior is not controlled by instructions about the value of tokens, the tokens can be given noncontingently a few times. Immediately after they are delivered, they can be exchanged or traded for a back-up reinforcer. For example, a retarded child may be given a few poker chips immediately before entering a dining room. A few seconds after having the tokens, an attendant at the door can take the tokens. Thus, the tokens (poker chips) are followed by access to food. By pairing tokens with other back-up events, their value is achieved.

Ayllon and Azrin (1965; 1968b) used token reinforcement with psychiatric patients. Tokens were earned for working on various jobs on or off the ward in the hospital. Reinforcers that could be purchased with tokens included selecting a bedroom on the ward, having a personal chair, attending religious services or movies, leaving the ward, visiting a neighboring town, listening to radio, watching TV, and having a private audience with a psychologist or social worker. The back-up reinforcers were available on a temporary basis so they had to be purchased repeatedly. For example, a patient could select and rent a particular bedroom. Patients who did not rent a special bedroom were placed in a free room. Tokens had to be paid daily to rent a special room.

Ayllon and Azrin (1965) demonstrated that patients would work on those jobs which paid tokens whether or not the job was one which they preferred performing. When one job no longer paid tokens while another job did, patients rapidly changed jobs. In one of the experiments reported, patients received tokens whether or not they worked on the job. Patients were given tokens daily before going to work. Figure 5–3 shows that when token reinforcement was not contingent upon working, the number of hours of work performed on the ward substantially decreased. Almost no work was performed. In the final phase, patients were told that the "vacation with pay" was over and tokens would be given at the end of the day depending upon how long an individual worked. Performance increased when reinforcement was contingent upon work.

Phillips (1968) reported a token program for predelinquent boys who had committed various offenses (e.g., thefts, fighting, school truancy, and academic failure). The program was conducted in a home-style cottage managed by houseparents. Performance of self-care, social, and academic behaviors were reinforced with points (tallied on 3- x 5-inch cards). Be-

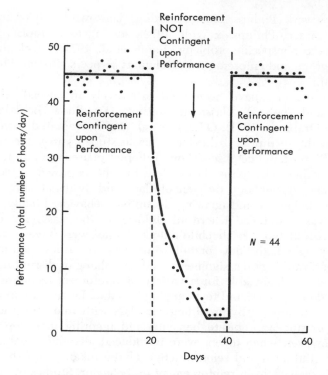

FIGURE 5–3 The total number of hours of the on-ward performance by a group of 44 patients. (Source: Ayllon, T. & Azrin, N. H. The measurement and reinforcement of behavior of psychotics. *Journal of the Experimental Analysis of Behavior,* 1965, **8,** 357–83. Copyright 1965 by the Society for the Experimental Analysis of Behavior, Inc. Additional information and related research can be found in *The token economy: A motivational system for therapy and rehabilitation* by T. Ayllon & N. H. Azrin, published by Appleton-Century-Crofts, 1968.)

haviors which earned tokens included watching the news, reading newspapers, keeping oneself neat and clean, performing chores around the house, receiving good grades at school, among others. However, points could be lost for poor grades, aggressive talk, disobeying rules, lying, stealing, being late, fighting, and other disruptive behaviors. Points purchased privileges such as staying up late, going downtown, watching TV, using tools, riding one's bicycle, and receiving an allowance. The token system was effective in controlling the use of aggressive statements, punctuality, room cleaning, completion of homework, academic achievement at school, poor grammar, saving money, and comprehension of daily news. The boys participated actively in running the program by supervising each other's work (Phillips, 1968), recording their own behavior and those of others (Fixsen, Phillips, & Wolf, 1972), serving as therapists to train peers to overcome specific problems (Bailey et al., 1971), developing rules of the program, and enforcing rule violations of peers (Fixsen, Phillips, & Wolf, 1973).

Token economies have been used extensively in special education, remedial, and "normal" classroom settings (Kazdin & Bootzin, 1972; O'Leary & Drabman, 1971). O'Leary et al. (1969) evaluated various procedures on the disruptive behavior of seven students in a second-grade classroom. After baseline observations, different phases were implemented such as providing rules to the class on how to behave, providing well structured lessons throughout the school day, and systematically praising appropriate behavior, and ignoring disruptive behavior. Finally, a token economy was introduced where all children in the class earned points placed in booklets on each child's desk. Points were given at various periods throughout the day for following classroom rules such as sitting in one's seat, working on assignments, and not talking or disrupting others. Tokens were exchangeable for a variety of reinforcers including candy, pennants, dolls, comics, and toys ranging in value. Disruptive student behavior was not altered by providing the class with rules or structure, or even by praising appropriate behavior and ignoring inappropriate behavior. However, when tokens were introduced, disruptive behavior decreased. Withdrawal and reintroduction of the token phase showed the strong influence of token reinforcement on behavior. Studies of classroom behavior have shown that academic performance (e.g., Brigham, Graubard, & Stans, 1972) and standardized achievement test scores (Chadwick & Day, 1971; Wolf et al., 1968) are accelerated with token reinforcement.

Token economies have been used extensively in a variety of settings (Kazdin, 1975; Kazdin & Bootzin, 1972). In psychiatric hospitals token programs have increased patient self-care behaviors such as grooming, eating, maintaining desirable personal habits, and participating in activities. In addition, patients have been trained to interact verbally with others and to decrease behaviors such as excessive crying, screaming, and delusional talking. Token programs in hospital settings have led to greater discharge rates of patients who have been hospitalized for long periods of time than have traditional treatment programs (Kazdin, 1975).

With the mentally retarded, token economies have been employed to alter academic skills, classroom deportment, self-care, social interaction, and work productivity. Token economies have been used effectively in other settings. For example, token economies have been implemented by parents in the home to alter child behavior (Christopherson et al., 1972). Similarly, spouses have used token reinforcement to alleviate marital discord (Stuart, 1969). Recently, the army has devised a token system to provide incentives for recruits going through basic training (Datel & Legters, 1970). (Chapter 10 presents additional programs.)

Important Considerations in Using Tokens. Tokens offer advantages over other reinforcers. First, tokens are potent reinforcers and can often maintain behavior at a higher level than other conditioned reinforcers such as praise, approval, and feedback (Kazdin & Bootzin, 1972). For example, in training reading skills, Staats, Staats, Schultz, and Wolf (1962) found that preschool children would work for only 15 or 20 minutes when they were praised for correct responses. The children became bored and restless. However, when additional reinforcers were introduced for reading, including tokens (exchangeable for toys), candy, and trinkets, they worked over twice as long without distraction.

A second advantage of tokens is that they bridge the delay between the target response and back-up reinforcement. If a reinforcer (e.g., an activity) cannot be delivered immediately after desirable behavior, tokens can be delivered immediately and used to purchase a back-up reinforcer later. Third, since tokens are backed up by a variety of reinforcers, they are less subject to satiation than are other reinforcers. If a client is no longer interested in one or two back-up reinforcers, usually there are many other reinforcers which are of value. Similarly, if an individual is satiated from food, nonfood items can be purchased with tokens. Fourth, tokens can be easily administered without interrupting the target response. Since the reinforcer does not require consumption (e.g., food) or performance of behaviors which may be incompatible with the target response (e.g., participating in a special activity), the delivery of tokens does not usually disrupt behavior. Fifth, tokens permit administering a single reinforcer (tokens) to individuals who ordinarily have different reinforcer preferences. Individual preferences can be exercised in the exchange of back-up reinforcers. Hence, there is less concern with the reinforcers being of value to only a few individuals in the setting. Sixth, tokens permit parceling out other reinforcers (e.g., activities) which might have to be earned in an all-or-none fashion. The tokens can be earned toward the purchase of the back-up reinforcer. For example, in one report a psychiatric patient could earn discharge from the hospital for accumulating a large sum of tokens (Linscheid, Malosky, & Zimmerman, 1974).

There are potential disadvantages in employing tokens. In some programs, back-up reinforcers are introduced which are extraneous to the setting. For example, in a classroom program tokens may be backed up with food. A potential problem is removing the token system after behavior gains have been made and transferring control of behavior to naturally occurring events such as privileges and activities. Food is not normally presented in a class and needs to be eventually eliminated. Of course, in a token economy, back-up reinforcers not normally available in the setting need not be introduced. Tokens can be used to purchase access to ordinary privileges, activities, and other events. Yet, introducing the tokens themselves may be disadvantageous. Tokens constitute a reinforcing event not available in most settings (excluding tokens such as money and grades). Because the delivery of tokens is clearly associated with reinforcement of desirable behavior, they may exert stimulus control over that behavior. Clients learn that the presence of tokens signals that desirable behavior is reinforced and the absence of tokens signals that desirable behavior is not likely to be reinforced. Once tokens are withdrawn, desirable behavior may decline. Specific procedures need to be implemented to withdraw the token program without a loss of behavior gains. In some settings, conditioned reinforcers normally available such as grades, money, and praise can be substituted for tokens. (Chapter 9 discusses techniques to maintain changes after a behavior modification program is withdrawn.)

A second possible disadvantage of tokens is that individuals in token economies may obtain tokens in unauthorized ways. For example, clients may steal tokens from each other. If tokens can be obtained without performing the target responses, their effect on behavior will decrease. To combat stealing, tokens can be individually coded so that they differ for each individual (e.g., Gates, 1972).

Types of Reinforcers: Summary.   The variety of reinforcers reviewed above provides a great deal of flexibility in devising reinforcement programs. At the very minimum, praise, activities, and privileges can be used in virtually any setting. The use of consumables may be limited by restrictions of the setting. For example, food may be too difficult to administer in a large group. Although tokens usually are the most powerful positive reinforcer, they may not be required to change behavior in most settings. Praise, privileges, and feedback should be used prior to implementing a token economy. A token economy is somewhat more difficult to implement (e.g., delivering tokens plus back-up reinforcers, keeping track of token earnings) and introduces problems (e.g., stealing or hoarding tokens, and withdrawing tokens from the setting) that may not occur with other programs. Hence, tokens should be introduced only when more easily implemented programs have been ineffective.

The discussion of types of reinforcers should not imply that various reinforcers have to be used independently. If a program relies on a consumable item, that does not mean that other events such as praise or activities cannot be used as well. In fact, a program which incorporates a variety of reinforcers is likely to be more effective than one in which only a few reinforcers are used. Token programs are effective because a variety of reinforcers are available. More than one type of reinforcer should be used for an additional reason. Programs using activities, feedback, consumables, or tokens should pair these events with praise. One goal of any program is to increase a client's responsiveness to his or her social environment. Developing responsiveness to praise is an important step in this process. When the client functions in nonprogrammed settings, social reinforcers are likely to be a major source of positive consequences which control behavior.

Contingency Contracts

Often reinforcement contingencies are designed in the form of behavioral contracts between individuals who wish behavior to change (e.g., parents, teachers, attendants) and those whose behavior is to be changed (students, children, patients) (Homme et al., 1969; Tharp & Wetzel, 1969). An actual contract is signed by both parties indicating that they agree to the terms. *The contract specifies the relationship between behaviors and their consequences.* Specifically, the contract specifies the reinforcers desired by the client and the behavior desired by the individual who wishes behavior change. Any of the reinforcers discussed above as well as idiosyncratic rewards may be used in the contract. When each participant signs the contract, the program is underway.

Ideally, contingency contracts contain five elements (Stuart, 1971). First, contracts should detail the privileges each party expects to gain from the contract. For example, parents may want a child to complete his or her work, attend school regularly, and so on. On the other hand, the child wants free time with friends, extra allowance, and other reinforcers. Second, the behaviors of the client must be readily observable. If parents or teachers cannot determine whether a responsibility has been met, they cannot grant a privilege. Thus, some behaviors may not readily be incorporated into the contract system. For example, parents often cannot easily monitor whether an adolescent visits certain friends so this would not be advisable to include in a contract. Third, the contract provides sanctions for a failure to meet with the terms. The client is aware of the conditions for failing to meet the responsibility and what consequences will follow. The aversive consequences for not meeting the contract terms are systematic and planned in advance (i.e., agreed to by all parties) rather than arbitrary and after the fact. Fourth, a contract can provide a bonus clause which reinforces consistent compliance with the contract. Bonuses (extra privileges, activity, or extension of curfew limit) can be used to reinforce desirable performance over a prolonged period. Consistent performance often goes unrewarded in everyday life. Since individuals expect such performance, it often is neglected. For a client whose behavior is recently developed, it is crucial to provide reinforcement for consistent performance. Bonuses written into the contract serve this purpose. Fifth, a contract should provide a means of monitoring the rate of positive reinforcement given and received. The records kept inform each party when reinforcement is to occur and provide constant feedback. Moreover, the records may cue individuals to make favorable comments about desirable behavior as earning of the back-up reinforcer is about to occur (Stuart, 1971).

Contracts need not be elaborate. A simple contract is presented in Figure 5–4. This contract was used for a 12-year-old boy who had "motivational" difficulties at home (Dinoff & Rickard, 1969). The boy's parents were concerned about his ability to accept responsibility. Hence, a contract was developed between the boy and his father. Some of the ideal features of contracts discussed above are included. For example, the behaviors desired by the agent (father) and reinforcers desired by the client (boy) are detailed, the target behaviors appear to be readily observable, and consequences are specified for failure to meet the terms.

MacDonald et al. (1970) used contingency contracting to decrease truancy of high school students. Absenteeism was 70% for students participating in one of the projects. The high rate of absenteeism was altered by having individuals important in the life of the students (e.g.,

CONTRACT

Between (Son's Name), and (Father's Name).

Son agrees to:
1. Carry out garbage pail each day.
2. Work six hours on Saturday every week. Work will consist of anything that he is capable of doing, such as hoeing, weeding, washing the car, or helping father, and so forth.

Father agrees to:
1. Pay $4 per week for above work each week (Saturday).

Both parties agree to the following conditions:
1. Penalty for failing to carry out garbage after being reminded will be reduction of 25¢ for each failure.
2. Penalty for not working on Saturday when work is available will be 40¢ per hour unless condition is covered by another condition.
3. When no work is available due to bad weather or father unable to supervise, $1 per Saturday will be paid.
4. Re-evaluation after a trial period of three weeks.
5. If son is sick there will be no penalty reduction on garbage detail, and $1 will be paid for Saturday. A total of $2 will be paid under this condition.

Signed:_____
                                          Father

Signed:_____
                                          Son

FIGURE 5–4 (Source: From Dinoff, M. & Rickard, H. C. Learning that privileges entail responsibility. In J. D. Krumboltz & C. E. Thoresen [Eds.], *Behavioral counseling: Cases and techniques.* New York: Holt, Rinehart and Winston, 1969.)

relatives, mother of a girl friend, pool hall proprietor) make deals with the students by contingently administering individualized reinforcers (e.g., access to family car, weekend privileges, time with a girl friend, and access to "fancy" clothing) for attending school. Attendance improved in a seven-week period. When the deals were discontinued and later reinstated, attendance decreased and improved respectively, indicating that the contracts controlled absenteeism.

Miller (1972) used a contract for an adult male alcoholic and his wife. Excessive drinking was a major source of marital conflict that had developed. For two weeks, baseline data were gathered on the daily number of alcoholic beverages consumed by the husband. A contract was devised which specified that the husband could have only one to three drinks a day (instead of average of seven to eight during baseline), and these could be consumed only before dinner. Any other drinking resulted in the husband paying $20 to the wife which she would spend as frivolously as possible. The wife agreed to refrain from negative verbal responses for her husband's drinking. She paid a $20 fine to the husband, if she failed to carry this out. Other conditions were included in the contract such as the increase of conversation between the mates. Drinking decreased abruptly and stabilized at a rate within the contract agreement. The effects were maintained after a six-month follow-up.

Contracts have been used to alter the weight of obese individuals (Mann, 1972), to control problem behaviors of delinquents and others on probation Liberman, 1971; Stuart & Lott, 1972), "emotionally disturbed" (Dinoff & Rickard, 1969), and public school children (Keirsey, 1969), to control drug abuse (Boudin, 1972), and to improve studying in college students (Bristol & Sloane, 1974). Various authors describe procedures for developing contracts for behavior disorders (Dinoff & Rickard, 1969; Tharp & Wetzel, 1969) and classroom management (Homme et al., 1969).

There are distinct advantages in using contingency contracts. First, when clients are allowed to have some input into designing or implementing the program, their performance may be better than if the program is imposed upon them (cf. Lovitt & Curtiss, 1969). Hence, programs may generally be more effective, if a contract arrangement is made rather than if a program is imposed upon the client. Second, the contingencies specified in a contract are not likely to be aversive to the client. The client can negotiate the consequences and the requirements for reinforcement. If the system is minimally aversive, the client is less likely to attempt to escape from the contingencies or from those who administer them. Third, contingency contracts are usually flexible in that participants can renegotiate the terms to make revisions (Stuart & Lott, 1972). Reinforcers delivered for particular responses can be adjusted, response requirements can be increased, and so on. Thus, signing a contract does not necessarily fix the program. Indeed, as soon as there is dissatisfaction of one signee, the negotiations can begin. Fourth, the contract makes the contingencies explicit. The specification of the contingencies serves as rules or instructions for the client on how to behave and what consequences will follow behavior. Research suggests that instructions alone are usually insufficient to effect long-term behavior change (e.g., Kazdin, 1973h; O'Leary et al., 1969; Phillips, 1968). However, instructions may increase the effect of reinforcement (Ayllon & Azrin, 1964). Fifth, the contract system is particularly useful in structuring the relationship between individuals who normally interact. For example, families of delinquents engage in a lower rate of positive exchanges than do nondelinquent families. Delinquent families may inadequately reinforce prosocial or nondelinquent behavior. The contract can ensure positive interaction (Stuart, 1971). A recent investigation suggested that the content of the contract (e.g., number of reinforcers, target responses, bonuses, and sanctions) is not related to success in changing behaviors of delinquents (Stuart & Lott, 1972). Rather, the contract per se may structure the family relationships toward successful resolution of problems.

Contingency contracting has not been widely studied. Thus, the limitations for effective application are not clear. Although different populations have been successfully trained with contracts, whether the contracts would be successful for a wide variety of client groups remains to be determined. Contract systems might not be feasible with groups such as severely and profoundly retarded whose understanding of the agreement may be impaired. Nevertheless, it is desirable to structure the reinforcement program in terms of a contract whenever possible so that the client plays a major role in planning the program.

Enhancing Client Performance in a Reinforcement Program

Although reinforcement programs have been very effective in altering behavior, on occasion a few individuals do not respond to the contingencies or respond only minimally (Kazdin, 1972b, 1973e). There are several procedures which can be incorporated into a reinforcement program to enhance performance. Specifically, procedures will be discussed which help clients initiate responses so that reinforcement can be delivered and increase the client's utilization of potential reinforcers in the setting. Additionally, procedures involving a client's peers can be used to enhance performance.

Response Priming.   In some programs the client does not perform the target behavior so reinforcement cannot be delivered. In the case of behavior deficits where new skills are required, shaping procedures can be employed. The terminal behavior is approached by reinforcing successive approximations, as discussed earlier. In many instances, the client can perform the response but simply does not. In these cases, the response can be primed.

Response priming refers to any procedure which initiates early steps in a sequence of responses. Prompts, such as instructions, serve a response-priming function because they initiate performance. However, response priming encompasses more than the use of prompts. As mentioned earlier, any act can be broken down into a sequence or chain of responses. The chain of responses is maintained by reinforcement which results from completing the sequence. The influence of the terminal reinforcer on earlier responses in the chain is much weaker than is its influence on responses later in the chain (Reynolds, 1968). For responses early in the sequence of behaviors, the final reinforcer is delayed, whereas for responses late in the sequence the reinforcer is immediate. For example, assume a person wishes his or her date would go to a distant restaurant to eat. The chain of responses includes all those behaviors leading up to and including eating in the restaurant. Food reinforcement along with any other reinforcing events in the restaurant may be too weak to provide an incentive for the responses early in the response chain. However, the likelihood of completing the chain is increased, if behaviors in close proximity of the final reinforcer are performed. If the individual would drive near the distant restaurant or walk inside, this would increase the likelihood of performing the final response (eating). The probability of eating at the restaurant would be increased because the strength of a response increases the closer one is to the reinforcer.

The notion of response priming suggests that performance of a given behavioral sequence can be facilitated by requiring the client to engage in the initial components of the sequence. By engaging in responses which are early in the sequence, the probability of performing the final behaviors in the sequence is increased.

Response priming has been used to initiate responses that otherwise have an exceedingly low frequency. For example, O'Brien, Azrin, and Henson (1969) used response priming to increase the frequency that chronic psychiatric patients made suggestions for managing the ward. The goal of the program was to involve patients more directly in their treatment by having them make specific suggestions regarding treatment procedures. Meetings were held in which patients were told to suggest anything they wished to have changed or improved on the ward. During baseline, staff sounded chimes on the ward and announced that patients could come to the meeting and make suggestions. After baseline rates of suggestions were gathered, the priming procedure was implemented. Patients were *required* to attend the meetings. If patients attended the meeting (an initial response in the chain of behaviors leading to a suggestion), suggestions should increase. Indeed, suggestions made by patients increased significantly when attendance was required. When priming was withdrawn and attendance was not required, the number of suggestions decreased. Later in the study, one group leader was told to follow the suggestions whenever patients made them at the meeting, whereas another group leader was told not to follow suggestions. When suggestions were followed (reinforced) they increased, whereas when they were ignored they decreased.

Response priming was used to increase the duration and frequency that three hospitalized patients visited with their relatives (O'Brien & Azrin, 1973). Normally, relatives of the patients could visit the psychiatric ward or request that the patients visit them at home for any length of time. This procedure resulted in virtually no visiting by the relatives. A written prompt was used to increase visits. Relatives received a letter each week inviting them to visit the hospital. However, the prompt did not increase visits over the normal procedure so an additional priming technique was used. Relatives were invited for a visit and were told that if a visit was inconvenient, the hospital would bring the patient to them for a short time. Patients were driven to their relatives weekly and stayed for a very short time. In fact, every 15 minutes during a visit a staff member who accompanied the patient said, "We should return to the hospital, now." The staff member and patient left unless the family objected to this statement. The priming procedure (transporting patients to their relatives) dramatically increased visits. During this phase, visits averaged over two hours per week for the three patients compared with less than an average of one minute per week during the normal visiting procedure. The relatives did not simply maintain the visit for the minimum 15-minute period. Even though the patients could have left at this time, the visits continued. Once visiting was primed, it continued for longer periods. A reversal of conditions demonstrated that without the priming procedure the visits decreased. After the priming procedure was reinstated, relatives for all three patients expressed a desire for the patients to be discharged and to live with them. In two of the three cases this was successfully accomplished.

Response priming has been used to improve self-medication. Individuals frequently forget to take medication at prescribed times. Azrin and Powell (1969) devised a pill box which signaled (with noise) when the pill should be taken. The noise, which sounded at the appropriate time, was terminated by turning a knob. When the knob was turned, the pill was automatically ejected. Use of a priming device improved self-medication above that achieved with a simple pill box and the use of a wristwatch.

In programs where the target responses are performed infrequently even though they are in the repertoire of the clients, a priming procedure can be used. Even where the responses are not in the clients' repertoire of responses, the priming procedure can initiate early response components and facilitate shaping.

Reinforcer Sampling.   Reinforcer sampling is a special case of response priming but warrants discussion in its own right. The responses primed are those involving utilization of a potentially reinforcing event. Utilization of a reinforcer can be viewed as a sequence of responses. If the initial responses in the sequence can be primed, the likelihood of completing the sequence is increased. To initiate the sequence, a client can engage in the initial part of or briefly *sample* the reinforcing event.

In reinforcement programs, it is very important that the clients utilize the available reinforcers when they are made available. The more frequently the reinforcers are used, the more the clients will engage in the appropriate target behavior required to obtain them. Yet, for many individuals, there may be few events which serve as reinforcers. There may be several potentially reinforcing events in the setting, but the clients may not engage in them. An event might be reinforcing, if the clients were familiar with it. Of course, even after familiarity with the event, it still may not serve as a reinforcer. However, the probability is increased that the event will be reinforcing after familiarity has been established. For other individuals, a given event may be reinforcing although it is not utilized frequently. The reason the event is not utilized frequently is unclear. It is not a matter of unfamiliarity because the event may be engaged in sporadically. Moreover, the event may appear to be enjoyable to the clients. The reinforcer may not be as potent as other reinforcers which are engaged in more frequently.

To develop or enhance use of a potential reinforcer, the individual can be provided with a sample or portion of that event. For example, Ayllon and Azrin (1968a) used reinforcer sampling to increase the frequency that psychiatric patients engaged in various activities on the ward. The activities were included in a large list of back-up reinforcers which could be purchased with tokens. In one project, patients were told twice daily that they could go for a walk on the hospital grounds. Payment of tokens was required to engage in the walk. After a few days of baseline, the reinforcer sampling procedure was implemented. Not only were walks announced, but all patients were required to assemble outside of the ward for a few minutes before deciding whether they would purchase the walk. Many cues associated with walking such as outdoor sights, sounds, and fresh air would be present before the patient decided to go back in the ward or go for a walk. While outside, patients were asked whether they wished to go for a walk. Those who decided not to go for a walk returned to the ward. The reinforcer sampling procedure increased the utilization of walks. For individuals who had or had not engaged in walks during baseline, the number of times walks were purchased increased. During a reversal phase, when the sampling procedure was discontinued, the frequency of walks decreased. However, some patients still continued to engage in a higher rate of walks than during baseline.

Reinforcer sampling was also used to increase attendance of patients to religious services in the hospital (Ayllon & Azrin, 1968b). Although many patients paid tokens to attend services without a sampling procedure, attendance increased markedly when all the patients were required to see five minutes of the service. Those who never attended the services before the sampling procedure, as well as those who were familiar with the services, increased in attendance. Similar results were found by using reinforcer sampling to augment the utilization of recreational and social events.

Sobell, Schaefer, Sobell, and Kremer (1970) used reinforcer sampling to increase eating of meals by psychiatric patients. Three sampling procedures were used. Patients either watched others eat, sampled one teaspoon of each type of food, or were given a free meal. All three procedures increased attendance at meals. Thus, even if an individual is given more than a small sample of the reinforcer, utilization of the reinforcer may be increased.

Importantly, the sampling procedure appears to initiate performance for those individuals who previously did not engage in the event. For these individuals, reinforcer sampling provides familiarity of the reinforcer which subsequently augments its use. However, reinforcer sampling provides more than familiarity. Individuals who are already quite familiar with the reinforcer and have utilized it on previous occasions are also affected by reinforcer sampling. After reinforcer sampling is terminated, participation in the event does not necessarily return to baseline levels. Clients may continue to utilize the reinforcer to a greater extent than they did during the baseline period. Thus, the effects of the sampling procedure are maintained (Ayllon & Azrin, 1968a, b).

In any situation in which it is possible to provide a small sample of the reinforcer, the sampling procedure should enhance performance. In utilizing reinforcer sampling, it usually is important to provide only a small sample of the event to avoid satiation. If an individual samples a large portion of the event such as food or an activity, there may be little incentive to earn and utilize the entire event. In fact, Sobell et al. (1970) found that giving an entire free meal instead of a sample of a meal temporarily *decreased* purchasing meals with tokens.

In applied settings, the effect of a reinforcement program may be relatively weak, in part, because the events selected by the staff as reinforcers are not utilized by the clients. Hence, the "reinforcers" provide little incentive to engage in the target behaviors. If the activity which is designed to serve as a reinforcer can be made more "valuable" to the client, the likelihood of engaging in the target behaviors to earn that activity is increased.

Vicarious Processes. Performance of a client can be altered by observing the consequences which follow the behavior of other individuals. Laboratory evidence has shown that individuals who observe others (models) receive reinforcing consequences for engaging in certain behaviors are more likely to engage in those behaviors. In contrast, individuals who observe models receive punishing consequences for engaging in certain behaviors are less likely to engage in those behaviors (Bandura, 1971; Rachman, 1972). These two processes are referred to as vicarious reinforcement and vicarious punishment, respectively.

Vicarious reinforcement has received the greater attention of the two processes in educational (Bolstad & Johnson, 1972; Broden et al., 1970; Kazdin, 1973c) and rehabilitation settings (Kazdin, 1973d). Investigations show that the behavior of one individual can be altered by reinforcing other individuals. For example, Broden et al. (1970) instructed an elementary school teacher to praise one of two boys for paying attention to the lesson. When one boy was praised for attending to the lesson, his behavior improved. However, an adjacent boy also increased in attentiveness. These results suggested that an adjacent peer imitated the behavior of the individual who received reinforcement. When he saw his peer receive praise for paying attention, he also increased in attention.

A recent investigation suggested that observing a model may not always be responsible for vicarious reinforcement effects. In a class of retarded children, praise was delivered to one child for paying attention. An adjacent individual who was not directly praised also increased in attentiveness. However, when the reinforced student was praised for *not* paying attention, the adjacent individual *increased* in attentiveness to the lesson (Kazdin, 1973c). Thus, whether one student was reinforced for attentive or inattentive behavior, the adjacent individual improved in attentiveness. A possible explanation is that whenever praise is delivered in a classroom, it is a cue to perform appropriate behaviors. Praise to one child is often a signal (S^D) that other children will be praised if they are behaving appropriately. Hence, children hearing praise may improve their behavior to increase the likelihood that they, too, will be reinforced.

One procedure to improve the behavior of a given individual is to provide reinforcement to others who are engaging in the target behavior. Of course, this is no substitute for providing direct reinforcement to the client himself. However, vicarious reinforcement can prompt behavior of one person because a model is reinforced for that behavior. Reinforcement of one individual signals others that certain behaviors are desired and will be reinforced. Investigators have shown vicarious punishment to occur in the classroom (cf., Kounin, 1970). When a teacher punishes one student, other students may behave more appropriately as well. Vicarious punishment has not been evaluated extensively in applied settings.

Group Contingencies. In group situations such as a classroom or institution each individual may be reinforced for routine behaviors. Sometimes the same performance criterion is applied to all individuals. Typically, the criteria for reinforcement are individualized. Obviously, it would be unfair to establish rigid criteria for all individuals given that initial performance levels differ. In any case, clients typically are reinforced on the basis of their own performance independently of how well others perform.

Although most programs are individualized, it is possible to employ peer group contingencies. Utilizing peers can enhance the effect of individualized contingencies and often is more potent in changing behavior. Peers can be used to enhance performance of individual clients in different ways. First, an individual may earn reinforcers for the entire group based on his performance alone. For example, in a classroom program (Patterson, 1965b), peers were enlisted to change the behavior of a nine-year-old "hyperactive" boy named Earl. The boy had been diagnosed as having minimal brain damage and had a history of skull injury, recurring convulsions, minor incoordination, and abnormal neurological signs such as electroencephalographic records. Earl was highly distractable, rarely worked on his lessons, and frequently talked and behaved aggressively. To decrease undesirable behavior, Earl received candy or pennies whenever he attended to his lesson. Earl's classmates were told to ignore him so that he could work, thus eliminating any distraction. To ensure that the class would support appropriate behavior, peers shared rewards that Earl earned. The group profited from Earl's appropriate behavior. This led to a great deal of peer encouragement from the class. In fact, at the end of each day, the results of Earl's behavior were announced to his classmates. Typically, they applauded his performance. Earl's behavior changed dramatically under this program. Unfortunately, the precise contribution of peer praise and encouragement to the program's effect was unclear.

In a classroom for low-achieving elementary school students, one particular child was frequently out of her seat (Wolf et al., 1970). To control this behavior, a program was devised where the student was given several points at the beginning of class. When a timer sounded (VI:10), she would lose some points, if she was out of her seat. Any points remaining at the end of the day could be exchanged for candy, snacks, clothes, and other back-up reinforcers. Although this procedure reduced out-of-seat behavior relative to baseline, she was still out of her seat a great deal. In the next experimental phase, the girl was told that any points she had left at the end of the day would be divided among herself and four peers. When the child earned points for her peers, her behavior improved drastically. A reversal phase showed that sharing points with peers was responsible for behavior change. Sharing of reinforcing consequences with peers has been used effectively in other programs when clients do not respond well to the initial program.

A second procedure in which peers are involved to help performance is conducted somewhat differently. In this procedure the performance of an individual determines what happens to the group and performance of the group determines what happens to a given individual. For example, in a psychiatric hospital (Olson & Greenberg, 1972), patients participated in group meetings to plan and administer their own treatment, to provide individual progress reports for patients, and to make decisions about the future treatment of individual patients (e.g., change in work assignment, discharge, or place in foster home). Patients on the ward received weekly sums of money in cash or ticket books which could purchase a variety of goods at a hospital canteen. Whether individual patients would have access to their funds or ticket books was determined by the performance of the group to which the individual belonged. The group's attendance at scheduled activities and the recommendations resulting from group meetings determined whether individuals could receive their reinforcers. The purpose of the group procedure was to increase peer pressure for individual participation in the groups.

An interesting program conducted in a fourth-grade classroom of 29 students used a group contingency to control excessive noise during a free-study period (Schmidt & Ulrich, 1969). A sound level meter was placed in the back of the room to monitor the noise level. An observer simply recorded the sound level from the apparatus. After several days of baseline recordings of the noise level, students were told that a timer would be set in the classroom for a 10-minute period. When the timer sounded, the class received two extra minutes added to their gym period plus a two-minute break to talk. If anyone became noisy during a 10-minute interval, a whistle sounded and the timer was reset. The program resulted in a decrease in noise level for the group as a whole.

A third procedure has been used to incorporate peers into the program. Specifically, peers can *implement* the contingencies. In a home-style setting for predelinquents, boys received points for keeping the bathrooms clean, among other behaviors (Phillips, 1968). During baseline, the boys were instructed to clean the bathrooms. In the next phase one boy was given managerial responsibility for cleaning the bathroom. He chose one or a few persons to do the cleaning and then paid or fined them points according to the quality of the work, as he judged it. When the bathroom was checked by the houseparents, the manager earned or lost points on the basis of how well the bathrooms had been cleaned. In a later phase, all boys were responsible as a group for the clean bathroom and subject to the same earnings and fines. The managerial program was extremely effective in maintaining high performance. When one of the boys had responsibility for the task and selected peers to execute the behaviors, the cleaning job was consistently well performed. This program involving peers incorporated other group procedures discussed above. Not only did a peer administer the program, but group performance determined the consequences which were delivered to an individual (the manager).

At the same facility for predelinquents, boys served as speech therapists to alter articulation errors (Bailey et al., 1971). Two boys had pronunciation errors such as substitution of "o" for "er" and saying "motho" for "mother" or omission of "l" from words and saying "probem" instead of "problem." Peers conducted therapy in special sessions set aside for this purpose. In some phases, peers received points for identifying errors and correct speech. In another phase, peers received points for the number of correct pronunciations made by the boys with speech problems. One peer function was to judge whether a particular word was pronounced correctly. The subjects lost points for errors (and sometimes earned points for correct pronunciation) depending upon the judgment of the peers. Peers were very effective in changing speech. The improvements in articulation were maintained after the program ended and generalized to performance outside of the training sessions.

In a classroom situation, a fourth-grade boy had a history of disciplinary problems (Axelrod, Hall, & Maxwell, 1972). The teacher was asked to attend to the boy when he behaved appropriately but apparently was unable to do so. One day the boy completed an assignment and took it to the teacher for grading. When the teacher ignored the boy, he took it to the outstanding student in the class who graded the paper. After the paper was graded, the boy asked the outstanding classmate to write "very good" on the paper. The investigators decided that the classmate might be able to execute the program and provide reinforcement. The seating in the class was rearranged so that the outstanding student sat next to the boy. After baseline observations of study behavior, the classmate was instructed to praise the student whenever he was studying. For a few sessions the classmate was cued by the experimenter when to deliver praise. Cueing was discontinued and the classmate carried this out on his own. Peer praise drastically increased study behavior. However, when peer reinforcement was withdrawn, the boy's study behavior returned to baseline levels.

Group programs sometimes exert greater control over the behavior of individuals than do programs which directly focus on the individuals themselves. However, there have been exceptions where individual and group programs are equally effective (e.g., Axelrod, 1973). One consideration in using a group program is the possibility of undesirable forms of peer pressure which can be used to coerce members of a group. For example, Axelrod (1973) noted that students in two special education classrooms made verbal threats to peers to perform appropriately during a group contingency. The threats themselves were disruptive to the class and possibly had detrimental effects on the students' interpersonal relationships. Similarly, Schmidt and Ulrich (1969) noted that peer pressure in the form of threatening gestures, arm movements, and facial expressions were used to control classroom noise when the group contingency was implemented. The prevalence of undesirable features of group programs has not been widely documented. Nevertheless, such features must be viewed as a possible product of the group system.

One potential advantage to the group contingency is that it may train clients to respond to the group. Group standards are responsible for a variety of behaviors in everyday life. Individuals in behavior modification programs utilizing group contingencies may develop a responsiveness to others. An individual performs in response to demands of the group. Additionally, an individual learns to influence the group to ensure that desirable consequences follow his own behavior.

Reinforcing Behaviors Incompatible with an Undesirable Response

Reinforcement is used to increase behavior, as shown in numerous illustrations in previous programs. In many situations in which behavior modification programs are used, the apparent goal of the program is to decrease undesirable behavior. Since reinforcement is discussed as a technique to increase behavior, individuals often believe that it is inappropriate to employ this technique to decrease behavior. Hence, punishment and extinction (to be discussed in the following chapters) are employed because they decrease response frequency directly. However, an undesirable target response also can be eliminated or decreased by reinforcing a behavior incompatible with that response. An incompatible behavior is one which cannot occur at the same time as the undesirable response. By increasing the frequency of an incompatible behavior, the undesirable response is decreased. It is usually quite easy to select incompatible responses which can be reinforced. For example, if a child fights with siblings at home, reinforcement can be delivered for behaviors such as reading quietly, playing games cooperatively, and watching television without arguing. If an institutionalized patient has violent outbursts, reinforcement can be delivered for talking or sitting quietly and interacting with peers in a calm demeanor, which are incompatible with outbursts.

Reinforcement can reduce undesirable behavior even when it is not delivered for behaviors which are physically incompatible with the undesirable target response. The frequency of a behavior may be decreased, if another behavior is reinforced because the reinforced behavior *displaces* the undesirable behavior in the individual's repertoire of responses. O'Brien and Azrin (1972b) used reinforcement to decrease screaming in a schizophrenic patient. Tokens were delivered to the patient for housekeeping tasks, grooming, and engaging in social behavior. As desirable behaviors increased, screaming decreased. Similarly, Hersen, Eisler, Alford, and Agras (1973) altered the behavior of three depressed neurotic patients in a hospital ward. The patients received tokens for engaging in a variety of behaviors related to personal hygiene and work on the ward. In a reversal design, ratings of depression of the patients decreased markedly as token earnings increased. Even though the contingencies did not focus on the depression per se, an increase in activity on the ward decreased depression. In a classroom project (Ayllon & Roberts, 1974), reinforcement was used to decrease discipline problems in fifth-grade boys by reinforcing performance of academic skills (correct performance on written assignments). Increases in academic performance were associated with marked decreases in disruptive behavior. These examples attest to the efficacy of strengthening adaptive behavior to decrease undesirable behavior. The importance of using positive reinforcement in programs designed to eliminate an undesirable behavior will be clearer in the discussion of punishment and extinction.

Conclusion

The effectiveness of positive reinforcement in increasing behavior depends upon the delay of reinforcement, the magnitude or amount of reinforcement, the quality or type of reinforcer, and the schedule of reinforcement. To maximize performance, reinforcement should be delivered immediately after a response. Moreover, a highly preferred reinforcer should be used. During acquisition, continuous reinforcement should be used until the response is well established. Subsequently, intermittent reinforcement can be substituted to enhance resistance to extinction.

Different types of reinforcers have been used effectively in applied settings such as food and other consumables, praise and attention, high probability behaviors, feedback, and token reinforcement. Each reinforcer has its own advantages and limitations such as dependence upon deprivation and satiation states, ease of administration, and relative effectiveness. Token economies usually incorporate a variety of back-up reinforcers and overcome some of the limitations which accrue to the use of any single reinforcer.

Contingency contracting refers to a way of structuring a reinforcement program. Each participant in the program formally agrees to the terms of the contract. The reinforcers for performing the target behaviors and penalties for failing to perform the behaviors are made explicit and agreed upon in writing in advance of the program. The primary advantage of a contract arrangement is that the client has an opportunity to develop his or her own behavior change program and to ensure that the terms are not coercive.

The effect of reinforcement programs often can be enhanced by various techniques. One technique is response priming which initiates performance of a target response. A related technique is reinforcer sampling which increases the frequency with which individuals utilize available reinforcers in the setting. Vicarious effects of reinforcement can also enhance performance. By reinforcing one individual, the behavior of others may be altered. Finally, an individual's peer group can be incorporated into a reinforcement program. Peers can share reinforcers earned by a given individual, the behavior of the group as a whole can determine the consequences for individual clients, or peers can administer the contingencies.

Each of these techniques has been used effectively in applied settings. In some programs, the major goal is to decrease performance of an undesirable behavior. Positive reinforcement of behaviors incompatible with the undesirable behavior can be used to achieve this end. Increasing the strength of behavior appropriate in a given setting, decreases the strength of behavior inappropriate in the setting.

6

Punishment and Negative Reinforcement

Aversive events play a major role in everyday life. Indeed, aversive techniques are deeply enmeshed in many social institutions including government and law (e.g., fines and imprisonment), education (e.g., failing grades on exams, expulsion, and probation), religion (e.g., damnation), international relations (e.g., military coercion), and normal social intercourse (e.g., discrimination, disapproval, humiliation, and social stigma). Routine interactions of most individuals with both physical and social environments result in aversive events ranging from a burn on a hot stove to verbal abuse from an acquaintance.

In applied settings, aversive events are used in two ways, namely, punishment and negative reinforcement. As mentioned earlier, punishment refers to a decrease in response rate when the response is followed by an aversive consequence. Negative reinforcement refers to an increase in response rate when the response is contingently followed by termination of an aversive event. Aversive events require careful consideration for at least two reasons. First, to apply punishment effectively, many specific requirements must be met. The requirements are often difficult to meet in applied settings. Second, undesirable side effects sometimes result from using punishment. Although a punishment contingency may be effective, unintended side effects may create new problems. Nevertheless, punishment of an "undesirable" behavior can be used effectively, particularly if supplemented with positive reinforcement as part of the behavior change program.

PUNISHMENT

Types of Punishment

As discussed earlier, punishment in the technical sense refers solely to the empirical operation (presentation or removal of events) which reduces the frequency of a response. Punishment does not necessarily involve physical pain. Indeed, events which may be painful (e.g., a spanking) may not necessarily decrease the responses they are designed to punish and may not qualify as punishing events. Alternatively, a variety of procedures which serve as punishment do not entail physical discomfort and are not odious to the client. On rare occasions a punishing event which effectively suppresses behavior even may be evaluated favorably by the clients (Adams & Popelka, 1971). Punishment may take one of two forms, the presentation of aversive events or the removal of positive events after a response. Each of these types of punishment encompasses a variety of specific procedures.

Presentation of Aversive Events.   After a response is performed, an aversive event such as spanking or a reprimand may be applied. There are two types of aversive events, primary and secondary or conditioned aversive stimuli. Primary aversive stimuli refer to those events which are inherently aversive. Stimuli such as electric shock, intense physical assault, bright lights, and loud noises are primary aversive stimuli. Their aversive properties are unlearned and are universal. Secondary or conditioned aversive stimuli acquire their aversive properties by being paired with events which are already aversive. For example, the word "no" serves as a conditioned aversive stimulus for many individuals. The word acquires its aversive value by being paired with events such as physical pain, loss of privileges, and so on. Conditioned aversive stimuli which typically control behavior include gestures, nods, frowns, and traffic tickets.

Stimuli may become aversive even if they are not paired with other specific aversive stimuli. When a stimulus is consistently associated with the absence of reinforcement, it too may become aversive. An event which signals that reinforcement will *not* be forthcoming was referred to earlier as a S^Δ and may serve as an aversive event (Azrin & Holz, 1966). The S^Δ serves as a signal that a period of nonreinforcement is in effect. For example, when a child breaks a valuable object, a parent may make a particular facial expression, become silent, and not respond to the child for a while. Nonresponsiveness of the parent denotes that the child will not be reinforced. During parental silence, virtually no behavior receives approval. The signal or cue (e.g., a facial expression) associated with nonreinforcement (silence) on the part of the parent becomes aversive in its own right.

A variety of aversive events has been employed to decrease behavior in applied settings. Reprimands constitute one type of aversive event which has been evaluated. Of course, reprimands form a major aspect of social interaction between teacher and student, parent and child, siblings, spouses, friends, and enemies. The major research on reprimands has been conducted in classroom settings. Behaviors suppressed with teacher reprimands include playing during lessons, being out of one's seat, talking without permission, and other disruptive acts (e.g., O'Leary et al., 1970). Reprimands which are delivered quietly and privately to the student suppress disruptive behavior, whereas loud reprimands shouted across the room often do not. Loud reprimands and disapproval or "negative attention" appear to draw attention to and reinforce disruptive behavior.

In one classroom study, the investigators instructed the teacher to increase her use of loud reprimands to examine the effect of reprimands on student behavior (Madsen et al., 1970). The teacher was instructed to increase her use of the reprimand, "sit down" when children were standing. The increased use of "sit down" *increased* out-of-seat behavior. Thus, the reprimand served as a *positive reinforcer* for the behavior it was intended to suppress. Not all studies show that shouting out reprimands reinforces behavior. Sometimes a reprimand such as "no" can exert strong control over disruptive student behavior (Hall, Axelrod, Foundopoulos, Shellman, Campbell, & Cranston, 1971). However, the lack of consistent effects with reprimands demands caution in their use.

Threats are frequently used to suppress behavior. When threats signal that some aversive consequence will follow if a given behavior is or is not performed, they become conditioned aversive events. Yet most threats in everyday life are "idle," that is, are not backed by the threatened consequences. Thus, threats lose their aversive effects. It is no surprise that threats often are ineffective when evaluated in behavior modification programs. For example, Phillips (1968) suppressed aggressive statements (e.g., "If you don't shut up, I'll kill you.") of predelinquents participating in a token economy. During one phase, threats were given periodically by telling the boys that if they continued aggressive statements, they would lose points. The threats were not enforced. Although the first few threats appeared to reduce behavior, their effectiveness decreased over time. To eliminate aggressive statements, fines were levied so that each statement cost points. Point loss effectively eliminated the statements. Other reports have also shown that threats do not suppress behavior unless they are consistently followed by the threatened aversive consequences (Kazdin, 1971a; Phillips, Phillips, Fixsen, & Wolf, 1971).

Aversive events other than reprimands and threats have been evaluated in applied settings. Electric shock has received some attention although it is used infrequently in applied settings. Shock has been used in cases where individuals have not responded to less intense aversive events or to procedures based on positive reinforcement. Shock is a primary aversive event and usually is very effective.

Risley (1968) used electric shock to suppress dangerous climbing in a six-year-old girl who exhibited several "hyperactive" and bizarre behaviors. The climbing previously had led to severe physical injury. Isolation of the child in the home and extinction (ignoring the behavior) in a laboratory setting did not reduce climbing, so shock was employed as a last resort. Shock (to the leg) was paired with "no" whenever the girl began to climb furniture in the laboratory setting. Although climbing was eventually eliminated in the presence of the experimenter in the laboratory, no change in climbing occurred at home. Subsequently, shock was used at home and climbing was suppressed there. At the end of the project, the child could avoid receiving shock by sitting in a chair for 10 minutes as punishment for climbing. This maintained a low rate of climbing. Other behaviors (e.g., the child's aggressive hitting of a sibling) were also eliminated with contingent application of shock by the mother.

Bucher and Lovaas (1968) suppressed self-injurious behavior in a seven-year-old boy who constantly hit his head. The boy usually was in physical restraints to deter self-injury. When restraints were removed, the boy hit himself about 3,000 times in a 90-minute period. Shock, delivered whenever the boy hit himself, effectively eliminated the behavior. Only 12 shocks were required even though the self-injurious behavior had been a long-standing habit (five years).

Shock was used to suppress uncontrollable sneezing in a female high school student (Kushner, 1968). The girl began to sneeze uncontrollably while she was hospitalized for treatment of a kidney infection. Before her discharge, the hospital corridors outside of her room were freshly painted. The onset of sneezing occurred at this time. The sneezing was quite frequent but stopped when she slept. Despite a variety of treatments including psychotherapy, hypnosis, trips to parts of the country with cleaner air, hospitalization and medication, her sneezing continued. After six months of continual sneezing, shock was used. Baseline observations were made of the frequency of sneezes for one 30-minute period. As shown in Figure 6–1, sneezing was quite high and averaged about one sneeze every 40 seconds. In the remaining 30-minute periods shock was used. Whenever the patient sneezed, shock was delivered to her fingertips. Although sneezing declined, shock was not working very well in the first few sessions (blocks 2, 3 and 4). However, during the initial sessions the electrodes were constantly coming off her fingertips. Essentially, the shock was not being applied. After the fourth treatment period in Figure 6–1, the electrodes were taped to the girl's fingertips so they would not come off. With the change in the procedure, sneezing decreased rapidly and was eliminated entirely. Since response suppression tends to be permanent with strong shock, withdrawal of the shock to show a reversal of behavior would probably not have increased sneezing. Indeed, 16 months following treatment, uncontrollable sneezing no longer occurred.

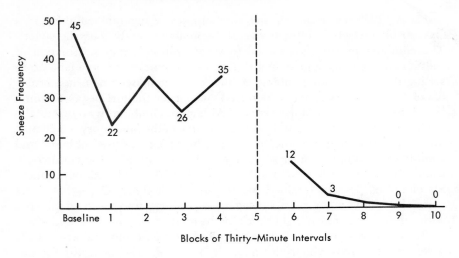

FIGURE 6–1 Decline in sneeze frequency when paired with contingent shock. (Source: Kushner, M. The operant control of intractable sneezing. In C. D. Spielberger, R. Fox, & B. Masterson [Eds.], *Contributions to general psychology: Selected readings for introductory psychology.* New York: Ronald Press, 1968.)

Other reports have confirmed the efficacy of shock in eliminating self-injurious behavior (Lovaas & Simmons, 1969), playing with dangerous equipment (Bucher & King, 1971), and persistent vomiting (Kohlenberg, 1970) in children. With adults, usually in outpatient settings, electric shock has been used to reduce or eliminate cigarette smoking, overeating, alcohol consumption, writer's cramp, stuttering, and various sexual responses such as homosexuality, transvestism, and fetishism (cf. Rachman & Teasdale, 1969).

Removal of Positive Events. Punishment often takes the form of removing a positive event after a response is performed. There are two forms of punishment by withdrawal of positive events, time-out from reinforcement and response cost. *Time-out from reinforcement* (or simply time-out) refers to the removal of all positive reinforcers for a *certain period of time.* During the time-out interval, the individual does not have access to positive reinforcers (Leitenberg, 1965). For example, an individual in an institution may be isolated for ten minutes. During the time period, the resident will not have access to staff or peer interaction, activities, privileges, and other reinforcers usually available. The removal of *all* reinforcement during a time-out interval is an ideal which is not always attained. In situations where time-out is used, reinforcement sometimes is uncontrolled during the time-out interval. For example, a child may be sent to his room for 20 minutes as punishment. Removal from the situation qualifies as time-out. However, all reinforcement has not been withdrawn since the child might engage in any number of reinforcing activities in his room (e.g., play, listen to music, or sleep).

Response cost refers to a loss of a positive reinforcer or to a penalty involving some work or effort. In response cost, there is no necessary time restriction for available reinforcement as there is with time-out (Kazdin, 1972a; Weiner, 1962). For example, a person may have to pay a fine for driving on the wrong side of the street. With the fine, there is no fixed period of time during which positive reinforcers are unavailable. Examples of response cost pervade everyday experience such as late fees for filing income tax beyond the due date and postage due for letters with too little postage. Both forms of positive reinforcer withdrawal, time-out and response cost, have been used in applied settings.

In one report, time-out was used to eliminate undesirable mealtime behaviors with severely and profoundly retarded adolescents (Barton et al., 1970). Undesirable behaviors included stealing food from others, spilling food, eating with fingers instead of utensils, and others. Two different time-out procedures were used. For some subjects, inappropriate mealtime behavior resulted in being removed from the dining area and isolated in a room for the remainder of the meal. For other subjects, time-out consisted of removing their food tray for 15 seconds. In the first time-out procedure, food was no longer available for the rest of the meal. In the second procedure, only a 15-second loss of the reinforcer occurred. Both procedures resulted in suppression of undesirable mealtime behaviors and an increase of appropriate eating behaviors (e.g., use of utensils).

An interesting application of time-out was used to reduce several tics (including spasmodic movement of neck, shoulder, chest, stomach, and facial muscles) in an adult male (Barrett, 1962). Music was selected as a positive reinforcer because the client was a part-time musician. During each session, the client sat in a chair listening to music. As soon as a tic occurred, the music was automatically interrupted for a short period of time (1.5 seconds). Tics decreased substantially with this time-out procedure although they were not completely eliminated.

Time-out has been effective in reducing stuttering. In one program, adult stutterers read out loud continuously until they stuttered (Adams & Popelka, 1971). As soon as they stuttered, a mild tone sounded for ten seconds. (The tone was considered "comfortably loud" and not sufficient to be punishing by itself.) During the tone, subjects were instructed to pause from reading. When the tone ended, subjects resumed reading. Subjects who received time-out showed a considerable reduction in stuttering compared to subjects who read without the interruption.

Time-out has been shown to be effective alone or in combination with other procedures in altering self-stimulation and self-destruction in retarded children and adults (Hamilton, Stephens, & Allen, 1967; Pendergrass, 1972), antisocial and disruptive behaviors of delinquent boys

(Burchard & Tyler, 1965), loud noise in a public school classroom (Schmidt & Ulrich, 1969), psychotic speech (Sanders, 1971), thumbsucking (Baer, 1962), toileting accidents (Azrin & Foxx, 1971), and aggressive behaviors (choking and grabbing others) (Vukelich & Hake, 1971).

Response cost has been used somewhat less extensively in applied settings than has time-out (Kazdin, 1972a). There are a variety of cost procedures. The most frequent use of response cost is in the form of a fine or token loss in a token economy program (Kazdin & Bootzin, 1972). Since tokens are delivered for desirable behavior, it is convenient (and usually effective) to subtract points or tokens when undesirable behavior is performed.

In one token program with psychotic patients, fines were levied whenever patients violated a rule of the ward (Upper, 1973). Infractions included getting up late in the morning, undressing or exposing oneself, shouting, sleeping in unauthorized areas, and several other behaviors As soon as a rule was broken, patients received a "ticket" which indicated that points were to be subtracted from their earnings. Violations dropped well below baseline rates. Similarly, in a token program with predelinquent boys (Phillips, 1968), loss of points reduced aggressive statements, tardiness, and use of poor grammar.

One especially interesting response-cost procedure was used to control classroom behavior of a child in a home for emotionally disturbed boys (Hall et al., 1971). At the beginning of class, the boy was given slips of paper each bearing his name. When the child cried, whined, or complained, a slip was taken away. Even though the slips of paper had no back-up value and could not be exchanged for rewards, their loss suppressed behavior.

Additional applications of response cost have included loss of privileges (e.g., television viewing) to alter disruptive behaviors in the home; loss of money or other personal possessions to reduce overeating or smoking; loss of tokens to reduce errors in speech, psychotic statements, teasing, whining, and bickering of children at home, and disruptive student behavior; and loss of minutes from recess for inappropriate classroom behavior (see Kazdin, 1972a for review).

Another form of response cost or penalty recently investigated is referred to as *overcorrection or restitution* (Foxx & Azrin, 1972, 1973). With overcorrection, the penalty for engaging in an undesirable behavior is performing some work in the situation. There are two components to overcorrection, namely, a correction of the environmental effects of the inappropriate behavior, and extensive rehearsal of the correct forms of appropriate behavior (Foxx & Azrin, 1972). For example, overcorrection was used with a 50-year-old profoundly retarded female adult who had been hospitalized for 46 years. For several years she had severe disruptive and aggressive behavior (especially throwing things). Overcorrection began after baseline observations were gathered on the number of objects thrown. When the client performed a disruptive behavior (e.g., overturning a bed), she was required to "correct" the physical effects of her behavior on the environment (e.g., turn the bed to its correct position and straighten the spread and pillows) and extensively rehearse the correct behavior (e.g., straighten *all* other beds on the ward). She had to correct the immediate consequence of whatever inappropriate behavior she performed and then practice doing the correct behavior throughout the ward. After 11 weeks of training, throwing objects no longer occurred. The behavior failed to return up to the fourteenth week after training began, at which time data were no longer gathered.

Overcorrection was also used with a brain-damaged female patient who screamed uncontrollably on the hospital ward (Foxx & Azrin, 1972). The consequences of a scream, of course, cannot be "corrected" in the same way as straightening beds in the above case. Although screams disturb other individuals, they do not result in a physical change in the environment. Overcorrection with this patient involved two procedures. When the patient screamed, she was taken to her bed where she had to stay and be very quiet for 15 minutes. Since screaming was the undesirable behavior, it could be corrected in part by becoming perfectly quiet. When the 15 minutes of quiet elapsed, the patient returned to the ward where she had to apologize to all staff and patients individually for having screamed. The authors reasoned that if screaming annoys and disrupts others, this can be "overcorrected" by having the patient reassure all individuals that she would behave appropriately. Overcorrection resulted in a reduction of screaming episodes from an average of ten per day during baseline to near zero after two weeks of training. In the last ten weeks of overcorrection, only four instances of screaming occurred.

In the above case, overcorrection included isolation for 15 minutes. Of course, isolation is a time-out procedure. Interestingly, the authors noted that isolating the patient for 15 minutes had been tried with no success. In fact, during "baseline" time-out had been used. The "overcorrection" contingency was added to a time-out procedure and appeared to change behavior.

Overcorrection has also been used to eliminate aggressive assaults by retarded adult patients on others (Foxx & Azrin, 1972) and ritualistic or self-stimulating behavior in retarded and autistic children (Foxx & Azrin, 1973). Relatively little is known about overcorrection and the components which contribute to its efficacy. Simply having an individual correct the effects of his misbehavior may not be sufficient to alter behavior (Foxx & Azrin, 1972). The client must extensively practice the correct behavior in several instances which "overcorrects" the environment. This is a desirable feature of overcorrection as a form of punishment. This procedure does not merely provide an aversive element to suppress behavior but provides the opportunity for practicing the correct response. Hence, when the individual is punished, he or she practices the response that can avoid punishment in the future. Also, when the correct response is performed, it can be positively reinforced. Practice of the correct response is an important ingredient which is omitted in other forms of punishment.

Important Considerations in Selecting Aversive Consequences. There are several considerations which need to be made in selecting aversive consequences. Each consequence has its own limitations and advantages. And, of course, the consequences are not equally effective.

Verbal statements such as threats, reprimands, warnings, disapproval and "no" are widely used. One limitation of these events is that they sometimes are ineffective. Indeed, as mentioned earlier, they may even function as positive reinforcers and increase the frequency of behaviors they are employed to suppress. On the other hand, verbal admonitions form a large part of naturally occurring events in everyday life. Hence, in treatment settings it is desirable to train clients to respond to disapproval, if they do not respond initially. By pairing verbal statements with aversive events such as shock (Birnbrauer, 1968), food removal, or physical restraint (Henriksen & Doughty, 1967), their efficacy as aversive events can be enhanced.

Electric shock has been shown to be effective as an aversive consequence. In fact, it is the most effective aversive event studied (Azrin & Holz, 1966). However, it has obvious limitations which militate against widespread use in applied settings. First, the administration of shock requires special equipment. Hence, shock has been generally restricted to laboratory or treatment settings where clients are seen individually. In an institution where individuals are treated in groups, it is not readily feasible to employ shock. Second, the person using shock must be particularly well skilled so that accidents due to misuse of equipment do not occur and so that shock intensity is not unnecessarily severe. Third, many people object to the use of shock and other forms of corporal punishment on ethical grounds. Certainly, less intense or painful forms of punishment are readily effective and should be tried before shock. Hence, as mentioned earlier, shock often has been restricted to those cases in which behaviors are not readily alterable with milder forms of treatment and the undesirable behaviors present some danger to the client (e.g., Lovaas & Simmons, 1969; Risley, 1968).

Time-out from reinforcement in the form of isolation or removal from the situation for a period of time has been effective in a number of studies. Usually short time-out durations such as a few minutes are effective in suppressing behavior (Bostow & Bailey, 1969). Longer time periods do not necessarily augment efficacy (White, Nielson, & Johnson, 1972).

Obviously advantages of time-out are that it can be relatively brief and that it does not involve pain. Long time periods could be highly disadvantageous. Removing individuals from the situation in which their performance is a problem reduces the opportunities for positive reinforcement in the situation. For example, in one program a child who constantly misbehaved in the classroom (talked, remained out of his seat, and threw objects) was immediately sent home (Shier, 1969). The child missed 26 of 83 days of school in about a five-month period. Although this treatment was partially effective in altering behavior, the time spent out of the classroom was lost for training other desirable behaviors. Thus, a potential disadvantage of time-out, particularly when long durations are used, is that time away from the training situation consumes time that might be used for reinforcing behaviors incompatible with the undesirable response. The above case is not a good example of time-out for another reason. Sending an individual home from school may not eliminate reinforcers but provide an opportunity for engaging in many reinforcing activities which are incompatible with study behavior, such as watching television or roaming around the community. The effective application of time-out depends upon removing the reinforcers available in the situation without introducing additional reinforcers to take their place during the time-out period.

An additional consideration in using time-out is that if the clients are "withdrawn" or do not interact socially, time-out may be undesirable. Removal from the social situation further isolates those individuals who have minimal social skills and are in need of behavior change in the social context. As a final consideration, time-out may not be effective in suppressing behavior for some individuals (Foxx & Azrin, 1972) and even serve as a positive reinforcer for others (Steeves, Martin, & Pear, 1970). In spite of the above, brief time-out is recommended in most applied settings because of the range of effectiveness across behavioral problems and the ease of implementation (Sherman & Baer, 1969).

Response-cost procedures, such as withdrawing privileges or tokens or requiring physical effort such as correcting the misbehavior, may be effectively used. Of the punishment procedures, these have been least well studied. Hence, problems associated with their use remain to be elaborated. Since the loss of points or tokens is the most common form of response cost, some problems have been discovered in this context.

One problem which may result from token loss is that individuals who lose points for misbehaving become deeply in debt so that no further points can be lost. If a client has no points because of previous fines, how can response cost be effectively employed? A requirement for response cost is that tokens are present so they can be withdrawn. Clients can be given tokens or points noncontingently (Hall et al., 1971) before losing them for inappropriate behavior. Even if the clients lose all of their points, additional ones can be given to them and then taken away (Kazdin, 1973b). However, this may be undesirable in the long run because tokens can exert greater control over behavior, if they are delivered contingently. Token loss and loss of privileges appear to be very effective in suppressing behavior. An advantage of using a fine (loss of tokens) is that it does not remove the client from the opportunity to receive positive reinforcement for desirable behaviors as is often the case with time-out.

Maximizing the Effectiveness of Punishment

As with reinforcement, the efficacy of punishment depends upon several conditions. However, the conditions which contribute to the efficacy of punishment have been somewhat less well investigated than have the conditions which contribute to reinforcement. Although punishment has been evaluated extensively in the laboratory (Azrin & Holz, 1966), most of the work has evaluated the presentation of aversive events, particularly electric shock. Removal of positive events has been less well studied (cf. Coughlin, 1972; Kazdin, 1972a; 1973i; Leitenberg, 1965). Nevertheless, general statements can be extrapolated from laboratory evidence regarding the conditions which should maximize the efficacy of punishment.

Intensity of Punishment. The greater the intensity of the aversive event, the greater the response suppression. Intense punishment with electric shock can result in complete and permanent suppression of a response (Azrin & Holz, 1966). Although this relationship has been established for electric shock, it may not apply to other aversive events in applied settings (e.g., reprimands).

The role of intensity of the aversive consequence is particularly unclear when the consequence is withdrawal of a positive reinforcer (Kazdin, 1973i). Even when a reinforcer is withdrawn for a short period of time (time-out), which does not seem to be an "intense" aversive event, response suppression may be dramatic. Yet, under certain circumstances the greater the duration of time-out (up to 15 or 30 minutes), the more effective the punishment tends to be (Burchard & Barrera, 1972; White et al., 1972). Similarly, for response cost (loss of tokens), larger costs tend to suppress behavior more than smaller ones do (Burchard & Barrera, 1972; Phillips, 1968).

Manner of Introducing the Aversive Consequence. Another feature regarding punishment intensity is important to note. Punishment is more effective when the aversive consequence is introduced at full strength or maximum intensity than when its intensity is increased gradually (Azrin & Holz, 1966). Punishment which is not very intense (e.g., a mild threat) may make a temporary reduction of behavior, but there is an adaptation to it so it quickly loses its punishing properties (Kazdin, 1971a; Phillips, 1968). Behavior recovers its prepunishment rate. More intense punishment will be required instead of the weak threat (e.g., a very firm threat). The individual will soon adapt to this latter event and it will lose its effectiveness. Eventually, a more severe form of punishment may be required (e.g., corporal punishment or isolation).

The effect of punishment can be enhanced by introducing the consequences at maximum intensity. Instead of beginning with a weak threat, and proceeding to a firm threat, corporal punishment, or isolation, it would be better if the final event were introduced initially rather than approached gradually. The notion of introducing aversive stimuli at maximum intensity for optimal effectiveness might justify severe punishment (e.g., imprisonment or torture) for minor offenses (e.g., traffic violations or being late for class or work). However, as discussed below, moderate or less intense forms of punishment can be very effective under certain circumstances.

Delay of Punishment.   Punishment, as positive reinforcement, is more effective when it is delivered immediately after the target response than when it is delayed (Azrin & Holz, 1966; Kimble, 1961). If punishment of the undesirable response is delayed, it immediately follows some other behavior. The other behavior may be desirable. For example, a child may receive punishment at the end of the day from a parent for some behavior performed earlier that day. However, prior to punishment the child may have done some particularly desirable behavior such as cleaning up his or her room. The punishment would be quite delayed and its effect on the undesirable behavior would be weak. However, the desirable behavior is performed in close contiguity with punishment and may be suppressed. Independently of the specific response that occurs during the delay period, punishment is not likely to be associated with the response which is to be suppressed, if there is a delay.

Schedule of Punishment.   Punishment is more effective when the punishing consequence occurs every time (continuous punishment) rather than once in a while (intermittent punishment). The greater the proportion of punished responses, the greater the response reduction. However, continuous punishment leads to greater recovery of the response when punishment is discontinued than does intermittent punishment (Azrin & Holz, 1966). For example, if time-out is to be used in the home, it should be delivered every time the behavior occurs. After the response has been suppressed, it can be delivered only intermittently to maintain control over behavior (cf. Clark, Rowbury, Baer, & Baer, 1973). At very high intensities of punishment (e.g., with electric shock), the relationship between punishment schedule and response suppression does *not* hold. There is no recovery even when punishment was previously delivered on a continuous schedule.

Source of Reinforcement.   If a punished response also is positively reinforced, punishment is less effective than if the response were not reinforced. That a punished behavior is performed at all suggests that some reinforcer is maintaining it, otherwise it would have extinguished. The effect of punishment can be enhanced by removing the source of reinforcement of the punished response (Azrin & Holz, 1966). For example, delinquents often provide peer social reinforcement to each other for committing deviant acts (Buehler, Patterson, & Furniss, 1966). Punishment of deviant acts is less effective when there is peer reinforcement of the acts than when there is no reinforcement. When using punishment, reinforcement for the punished response should be eliminated. In practice, it is sometimes difficult to identify the source of reinforcement maintaining a deviant behavior (Johnston, 1972). However, in many instances it is evident that teachers (Hall et al., 1968; Wahler, 1969) and parents (Wahler, Winkel, Peterson, & Morrison, 1965; Zeilberger et al., 1968) socially reinforce those behaviors they wish to suppress. When reinforcement of the deviant behavior is removed, positive reinforcement should be provided for desirable behavior. If peer attention and recognition are delivered for inappropriate behavior, the situation should be arranged so that peer attention is still available but for appropriate behavior. The reinforcer is not withdrawn. It is only shifted so that it follows desirable rather than undesirable behavior.

Timing of Punishment in the Response Sequence. Punishment tends to be more effective the earlier it is delivered in the response chain (e.g. Aronfreed & Reber, 1965). An undesirable response is not a single behavior but a chain or sequence of behaviors which culminates in an act considered undesirable. For example, a child's "theft" of a cookie prior to dinner may consist of a series of behaviors such as walking into the kitchen, climbing onto a chair, reaching for the cookie jar, opening the jar, taking a cookie, and eating it. Punishment for going into the kitchen or climbing onto a chair will reduce stealing cookies to a greater extent than punishment after the cookie is taken and eaten.

The importance of the timing of punishment can be readily explained. If the response chain is completed, the terminal behavior is positively reinforced (e.g., cookie consumption). Punishment is then used to suppress a reinforced response. Moreover, reinforcement of the undesirable response is more immediate than the punishment, if the chain is completed. As mentioned above, punishment is more effective when the response to be suppressed is not reinforced than when it is reinforced. Hence, if a response is punished before it is reinforced, punishment should be more effective. Responses early in the chain of behavior may still be reinforced since behaviors in a chain reinforce prior behaviors in the sequence. Yet, the further back a behavior is in the chain from the terminal reinforcer, the less potent the reinforcement. Behaviors early in the sequence are further removed from behaviors later in the sequence and the terminal reinforcer so their conditioned reinforcing properties are less, and they are more readily suppressed when punishment is applied.

A potential problem in applying punishment to initial behaviors in a response sequence is that the behaviors at this point in the chain are also part of other response chains which constitute appropriate behavior. To continue the above example, punishment of cookie theft might be very effective, if delivered when the child enters the kitchen. However, entering the kitchen may be a part of other chains which are appropriate such as washing dishes, feeding a pet, or washing one's hands.

Reinforcement of Alternate Responses. Punishment is most effective when the individual is reinforced for performing desirable or prosocial behaviors while being punished for an undesirable response (Azrin & Holz, 1966). When an alternate response is reinforced, the punished response is more likely to be suppressed (e.g., Kircher, Pear & Martin, 1971). Aversive events of relatively weak intensity can effectively suppress behavior, if reinforcement is provided for an alternate response. Thus, intense punishment is not always required or even necessarily desirable. Mildly aversive events (e.g., grimaces, statements of disapproval, or "no") may only temporarily suppress behavior. However, their suppressive effect will be enhanced by delivering reinforcement for another behavior.

Even aversive consequences which are not effective by themselves can be effective when combined with reinforcement for alternate forms of behavior (Azrin & Holz, 1966). As an example, in one program an attempt was made to train a profoundly retarded child to walk. Whenever the child crawled, he was restrained (held at the waist for five seconds) (O'Brien, Azrin, & Bugle, 1972). This procedure did not decrease crawling nor increase walking. The investigators added a positive aspect to the restraint procedure. Whenever the child crawled, he was restrained as before but then was aided in walking for a few seconds. By reinforcing an alternate response (continued movement in an upright position), crawling dramatically decreased and walking increased. Restraint alone subsequently was effective once walking had been established.

Most studies of punishment include reinforcement for desirable behaviors to augment behavior change. In the report of electric shock to suppress a child's climbing (Risley, 1968), food reinforcement was also used to increase sitting appropriately and making eye contact with the experimenter. Mild shock for incorrect responses has been combined with token reinforcement for correct responses in teaching language to retarded children (Kircher et al., 1971). O'Brien and Azrin (1972a) used verbal reprimands and time-out to maintain previously trained mealtime behaviors of institutionalized retardates. When residents failed to eat appropriately the trainer said, "No!" If the error occurred again, the trainer removed the food for 30 seconds (time-out). However, reinforcement was also used in the form of verbal praise for appropriate eating and, of course, food reinforcement.

Bostow and Bailey (1969) combined time-out and reinforcement to control the severely aggressive behavior of a retarded boy who had to be isolated from others. Aggressive behavior (e.g., hits, bites, kicks, and scratches) resulted in two minutes in an isolation booth. On the other hand, for every two minutes outside of time-out without an aggressive response, a small amount of either milk, soft drink, or cookies was delivered.

In some of the above studies, punishment alone might have been used to suppress the undesirable behavior. However, suppressing an undesirable behavior does not guarantee that a desirable behavior will take its place. *Punishment trains an individual in what not to do rather than in what to do* (Thorndike, 1932). For example, suppression of food spilling during a meal does not necessarily result in desirable mealtime behavior (e.g., eating with utensils). Similarly, suppression of fighting in a delinquent does not guarantee that desirable social behaviors will appear. It is advisable to use positive reinforcement whenever punishment is employed, for three reasons. First, reinforcement for alternative responses increases the efficacy of punishment (Azrin & Holz, 1966). Second, reinforcement can develop appropriate behaviors to displace those inappropriate behaviors which are to be eliminated. Third, positive reinforcement combined with punishment may eliminate any undesirable side effects which might result from the use of punishment alone (see below). Punishment in the form of withdrawal of a positive event (time-out or some forms of response cost) can be readily combined with reinforcement. If a positive event is to be withdrawn, it has to be given to the client in advance. The positive reinforcer can be contingent upon a desirable response and its loss can be contingent upon an undesirable response. For example, in token economies with a variety of populations tokens are usually delivered for desirable behaviors and withdrawn for undesirable behaviors (Kazdin, 1975).

Possible Side Effects of Punishment

An argument against the use of punishment is that there may be undesirable side effects. Even though the target behavior may be eliminated, other consequences resulting driectly from punishment may be worse than the original behavior or at least be problematic in their own right. Laboratory research, usually with infrahuman subjects, provides evidence for various undesirable side effects (Azrin & Holz, 1966). The side effects of punishment with humans in applied settings has received somewhat less attention (Bucher, 1969; Johnston, 1972; Kazdin, 1972a).

Emotional Reactions. Undesirable emotional reactions may result from punishment. The emotional states may be temporarily disruptive to the individual. For example, when a child receives a spanking, crying, anger, and other similar emotional states will probably occur. These states are not essential ingredients of punishment but undesirable concomitant effects. They are undesirable, in part, because they may interfere with new learning. The child may be temporarily unresponsive to his social environment until he is no longer upset. An additional consideration is that undesirable emotional states may be frequently paired with cues in the punishment situation. Eventually the cues themselves (e.g., a given individual such as a parent or teacher or a situation such as the home) may elicit similar emotional reactions in the absence of punishment.

Escape and Avoidance. One side effect of punishment is that it can lead to escape from or avoidance of the punishment situation. If a situation is aversive, an individual can terminate the aversive condition by escaping. Successful escape from a situation associated with punishment is negatively reinforced because it terminates an aversive condition. Even if the punishing event is only mildly aversive and too weak to be very effective in suppressing behavior, it may result in escape behavior (Azrin & Holz, 1966). Hence, the use of aversive stimuli fosters escape and reinforcement of escape behaviors. For example, reliance upon punishment in the home may result in attempts to avoid or escape from the home.

Stimuli associated with the aversive situation may also lead to escape. Recall that any event associated with an aversive event becomes aversive in its own right. If one person is constantly punishing someone else, the punishing agent will take on properties of a conditioned aversive stimulus. The individual who is punished will attempt to escape from or avoid the punishing agent because of these aversive stimulus properties. This side effect is undesirable because if individuals (e.g., children) escape or avoid punishing agents (e.g., parents and teachers), the agents will be unable to provide reinforcement to train desirable responses. Perhaps, the most pervasive example of escape and avoidance behavior is evident in the responses and attitudes that the police evoke from the public. For most people, the police are associated with punishment more than anything else. It is no surprise that for many individuals the police become a conditioned aversive stimulus to be avoided or escaped whenever possible.

Aggression. In laboratory work, punishment sometimes results in one organism attacking another or attacking the source of punishment (Azrin & Holz, 1966). These phenomena have not been demonstrated with the wide range of punishing events used in applied settings but only with painful stimuli. Yet in using punishment of any kind there is the possibility that the punished individual will aggress toward the punishing agent. By attacking the agent, the source of punishment may be temporarily removed. Hence, the individual's aggression toward the punishing agent is *negatively reinforced* by terminating an aversive state. For example, protesters may be reinforced for attacking police because attacking police may temporarily reduce aversive events (e.g., tear gas or physical assault). Of course, the same contingencies operate to control aggressive behavior of police.

Modeled Punishment. The punishing agent *models* or provides an example of certain behaviors, namely, the use of aversive behavior control techniques, which may be learned by the individual who is punished (Bandura, 1969). If a parent uses physical punishment with a child, the likelihood of the child engaging in physically aggressive behaviors is increased. Aggressive behavior patterns can be readily learned from adult models (Bandura, 1965). Moreover, children appear to use behavioral control techniques in interactions with their peers that are similar to those techniques used by their parents to control them (Hoffman, 1960). In addition, children respond to their own behavior on the basis of the consequences they see others provide themselves (Bandura, Grusec, & Menlove, 1967). Children of punitive parents may learn to criticize and punish themselves through modeling. Certainly, a degree of caution is required in using aversive techniques, particularly physical punishment, because of the modeling influences which may result.

Perpetuation of Punishment.   Another undesirable side effect of punishment is that agents who use punishment are reinforced for punishing. Punishment usually results in rapid reduction of the target response (Azrin & Holz, 1966). If a parent shouts at a child, the child's behavior usually is altered immediately. The parent's behavior (shout) is *negatively reinforced* (termination of some undesirable child behavior). Since reinforcement is a powerful technique, particularly if it is immediate, the parent is likely to increase in the frequency of delivering punishment. Even though the child's behavior may not be altered for very long, the obvious failure of punishment is delayed, whereas the short-term effect is immediate. Hence, the parent is likely to rely increasingly on punishment and runs the risk of encountering the side effects discussed above.

Evidence for Side Effects in Applied Settings

The evidence for side effects of punishment in humans is relatively sparse. Not all of the problems demonstrated in the laboratory have been found with punishment in applied settings (Bucher, 1969; Johnston, 1972; Kazdin, 1972a).

A few studies have reported results which may be analogous to the side effects demonstrated in the laboratory. For example, in one program hospitalized delinquent soldiers who lost tokens for not attending meetings on the ward *increased* in absenteeism (Boren & Colman, 1970). This suggests that the aversive contingency for nonattendance increased *escape* from the situation. In another project in which individuals were to shock themselves for cigarette smoking, 50% dropped out of the project (Powell & Azrin, 1968). Many subjects said they wanted to stop smoking but not at the expense of experiencing shock. Hence, they *avoided* participation. Tate and Baroff (1966) reported that shock suppressed self-injurious behaviors in a retarded boy. However, for several days the boy appeared upset and sometimes refused to eat. Similarly, Meichenbaum et al. (1968) noted negative reactions of delinquent girls when they lost money for inappropriate classroom behavior. These reports suggest *emotional side effects* may be associated with punishment.

Using overcorrection to suppress aggressive behavior in a retarded adult, Foxx and Azrin (1972) reported that for the first few days of punishment the client attacked the punishing agent. This provided an example of *aggression* toward the punishing agent, found in laboratory research. However, aggressiveness abated rapidly. Temporary aggression toward the experimenter has also been noted in the use of time-out from reinforcement with children (Pendergrass, 1972).

In spite of the above reports, many studies in applied settings have attempted to assess undesirable effects without finding them (Kaufman & O'Leary, 1972; Kazdin, 1972a). Indeed, *desirable* side effects are often associated with punishment. Using electric shock to suppress self-destructive behavior in retarded children sometimes increases social behaviors such as attentiveness to and physical contact with the experimenter and smiling and decreases inappropriate behavior such as whining and fussing (Bucher & Lovaas, 1968; Lovaas & Simmons, 1969; Tate & Baroff, 1966).

Risley (1968) noted that eye contact of a child increased when the child was shocked for dangerous climbing. Similarly, when the child's autistic rocking was punished (with reprimands and physical shaking), the child increased imitative behaviors which facilitated the acquisition of new desirable behaviors. Foxx and Azrin (1972) reported increased social interaction and participation in activities and increased interest in personal appearance after punishment suppressed aggressive behavior in one retarded adult.

It is clear that undesirable side effects are not necessary concomitants of the use of punishment procedures. Perhaps, a major reason that undesirable side effects have been less apparent in the research with humans in applied settings is that reinforcement for alternate responses is usually used in conjunction with punishment. If some behavior is reinforced, even though others are punished, it is less likely that the situation and punishing agent will be as aversive as would be the case if punishment were administered in the absence of reinforcement. Hence, less escape and avoidance on the part of the client would be evident. In addition, if a punishing agent also delivers reinforcement, the negative effects of modeling will be alleviated. Another reason that undesirable side effects have not been widely found is that mild forms of punishment are usually used in applied settings. Mild forms of punishment are effective in suppressing behavior when reinforcement is delivered for other behaviors. Of course, when mild intensities of punishment are used it is likely that fewer unde-

sirable side effects would result. Emotional disruption and aggressive behavior are less likely to result from mild forms of punishment than from
intense forms resulting from painful stimuli.

Characteristics of the Punishment Process

Immediacy of Effects. A reduction in response rate following punishment usually occurs immediately (Azrin & Holz, 1966; Kushner, 1970).
Using punishment for prolonged periods may result in further suppression.
However, if there is no immediate effect, it probably is not advantageous
to continue the aversive contingency. It is difficult to specify precisely
how immediate the effect of punishment should be to justify being continued. Laboratory work has shown that some response suppression occurs
as soon as the punishing stimulus is delivered a few times (Azrin & Holz,
1966). Yet, several factors determine the immediacy of punishment effects.
The most important factor is intensity of the aversive event, with greater
intensities associated with more immediate response suppression. Other
conditions for maximizing the efficacy of punishment described above, presumably also contribute to the immediacy of response suppression.

In applied settings, the rapidity of punishment effects has been especially evident with shock. In a matter of a few sessions and only a few
applications of shock, behaviors are reduced and sometimes eliminated
(Bucher & Lovaas, 1968; Risley, 1968). Immediate effects also occur with
less intense forms of punishment. For example, in classroom programs,
reprimands, response cost, and staying after school substantially decrease
inappropriate behaviors, often after only one day of punishment (Hall
et al., 1971). Similarly, time-out (Barton et al., 1970; Pendergrass, 1972),
fines (Kazdin, 1973b), and overcorrection (Foxx & Azrin, 1973) have resulted in dramatic response suppression after one or a few days of punishment in institutional and day-care settings. There certainly are exceptions
to the above studies. Not all programs or aversive procedures show response reductions in one or two sessions. Nevertheless, some effect usually
occurs within the first few days of the punishment contingency.

Specificity of Effects. Punishment often leads to effects which are
specific to the situation in which the response is punished. The punished
behavior may be suppressed only in the presence of the punishing agent or
the setting in which punishment took place (Bucher & Lovaas, 1968).
Punishment training usually has to be extended in a variety of situations
to ensure that the target response will not be performed in each of those
situations.

Investigators have noted that punishing a response in a treatment setting
does not influence behavior at home. Punishment has to be extended to
the home (Risley, 1968). Similarly, Bucher and King (1971) suppressed
the child's touching and playing with electrical appliances by shocking

the child's arm when he approached appliances. When the situation was changed (different settings and different appliances), the undesirable response still was performed. However, when responses in the new situations were shocked, they rapidly diminished. It is likely that when punishment is used in one situation, it will need to be extended to other situations. Usually, when punishment is extended to new situations responses are suppressed with increasing rapidity.

The effect of punishment may be restricted to the presence of the person who previously administered it. For example, verbal warnings and reprimands are sometimes effective when given only by persons previously associated with administration of more severe punishment (Birnbrauer, 1968). Response suppression may occur only in the presence of the experimenter who administered punishment and not in the presence of non-punishing adults. When punishment is carried out by more than one adult, responses may be suppressed across other adults who have not administered punishment (Lovaas & Simmons, 1969).

Recovery after Punishment Withdrawal. The effects of punishment often are quite rapid so that the frequency of a behavior is reduced in a short time. However, the effect of punishment may not last so that when the punishment contingency is withdrawn, behavior recovers or returns to its baseline rate. Recovery is likely to occur when punishment has not completely suppressed the response while the contingency was in effect (Azrin & Holz, 1966) and reinforcement has not been used to develop an alternate response. As mentioned earlier, whether punishment is highly effective in suppressing behavior depends upon a variety of factors. For example, use of electric shock to suppress self-destructive behavior can completely eliminate that behavior with a few shocks. Moreover, the suppression is complete and the response does not recover even though the contingency is withdrawn.

Since shock typically is not used to suppress behavior in applied settings, factors other than intensity of the aversive event must be considered to ensure response suppression and little or no recovery. Ordinarily mild forms of punishment will result in recovery after the punishment contingency is withdrawn. Indeed, even when punishment is in effect the individual may adapt to mild punishment so it loses its suppressive effects (Azrin & Holz, 1966). For example, threats lose their suppressive effects the more frequently they are used (Phillips, 1968; Phillips et al., 1971). To maximize response suppression with punishment and to minimize recovery, reinforcement can be provided for behaviors incompatible with the punished response (Boe, 1964). When the punishment contingency is removed, the reinforced response will be of a higher relative frequency than the punished response. The reinforced response will have replaced the previously punished response and can be maintained with continued reinforcement.

When and How to Use Punishment

In light of the above discussion, punishment is a procedure to be used cautiously because of possible undesirable side effects. In general, other procedures should be employed in advance of punishment. In many situations response suppression can be achieved without using punishment. Behaviors incompatible with the undesirable response can be reinforced, which may be sufficient to eliminate the undesirable response. Along with reinforcement for incompatible behaviors, the undesirable response can be extinguished by ensuring that no reinforcement is maintaining the response. Reinforcement combined with extinction can effectively alter behavior while minimizing the risk of side effects outlined above.

Nevertheless, there are several situations in which punishment will be useful, required, and, in many cases, essential. First, punishment is essential when the inappropriate behavior may be physically dangerous to oneself or others. Some immediate intervention is required to suppress responses before the relatively delayed effects of reinforcement and extinction might operate.

Second, punishment is useful when reinforcement of a behavior incompatible with the disruptive behavior cannot be easily administered. For example, if a "hyperactive" student is literally out of his seat all of the time, it will be impossible to reinforce in-seat behavior. Punishment (along with shaping) may be helpful in initially obtaining the desirable response. Eventually, of course, punishment can be faded with increasing reliance upon shaping with positive reinforcement and extinction.

Third, punishment is useful in temporarily suppressing a behavior while another behavior is reinforced. This latter use may be the most common application of punishment in applied settings. However, it should be remembered that mild forms of punishment (e.g., quiet reprimands, brief time-out durations, and small penalties or costs) usually are sufficient to suppress behavior as long as reinforcement for alternate responses is provided. Indeed, mild punishment can sometimes enhance the effect of reinforcement.

In one program, reinforcement was used to control the behavior of an extremely stubborn and disobedient child in the home (Wahler et al., 1965). Differential reinforcement was used whereby the mother praised cooperative behavior and ignored a failure to comply with requests. However, cooperative behavior had only increased slightly, so punishment was added. Whenever the boy was uncooperative, he was isolated in his room for five minutes. During the reinforcement-punishment program, cooperative behavior increased dramatically. This example suggests that punishment can augment the effect of reinforcement. In some reports the combination of punishment and reinforcement is more effective than either procedure used alone (Phillips et al., 1971; Walker, Mattson, & Buckley,

1971). Yet in many cases, positive reinforcement combined with extinction will be effective without the addition of punishment.

It should be clear that the best use of punishment in applied settings is as an ancillary technique to accompany positive reinforcement. At best, punishment will only suppress undesirable responses but not train desirable behaviors. Reinforcement is essential to develop appropriate behaviors which replace the suppressed behaviors.

NEGATIVE REINFORCEMENT

A behavior is increased or strengthened through negative reinforcement when it results in escape from or avoidance of an aversive event. Escape occurs when a response terminates or eliminates the aversive event. In an escape situation the individual comes in contact with the aversive event and the appropriate behavior eliminates the event. Many behaviors in everyday life are maintained by negative reinforcement through escape. For example, leaving the house to escape from an argument with one's roommate or spouse, turning off an alarm to escape from a loud noise, screaming to quiet noisy neighbors, and taking medicine to alleviate pain all represent escape.

Avoidance behavior allows the individual to prevent or indefinitely postpone contact with the aversive event. As mentioned in Chapter 2, avoidance learning may develop after an individual learns to escape an aversive event. Through classical conditioning, a previously neutral event acquires the capacity to elicit escape behavior. The escape behavior is automatically reinforced by terminating the conditioned aversive event. Thus, avoidance involves classical and operant conditioning. Avoidance refers to escape from a conditioned aversive event.

Most avoidance behavior is acquired without direct experience with the aversive event. Verbal cues from other individuals instruct us that certain things are to be avoided. The cues are discriminative stimuli indicating certain untoward consequences may follow, if we behave in a particular way. Examples of avoidance based on verbal cues are present in everyday experience. For example, one can avoid personal harm by responding to a threat of an impending flood. Avoidance of the flood is escape from or elimination of the threat. When a threat portends an aversive event if certain behaviors are (or are not) performed, avoidance conditioning is operative. Behavior which reduces the threat is strengthened through negative reinforcement. Other examples of negative reinforcement through avoidance include parking one's car in a particular place to avoid a traffic fine, wearing a coat to avoid a chill, drinking alcohol sparingly to avoid a driving mishap, and leaving a sinking ship to avoid drowning.

Negative reinforcement, in the form of escape from an aversive event, has not been widely used in applied settings for various reasons. First, when the treatment goal is to increase behavior, positive reinforcement is usually employed. By selecting positive instead of negative reinforcement, one can avoid all of the potentially undesirable features of aversive consequences outlined above. Negative reinforcement need only be employed when positive reinforcement and shaping have proved inadequate or when there is a paucity of positive events that serve as reinforcers. Second, negative reinforcement requires an ongoing aversive event which can be terminated when the desired target response occurs. This means that aversive events must be delivered frequently before reinforcement can occur. The extensive use of aversive events may be even more likely to result in undesirable side effects than if the aversive event were applied less frequently in the form of punishment. Third, the termination of the aversive state must be carefully controlled so that the appropriate response is reinforced. Usually this requires carefully monitoring behavior, often with certain apparatus. For the above reasons, it is no surprise that negative reinforcement has been restricted to relatively few settings.

Yet, negative reinforcement has been used in some cases to alter behaviors not readily amenable to change with other techniques. As mentioned earlier, negative reinforcement has been used to develop behaviors in schizophrenic children using shock as the aversive event (Lovaas et al., 1965). Shock removal negatively reinforced social behaviors such as approaching or hugging and kissing adults. Termination of the shock after these behaviors increased their probability.

Electric shock was used to increase a retarded child's use of toys (Whaley & Tough, 1970). The use of toys was important since it permitted the child to do something with his hands other than severely beating his head. Touching the toys was incompatible with head pounding. A toy truck was placed in front of the child. A buzzer and shock were presented to the child to provide an ongoing aversive event. The experimenter guided the boy's hand to the truck which resulted in cessation of the shock. Soon the boy avoided the shock by holding onto the toy truck. Additional toys were substituted and the buzzer alone, which had been previously paired with shock, served as the aversive stimulus. When the toy was released, the buzzer sounded. The buzzer was terminated when the toy was held. The child eventually used several toys and did not resume self-inflicted headbanging.

Flanagan, Goldiamond, and Azrin (1958) evaluated the effect of negative reinforcement on stuttering. The purpose of this report was merely to determine whether stuttering could be altered by manipulating the consequences which followed instances of blocking in speech rather than whether therapeutic improvements in stuttering could be achieved. Negative reinforcement consisted of removing a loud noise for five seconds when the client stuttered. The frequency of stuttering increased, as expected.

In many cases, negative reinforcement is combined with punishment to alter behavior. If aversive stimuli are to be employed, it is probably desirable to use negative reinforcement rather than punishment alone. Negative reinforcement can increase some adaptive behavior and thereby enhance the efficacy of punishment (Sanders, 1971).

In one report, loud noise was used as the aversive event to increase conversation in a group therapy session for psychotic patients (Heckel, Wiggins, & Salzberg, 1962). When the group was silent for more than one minute, a loud noise sounded through a speaker hidden in an air conditioning vent. The noise continued until one patient broke the silence (negative reinforcement). Patient conversation increased dramatically under this regime.[1]

Winkler (1971a) used negative reinforcement to control behavior of institutionalized psychiatric and retarded patients. The aversive event was time-out from reinforcement during which tokens could not be earned for any behavior for a period of time on the ward (one day). Time-out was imposed for not performing routine ward behaviors (e.g., making the bed). A patient could terminate time-out any time by performing the desired response. Removal of the aversive state after a response exemplifies negative reinforcement.

Television distortion was used as an aversive event to control work behavior of a retarded adult (Greene & Hoats, 1969). Whenever work dropped below a certain rate, the TV picture he was viewing became grossly distorted (punishment). To remove the distortion, he had to increase his speed to the appropriate rate. Weekly work rates increased under the punishment and negative reinforcement contingency.

An interesting use of punishment and avoidance was employed in a sheltered workshop for multiply handicapped retarded clients (Zimmerman, Overpeck, Eisenberg, & Garlick, 1969). Clients worked on a piece-work assembly job. To increase performance, a client was told that if he failed to complete a certain number of work units per day, he had to work at a table isolated from others. Hence, punishment was delivered for a slow work rate. The client could avoid isolation by producing work rates above an individually determined criterion. Avoidance of the anticipated aversive event could be achieved by performing the desired response (working at a relatively high rate). Interestingly, the procedure dramatically increased work. When the avoidance contingency was withdrawn, high rates of work behavior were maintained.

Negative reinforcement has been effectively combined with positive reinforcement. For example, Ayllon and Michael (1959) described a psy-

---

[1] Strictly speaking, this example does not entail punishment. Technically, presentation of an aversive event must follow a response to qualify as punishment. Since silence is not a response (but rather lack of a response), presentation of the aversive event is not punishment (Azrin & Holz, 1966).

chiatric patient who had to be spoon-fed at each meal. The patient liked to have clean clothes so the investigators developed an aversive contingency in which her clothes were soiled whenever she was spoon-fed. While the nurse fed her, she periodically spilled food on the patient. The patient could avoid this by feeding herself, which she quickly did. As soon as the patient began to feed herself, the nurse positively reinforced her by attending to and talking with her.

Negative reinforcement has had its greatest application as part of the therapy techniques used to alter behaviors such as alcoholism, overeating, and sexual deviance including homosexuality, transvestism, and fetishism (Rachman & Teasdale, 1969). In such applications, aversive stimuli are used to build avoidance responses. The procedure entails both classical and operant conditioning. Thus, negative reinforcement is not the only element operative. For example, in the treatment of male homosexuals who wish to change their sexual orientation, homosexual slides are viewed (Feldman & MacCullough, 1965). While a client is viewing a slide, shock is delivered. The procedure to this point illustrates classical conditioning. By pairing the homosexual scene (conditioned stimulus) with the shock (unconditioned stimulus), the scenes alone should eventually elicit an avoidance reaction. The procedure includes other aspects as well. The shock, which is initiated in the presence of the homosexual slide, can be terminated by turning off the slide. Thus, the client can escape shock by quickly turning off the homosexual slide. Indeed, the client can avoid the shock entirely if he turns off the slide a few seconds after it is shown. The client is negatively reinforced for turning off the slide. The shock is avoided entirely. Escape from or avoidance of the shock is sometimes associated with heterosexual slides. If the termination of shock is associated with a heterosexual scene, that scene may become positively valenced.

Similarly, for alcoholics, various procedures include negative reinforcement. One form of treatment requires that clients ingest a drug, disulfiram (trade name Antabuse) which, when followed by alcohol consumption within a 24-hour period, results in violent illness. The drinking response is immediately punished by nausea. The aversive consequence can be avoided by not consuming alcohol. Of course, the person also can avoid the aversive contingency altogether by failing to take the drug. As mentioned earlier, avoidance conditioning includes classical and operant conditioning components. In aversive conditioning treatments, there is a great deal of dispute whether certain procedures are primarily classical or operant in nature (Rachman & Teasdale, 1969).

Evaluation of Negative Reinforcement

A major restriction in using negative reinforcement is the risk of undesirable side effects. From the standpoint of designing a behavior modification program, aversive stimuli should be avoided or minimized. When they are used, emphasis should be placed upon positive reinforcement for desirable behavior. In many examples of negative reinforcement reviewed above, strong aversive stimuli were required because other procedures had failed or because the response (e.g., sexual deviance) was strongly reinforced. In such instances, aversive stimuli including punishment and/or negative reinforcement constitute a last resort.

Conclusion

A variety of aversive events are available for suppressing (punishment) or increasing behavior (negative reinforcement). Punishment consists of presenting aversive events such as shock or verbal reprimands and disapproval or removing positive events through time-out from reinforcement and response cost. Punishment needs to be used carefully to ensure that the procedure will be maximally effective. The most important element when punishment is used is to provide positive reinforcement for behaviors incompatible with the punished response. By reinforcing an alternate response, even mild forms of punishment can change behavior dramatically.

Use of punishment can lead to side effects which may be undesirable, such as emotional reactions, escape from the situation or from the person who administers punishment, aggression, the use of punishment by the individual who is punished, and overreliance upon aversive control procedures. These undesirable side effects have not been widely demonstrated in applied settings. Indeed, in some instances positive side effects result from suppressing deviant behavior. Nevertheless, at the present time, the possibility of adverse side effects makes extensive reliance upon aversive procedures somewhat hazardous. Additionally, punishment effects may be very specific both in the responses that are altered and the situations in which behavior change occurs. Negative reinforcement is not widely used as a behavior change technique in most applied settings. This is due, in part, to reliance upon positive reinforcement to increase behavior whenever possible. Nevertheless, negative reinforcement has been used successfully, particularly in those instances where positive reinforcement has not been effective or has been difficult to administer.

7

Extinction

Extinction refers to withholding reinforcement from a previously reinforced response. A response undergoing extinction eventually decreases in frequency until it returns to its prereinforcement level or is eliminated. Numerous examples of extinction are evident in everyday life. For example, trying to start a defective automobile extinguishes after several unsuccessful attempts; warmly greeting an acquaintance each day decreases, if he or she repeatedly does not reciprocate; and raising one's hand in class will cease, if it is never followed by teacher attention. In each case, the behavior decreases because the reinforcing consequence no longer occurs.

Extinction in applied settings usually is used for behaviors which have been *positively* reinforced. In fact, each of the above examples refers to behaviors maintained by positive reinforcement. However, extinction can also be used with responses maintained by negative reinforcement. Extinction of responses developed or maintained through negative reinforcement is somewhat different from extinction of responses maintained with positive reinforcement.

EXTINCTION OF NEGATIVELY REINFORCED RESPONSES

As discussed earlier, many behaviors are performed to avoid anticipated aversive consequences and hence are maintained by negative reinforcement. For example, a student may study for exams to avoid poor grades. Similarly, some people spend money judiciously to avoid a lack of funds at the end of the month. Many behaviors are maintained by their success in avoiding the occurrence of anticipated undesirable consequences.

Laboratory research has shown that avoidance behaviors are highly resistant to extinction. In classic experiments, Solomon, Kamin, and Wynne (1953) trained dogs to avoid brief electric shocks by responding to a buzzer which preceded the shock. A dog could avoid the shock by jumping over a barrier in the middle of the compartment when the buzzer sounded. The avoidance training procedure was repeated in each side of the compartment. At the beginning of training, the animal was shocked and escaped over the barrier. In a short time, the dog repeatedly jumped back and forth over the barrier in response to the buzzer. Although the shock eventually was completely withdrawn from the situation, the avoidance responses did not extinguish. The dog never remained in the situation long enough to find out that extinction (removal of shock) began.

Anxiety is presumed to play a role in the development and maintenance of avoidance responses. A previously neutral stimulus elicits anxiety and escape through the process of classical conditioning, described earlier. Cues associated with the unconditioned aversive event can elicit the anxiety and escape response. In the case of avoidance in animals, anxiety or fear increases when the buzzer sounds because the buzzer preceded shock. Escape from the buzzer reduces fear. Thus, anxiety reduction, by termination of the unconditioned aversive event, negatively reinforces escape. Although the unconditioned aversive event (shock) no longer occurs, successful escape from the anxiety-arousing conditioned aversive event maintains avoidance behavior. For example, a fearful individual rarely places himself in the fear-provoking situation which would permit escape and avoidance behaviors to extinguish. The original traumatic event which may have led to the fear may no longer provide a threat. However, extinction cannot begin to take effect because the person does not enter the situation in which escape and avoidance were conditioned. The complete explanation of avoidance behavior and resistance to extinction remains unsettled. Nevertheless, effective treatments for avoidance responses have been developed (Bandura, 1969; Kanfer & Phillips, 1970; Wolpe, 1969; Yates, 1970).

As mentioned earlier, one technique which has been widely used to extinguish avoidance responses is systematic desensitization (Wolpe, 1958, 1969). Derived from a classical conditioning framework, desensitization attempts to alter the valence of conditioned stimuli so they no longer elicit anxiety. Anxiety-eliciting conditioned stimuli are paired with non-anxiety states of the client. To achieve a nonanxiety state, the client is usually trained to relax deeply. The relaxation is paired with *imagination* of anxiety-provoking situations. While the client is relaxed, he imagines himself in situations which are only mildly anxiety provoking. As treatment progresses and the individual has successfully associated relaxation with these scenes, increasingly more arousing scenes are imagined. Eventually, the client can imagine these scenes without anxiety. The previously anxiety-provoking stimuli no longer elicit anxiety. The changes made in the client's anxiety responses are not restricted to images of or thoughts about the situations but extend to the actual situations themselves. Thus, the changes made in therapy carry over to actual situations encountered by the client. Desensitization has been used to treat a variety of specific fears and other anxiety reactions (Bandura, 1969; Kanfer & Phillips, 1970; Paul, 1969b).

Operant procedures have been used to extinguish avoidance responses. In one case, a seven-year-old boy named Karl would not stay at school unless his parents remained with him (Patterson, 1965a). Karl was seen at a clinic to treat his "school phobia." A doll-play situation was used in several therapy sessions where a male doll "enacted" situations which were problematic for Karl. Karl was asked questions about the boy doll (e.g., "Is he afraid?") and was reinforced with praise and candy when he indicated the doll had little difficulty in going places, leaving his mother, receiving minor injuries, and engaging in other normally routine behaviors. After ten sessions, Karl's behavior was shaped at school. At first, the child went to school with a teacher near him at all times. Eventually, he was left alone for increasingly longer periods. Karl's family praised him for progress at school. In a few weeks, the boy was at school full time with no difficulty. Three months later the boy was continuing to attend school with no apparent fear.

To extinguish avoidance responses, classical and operant conditioning procedures have been combined in the treatment of another school phobic child (Lazarus, Davison, & Polefka, 1965). A nine-year-old boy named Paul had a history of absenteeism from school. The boy's parents reported that each morning the boy became dejected, fearful, and withdrawn as the hour of departure approached. Attempts to reassure, coax, and coerce him were unsuccessful in getting Paul to go to school. The authors initially attempted to reduce avoidance by using desensitization in the actual situations which bothered Paul. A graded hierarchy of steps leading toward school attendance was constructed. Paul was exposed to each step in a gradual fashion in an attempt to minimize anxiety. Initially, Paul was accompanied by the therapists to school on a Sunday. The therapists allayed Paul's anxiety by humor and distraction. Next, Paul was accompanied by one of the therapists from his home to the school yard. His anxiety was reduced by encouragement and by having him imagine pleasant experiences (e.g., Christmas and visiting Disneyland). Gradually, Paul performed increasingly difficult steps including sitting in class after school was over, visiting with other children immediately before class began, spending the entire morning in class with the therapist present, and spending increasingly greater portions of the day without the therapist. At one point, a mild tranquilizer was used to decrease anxiety in the mornings before school. To encourage school attendance in the absence of the therapist, Paul could earn reinforcers (comic books and tokens toward a baseball glove). After three weeks of the reward procedure, Paul earned enough tokens to buy the glove. He then agreed with his parents that special rewards were no longer necessary. Treatment had lasted a total of four-and-one-half months. Although behavior changed in this time, it is unclear precisely what was responsible for change. Nevertheless, the example shows an attempt to combine procedures based upon classical conditioning (extinction of avoidance behavior toward school) and operant conditioning (shaping school attendance with positive reinforcement).

Responses maintained by negative reinforcement can be extinguished by exposing the individual to the situation which is usually avoided, thereby preventing the avoidance response. Avoidance behavior extinguishes because no untoward consequences actually occur in the situation. Extinction of avoidance responses occurs in counseling and psychotherapy interviews. Clients participating in therapy frequently express feelings and thoughts which typically elicit anxiety and guilt in themselves presumably because of a previous history of punishment for these feelings. Certain feelings and thoughts may be avoided as topics in therapy because of the anxiety they evoke. Therapists typically respond in a permissive and nonpunitive fashion so that inappropriate emotional responses extinguish. As therapy progresses, the physiological arousal associated with anxiety-provoking topics, such as sex, decreases over time (Dittes, 1957).

Behavior modification techniques to extinguish negatively reinforced behaviors are not widely employed by parents, teachers, attendants, and others in applied settings. Usually professional treatment is administered in an outpatient setting and is sometimes supplemented by assistance from relatives and others in daily contact with the client. The major use of extinction in applied settings is the elimination of behaviors maintained by positive reinforcement. The remaining discussion of extinction will be devoted to behaviors maintained by positive reinforcement.

EXTINCTION OF POSITIVELY REINFORCED RESPONSES

Initial Considerations in Using Extinction

Extinction of positively reinforced behaviors is almost always used in a behavior modification program. For example, in a reinforcement program, when a target response is reinforced, implicitly, nontarget responses which are no longer reinforced are undergoing extinction. Although extinction is an ingredient in most programs, it may be used as the major technique to decrease undesirable behavior. When relied upon as the major technique, various factors determine whether it will be effective.

Schedule of Reinforcement. The efficacy of extinction and the speed with which response reduction is achieved depends upon the schedule of reinforcement which previously maintained the response. As mentioned in the discussion of reinforcement, a response reinforced every time (continuous reinforcement) rapidly extinguishes once the reinforcer is withheld. In contrast, a response reinforced once in a while (intermittent reinforcement) extinguishes less rapidly when the reinforcer is withheld. The more intermittent the schedule (or less frequent the reinforcement), the greater the resistance of the response to extinction.

The relationship of reinforcement schedules and extinction creates a major problem for programs relying primarily on extinction because most behaviors are maintained by intermittent reinforcement. For example, incoherent verbalizations in psychiatric patients often are attended to but sometimes are ignored. Decreasing the frequency of these behaviors may be difficult because of the intermittent schedule on which they have been maintained. If all the sources of reinforcement were removed from a behavior previously maintained by intermittent reinforcement, the behavior would eventually decrease and perhaps be eliminated. Intermittent reinforcement *delays* the extinction process. Yet, the delay may be unfortunate. While the long extinction process is underway, it is possible that the response will be *accidentally reinforced*. The possibility of accidental reinforcement during extinction is always a problem and is only exacerbated with a long extinction period.

An example of accidental reinforcement was mentioned earlier in a program where parents eliminated a child's tantrum by no longer providing attention for this behavior (Williams, 1959). Extinction proceeded uneventfully until tantrums were nearly eliminated within a few days, as shown in Figure 7–1. However, one night the child fussed when put to bed by his aunt. The aunt provided a great deal of attention to the tantrum by staying with the child until he went to sleep. The tantrums had to be extinguished a second time. After tantrums were eliminated the second time, they did not occur in the following two years.

Other Variables Affecting Extinction. The effects of reinforcement schedules on extinction have been more thoroughly studied than the influence of other variables. Yet, general statements can be extrapolated from laboratory research on variables which contribute to resistance to extinction (Kimble, 1961; Reynolds, 1968). First, the amount or magnitude of reinforcement used to develop the response affects extinction. The greater the amount of a particular reinforcer given for a response, the greater the resistance of the response to extinction. Similarly, the longer the period of time that the response has been reinforced, the greater the resistance to extinction. Finally, the greater the number of times that extinction has been used in the past to reduce the behavior, the more rapid extinction will be. The individual learns to discriminate periods of reinforcement and extinction more rapidly. If a strong or powerful reinforcer is maintaining a response, and if the response has been sustained over a long period, it is likely to be more resistant to extinction than if weak rein-

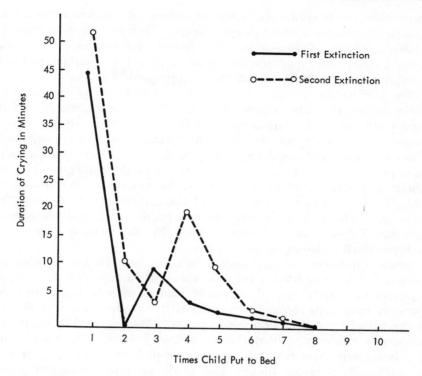

FIGURE 7–1 Length of crying in two extinction series as a function of successive occasions of being put to bed. (Source: Williams, C. D. The elimination of tantrum behavior by extinction procedures. *Journal of Abnormal and Social Psychology,* 1959, **59,** 269. Copyright 1959 by the American Psychological Association. Reprinted by permission.)

forcers were used and reinforcers were delivered over a short period of time. Of course, these effects act in concert with the schedule of reinforcement in influencing extinction.

Identifying the Reinforcer Maintaining Behavior. Extinction requires that the reinforcer(s) maintaining behavior be identified and withheld when the response is performed. While this appears simple enough, in practice it may be difficult to isolate the reinforcer. For example, an "emotionally disturbed" child may behave aggressively with peers. Various reinforcers might maintain aggressive behavior, such as the control aggressive behavior exerts over peers, a submissive response of the victim, admiration from friends, or special attention from a teacher or parent. It is difficult to identify which potential reinforcer or combination of reinforcers is maintaining behavior. Extinction may be attempted by removing teacher and parent attention without decreasing aggressive behavior because other reinforcers are operative. For example, in a classroom program, an attempt was made to extinguish disruptive behavior by withdrawing teacher attention (Madsen et al., 1968). However, disruptive behavior increased. Apparently, reinforcement resulting from peer attention or from disruptive acts themselves maintained inappropriate behavior.

The only method for determining which reinforcer is maintaining behavior is empirical observation. By repeatedly observing events which consistently follow the target response, the consequence which appears responsible for maintaining behavior can be examined. The consequence is removed while data on the frequency of the response are continuously gathered. It is useful to record the frequency of the consequence (e.g., teacher or parent attention) to ensure that the consequence is consistently withheld. If the response declines and the consequence is consistently withheld, the consequence served as a positive reinforcer and maintained behavior. This can be evaluated carefully by employing a reversal or multiple-baseline design, outlined earlier.

In many instances, the reinforcer maintaining behavior may be difficult to identify because it follows behavior very infrequently. For example, in a psychiatric hospital disruptive patient behavior may be maintained by attention from a psychiatrist or psychologist. However, the psychiatrist or psychologist may have little interaction with the patient. Yet, the interaction may follow particularly bizarre patient behavior. The interaction may be so infrequent that it is assumed not to be responsible for maintaining bizarre behavior. Identification of the reinforcer maintaining behavior is likely to be delayed. If the reinforcer is not quickly identified, there can be considerable delay in beginning the extinction process. For this reason, it is desirable to supplement extinction with other procedures (e.g., reinforcement for appropriate behavior), as will be elaborated below.

Controlling the Source of Reinforcement. Once the reinforcer maintaining an undesirable behavior has been identified, a major problem may be withholding it after behavior. As mentioned earlier, extinction requires very careful control over reinforcers. Any accidental reinforcement may rapidly reinstate the inappropriate behavior and prolong the extinction process.

An example of the problem in controlling reinforcement delivery was reported by Ayllon and Michael (1959). These investigators used extinction to decrease delusional talk of a hospitalized psychotic patient. The patient consistently talked about her illegitimate child and the men she claimed were always pursuing her. Her psychotic talk had persisted for at least three years. Typically, nurses responded to the delusional talk by listening to understand and get at the "root" of the problem. When extinction was implemented, the nurses did not attend to the psychotic talk and provided attention for sensible talk. At three different times during the extinction phase, delusional talk was accidentally reinforced. Once a social worker attended to psychotic talk. On two other occasions, when another employee and volunteers visited the ward, the extinction procedure again was sacrificed. Although extinction decreased behavior, the accidental reinforcement appeared to account for temporary increases.

Reinforcement is particularly difficult to control when it is delivered by peers. Peers reinforce each other without staff members knowing it. For example, often institutionalized delinquents reinforce each other for deviant acts that the staff would like to extinguish (cf. Buehler et al., 1966). Constant surveillance is required to ensure that no peer reinforcement occurs. The resources for such surveillance are rarely available in applied settings.

One alternative is to enlist peers so that they ignore (extinguish) the deviant behavior of a particular individual. For example, in one classroom program (Pierce, 1971), a 12-year-old girl engaged in bizarre behaviors including frenzied hand flapping, aimless running, "crazy" talk referring to fictitious events, and paralysis. The teacher instructed the girl's classmates that the student had trouble with her imagination and needed their help. They were told that her "acting crazy" would probably continue, if people paid attention to her. The classmates were instructed to ignore bizarre behavior and to reinforce appropriate behavior. The girl was reported to have changed considerably although the program was not rigorously evaluated.

Peers can be reinforced for systematically ignoring certain behaviors. By providing a strong peer incentive for extinguishing a response, it is likely that there will be little or no accidental reinforcement. For example, students in one elementary classroom received candy if they ignored a peer who had severe tantrums which consisted of profane screaming and throwing objects (Carlson, Arnold, Becker, & Madsen, 1968). By reinforcing the peers, these authors decreased the likelihood of any uncontrolled reinforcement.

It is virtually impossible to control reinforcement for some behaviors. For example, criminal acts such as theft are reinforced intermittently. It is not readily feasible to design society so that reinforcers are never provided for theft. All objects for which thefts are committed cannot be locked up. So theft is likely to be reinforced once in a while and maintained. Extinction alone is exceedingly unlikely to control theft and other crimes where the source of reinforcement cannot be controlled.

Characteristics of the Extinction Process

Gradual Reduction in Behavior. Although extinction effectively decreases and often eliminates behavior, *the process of extinction is usually gradual.* Unlike the effects of punishment, described in the last chapter, extinction typically does not show an immediate response reduction.

Rather, several unreinforced responses are performed prior to demonstrating an effect.

When the undesirable behaviors are dangerous or severely disruptive, the delayed effects of extinction can be deleterious either to the individual himself or to others. For example, self-destructive behavior of retarded and autistic children often is severe enough to render serious self-inflicted physical damage. Ignoring the behavior may reduce its frequency. Yet the physical damage rendered in the process may be unfortunate. One child who engaged in self-inflicted headbanging had multiple scars over his head and face from the injuries (Lovaas & Simmons, 1969). During extinction, the child was taken out of physical restraints and placed in a small room with no adults who could reinforce (attend to) the destructive behavior. The child's behavior, observed through a one-way mirror, eventually extinguished in ten sessions over a total of 15 hours. However, from the beginning of extinction until the response finally decreased to zero, the child had hit himself almost 9,000 times. Thus, a great deal of self-inflicted injury occurred during the course of extinction. Although extinction can reduce behavior, dangerous behavior requires an intervention with more rapid results than extinction usually provides.

Extinction Burst. At the beginning of extinction, the frequency of the response may increase compared to what it was while the response was reinforced. The response may be performed several times in rapid succession. The increase in responding at the beginning of extinction is referred to as a "burst" of responses. Numerous examples of a burst of responses at the beginning of extinction pervade everyday experience. For example, turning on a radio is usually followed by some sound (e.g., music or news). If the radio no longer works so that no reinforcement (sound) occurs, eventually attempts to turn the radio on will extinguish. However, before this occurs, the response may temporarily increase in frequency (several on-off turns) and intensity or vigor. These responses will eventually cease, if the radio does not work.

A burst of responses at the beginning of extinction sometimes occurs in behavior modification programs. Allen, Turner, and Everett (1970) used extinction to decrease the tantrums of a four-and-one-half-year-old boy in a Head Start classroom. The boy's outbursts and aggressive attacks on others disrupted the entire class. Baseline observations revealed an average duration of five minutes for each tantrum. After baseline, the teacher agreed to ignore each tantrum no matter how severe it was. The first tantrum during extinction was much more severe than previous tantrums and lasted 27 minutes. While this tantrum was occurring, the teacher anticipated that it might last a long time so she took the other children out to the playground. This prevented accidental peer reinforcement of tantrum behavior. On the second day of extinction the one tantrum that occurred lasted about 15 minutes and on the third day there was one mild tantrum of 4 minutes. From that point on no further tantrums occurred. Thus, extinction eliminated behavior but not until behavior became worse for a short time.

When extinction is used as a treatment strategy, it is important to prepare those persons who will ignore the behavior for a possible burst of responses so that obstreperous behavior will not be reinforced when it becomes worse. In the above report (Allen et al., 1970), the investigators prepared the teacher for the increase in response intensity. However, in another classroom project, the teacher who ignored disruptive classroom behavior was unprepared for the consequences. At the beginning of the extinction phase, the class reportedly became worse and she was very upset (Madsen et al., 1968).

A burst of responses is especially serious with physically dangerous behavior. Lovaas and Simmons (1969) noted that self-injurious behavior in children initially increased at the beginning of extinction over their dangerously high rate. For one child, the burst of self-destructive responses at the beginning of extinction led to considerable bleeding and physical discomfort. The investigators decided against the use of extinction for another child who already had physical damage from self-destructive behaviors over concern with further damage.

With behaviors that are not physically dangerous, a burst of responses may still be undesirable. It may be exceedingly difficult for someone to tolerate the undesirable behavior as it intensifies at the beginning of extinction (Patterson & Reid, 1970). Thus, during a burst of responses, the likelihood that reinforcement will occur is increased. For example, a tantrum may become worse when parents systematically ignore the behavior. When the tantrum is worse, the parents may give in to the child and provide attention and comfort. Parental reinforcement will increase the probability of intense tantrums because reinforcement is provided when the behavior is worse than usual. To the parents, of course, extinction may appear to be failing because behavior has become worse. However, the effect of extinction is merely beginning. It is likely that reinforcement during a burst of responses is a basis for behaviors such as protracted whining and excessive demands for attention often seen in children. It should be noted that an initial burst of responses does not always occur. However, when the burst occurs, the possibility of reinforcement adds to the risk in relying on extinction in the absence of other procedures.

Spontaneous Recovery.   After extinction has progressed, the response may temporarily reappear even though it has not been reinforced. The temporary reoccurrence of a nonreinforced response during extinction is referred to as spontaneous recovery (Kimble, 1961). When the response recovers during extinction, its strength ordinarily will be less than it was prior to extinction. For example, if a child's tantrum is ignored, the frequency of tantrums probably will decrease over time, possibly, after an initial burst of responses. However, there may be a tantrum that occurs after extinction has progressed for some time. The tantrum is likely to be of a lower intensity or magnitude than the original tantrums during baseline (cf. Williams, 1959).

As with extinction burst, a major concern with spontaneous recovery is that the response will be reinforced. Spontaneous recovery occurs after several responses have not been reinforced. If reinforcement is provided, it follows a long series of nonreinforced responses. This is tantamount to a highly intermittent reinforcement schedule which may further increase resistance to extinction (Slamecka, 1960). If extinction continues and no accidental reinforcement occurs, the frequency and intensity of the spontaneously recovered response decreases. It is important to realize that extinction may include the spontaneous reoccurrence of the response. A reoccurrence is less likely to be interpreted as the inefficacy of the procedure but rather a characteristic of the extinction process.

Possible Side Effects. Another characteristic of extinction is that the cessation of reinforcement may result in "emotional responses" such as agitation, frustration, feelings of failure, or rage (cf. Lawson, 1965; Miller & Stevenson, 1936; Skinner, 1953). In addition, aggressive behavior is sometimes produced when reinforcement is discontinued (e.g., Hutchinson, Azrin, & Hunt, 1968). Apparently the transition from positive reinforcement to extinction is aversive (cf. Azrin, 1961).

Examples of emotional reactions in response to extinction abound in everyday experience. For example, after individuals place money into a malfunctioning vending machine (i.e., reinforcement no longer delivered), exhortations of frustration and aggressive attacks on the machine are common events. For individuals who have experienced repeated reinforcement of certain responses, the cessation of reinforcement may be experienced as failure. For example, when an athlete performs poorly he or she may swear, express feelings of failure, and throw something to the ground in disgust. The notion of being a "poor loser" denotes that emotional behavior occurs when a person's responses are not reinforced in a contest, that is, the person loses (Staats & Staats, 1963).

The emotional effects of extinction have not been widely studied in applied settings. Nevertheless, extrapolation from laboratory evidence suggests that the emotional effects may only be temporary and diminish as the response decreases. However, if the response is performed for a long period during extinction, emotional responses may also continue for some time (Hutchinson et al., 1968).

An important consideration is that a situation which is no longer reinforcing may become aversive. An aversive situation can result in escape and avoidance and reduce the opportunity for providing the client with positive reinforcement for desirable behavior. To avoid this, reinforcement should be delivered for an alternate response from the one to be eliminated. Thus, there is no net loss in reinforcement for the client. Rather, the reinforcement is provided for a new behavior.

Applications of Extinction

Extinction has been applied to diverse problems. In a psychiatric hospital, extinction was used to reduce the frequency that a patient visited the nurses' office (Ayllon & Michael, 1959). The visits, which had been going on for two years, interfered with the nurses' work. The nurses usually paid attention to the patient when she visited and frequently pushed her back into the ward. After baseline observations, the nurses were instructed not to provide attention to the patient when she visited. Extinction decreased visits from 16 times a day during baseline to 2 per day at the end of seven weeks.

An interesting case of extinction was reported for a 20-year-old woman who suffered from neurodermatitis on her neck for two years (Walton, 1960). She persistently aggravated the condition by scratching it. Various treatments such as x-ray therapy, lotions, ointments, and pills had proved unsatisfactory. Scratching appeared to receive a great deal of attention from her family and her fiance including the routine applications of ointment. The family and fiance were instructed to discontinue attention for scratching. At the end of three months of extinction, scratching was eliminated and the skin condition disappeared. A subsequent examination of the patient four years later revealed no recurrence of the problem.

Extinction was used with a patient in a psychiatric ward who had a 10-year history of vomiting after meals (Alford, Blanchard, & Buckley, 1972). Chemical therapy had not suppressed vomiting. To begin the extinction program, the patient ate in the presence of two staff members. Vomiting was frequent when staff members attended to her and engaged in conversation after vomiting. As soon as staff members failed to attend to her when she vomited (e.g., left the room), vomiting ceased. To ensure that treatment effects would be maintained, other patients on the ward were told to ignore her when she vomited or even spoke of feeling nauseous. Since the patient failed to vomit, the program was terminated. A follow-up interview with the patient and her parents revealed that she only vomited once in the seven months after discharge.

Extinction usually is used in conjunction with reinforcement. For example, Ayllon and Haughton (1962) trained self-feeding in 32 psychiatric patients. Normally patients had been fed by nurses. The nurses reinforced dependent behavior by individually escorting patients to the dining room and feeding them. In short, a great deal of attention was provided to the patients for *not* attending the dining room and self-feeding. To develop self-feeding, patients were told that they had to come to the dining room within a half hour after it opened for mealtime, otherwise they could not eat. Hence, coming to meals would be reinforced with food whereas remaining in the ward (not coming to meals) would be extinguished (food no longer provided). Moreover, staff attention was not given for refusal to eat as it had been previously. Although some patients missed a few meals, all learned to attend the dining room and feed themselves.

Ayllon and Haughton (1964) used extinction and reinforcement to modify psychotic verbal behavior in a hospitalized schizophrenic patient. The patient's verbal statements included frequent references to "Queen Elizabeth," "King George," and the "Royal Family" and statements such as "I'm the Queen. Why don't you give things to the Queen . . . How's King George. . . ?" Her psychotic verbal behavior had a history of 14 years in the hospital. Baseline observations were made of both the frequency of psychotic and neutral verbalizations. Neutral verbal responses included statements which were not psychotic (e.g., "It's nice today.").

To determine whether consequences provided by staff could control the patient's verbal behavior, staff temporarily ignored neutral talk and reinforced psychotic verbalizations. When the patient made a psychotic statement, staff provided attention and cigarettes but ignored her for neutral statements. Figure 7–2 shows that after baseline, neutral statements were extinguished whereas psychotic statements increased. In the last phase, the contingencies were reversed. Psychotic verbalizations were ignored whereas neutral statements were attended to and followed with cigarettes. The combined effect of extinction and reinforcement was dramatic.

Extinction and reinforcement were combined to control a 15-year-old handicapped, retarded boy in a junior high classroom (Hall, Fox, Willard, Goldsmith, Emerson, Owen, Davis, & Porcia, 1971). The boy argued constantly with his teacher. After a baseline period of several days, the teacher simply ignored and walked away from the boy when he began to argue. Praise was delivered when he worked on his assignment without arguing. The combination of extinction and reinforcement markedly reduced the number of arguments from seven per day during baseline to less than one per day a few days after the contingency was in effect. Six weeks after the experiment had terminated, the teacher reported that arguments were no longer a problem.

In a preschool classroom, a 4-year-old girl isolated herself from other children and received adult attention for this behavior (Allen, Hart, Buell, Harris, & Wolf, 1964). Playing with peers was selected as the target behavior to increase social interaction. The teacher ignored any isolated behavior and praised her when peer play was initiated. Since peer interactions did not occur frequently, approximations of peer interaction had to be reinforced initially such as standing near or playing beside another child. Social interaction with peers increased markedly. During a reversal phase, the child received attention for isolate play and was ignored for peer interaction. As shown in Figure 7–3, peer interactions decreased when

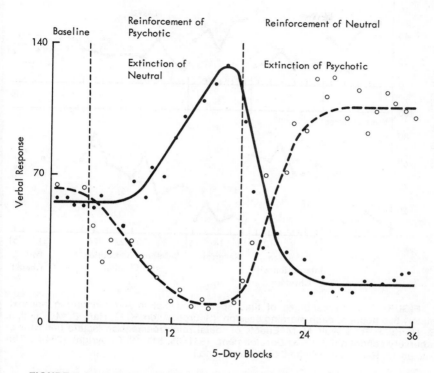

Psychotic Verbal Response •━━━•

Neutral Verbal Response o━ ━ ━o

FIGURE 7-2 Verbal responses of a psychotic patient as a function of reinforcement and extinction procedures. (Source: Ayllon, T., & Haughton, E. Modification of symptomatic verbal behavior of mental patients. *Behaviour research and
therapy,* 1964, **2,** 87–97. Reprinted with permission from Pergamon Press.)

they were ignored and increased when they were reinforced. After the
program was terminated during the last month of school, a high rate of
peer interaction was maintained.

Other reports have shown behavior change in classroom settings when
teachers ignore disruptive behavior and praise attentive or work behavior
(Becker, Madsen, Arnold, & Thomas, 1967; Kazdin, 1973c; Kazdin & Klock,
1973; Madsen et al., 1968) with some exceptions (O'Leary et al., 1969).
Extinction of disruptive behavior is less effective when used alone than if
it is combined with praise for appropriate behavior (Madsen et al., 1968).

Extinction alone or in conjunction with reinforcement has been used to
decrease chronic hypochondriacal complaints (Ayllon & Haughton, 1964),
persistent vomiting (Wolf, Birnbrauer, Williams, & Lawlor, 1965), stub-

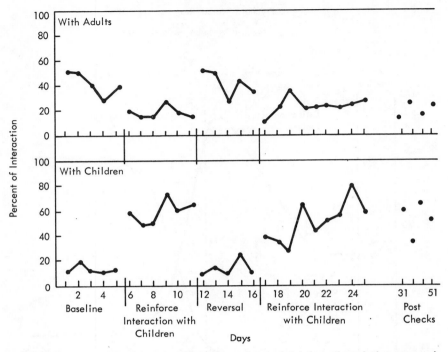

FIGURE 7–3 Percentages of time spent in social interaction during approximately two hours of each morning session. (Source: Allen, K. E., Hart, B. M., Buell, J. S., Harris, F. R., & Wolf, M. M. Effects of social reinforcement on isolate behavior of a nursery school child. *Child Development,* 1964, **35,** 511–18. Copyright 1964 by The Society for Research in Child Development, Inc.)

bornness (Wahler et al., 1965), self-injurious scratching (Allen & Harris, 1966), and persistent crying in children (Hart, Allen, Buell, Harris, & Wolf, 1964) and infants (Etzel & Gewirtz, 1967). The above reports are particularly noteworthy because they reveal that several deviant behaviors are maintained by social consequences.

When and How to Use Extinction

Extinction as a behavior change procedure is useful in those situations where the reinforcer which maintains behavior can be readily identified and controlled. In some situations, it is plausible that only one or a few reinforcers maintain behavior. For example, parents may attend to a child's tantrum before the child goes to bed. The reinforcers for tantrums may include attention and food, if a snack is given to placate the child. In this example, the reinforcers maintaining behavior probably are limited to attention and food. Each can readily be withdrawn to test this notion. Of course, if there are other relatives in the house (e.g., siblings and grand-parents) who can inadvertently provide reinforcement, identifying and controlling available reinforcers are more difficult. Another consideration in using extinction is whether the burst which may occur will be harmful to the client himself or to others or tolerable to the agents responsible for the client. If the above conditions for extinction can be met, extinction may eliminate the target behavior so that it is unnecessary to employ other procedures (e.g., punishment).

Extinction is enhanced tremendously when combined with positive re-inforcement for behavior which is incompatible with the response to be extinguished. There are many reasons to combine reinforcement with ex-tinction. First, the problems of executing extinction effectively are miti-gated. Identifying and controlling reinforcement which maintains the undesirable response are not as essential, if other reinforcers are provided to develop desirable behavior. Second, the potentially undesirable side effects of extinction and the problematic characteristics of the course of extinction are less likely to occur, if reinforcement is provided for alternate responses. By providing reinforcement, the side effects which result from reinforcer loss should not appear. In addition, a burst of responses and spontaneous recovery may not occur, if the reinforced response replaces the extinguished response. Third, extinction may effectively decrease be-havior but it does not ensure that a desirable behavior will replace the be-havior that has been eliminated. However, reinforcement can effectively strengthen behavior. If certain undesirable behaviors are extinguished and desirable behaviors are not simultaneously reinforced, extinction may not be very effective. When extinction is terminated, the undesirable behavior is likely to return because no alternate responses have been developed and no alternate means of obtaining reinforcement have been provided. Thus, the recommendations made for using punishment apply to extinction. *When extinction or punishment is used, reinforcement should be delivered to develop a behavior to replace the response to be eliminated.*

Conclusion

Extinction often is an effective procedure to eliminate behavior. The effectiveness of withholding reinforcement for a response depends pri-marily upon the schedule of reinforcement on which the response has been maintained. Behavior maintained with highly intermittent reinforcement is particularly resistant to extinction. In practice, extinction can be difficult to implement because the source of reinforcement maintaining behavior cannot always be readily identified and controlled. Several features of extinction warrant consideration.

First, for behaviors which are dangerous (e.g., self-destruction) or highly disruptive (e.g., shouting and screaming), extinction is not recommended.

Since the decrease in behavior is usually *gradual* during extinction, a large number of responses may be performed before the undesirable behavior is eliminated. If an immediate intervention is required, extinction may be too slow to effect change. A second consideration is that responses may increase at the beginning of extinction. During this burst of responses, behavior may be reinforced inadvertently. If behavior is reinforced when it becomes worse, increasingly deviant behavior may result. Third, extinguished behavior sometimes recovers spontaneously even though responses are not reinforced. Again, a potential problem is that inadvertent reinforcement will reinstate the behavior when spontaneous recovery occurs. Fourth, extinction may be accompanied by undesirable emotional side effects such as anger or frustration. These states are not necessarily inherent in response reduction but are side effects which are likely to occur when alternate means of reinforcement are not provided.

While extinction can decrease or eliminate behaviors, it cannot develop new prosocial behaviors to replace those responses which have been extinguished. The most effective use of extinction is in combination with positive reinforcement for behaviors which are incompatible with or which will replace the undesirable behavior. This latter use of extinction is included in most behavior modification programs.

8

Self-Control

The principles of behavior modification describe lawful relations between various environmental conditions and behavior. These lawful relations and the techniques derived from them hold independently of who actually uses them (Homme, 1965). The techniques discussed previously represent instances in which one individual (the agent) manages the contingencies to alter the behavior of someone else (the client). Yet, the techniques can be applied by the client himself to control his own behavior. The present chapter will focus on self-control or the application of behavioral principles to modify one's own behavior.

In virtually every behavior modification program, external agents administer the reinforcing or punishing consequences. There are potential disadvantages in relying entirely on staff-administered contingencies (Kazdin, 1971b). First, teachers, parents, and other agents usually miss a great deal of behavior when applying reinforcement. Monitoring several clients in a group situation makes it virtually impossible to notice, not to mention reinforce, all instances of a target response. Second, agents who administer the contingencies may become a cue for performance of the target behavior because of their association with reinforcement and punishment. Behavior may be performed only in the presence of those who administer reinforcers (cf. Redd, 1969; Redd & Birnbrauer, 1969). Third, and related to the above, behaviors may not be performed as readily in situations in which external agents are not administering reinforcement because the client can easily discriminate different contingencies across situations. Fourth, individuals sometimes perform better when they are allowed to contribute to the planning of the program or choose the behaviors they are to perform rather than having the contingencies imposed upon them (e.g., Lovitt & Curtiss, 1969). Thus, performance may be enhanced by allowing the client some control over his own behavior (Kazdin, 1973e).

Aside from the possible limitations of externally administered contingencies, there are other reasons for interest in self-control. Almost all problems for which people seek therapy are not readily accessible to the therapist. For example, overeating, deviant sexual behavior, obsessive thoughts, phobic responses, and marital discord are not easily observable to the therapist. Of course, there are problems which therapists can readily observe such as tics, "free-floating" anxiety, and stuttering which are likely to be present both in the therapy session as well as extratherapy settings.

There is one area where only the client has access to the problem. Many problems for which individuals seek therapy entail *covert* or *private events* which include thoughts, images, fantasies, hallucinations, and dreams which are not "observable" by anyone other than the individual to whom they occur. As noted earlier, it has been suggested that covert events can be viewed as covert operant responses (referred to as coverants) (Homme, 1965). As overt operant responses, covert responses can be altered by varying the consequences which follow them. Since the client himself is the only one who can identify the occurrence of the coverant, he is in the best position to provide contingent consequences. Thus, for therapeutic problems involving private events, only the client can manage the contingencies.

Whether the behavior to be changed is overt or covert, behavior change in the situation in which the problem is occurring is the goal of therapeutic intervention. The therapist may ask the client to collect data on the extent of the target behavior, such as the number of cigarettes smoked, number of hours studied, or number of obsessive thoughts. After a clear rate of behavior has emerged, procedures are implemented in the client's everyday life to control performance outside of the therapy setting. Frequently individuals in the client's environment can serve this function and alter behavior (Ayllon & Wright, 1972; Guerney, 1969). However, the person in the best position to monitor behavior and provide consequences is the client himself. The client consults with the therapist for directions on precisely how this is done. The function of the therapist is to teach the client to alter his environment and serve as his own therapist. Therapy is instigated by the therapist but ultimately conducted entirely by the client (Kanfer & Phillips, 1966). Thus, to change behavior in the actual setting in which it is problematic, self-control techniques are helpful.

There is one additional reason for interest in self-control. The goal of behavior modification is to train an individual to control his or her own behavior and achieve self-selected goals. To require continuous control over a client by an external agent is not an end in itself. Whenever possible, external control is a means to achieve self-control. Self-control and external control can be viewed as opposite ends on a *continuum* rather than discrete procedures. Behavior modification programs vary in the degree to which the client has control over the contingencies and the administration of reinforcing or punishing consequences. Programs discussed in this chapter attempt to maximize the control the individual has over the training procedure. Of course, external control in some form is essential to initiate the program. Therapists train clients to exert self-control by providing recommendations, strong advice, systematic praise, and feedback, all of which are external influences on client behavior. Hopefully, after training the consequences which follow them. Since the client himself is the alter new behaviors across different situations. When this final stage is complete, self-control has been achieved.

Self-Control in Everyday Life

Individuals exert control over their own behavior in everyday actions such as selecting a course of action, abstaining from particular excesses, adhering to various rituals to sustain or recover health, and acting in ways which appear to violate self-interest. Yet, an individual controls his own behavior using techniques which resemble those he would use to control the behaviors of others, viz., by altering the antecedent and consequent conditions which control behavior (Skinner, 1953).

Skinner has noted that individuals control their own behavior in everyday life with a variety of techniques. First, an individual uses *physical restraint* such as clasping one's mouth to stifle a laugh, covering one's eyes to avoid seeing something, and clasping one's hands to avoid nailbiting. With this technique, the individual physically places restrictions on himself to achieve a particular end. Second, *changing the stimulus conditions* or cues which occasion the response is used to control behavior. For example, an individual usually selects a place to relax where there are few cues associated with work. Also, one lists appointments or important dates on a calendar so that these stimuli will increase the probability of engaging in certain behaviors at a later date. The cues (relaxing environs or written reminders) increase the likelihood that certain behaviors are performed. Third, *depriving or satiating* oneself can be used as a self-control technique. A person may deprive himself or herself of lunch in anticipation of a special dinner or prior to participation in an athletic event. Fourth, *emotional reactions* can be altered. A person can prevent an emotional reaction such as laughing by eliciting an incompatible response such as biting one's tongue. Pleasant or unpleasant feelings can be reinstated by conjuring up emotive memories and images. Fifth, people use *aversive events* in the environment to control behavior. For example, setting an alarm clock ensures that an aversive event (noise) will be presented. An individual may also make threatening statements to himself or herself such as, "If I don't do this, I will be late." Sixth, *drugs, alcohol, and stimulants* may be ingested specifically for self-control purposes. Alcohol may be consumed to alter one's mood or alleviate anxiety. Coffee may be consumed to increase alertness during studying or driving. Seven, *self-reinforcing and self-punishing operations* are employed to control behaviors. A person may derogate himself after failing to achieve a goal or verbally praise himself after accomplishing a feat. Finally, *doing something else* is a technique commonly used to control one's own behavior. An individual can engage in behaviors other than the one which leads to aversive consequences. For example, one can alter topics in the middle of the conversation to avoid an argument or whistle a happy tune whenever one feels afraid. Similarly, one can count sheep to avoid anxiety-provoking thoughts prior to going to sleep.

The above techniques used in everyday life allow the individual to control his own behavior. Most of the techniques operate by having the individual perform one behavior (a *controlling* response) which alters the probability of another behavior (a *controlled* response). Thus, a person may chew gum (controlling response) to reduce the likelihood of smoking cigarettes (controlled response). On the other hand, a person may wear a blindfold (controlling response) in a well-lighted room to increase the likelihood of sleeping (controlled response). In self-control training, the client is taught not only how to control a particular response, but also a technique which may be applied to new situations and behaviors as the client deems necessary.

Definition of Self-Control

Self-control refers to *those behaviors an individual deliberately undertakes to achieve self-selected outcomes*. The individual himself chooses the ends or goals and implements the procedures to achieve these goals. There may be external pressures brought to bear on an individual such as influence or coercion by one's parents, peers, or spouse to control certain behaviors. However, to qualify as self-control an individual must commit himself to that goal and apply the procedures to himself (Cautela, 1969; Goldfried & Merbaum, 1973; Kanfer & Phillips, 1970; Thoresen & Mahoney, 1974).

The notion of self-control usually is used to refer to the regulation of behaviors which have conflicting consequences, that is, which result in both positive reinforcement and punishment. There are two cases where consequences conflict (Kanfer & Phillips, 1970). In the first case, the reinforcing consequences which follow behavior are immediate and the punishing consequences are delayed. Behaviors in this category include excessive consumption of food, cigarettes, alcohol, and drugs. For example, excessive eating results in immediate positive reinforcement derived from the food. However, aversive consequences which follow overeating such as physical discomfort, obesity, and social ostracism attendant upon being overweight are delayed. In the second case, aversive or potentially aversive consequences which follow behavior are immediate and the reinforcing consequences, if present at all, are delayed. Behaviors in this category include heroic, altruistic, and charitable acts.

Self-control procedures have been applied primarily to behaviors which appear to have immediate positive reinforcing consequences and delayed aversive consequences. An individual performs a response which counteracts (or at least appears to counteract) the natural effects of external reinforcers. Indeed, self-control behaviors are sometimes considered to be defined by the absence of any external reinforcement (Kanfer & Phillips, 1970). (Of course, for any given behavior it is difficult to rule out the influence of external reinforcement contingencies. The absence of external contingencies may be more apparent than real in any given case.)

Development of Self-Control

Self-control is assumed to be a behavior learned in much the same way that other behaviors are. Individuals learn to control their own behavior according to the principles of learning, discussed earlier. As any other behavior, self-control may be specific to particular situations or somewhat general across many situations. For example, an athlete may adhere to a rigorous self-planned training regimen. Yet, the same individual may evince little or no "control" in other areas such as completing academic assignments. Alternatively, some athletes adhere both to rigorous athletic and academic schedules and perform well in both areas.

In early development, a child's behavior is controlled by external agents such as parents and teachers who set standards and provide consequences for performance. The standards vary for different behaviors. Some parents set high standards for musical or academic achievement but not for mechanical or social skills, or household chores. Indeed, standards may vary for different sex siblings within the same home. Positive reinforcement is provided when the child achieves the standard, whereas punishment (or lack of reward) is provided for performance below the standard. As training continues, achieving a particular standard may take on reinforcing consequences because achievement in the past was paired with external reinforcement. Conversely, the failure to achieve a standard may become aversive by being paired with punishment or lack of reward. Thus, attainment or lack of attainment of an externally or self-imposed standard may contain its own reward or punishment (Bandura, 1969). Through early training, the process of standard setting and providing consequences for achievement eventually becomes independent of external consequences.

The above interpretation of how self-reinforcement and punishment patterns of behavior develop has received some support (Bandura, 1969).

Laboratory research has shown that patterns of standard setting and self-reinforcement can be transmitted in ways consistent with that interpretation. For example, a person can learn to evaluate his or her own performance based upon how others evaluate that performance. Individuals who are rewarded generously by others are more generous in rewarding themselves (Kanfer & Marston, 1963). Thus, one administers reinforcers to oneself consistent with the way others have provided reinforcement.

Modeling also is extremely important in transmitting self-control patterns. For example, children adopt standards of reinforcement they observe in a model. If a child is exposed to a model who sets high or low standards for self-reinforcement, the child adopts similar standards for himself (Bandura & Kupers, 1964; Mischel & Liebert, 1966). Individuals exposed to models who have had low achievement standards tend to reward themselves highly for relatively mediocre performance (Bandura, 1969). The self-rewarding and self-critical statements made by a model are transmitted to and made by observers (Bandura & Kupers, 1964; Liebert & Allen, 1967).

Self-held standards and self-administered consequences for achievement also are regulated by others in everyday interaction. For example, self-reinforcement for achieving consensually low standards of performance is not looked upon favorably. Students rarely flaunt a "D" grade-point average in part because consensually the standard is low. Thus, standards of performance in self-reinforcing patterns are conveyed both through modeling, direct reinforcement, and social control (Bandura, 1971; Mischel & Liebert, 1966).

Techniques of Self-Control

Self-control patterns of behavior can be developed through behavior modification techniques to achieve specific therapeutic ends. There are five major techniques an individual can be trained to use to control his or her own behavior. The techniques are stimulus control, self-observation, self-reinforcement and self-punishment, self-instruction, and alternate response training. Although other techniques are available, they are less commonly employed than these five. Detailed accounts of other techniques can be obtained from various texts (Goldfried & Merbaum, 1973; Kanfer & Phillips, 1970; Thoresen & Mahoney, 1974; Watson & Tharp, 1972).

Stimulus Control. Specific behaviors are performed in the presence of specific stimuli. Eventually, the stimuli regularly associated with a behavior serve as cues and increase the probability that the behavior is performed. Three related types of behavioral problems result from maladaptive stimulus control. First, some behaviors are under the control of stimuli the client wishes to change. For example, cigarette smoking may be under the control of many stimuli, such as getting up in the morning, drinking coffee, talking with friends, studying, and being alone. Smoking is cued by a variety of situations because it has been associated with these situations. The therapeutic goal is to eliminate the control which these stimuli exert over smoking. Second, some behaviors are not controlled by a narrow range of stimuli when such control would be desirable. For example, students who have difficulty studying often have no particular setting, time, or cues associated with studying. Studying is not consistently performed in the presence of any particular stimuli. The therapeutic goal is to develop stimulus control over study behavior. Third, some behaviors are under control of inappropriate stimuli. Sexual deviance such as exhibitionism and fetishism are included in this category. In these behaviors, sexual responses are controlled by stimuli which deviate from appropriate stimuli as determined by social standards.

The three types of problems resulting from stimulus control are not easily separable in a given instance. For example, the eating behavior of obese individuals is controlled by many stimuli, rather than a narrow range of stimuli, in the external environment (Schachter, 1971). However, the stimuli are external cues (e.g., sight of food) rather than internal cues (e.g., hunger pangs), so inappropriate stimulus control is also operative.

An individual who is aware of how certain stimuli control his behavior can structure his environment so that he performs the behavior he wishes. For example, avoiding a bakery is one example of using stimulus control as a self-control technique. When going by the window of a bakery, a person may not be able to "control himself" from entering and purchasing pastry. However, not walking by the bakery or crossing the street right before approaching the bakery can remove the sight of the tempting stimuli (pastries) in the window so they cannot exert their influence. Self-control can be attained in the actual tempting situation by gradually approximating the original controlling stimulus in mild doses. The individual tempted by the bakery window can pass the window when the bakery is closed, walk by the bakery quickly when it is crowded, walk by while looking away, and stopping by the window after eating a large meal. By not entering the bakery in the presence of increasingly tempting cues, the bakery may no longer exert its influence over behavior.

Employing stimulus control usually requires that the therapist initially consult with the client to explain learning principles and various techniques useful in controlling the client's behavior. Stimulus control has been used along with other procedures to control excessive eating (Ferster, Nurnburger, & Levitt, 1962). For example, one adult male who wished to reduce his weight was told to eat at his "heart's content" (Goldiamond, 1965). However, when he ate, he was to sit at a table with a place setting in from of him and not to engage in any other activity. Within one week, the individual eliminated all between meal snacks and began to lose weight. Not engaging in other activities along with eating may have two effects. First, the act of eating is dissociated with other reinforcing events which can maintain undesirable (e.g., between meal) eating. Second, activities associated with eating may become cues for eating. For many individuals, eating occurs while they are watching television or a movie, reading, or talking on the phone. These activities can become stimuli which serve as the occasions for eating. To control eating, one should eat under a very narrow range of stimuli so that these other activities lose their power to control eating.

Stimulus control has also been used to develop study habits in college students (Fox, 1962). Poor study behavior often is associated with the absence of situations or environmental cues which are consistently paired with studying. In fact, "study-related" cues are associated with behaviors incompatible with studying such as talking with friends in the library, taking coffee breaks, and daydreaming. One student who had poor study habits was instructed to go to the library at a certain time each day and study in a particular room (Fox, 1962). Initially, the student took materials for only one subject. The student was told that he was to stay in the room, only if he was studying. If he daydreamed or felt disturbed, he was to leave. Before leaving, the student was to complete a small amount of work (e.g., read one page). Gradually, the assignment before leaving was increased to shape long periods of successful studying. The student could leave anytime nonstudying occurred. Although the procedure began with only a short amount of studying, eventually the student studied one hour per day for each course.

Insomnia has been treated using stimulus control. For whatever reasons insomnia develops, it follows a well-known pattern. The individual may be tired before retiring. As soon as he goes to bed, he may begin to ruminate and worry about the day's activities before going to sleep. The stimuli which are usually associated with sleeping (bed, darkness, and a specific time and place) become associated with behaviors incompatible with sleeping. For example, one adult insomniac went to bed about midnight, but was unable to fall asleep until approximately 3 A.M. or 4 A.M. (Bootzin, 1972). Before sleeping, he worried about several mundane problems and finally turned on television. He fell asleep while the television was still going. Treatment attempted to bring sleep under control of the stimuli associated with going to bed. The client was told to go to bed when he felt sleepy but not to read or watch television. If unable to sleep, he was to go into another room and stay up as long as he liked. When he again felt sleepy, he was to return to the bedroom. If he still could not sleep, he was to repeat the procedure continuously. For the first few days of treatment, the client got up four or five times each night before going to sleep. Yet after two weeks, he no longer got up at all. When he went to bed, he stayed there and fell asleep. The client reported sleeping much better as well as getting much more sleep each night. During a follow-up period conducted up to two months after treatment began, the client got up during the night less than once a week. Thus, the treatment appeared to work very well. Of course, since the procedure was not evaluated experimentally, one cannot be sure whether the stimulus control procedure accounted for the change. Nevertheless, the rationale of stimulus control and the ability of a client to apply the procedure to himself are nicely illustrated. Interestingly, the therapist who directed this case never had any contact with the client. The client's wife was responsible for explaining the procedure and reporting the results.

Stimulus control was used to treat a male college student who experienced sexually arousing sadistic fantasies (Davison, 1968). His fantasies, which involved inflicting torture on women, precipitated sexual arousal and masturbation. Thus, sexual arousal was under the control of sadistic fantasies. To associate more acceptable cues with sexual arousal, the client was instructed to masturbate while looking at either *Playboy* pictures or "real life" pictures of girls in lingerie or bathing suits. By repeated association of sexual arousal and orgasm with these stimuli, arousal eventually was controlled by these stimuli rather than by sadistic fantasies. Ultimately, the sadistic fantasies no longer were sexually arousing. Heterosexual arousal has also been developed in homosexuals by bringing masturbation under control of heterosexual fantasies.

Although stimulus control requires the therapist to explain the principles and techniques and recommend applications to the client, the client himself applies the procedures in his daily life. Of course, the client can extend use of stimulus control beyond the original area which served as the impetus for seeking counseling (Goldiamond, 1965; Kanfer & Phillips, 1970).

Self-observation. Control over behavior can be enhanced by observation of one's own behavior. As mentioned earlier, individuals adhere to certain standards of performance for various tasks and activities. When behavior departs from one's own standard or from a consensually held standard, the individual may attempt to control his behavior (Kanfer & Karoly, 1972; Kanfer & Phillips, 1970). For example, individuals who feel they are overweight, whether or not they are by medical standards, try to regulate their eating by carefully watching what they eat.

Most people are not entirely aware of the extent to which they engage in various behaviors. Habitual behaviors are automatic. People rarely observe their own behavior in a systematic fashion. However, when people are provided with the opportunity to observe their own behavior carefully, dramatic changes often occur. Careful observation of a response provides feedback to the individual, which can be compared with the standard the individual believes is appropriate. If behavior clearly departs from a cultural or self-imposed standard, self-corrective procedures begin to be employed until an acceptable level of behavior is met (Kanfer & Phillips, 1970). Thus, self-observation is effective insofar as it initiates other action on the part of the individual. The act of observation itself may be reinforcing or punishing (Homme, 1965). For example, for an individual who wishes to stop smoking, each time he records having smoked a cigarette may serve as mild punishment. On the other hand, for the individual who records hours of study behavior, each hour tallied may provide reinforcement. Although it is not entirely clear why self-observation is effective, it has been widely applied as a therapy technique (Kazdin, 1974c).

The use of self-observation in applied settings has been relatively sparse. In two junior high school classrooms, self-monitoring was used to control undesirable student behaviors (Broden, Hall, & Mitts, 1971). Observations were made of the study habits of an eighth-grade girl who was performing poorly on class assignments. After baseline, the girl was given a slip of paper and told that when she thought of it, she was to mark on the sheet whether she had been studying for the last few minutes (by marking a $+$) or whether she had not been studying (by marking a $-$). Figure 8–1 shows that when the girl recorded behavior, study time increased dramatically.

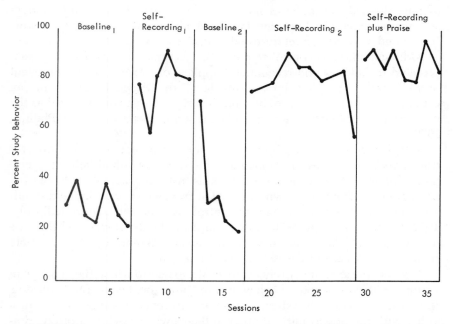

FIGURE 8–1 A record of Liza's study behavior during: *Baseline*₁—Before experimental procedures; *Self-Recording*₁—Liza recorded study or non-study on slips provided by counselor; *Baseline*₂—Self-recording slips withdrawn; *Self-Recording*₂ Self-recording slips reinstated; *Self-recording Plus Praise*—Self-recording slips continued and teacher praise for study increased. (Source: Broden, M., Hall, R. V., & Mitts, B. The effect of self-recording on the classroom behavior of two eighth-grade students. *Journal of Applied Behavior Analysis,* 1971, **4,** 191–99.)

When self-observation was temporarily discontinued, study behavior returned to baseline levels. When self-observation was again reinstated, study behavior again increased.

Another child in a different classroom talked out inappropriately in class (Broden et al., 1971). Observations were made of the number of incidents in which the boy talked inappropriately. After baseline, the boy was given a slip of paper and was told to put a mark on the sheet whenever he talked without permission. When the boy observed his behavior, his talk-outs per minute declined. Although self-observation initially had an effect, the frequency of talk-outs eventually was no different from the original baseline albeit the boy still recorded his own behavior. Other reports have also noted that the effects of self-observation sometimes attenuate over time (cf. Kazdin, 1974c).

Self-observation was used effectively to train two mothers to use behavior modification to control behavior of their "hyperactive" children at home (Herbert & Baer, 1972). Observers in each home recorded behavior of both the mother and child. The mothers attended to a variety of undesirable behaviors which probably contributed to the high frequency of breaking things, pounding on or marking furniture, stealing food, screaming, shouting, making threats, hitting others, among other disruptive behaviors. The mothers were told to observe the number of times they attended to appropriate behavior of their children and record their own behavior on a wrist counter that each mother wore. When the mothers observed their own behavior, their attention to appropriate child behavior increased. In addition, the children engaged in greater appropriate behavior. At the end of the program, one mother continued to monitor her behavior once in a while, whereas another mother stopped monitoring altogether. However, both mothers continued to attend to appropriate child behavior which remained at a high level.

Investigations have shown that self-recording behavior can influence smoking, overeating, tics, studying, and oral participation in class (Kazdin, 1974c). However, the effectiveness of self-observation has been inconsistent. A number of studies show that self-observation does not affect behavior. At the present time it is unclear why self-observation alters behavior in some situations but not in others. Nevertheless, self-observation can be used as a self-control technique in its own right or as part of other self-control techniques. For example, self-observation of one's behavior may be used along with self-reinforcement and self-punishment. Indeed, to apply consequences to one's own behavior one needs to know when and how frequently the behavior is occurring.

Self-reinforcement and Self-punishment.   Providing reinforcing or punishing consequences to oneself is used increasingly as a self-control technique. The client is trained to administer consequences to himself contingent upon behavior rather than to receive consequences from an external agent. Self-reinforcement has received more attention than self-punishment. As emphasized earlier, when the goal is to decrease a behavior, reinforcement of incompatible responses is especially important. This applies whether the individual himself or an external agent administers the contingencies.

The major requirement for self-reinforcement is that the individual is free to reward himself at *any time* whether or not he performs a particular response (Skinner, 1953). If an external agent influences or partially controls the delivery of reinforcement, then this is not complete self-control. The individual who reinforces himself must not be constrained to perform a particular response. To qualify as reinforcement, the behavior which is followed by a positive self-administered consequence must increase in probability. Similarly, a behavior followed by self-administered aversive events must decrease to qualify as punishment.

In most applications of self-reinforcement, two different procedures are used. First, the individual can determine the response requirements for a given amount of reinforcement, that is, when to deliver reinforcement and the amount to be delivered. When the individual determines the criteria for reinforcement, this is referred to as *self-determined reinforcement* (Glynn, 1970). Second, the individual can dispense reinforcement for achieving a particular performance criterion, which may or may not be self-determined. When the individual administers the reinforcers to himself, this is referred to as *self-administered reinforcement*. Who administers the reinforcers (oneself or someone else) is not crucial. The crucial element is determining when to deliver reinforcement and for what behaviors. However, if an individual is not permitted to self-administer reinforcers, there may be constraints from external agents which influence self-reinforcement. Thus, self-reinforcement is probably best achieved by allowing the individual to self-determine and self-administer reinforcement. Self-reinforcement usually requires the individual to observe and record his behavior to determine whether it has met a criterion. Thus, self-reinforcement usually involves self-observation which may also contribute to the overall effectiveness of self-reinforcement.

Self-reinforcement has only recently been used in applied settings. The applications have been restricted mainly to classroom settings. Glynn, Thomas, and Shee (1973) had elementary school students record whether they were paying attention whenever a "beep" sounded from a tape recorder. A beep sounded at randomly selected intervals so that the students could not predict their occurrence. Each time a student self-recorded paying attention, he earned one minute of free time. When students recorded their own behavior and thereby determined their own reinforcement, the rate of paying attention was high. When self-reinforcement procedures were withdrawn, attentiveness declined. Similar findings have been reported in other classrooms where students reward themselves with points exchangeable for back-up rewards (Bolstad & Johnson, 1972; Glynn, 1970; Lovitt & Curtiss, 1969).

In a psychiatric hospital, "emotionally disturbed" children participated in a classroom project in the hospital (Santogrossi, O'Leary, Romanczyk, & Kaufman, 1973). The effects of teacher-determined versus self-determined points were evaluated on disruptive student behavior. The points each child received were exchangeable for snacks, fruits, and prizes. When the teacher administered points, disruptive classroom behavior decreased. However, when the students were given the opportunity to reward themselves, they did so *noncontingently* and disruptive behavior increased. Thus, self-reinforcement led to administration of rewards for undesirable behavior.

Self-reinforcement has been used in outpatient treatment. Mahoney, Moura, and Wade (1973) compared different self-control techniques for weight loss. Self-reward clients initially deposited money with the experimenter. At each weigh-in, clients could reward themselves by taking back some of the money they had deposited. Self-punishment subjects fined themselves money that they had initially deposited with the experimenter when they did not lose weight. Specifically, they determined how much money would be permanently lost. Another group could self-reward or self-punish. A final self-control group simply monitored their weight and eating habits daily. After four weeks of treatment, only the self-reward group showed a greater reduction in weight relative to the self-monitoring group and another group that only received information about weight-loss. Weight-loss was maintained after four months of treatment.

Self-reinforcement has been used to develop social responses in male college students who had difficulty in meeting and dating girls (Rehm & Marston, 1968). Self-reinforcement subjects selected tasks involving social interaction with females, such as sitting next to a female in class, calling up a girl for a date, expressing affection, among others. Students were told to engage in the tasks and to deliver points to themselves depending upon how well they did. The therapist praised the students at weekly therapy sessions depending upon how many points were self-administered. Self-reinforcement subjects showed a reduction in anxiety and an increase in social interaction at the end of treatment. These gains were maintained when last checked, seven to nine months after treatment.

Self-punishment has been used primarily in outpatient settings. For example, to control overeating, clients are trained to administer aversive consequences to themselves (Ferster et al., 1962; Harris, 1969). At the beginning of treatment, clients were told to compose a list of those ultimate consequences of eating which they found especially aversive. Consequences such as being rejected socially, overhearing verbal references of other people to obesity, incurring physical diseases, and having problems in attracting a mate were some of the reasons listed and served as the aversive consequences of overeating. These aversive consequences are used to suppress undesirable kinds of eating by applying them before eating. For example, when an individual sits down to eat a rich dessert, he can vividly imagine and recite the aversive consequences of overeating which he regards as important. The aversive consequences which are normally delayed can be brought close to the actual act of eating. In this way, self-punishment can be used to suppress behaviors leading to overeating. Self-punishment usually is combined with several other procedures such as stimulus control, nutritional training, and reinforcement for weight loss.

In another self-punishment technique, the client *imagines* both the behavior he wishes to decrease and the aversive consequence. The client can imagine himself engaged in an undesirable behavior (e.g., overeating or alcohol consumption). When this is vivid, he can imagine an aversive consequence associated with the behavior (e.g., feeling nauseous). The procedure is referred to as *covert sensitization* (Cautela, 1966, 1967). Covert sensitization builds up an aversion to stimuli which previously served as a source of attraction. It is a *covert* technique because the procedure is conducted entirely in the client's imagination. Thus, the client does not have to actually engage in the behavior. Both the target behavior and punishment of the behavior are rehearsed in imagination. An example of a scene used for the treatment of an alcoholic is presented below (Cautela, 1967). The alcoholic imagined himself entering a bar or drinking which was followed by aversive consequences.

> You are walking into a bar. You decide to have a glass of beer. You are now walking toward the bar. As you are approaching the bar you have a funny feeling in the pit of your stomach. Your stomach feels all queasy and nauseous. Some liquid comes up your throat and it is very sour. You try to swallow it back down, but as you do this, food particles start coming up your throat to your mouth. You are now reaching the bar and you order a beer. As the bartender is pouring the beer, puke comes into your mouth. You try to keep your mouth closed and swallow it back down. You reach for the glass of beer to wash it down. As soon as your hand touches the glass, you can't hold it down any longer. You have to open your mouth and you puke. It goes all over your hand, all over the glass and the beer. You can see it floating around in the beer. Snots and mucous come out of your nose. Your shirt and pants are all full of vomit. The bartender has some on his shirt. You notice people looking at you. You get sick again and you vomit some more and more. You turn away from the beer and immediately you start to feel better. As you run out of the bar room, you start to feel better and better. When you get out into the clean fresh air you feel wonderful. You go home and clean yourself up [pp. 461–462].

Aside from the punishment component, negative reinforcement is included in the scenes. The aversive events are *withdrawn* when the individual leaves the setting. Although treatment in covert sensitization initially is guided by the therapist, the client learns to apply the imagination procedure to himself at home or in problematic situations. Also, new behaviors a client wishes to decrease and eliminate can be treated in this fashion. Covert sensitization has been used to alter homosexuality, obesity, drug addiction, smoking, and obsessive-compulsive behaviors (cf. Cautela, 1972).

Self-administered shock has also been used as a self-punishment technique for craving drugs (Wolpe, 1965), engaging in deviant sexual behavior (McGuire & Vallance, 1964), and smoking cigarettes (Powell & Azrin, 1968). In some cases, self-shock is delivered in therapy situations, whereas in others the client carries a portable shock device with him. Other self-applied aversive events include tearing up dollar bills and giving up money to charity each time an undesirable target response is performed (Axelrod et al., 1974).

Self-instruction. Language directed toward oneself has been considered important in controlling one's own behavior (e.g., Dollard & Miller, 1950; Luria, 1961; Skinner, 1953). Indeed, psychotherapy sometimes focuses on self-defeating verbalizations a person makes to himself which contribute to maladaptive and irrational behavior.

Developmental psychologists have proposed that the speech of external agents (e.g., parents) controls and directs behavior in early childhood. The child eventually develops a self-directed verbal repertoire which derives from the speech of these external agents. For example, children self-administer verbal praise and criticism which they observe in the behavior of adult models (Bandura & Kupers, 1964; Liebert & Allen, 1967). Similarly, children verbally administer self-instructional statements to guide their actions. While the instructions of others continue to influence behavior throughout life, the self-instructional statements also exert control. Self-instructional statements, while usually private or covert, are sometimes evident in everyday life when an individual "thinks out loud" and describes a particular course of action he believes he should pursue. For example, in preparation for asking an employer for a raise, an individual may tell himself what he would say when the situation arises. Indeed, the self-verbalizations may be used while the individual performs the actual conversation.

Self-instruction training has been used directly to develop self-control. The individual is trained to control his behavior by making suggestions and specific comments which guide his behavior in a fashion similar to being instructed by someone else. Investigations have shown that children use or can be trained to make statements to themselves which guide their behavior. In one report, elementary school boys were allowed to earn prizes by working on a task (O'Leary, 1968). The likelihood of earning a prize could be enhanced by cheating on the task and taking tokens (exchangeable for prizes) at an inappropriate time. All children were made aware of the "right" and "wrong" behaviors. Some children were told to tell themselves whether they *should* make the response before actually responding. Other children did not instruct themselves. The self-instruction group showed fewer transgressions than those who did not self-instruct themselves. Thus, self-instructions restrained cheating.

Meichenbaum (1969) trained schizophrenic patients to talk rationally. Training consisted of delivering praise and token reinforcement for coherent talk without any self-instructional training. At the end of training, patients showed a reduction in inappropriate talk. As a test for generalization of training, patients were given a new task, namely, the interpretation of proverbs. Patients previously trained to speak appropriately gave more coherent interpretations of the proverbs. Interestingly, some patients trained to emit coherent talk *spontaneously* repeated the experimenter's instructions to themselves when presented with the generalization task. Patients said to themselves, "give 'healthy' talk, be coherent and relevant," while interpreting the proverbs. Self-instruction appeared to aid the patients with the proverb task. Patients appeared to attend to the task as a result of their own instructions even though they were not explicitly trained to instruct themselves.

Self-instructional training was used with "impulsive" and "hyperactive" children (Meichenbaum & Goodman, 1971). The children tended to make errors that resulted from performing tasks quickly without deliberation. To train methodical work habits, the experimenter modeled careful performance on tasks such as coloring figures, copying lines, and solving problems. As the experimenter performed the tasks, he talked out loud to himself. The verbalizations modeled by the experimenter included: (1) questions about the nature of the task, (2) answers to these questions by mentally rehearsing and planning his actions, (3) self-instructions in the form of self-guidance, and (4) self-reinforcement. Essentially, the experimenter modeled "thinking out loud." Then the impulsive children were trained to do the task while instructing themselves out loud just as the experimenter had done. Eventually they were trained to do the task while whispering the instructions and then saying them covertly (privately) without lip movements or sounds. Training in self-instruction resulted in a reduction of "impulsive" errors. Children who met with the experimenter and practiced the tasks but did not receive self-instruction training failed to improve.

Self-instructional training has also been used to train schizophrenic patients to pay attention while performing motor and verbal tasks (Meichenbaum & Cameron, 1973). Behavioral gains resulting from training were maintained three weeks after training. Moreover, the effects of self-instructional training transferred to tasks not originally included in training. Anxiety stemming from fear of animals, delivering speeches, and taking tests have all been ameliorated effectively with self-instructional training

(Meichenbaum, 1973). In each situation, the client is trained to recognize the self-defeating verbalizations in which he engages. Further, new adaptive self-verbalizations which can guide behavior are substituted.

Alternate Response Training. The final self-control technique to be discussed is training an individual to engage in responses which interfere with or replace the response which is to be controlled or eliminated. To achieve this, the individual must have an alternate response in which to engage. For example, an individual can think of pleasant thoughts to control worrying or can relax to control tension. Similarly, a person can tolerate greater pain levels if he engages in nonpain related (i.e., distracting) activities rather than not engage in other activities (Kanfer & Goldfoot, 1966).

The most frequent application of alternate response training is to control anxiety. Relaxation has been widely used as a response which is incompatible with and therefore an alternative to anxiety. Typically, a client is trained by a therapist to relax deeply. Different methods have been used to achieve deep relaxation. Usually a client is trained to alternately tense and relax individual muscle groups (Jacobson, 1938). Alternately tensing and relaxing helps the individual discriminate different levels of muscle relaxation. Within a few sessions, the client can become deeply relaxed (Paul, 1966; Wolpe, 1958, 1969). A client may also be trained to provide suggestions to himself (i.e., self-instructions) of feeling warmth and heaviness in the muscles to help relaxation (Schultz & Luth, 1959). Once relaxation is developed, the client can apply the skill in any situation which is anxiety provoking. Relaxation has been self-applied to overcome anxiety toward the opposite sex (D'Zurilla, 1969), fear associated with natural childbirth (Kondas & Scetnicka, 1972), anxiety associated with public speaking (Migler & Wolpe, 1967) and interviews (Zeisset, 1968), and to inhibit the tendency to exhibit oneself (Hutchinson, 1962).

In a recent report, relaxation was used to help an 11-year-old girl control insomnia (Weil & Goldfried, 1973). The girl spent approximately two hours awake each night trying to go to sleep. She ruminated about the previous day's activities and was sensitive to external noises which interferred with sleep. She was also upset whenever her parents left for the evening and remained awake until they returned. Focusing on the insomnia, a therapist visited one night while the girl was going to sleep and gave her relaxation instructions. The therapist told her to tense and relax her muscles and gradually become more and more relaxed. The girl eventually went to sleep within one hour rather than the usual two hours. A 30-minute tape with relaxation instructions was given to her. She used it for a few weeks before going to bed each night. Tapes of a shorter duration were eventually substituted until the final one which was only five minutes long. After a total of five weeks of treatment, the tape was withdrawn. The girl was told to concentrate on self-relaxation when she went to bed. She reported going to sleep immediately. Going to sleep was not a problem when checked six months after treatment. Initially, the therapist provided a technique to help the child. Yet, the child eventually applied the procedures to herself.

Engaging in an alternate behavior was used to control persistent scratching of a 21-year-old woman (Watson, Tharp, & Krisberg, 1972). Since the age of four, the woman had suffered from itchy rashes on her legs, arms, and hands. Prior to treatment, the woman recorded the daily number of instances of scratching. Initially, self-observation led to a decrease in scratching. Yet, after a week, behavior returned to its initial high level. For two weeks, the client was told to substitute another response in place of scratching. She was instructed to stroke herself, every time she felt like scratching. Scratching and stroking were both observed. Figure 8–2 shows that during the first treatment phase (Plan 1) after baseline, the use of an alternate response was associated with decreases in scratching. In the next phase (Plan 2), the client devised a reinforcement program where she awarded herself points when she stroked instead of scratched. Points were used to purchase her daily bath. In the next phase (Plan 3), she substituted patting for stroking herself. Figure 8–2 also shows the frequency of patting. By the last few days of the program, no further scratching occurred. Dur-

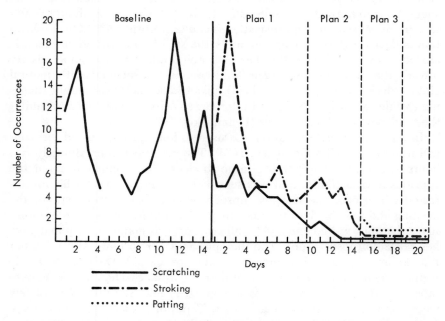

FIGURE 8–2 Occurrences of scratching, stroking, and patting during the different experimental procedures. (Source: Watson, D L., Tharp, R. G., & Krisberg, J. Case study in self-modification: Suppression of inflamatory scratching while awake and asleep. *Journal of Behavior Therapy and Experimental Psychiatry,* 1972, **3,** 213–15. Reprinted with permission from Pergamon Press.)

ing the one-and-one half years following treatment, scratching had returned twice but was eliminated with the self-application of behavioral techniques.

Important Considerations of Self-Control Techniques

In each of the self-control strategies reviewed above, an external agent or therapist was required to initiate the procedure. At the very minimum, the client was trained briefly in the techniques and principles which he or she subsequently applied in everyday situations. Training sometimes requires a number of sessions where the individual consults with a therapist. In applied settings such as a classroom, self-control training may be conducted over a period of weeks at which time control by the teacher is gradually withdrawn (Drabman, Spitalnik, & O'Leary, 1973).

Some authors (Morgan & Bass, 1973; Stuart, 1972) have questioned whether self-control has really been studied. In all investigations, there seems to be considerable external control over the "self-control" program. Investigations of self-reinforcement illustrate that control exerted by an external agent may play a *major* role. Recall that the requirement for self-reinforcement is that the individual can administer the reinforcer at any time, for any response as he sees fit (Skinner, 1953). Yet, in self-reinforcement studies recommendations are made to the client when the individual should administer the consequences to himself and what standards of performance should be invoked (Bolstad & Johnson, 1972; Mahoney et al., 1973). For example, in some studies the individual is told that he can give himself a reinforcer for performing *correctly* on a task (Felixbrod & O'Leary, 1973), for *losing* weight (Mahoney et al., 1973), or for *interacting* socially (Rehm & Marston, 1968), and that only a *certain amount* of the reinforcer should be taken (Mahoney et al., 1973). Thus, the reinforcement which is to be controlled by oneself is subjected to external contingencies (Stuart, 1972) and constraints by others (Morgan & Bass, 1973). At the present time, it is unclear to what extent an individual can carry out aspects of the contingencies without external control by others. Yet, as mentioned earlier, self-control should be considered a matter of *degree* where external control is minimal or intermittent. As external control over behavior is withdrawn and the individual exerts more control over himself, two major questions remain. To what extent will an individual continue to apply the consequences to himself contingently? Second, what is the range of populations which will be able to continue self-administered contingencies with minimal control by external agents?

Applying Consequences Contingently. Administration of consequences to oneself for certain behavior raises important questions. Will an individual reward himself for meeting a predetermined performance criterion and deliver punishment for failing to meet the criterion over a long period of time? Although the client may reinforce himself for performance for a specific target behavior, there is no automatic penalty for reinforcing oneself without performing that behavior (Morgan & Bass, 1973). Indeed, if the individual "weakens" just once by lowering standards for self-reinforcement or administering the reinforcer without performing the target response, he will be reinforced for *ignoring* the contingency. The effect will be to increase the probability of violating the contingency. For example, if an individual devises a contingency whereby he will only watch television (high probability behavior) after exercising (low probability behavior), this would be an example of self-reinforcement. The individual allows himself access to the reinforcer after exercising. However, one day he may decide to watch television without exercising. Television will reinforce violation of the original contingency, that is, not exercising. The likelihood of nonexercising will increase (Morgan & Bass, 1973).

In a program to develop study skills of college students with low grades (McReynolds & Church, 1973), students devised "self-contracts" where they specified small response requirements over a few days (e.g., study for a few minutes each day) to acquire reinforcers (e.g., cigarettes or attending a sports event). A new contract was drawn up at the end of a few days as behavior met the previously specified criteria. Despite the fact that students devised the response criteria themselves—or perhaps because of it—many subjects rewarded themselves even though the requirements for the behavioral contract had *not* been met.

Recently, classroom studies suggest that children who are permitted to reinforce themselves sometimes become lenient over time. For example, in one project students were told they could determine the number of points (exchangeable for prizes) earned for correct arithmetic answers. Students who determined the number of points per correct answer did as well as those who had a fixed number of points assigned for correct responses. However, those who selected their own standards for earning rewards were more lenient and became increasingly lenient over time (Felixbrod & O'Leary, 1973). Similarly, children reinforced themselves noncontingently when given control over the contingencies in a classroom setting. Students performed disruptively but continued to reward themselves (Santogrossi et al., 1972).

In light of the above reports, it is possible that allowing the individual to reward himself may lead to the noncontingent delivery of reinforcers, a procedure which is not usually associated with improvements in behavior. Alternative strategies are available to decrease the likelihood that individuals will self-reinforce themselves noncontingently. First, in most classroom studies, students are reinforced by the teacher or an external observer for a period of time before the self-reinforcement program begins. During the external reinforcement phase, the expected requirements for self-reinforcement are made explicit to the children. As mentioned earlier, standards of performance and reinforcement can be conveyed from the behavior of others. Thus, when students are reinforced by a teacher, they probably temporarily acquire a standard of self-reinforcement. This would explain why students initially may not reinforce themselves more generously than external agents (Glynn, 1970). A second strategy to discourage the noncontingent self-administration of reinforcers is to reinforce individuals for their contingent delivery of reinforcers. In a recent report, also in a classroom, children were reinforced for reinforcing themselves contingently (Drabman et al., 1973). Thus, the children were trained not to be lenient when they had the opportunity to self-reward. This procedure was successful for the short period in which the children could self-reward. Although providing externally controlled consequences is effective in ensuring the contingent delivery of self-reward, it challenges somewhat the notion of "self-control" as usually conceived.

Delivering aversive events to oneself also introduces the problem of leniency. As mentioned earlier, an aversive event administered by an external agent may result in escape or avoidance. There is no reason to believe that a similar phenomenon will not take place with self-administered aversive events. The individual may avoid applying the aversive event to himself. The client can avoid the self-administered aversive event in one of two ways. The aversive event can be avoided either by not performing the undesirable behavior or by simply performing the behavior but not applying the aversive event afterwards. For example, for one client, a self-administered punishment contingency to reduce smoking consisted of destroying a one-dollar bill for each cigarette smoked (Axelrod et al., 1974). To avoid losing money, the individual could stop smoking. Alternatively, she could smoke but not destroy the money. Of course, the second procedure is not self-punishment and is not likely to alter smoking. However, *both* procedures are effective in avoiding the aversive event. Which one will be performed?

With both self-reinforcement and self-punishment, the clients may discontinue the contingency at any time because it is under their complete control. If the client suspends the contingency, even temporarily, he will be reinforced (obtain the positive reinforcer or avoid the aversive event). Hence, a concern with self-control procedures is what will maintain adherence to the contingency. Hopefully, the delayed reinforcing consequences or intended goal of the program (e.g., being thin to a previously obese individual) will sustain self-control. Everyday experience suggests that delayed consequences are not sufficient to maintain adherence to self-imposed contingencies. More often than not, individuals appear to go off diets, resume cigarette smoking, or give up some other contingency they originally designed. It is possible to train individuals to delay reinforcement so that they are not tempted by reinforcers immediately available (Mischel & Ebbesen, 1970). Development of the ability to delay reinforcement may be necessary to ensure that self-administration of consequences is contingent upon behavior. In addition, it may be important to provide individuals with some external reinforcement (perhaps delivered by friend, relative, or spouse) for adherence to the "self-control" contingency. Gradually, external reinforcement might be delivered increasingly intermittently, and eventually eliminated altogether.

Range of Application of Self-control Techniques. Another issue is whether self-control techniques can be extended to populations seen in diverse applied settings. Perhaps, self-control techniques are limited to clients who have enough control to initiate the procedures. As mentioned earlier, most of the self-control procedures have been carried out with adults on an outpatient basis (Goldfried & Merbaum, 1973). However, outpatient groups characteristically show initial control by seeking treatment of some kind and attending therapy. Inpatient populations such as institutionalized retardates, the "emotionally disturbed," psychiatric patients, delinquents, and others might not be able to carry out self-control techniques. For many of these groups, treatment is not initially sought but rather imposed. Hence, there may be little incentive to initiate or carry out the self-control contingencies.

Yet, even at this early stage of self-control research, the results have been encouraging for different treatment populations. Treatment groups using the self-control procedures discussed earlier have included adult (Meichenbaum & Cameron, 1973) and adolescent hospitalized psychiatric patients (Kaufman & O'Leary, 1972; Santogrossi et al., 1973), and children in elementary and junior high school classes (Broden et al., 1971; Drabman et al., 1973: Glynn, 1970; Glynn et al., 1973; Lovitt & Curtiss, 1969). There is a paucity of work with delinquents and retarded clients using self-control techniques. Preliminary evidence indicates that delinquents can play a major role in self-government in a home-style training facility (Fixsen et al., 1973). Whether there is any treatment population for whom self-control techniques are unsuited remains to be determined.

The application of self-control techniques raises important questions which remain to be solved before the procedures will enjoy widespread use. Yet, even at this early stage of development, self-control procedures represent promising means to help an individual gain increasingly greater control over his own behavior. Whether the individual's goal is to eliminate debilitating behavior or to develop socially appropriate behaviors, self-control can be acquired to achieve the end.

Conclusion

Self-control refers to those behaviors an individual deliberately undertakes to achieve self-selected outcomes. Behavioral techniques are applied by the individual himself rather than by an external agent. Laboratory work has shown that patterns of self-reinforcement and punishment can be developed according to the principles which control other behaviors. Direct reinforcement and modeling can convey performance standards by which an individual evaluates his or her own behavior and provides reinforcing and punishing consequences.

Five techniques of self-control were discussed. First, *stimulus control* allows an individual to control his or her own behavior by altering environmental and situational events which serve as cues for behaviors. The client can design the environment so that certain cues increase the likelihood that specific behaviors are performed and other cues which have an unwanted controlling effect no longer influence behavior. Second, *self-observation* requires that an individual keep a careful record of the target response. Often merely observing one's behavior leads to a systematic change. Third, *self-reinforcement and self-punishment* require that a person apply certain events to himself following behavior. The crucial aspect of self-reinforcement or punishment is that the individual is entirely free to partake of the reinforcer or not apply the punishing event but does so of his or her own accord. Fourth, *self-instructional training* develops patterns of instructing oneself how to perform. The instructions allow an individual to analyze a situation and specify the requirements for his or her own performance. Once the instructional set is learned, the individual can apply the technique across a variety of situations. Finally, *alternate response training* requires that an individual engage in a response which interferes with or replaces the response the client wishes to control. In each of the self-control techniques, some preliminary training is required to convey to the client the principle behind the technique and the requirements for effective application. However, once the basic principle is understood and initial training is completed, the client can control the program and determine what behaviors to change.

Two potential limitations of self-control techniques were discussed. First, since the client himself has complete control over the contingencies, it is possible that he will not adhere to them. For example, the individual may reinforce himself even though he has not engaged in the target behavior. Not carrying out the contingency faithfully will be reinforced, if the client so chooses. Thus, it is not clear whether long-term effects of self-control procedures will be sustained. A second issue is whether a wide range of populations can be trained to use self-control procedures. The majority of studies are restricted to outpatient populations who initially seek treatment, that is, show some initial "self-control" to begin with. However, there are some demonstrations in school settings and with institutionalized psychiatric patients. Self-control appears to include a set of promising techniques for decreasing the influence of external agents and allowing the client greater autonomy in guiding his or her own behavior.

9

Response Maintenance and Transfer of Training

It is an achievement to dramatically reduce deviant behavior and to develop socially desirable behavior as behavior modification techniques have done. Yet the significance of the achievement is minor, if behavior reverts to its preprogram level after the program is withdrawn. What happens when the program is discontinued? Further, if the clients leave the setting in which behavior was altered, will the changes carry over to the new setting? The issues raised by these questions are referred to as response maintenance or resistance to extinction and transfer of training, respectively.

Response maintenance is an obvious problem in behavior modification programs. When the reversal design is used to demonstrate a causal effect of the program, appropriate behavior usually declines. As discussed earlier, the effects of a program can be demonstrated by returning to baseline conditions, after the program has been in effect. If desirable behavior declines when the program is withdrawn and improves when the program is introduced, a causal relationship is demonstrated. Withdrawing the program to show a reversal in behavior provides a preview of the conditions the individual will face once the program is completely terminated. If behavior reverses and the program is withdrawn or altered in some way, behavior change must be transient. This conclusion seems warranted in light of the frequent successful demonstrations using the reversal design.

Transfer of training represents another concern. Do the behaviors altered in one situation transfer to other situations in which the program has never been in effect? For example, does administration of reinforcement for cooperative behavior in the home transfer to behavior in the classroom, on the playground, at camp, and other situations? Since behavior is often situation specific, transfer of training should be as much a problem as response maintenance. Indeed, this is reflected in the use of the multiple-baseline design across situations. As discussed at length earlier, in this version of the multiple-baseline design the contingency is introduced to control a particular behavior across different situations. The contingency is introduced in the situations at different points in time. The design relies upon the failure of behavior change in one situation to generalize to other situations. The contingency can only be considered responsible for change, if behavior does not change in a given situation, until the contingency is introduced.

Response maintenance and transfer of training usually are not separate problems. In most instances, both of them are at issue simultaneously. For example, if a psychiatric patient leaves the hospital and returns home, both resistance to extinction and transfer of training are important. Reinforcement is no longer forthcoming (i.e., extinction) and the setting is different from the hospital where the program was conducted (i.e., transfer). Transfer of training does not always include resistance to extinction. For example, reinforcement programs are often implemented in classroom situations at one time of the day only (e.g., morning). Transfer of training can be studied by determining whether behavior changes during other periods (e.g., afternoon). Resistance to extinction is not relevant here because the target behavior is still reinforced in the morning. The issue is whether the reinforced behaviors transfer or generalize to other situations while the program is in effect. The present chapter will focus on the evidence bearing on both response maintenance and transfer of training. Additionally, procedures will be discussed which can be used to increase the likelihood that behaviors will be maintained and carry over to new situations.

Response Maintenance

Although reversal designs are used extensively, behaviors do not always revert to preprogram levels once the program is withdrawn. For example, in a reinforcement program for elementary school students, children were reinforced for working on their assignments (Surratt et al., 1969). After reinforcement was no longer provided, three of four students continued to perform better six weeks after the program than they had during the initial baseline. Thus, for almost all of the students the effects of the program were maintained. Other investigators have reported response maintenance after removing programs in classroom settings (Hewett et al., 1969; Whitman et al., 1970).

In hospital settings, behavior changes are sometimes maintained for long periods after the program has been terminated. One psychotic patient, treated for excessive hoarding of towels, no longer hoarded one year after the program had been withdrawn (Ayllon, 1963). Another patient displayed "normal" eating behavior (going to the hospital dining room and eating without assistance) two years after the program was terminated (Ayllon, 1965). Appropriate eating was maintained in an institutionalized retarded girl one year after training (Hamilton & Allen, 1967). In day-care facilities for the retarded, changes in productivity and bizarre behavior have been maintained after the programs are withdrawn (Kazdin, 1971a; Zimmerman et al., 1969). Despite the above investigations, behaviors *usually* extinguish when a program is withdrawn.

When responses are maintained after consequences have been withdrawn, the precise reason is usually unclear. A behavior should reflect the contingencies which operate in the environment. When the contingencies are withdrawn, one can only speculate why the response is maintained. Various explanations have been offered. First, it is possible that behaviors developed through a reinforcement program may come under control of other reinforcers in the setting (Baer et al., 1968; Bijou et al., 1969). Events associated with the delivery of reinforcement acquire reinforcement value (Medland & Stachnik, 1972). Even though the programmed reinforcers are withdrawn, behavior may be maintained by other reinforcers. For example, behaviors may be maintained in a classroom in which token reinforcers were previously used because the teacher has been consistently associated with token reinforcement. The teacher may be a more powerful reinforcer after the program and maintain performance of the students without using other reinforcers such as tokens (Chadwick & Day, 1971).

A second and related explanation of response maintenance is that after reinforcers are withdrawn, reinforcers which result directly from the activities themselves maintain behavior. Many behaviors result in their own reinforcement. For example, reading, social or eating skills may be maintained because once they are developed, they are reinforced by their normal consequences. In one report, a preschool child was reinforced with praise and teacher attention for using outdoor play equipment in an attempt to develop her social contact with other children and motor skills (Buell et al., 1968). Interestingly, social interaction (e.g., talking with and touching other children) increased even though it was not directly reinforced. When social reinforcement was withdrawn for playing with equipment, this behavior decreased in frequency. However, the child continued to interact socially with others. Possibly, social contact of the child was maintained by the reinforcing aspects of interacting.

A final explanation of response maintenance is that even though the program is terminated and reinforcers are withdrawn, the agents administering the program (parents, teachers, and staff) have changed in their behavior in some permanent fashion. The agents may continue to use the principles of behavior modification even though a specific program has been withdrawn (cf. Patterson, Cobb, & Ray, 1973). For example, if a contingency contract system in the home is withdrawn, a child's desirable behavior may still be maintained at a high level. Although the contract is terminated, the parents may provide reinforcement (allowance and praise) and punishment (loss of privileges) more systematically than they had prior to the contract system. Unfortunately, there is almost no evidence showing that the behavior of those who administer a behavior modification program is permanently altered (see Kazdin & Moyer, 1975). As soon as a program is withdrawn, the agents who administer the program frequently revert to behaviors previously used to control client behavior (e.g., Cooper, Thomson, & Baer, 1970; Panyan, Boozer, & Morris, 1970; Katz, Johnson, & Gelfand, 1972).

Each of the above explanations of response maintenance is usually offered *post hoc*. After behavior fails to reverse when the program is withdrawn, an investigator may speculate why this occurred. Any of the explanations may be correct in a given instance. Yet, maintenance of behavior is more clearly understood when it is *predicted* in advance on the basis of using procedures to develop resistance to extinction, rather than when extinction does not occur and has to be explained.

In spite of the above examples and explanations of response maintenance, removal of the contingencies usually results in a decline of performance to or near baseline levels. A reversal of behavior to baseline conditions has been shown after the program is withdrawn across a wide range of settings and clients (Kazdin & Bootzin, 1972; Kazdin & Craighead, 1973; O'Leary & Drabman, 1971). If response maintenance is a goal of the program, it has to be systematically programmed into the setting rather than assumed to occur automatically (Baer et al., 1968).

Transfer of Training across Situations

In most behavior modification programs, alteration of behavior in one situation does not result in a transfer of those changes to other situations either while the program is in effect or after it has been withdrawn (Kazdin & Bootzin, 1972). Indeed, the range of stimulus conditions controlling behavior often is quite narrow. Typically, behavior changes are restricted to the specific setting in which training has taken place and to the presence of those who administered the program (Lovaas & Simmons, 1969; Redd, 1969; Redd & Birnbrauer, 1969; Risley, 1968). However, examples of generalization of behavior across situations have been reported.

In a psychiatric hospital, two patients were reinforced for talking with each other during daily sessions conducted in a special treatment room (Bennett & Maley, 1973). Dramatic changes were made in talking during the sessions. In addition, social interaction on the ward increased even though it was not reinforced. When reinforcement was withdrawn in the individual sessions, performance on the ward was maintained. The social responses were maintained after training and transferred to the ward.

In the classroom, programs altering behavior during one part of the day such as the morning or afternoon period, sometimes demonstrate behavior change at other periods of the day even though performance during these other periods is not reinforced (Kazdin, 1973h; Walker et al., 1971). Additionally, in programs for predelinquents, altering speech behavior in one situation has resulted in behavior change in situations in which the program has not been carried out (Bailey et al., 1971). Despite a few encouraging findings of transfer of training to settings in which the program has not been conducted, they are in the minority. Transfer of training usually does not occur (Isaacs et al., 1960; Meichenbaum et al., 1968; O'Leary et al., 1969) unless the program is continued across settings (Wahler, 1969; Walker & Buckley, 1972).

Programming Response Maintenance and Transfer of Training

Response maintenance and transfer of training have only recently received attention in behavior modification programs. For some time it has been thought that the "natural environment" that is, everyday experience, will support adaptive behavior change. Specifically, "natural reinforcers" or those reinforcers that normally follow behavior in everyday life are considered sufficient to maintain behavior once behavior is well established. Thus, behaviors should transfer to settings in which no program is in effect because of the consequences which ordinarily are provided. Naturally occurring reinforcing events refer to social reinforcers such as praise, and attention, as well as reinforcers which follow directly from the behavior itself such as in reading and eating.

The advice to those initiating behavior modification programs has been to select a behavior that is likely to be maintained by natural consequences in the environment (e.g., Ayllon & Azrin, 1968b). For example, behaviors important in everyday living, such as grooming oneself, eating appropriately, and conversing with others, should be maintained by the consequences normally delivered for such behaviors.

Recently, the assumption that behaviors which appear to be important in everyday living will be maintained by the environment and transfer to everyday situations has been brought into question. Behaviors which appear to be the kind that the environment would normally support such as appropriate social interaction skills in adults (Kazdin & Polster, 1973) and children (Buell et al., 1968) or appropriate eating skills (O'Brien et al., 1972) are not automatically maintained once a program is terminated. It is difficult to select behaviors which one can be assured will be maintained after the program is withdrawn. A given behavior such as paying attention to the lesson is maintained in some classrooms (e.g., Hewett et al., 1969; Kazdin, 1973h) but not in others (e.g., Bushell, Wrobel, & Michaelis, 1968; Kazdin & Klock, 1973; O'Leary et al., 1969). Similarly, smiling in individuals who appear depressed may be maintained at a high level after programmed reinforcement is withdrawn (Hopkins, 1968) or it may decline (Reisinger, 1972). Thus, there is little consistency, at least at present, in the *behaviors* which will be maintained automatically by the environment.

It is unlikely that very many behaviors would be automatically maintained by reinforcement from the social environment after a behavior modification program is withdrawn. The everyday social environment does not usually provide consequences as systematically as does the programmed environment in which a behavior modification program is conducted. Typically, desirable behaviors go unreinforced in the natural environment. Rather, punishment is delivered for not performing desirable behaviors. For example, one is rarely reinforced (at least immediately) for coming to work or class on time. These behaviors are expected and their nonoccurrence may result in social censure and additional undesirable consequences. Similarly, policemen rarely reinforce obedience to the law but rather punish disobedience. An individual who leaves a programmed setting in which reinforcement was delivered might not respond in a similar fashion in the community where reinforcement is very intermittent and unsystematic. The transition from a highly programmed treatment setting to the community is too abrupt.

Socially appropriate behaviors may not be automatically maintained by the social environment after programmed contingencies are withdrawn for another reason. Behaviors which are deviant or disruptive are likely to receive attention or notice in everyday settings such as at home and at school (Allen et al., 1964; Wahler, 1969). Bizarre behaviors may be reinforced rather than extinguished in the natural environment because of the attention they receive. Thus, it is no surprise that appropriate behaviors usually are not maintained once a behavior modification program is abruptly withdrawn and do not transfer to everyday situations.

Most behaviors of individuals functioning adequately in society are resistant to extinction and do not require carefully programmed, immediate consequences for their continued performance. Various features of the environment and the individual's background over years of training may contribute to sustained performance. First, behaviors often are maintained by highly intermittent reinforcement schedules and exceedingly delayed consequences. Second, a variety of behaviors are maintained by the avoidance of aversive consequences rather than by positive reinforcers. The absence of certain behaviors (e.g., table manners) results in untoward social consequences (e.g., ridicule). Behaviors maintained by the avoidance of undesirable events are highly resistant to extinction. Third, prolonged performance of particular behaviors (e.g., mastery of a musical instrument) may be a function of self-control processes including standard setting, self-reward, and self-punishment. Fourth, subtle stimulus control features of the environment may contribute to performance of various behaviors. Prompts, models, and vicarious consequences, all of which are provided by the media, for example, provide cues of expected behavior and illustrate the immediate and long-term consequences of performing or failing to perform certain responses. Of course, the specific influences which actually maintain performance of various behaviors in the absence of extrinsic consequences are a matter of speculation.

In many instances, the external consequences (e.g., money and grades) which contribute substantially to performance are obvious because their absence results in a cessation of behavior. For example, it is doubtful that individuals would continually work when wages (token reinforcers) are terminated for performance (cf. Ayllon & Azrin, 1965). Similarly, it is likely that reading, a behavior frequently associated with pleasurable consequences, declines somewhat after a student leaves college, in part, because of the termination of external consequences (e.g., grades) for performance. Thus, for many behaviors, direct consequences normally present in the environment appear to contribute to sustained performance.

For individuals functioning normally in society, many adaptive behaviors *are* maintained by the natural environment. Yet, most individuals have received extensive social training and respond to a variety of subtle external and self-imposed influences. In contrast, individuals in treatment, rehabilitation, and educational settings for whom most behavior modification programs are conducted are trained to respond to external consequences in carefully programmed situations. It is no surprise that their behaviors are not maintained when the consequences are withdrawn and they are placed into a social situation for which they have not been prepared.

Specific procedures have to be employed to achieve response maintenance and transfer of training. Several procedures can be employed to serve this purpose after a program has been withdrawn. The evidence for many of the procedures is not sufficiently clear so that unequivocal statements can be made about their efficacy. Nevertheless, preliminary evidence suggests that they may be effective in ensuring response maintenance and transfer of training. Although some procedures to be discussed are more suited to either response maintenance or transfer of training, in most instances these goals and the procedures used to obtain them are difficult to separate.

Substituting "Naturally Occurring" Reinforcers. In many programs, events are used to alter behavior which are not usually available in the setting or do not usually follow behavior contingently. For example, tokens, candy, or electric shock are used to alter behavior. They do not normally serve as events which follow behavior in settings such as classrooms, hospitals, and the home. An issue in such programs is how to maintain behaviors after these events are withdrawn. Consequences which normally are available in the environment can replace those extraneous events initially used to alter behavior. For example, depression was decreased in a female patient by reinforcing her with tokens for smiling, and taking tokens away for crying (Reisinger, 1972). At the end of treatment, tokens were eliminated entirely. Social reinforcement alone was delivered for smiling whereas crying was merely ignored. This effectively maintained smiling for four weeks at which time the patient was released from the hospital. In a project mentioned earlier (Hopkins, 1968), a boy was reinforced with food for smiling. Eventually food was eliminated and smiling was maintained by the attention he received from others.

If "naturally occurring" consequences can be programmed to maintain behavior, the question arises whether they could have been used to change behavior in the first place without introducing extraneous events (O'Leary & Drabman, 1971). Although events such as praise, activities, and privileges which are readily available in the normal environment usually effectively alter behavior, a more powerful extrinsic reinforcer sometimes is needed. For example, in one report, parents praised their children for playing cooperatively in an attempt to reduce obstreperous behavior (Wahler, 1968). Praise was not effective initially. The parents then reinforced the children with points which could be exchanged for toys. Praise was paired with and eventually replaced the tokens. Although praise was not effective initially, it became a reinforcer after being paired with points. Thus, extrinsic reinforcers are sometimes necessary to enhance the reinforcing properties of naturally occurring events. Eventually, reinforcers within the setting can be used to maintain behavior. Of course, if behaviors are maintained with reinforcers present in the setting, the program is not really withdrawn. Rather, one program is substituted for another one. Other procedures may still be required once all programmed consequences are withdrawn.

Training Relatives or Other Individuals in the Client's Environment. When a program is carried out in a particular setting, a major concern is whether the behaviors will be performed when the client leaves the setting. The effects of a program can be maintained, if individuals in the client's environment are trained to use behavior modification techniques. Of course, training individuals in the client's environment such as parents, teachers, and peers is an effective procedure for changing behavior initially (Ayllon & Wright, 1972; Guerney, 1969). However, training those individuals not included in the implementation of the *initial* program can ensure that the program's effects will be maintained.

In one program, investigators altered the behavior of an aggressive, "hyperactive" child in the home by providing candy, social, and token reinforcement for behaving cooperatively (O'Leary, O'Leary, & Becker,

1967). After cooperative behavior had been established, the mother was trained to continue the reinforcement program on her own. Although some deviant behaviors remained, the cooperative behaviors were maintained.

Transfer of training is unlikely to occur unless significant others in the client's environment do carry out the procedures. For example, Wahler (1969) reported that training parents to attend to cooperative play and to punish uncooperative play behavior effectively improved behavior at home. However, the child's behavior at school did not change until the teacher also carried out the contingencies.

Relatives of the clients in institutional settings sometimes are trained in behavior modification so that the gains achieved in the institutional setting will be maintained after release (Henderson & Scoles, 1970). The importance of training individuals in the client's environment in behavior modification procedures cannot be overstated. Recently, a follow-up assessment of the behavior of autistic children one to four years after treatment had been terminated showed that the posttreatment environment was extraordinarily important (Lovaas, Koegel, Simmons, & Long, 1973). The children of parents who were trained to carry out behavior modification procedures maintained their behavior gains outside of the treatment facility and indeed, slightly improved, whereas children who had been institutionalized regressed, that is, showed a great loss of those gains previously achieved in treatment.

Gradually Removing or Fading the Contingencies.   Losses of behavioral gains following a behavior modification program may result from abruptly withdrawing the consequences (reinforcing or punishing) which follow behavior. The gradual removal of the consequences is less likely to be as discriminable to the client than is the abrupt withdrawal of consequences. Eventually, the consequences can be eliminated entirely without a return of behavior to its baseline rate. Of course, it is important that the consequences be withdrawn only after behavior is well established and performed consistently.

In institutional programs, consequences have been faded to reduce or eliminate dependence upon an elaborate program. For example, in psychiatric hospitals, programs have been devised so that when an individual consistently engages in the target behaviors such as attending activities and grooming oneself, the consequences are free rather than contingent upon performance (Atthowe & Krasner, 1968). Similarly, in a program for predelinquents, boys initially are placed in a token economy (Phillips et al., 1971). After performance of desirable behavior is consistent for several weeks, the client is advanced to a "merit" system where privileges and activities are "free" as long as appropriate behaviors are maintained at a high level.

Sometimes programs are divided into levels. In a leveled program, clients participate at one level and, as they progress, advance to different levels. Each level requires more complex behavior and consistent performance for longer periods of time. At higher levels, more reinforcers are available so there is an incentive to progress. Higher levels are also characterized by less structured contingencies. At the highest level, the contingencies are completely withdrawn and the client may leave the setting (Kazdin, 1975).

In some institutional programs, the contingencies are gradually faded by requiring the client to spend increasingly greater portions of time out of the program into the community. For example, in one program male psychotic patients participated in a token economy in a residential setting located in the community (Kelley & Henderson, 1971). As a patient's behavior (social, vocational, and countersymptom) improved, the system was gradually withdrawn. The patients were required to participate in community activities such as attending social functions and securing employment.

Gradually withdrawing the contingencies is a useful technique because it prepares a client for the conditions under which he must normally function. In everyday living, the contingencies often are unsystematic and the consequences for performance are delayed, if present at all. The gradual withdrawal of contingencies provides a transition between a highly programmed environment and one which is less well programmed with regard to given target behaviors.

Varying the Conditions of Training.   One reason that behaviors are not maintained and do not transfer to new settings is that the clients readily form a discrimination between conditions in which reinforcement (or punishment) is and is not delivered. Behavior becomes associated with a narrow range of cues. As soon as the program is withdrawn or the setting changes, clients discriminate that the desirable behavior is no longer associated with certain consequences. Thus, responses are not maintained and do not transfer to new situations. One way to program response maintenance and transfer of training is to develop the target behavior in a variety of situations and in the presence of several individuals. If the response is associated with a range of settings, individuals, and other cues, it is less likely to be lost when the situations change.

Goocher and Ebner (1968) varied stimulus settings extensively in developing appropriate classroom behavior in a deviant child. Initially, training was carried out in the presence of a single experimenter in a special room set aside for training. The child was praised and received candy for paying attention to the task. Gradually, planned distractions such as television and other individuals passing by were introduced in the setting. Training was shifted to the classroom itself in the presence of other children. Throughout training, deviant behavior increased whenever distracting stimuli were introduced, but it quickly extinguished. Appropriate behavior was maintained in the classroom for nine months after training had been terminated.

A psychotic patient who had been mute for several years was trained to speak (Isaacs et al., 1960). However, speech was limited to conversation with the therapist who previously administered reinforcement. To develop generalization of the patient's verbal behavior to different individuals, a nurse was included in the speech-training sessions. Eventually, the patient also communicated verbally with her.

Similarly, when self-destructive behavior of retarded children was punished, the behavior decreased only in the presence of the experimenter who had delivered shock (Lovaas & Simmons, 1969). The behavior continued to be performed in the presence of other individuals. When one of these other individuals administered shock, the self-destructive behavior ceased and was not performed in the presence of new individuals who had not used punishment. Having a few individuals administer consequences led to generalization across individuals.

The above results suggest that consequences should be provided for behavior in a variety of training settings and situations. A consistent pattern of responding will be established across situations and individuals. The stimuli which exert control over behavior will become broad rather than narrow. Once behavior is consistently performed in a few situations or in the presence of a few individuals, the likelihood that the behavior will be performed in a variety of situations or in the presence of a variety of individuals is increased (Koegel & Rincover, 1974; Lovaas & Simmons, 1969).

Schedules of Reinforcement. As mentioned earlier, resistance to extinction can be enhanced by using intermittent reinforcement. After behavior is well established, reinforcing consequences can be delivered intermittently. The intermittency of the reinforcement can be increased so that very little reinforcement is provided for behavior. Resistance of behavior to extinction once reinforcement is withdrawn is a function of the intermittency of the reinforcement. The more intermittent or thinner the reinforcement schedule, the greater the resistance to extinction.

Intermittent reinforcement has been used to maintain behavior in several projects. Kale et al. (1968) trained three schizophrenic patients to greet staff on the ward. Whenever patients greeted a staff member (e.g., "Hello, Mr. _____," or "Hi!"), they were given cigarettes and praised. After greetings were performed at a high rate, reinforcement was thinned so that not all responses were reinforced. For example, for one patient a variable ratio schedule was used so that on the average every second response was reinforced. The ratio was gradually increased so that many responses (e.g., on the average 20) were required for a cigarette. After reinforcement had been delivered intermittently for a few weeks, reinforcement was withdrawn completely. Yet, behavior was maintained at its reinforced level. A follow-up conducted approximately three months after treatment showed that greeting responses were maintained at the high level which was developed during treatment.

Kazdin and Polster (1973) used intermittent reinforcement to maintain social behavior. In a sheltered workshop, two male adult retardates who engaged in little social interaction received tokens for talking to peers. During three work breaks the clients were told that they would receive tokens for each person they interacted with socially. An interaction was defined as a verbal exchange in which the client and a peer each made at least one statement to the other person. The statement had to reflect some content area such as information in the news, sports, television, and weather, rather than general greeting statements and replies such as "Hi, how are you?" "Fine!" Peers were queried after each break to ensure that the client reported the conversation accurately. If a peer noted that the client had not spoken with him, or if the peer forgot the conversation, the client did not receive a token. Each of the two clients received a token for each peer they had spoken with during each break. Every interaction was reinforced. Figure 9–1 shows that during the first phase in which reinforcement was given, the daily average number of interactions gradually

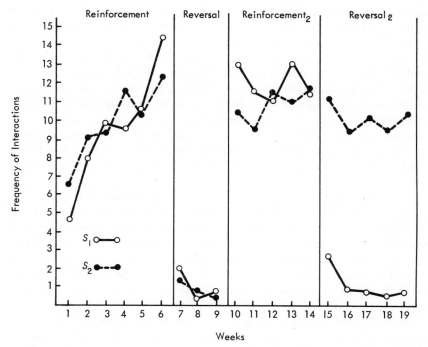

FIGURE 9–1 Mean frequency of interactions per day during Reinforcement, Reversal, Reinforcement$_2$, and Reversal$_2$ for subject 1 (S$_1$) and subject 2 (S$_2$). Source: Kazdin, A. E., & Polster, R. Intermittent token reinforcement and response maintenance in extinction. *Behavior Therapy,* 1973, **4**, 386–91. Reprinted with permission from Academic Press, Inc.)

increased for both clients. Yet, during a reversal phase in which tokens were withdrawn, interactions decreased. When reinforcement was reinstated, one client (S_1) received reinforcement as he had before (i.e., continuous reinforcement). The other client (S_2) was told that he would receive tokens only once in a while (i.e., intermittent reinforcement). At first, the client received tokens at two of the work breaks, and after three weeks at only one of the three daily breaks. The client never knew for sure which break would be reinforced since the scheduled reinforcement varied each day. Eventually, all token reinforcement was withdrawn. As Figure 9–1 shows, the client who had been reinforced continuously showed an immediate decline in social interaction. However, the client who had been reinforced intermittently maintained a high rate of interaction for the final five weeks of the project. Thus, intermittent reinforcement appeared to help maintain behavior.

Some investigators continue the use of intermittent reinforcement to maintain behavior at a high level rather than eliminate all reinforcement. Intermittent reinforcement is quite effective, of course, while the reinforcement is still in effect. For example, Phillips et al. (1971) gave or withdrew points on the basis of the degree to which predelinquents cleaned their rooms. When the points were given, daily room cleaning was maintained at a high level. After the behavior was well established the reinforcing and punishing consequences became increasingly intermittent. The rooms were checked daily but reinforcement or punishment occurred only once in a while. When the consequences were delivered, the number of points given (or lost) on the basis of that day's performance was multiplied by the number of previous days that consequences had not been given. Although the consequences were delivered on only 8% of the days checked, behavior was maintained at a high level. The consequences were not completely withdrawn so the effect of intermittent reinforcement on extinction was not evaluated.

Intermittent reinforcement can be readily incorporated into all programs. It is important to make the schedule of reinforcement increasingly intermittent. Resistance to extinction can be delayed after the program is withdrawn. At the present time, it is unclear whether highly intermittent reinforcement only forestalls extinction temporarily or can virtually eliminate extinction even after a long extinction period. Behaviors reinforced intermittently have been maintained at least up to three months of extinction (Kale et al., 1968).

Delay of Reinforcement. Behavior might also be maintained by gradually increasing the delay between reinforcement and the target behavior. When behavior is initially developed, immediate reinforcement usually is essential to ensure a high rate of responding. As behavior stabilizes and is well established, the delay between behavior and the reinforcing consequences can be increased without a loss in performance.

In token economies, it is possible to delay reinforcement in one of two ways. First, the delay between behavior and the delivery of tokens can be increased. Initially, the client receives tokens as soon as the target response is performed. Eventually, the delivery of tokens is delayed. Second, the delay between token delivery and exchange of tokens for back-up reinforcers can be increased. Initially, the client can exchange tokens for back-up reinforcers almost immediately after receiving them. Eventually, the delay between receiving tokens and their exchange is increased.

The effectiveness of delayed reinforcement in maintaining behavior has not been widely studied. In a classroom program (Cotler et al., 1972), tokens were delivered to the class for studying and completing academic tasks. The tokens could be cashed in for toys or candy only after studying for a 30-minute period. After study behavior stabilized at a high level, the delay between token earning and exchange of tokens for other reinforcers was increased to every other day and then to every four days. In spite of the delay, study performance was maintained at a high level. Of course, it is unclear what effect increasing the delay beyond four days or eliminating reinforcement altogether would have had.

As mentioned earlier, most reinforcers available in the social environment are delayed. Thus, it is important to wean a client from immediate reinforcement. Behavior should be well established prior to invoking long delays. When delayed reinforcement is employed, performance should be observed to ensure that there is no loss of behavior gains. Eventually, reinforcement may be withdrawn entirely or delivered only after a long delay.

Self-control Procedures.   One strategy which may be employed to enhance response maintenance and transfer of training is to train the client to control his or her own behavior. Specifically, the client can be trained to administer prompts (instructions) or deliver reinforcing and punishing consequences to himself. If an individual is trained to control his own behavior, it is unlikely that behavior gains will be lost once the program is withdrawn. The client can continually monitor his behavior and keep the contingencies in effect over time and across situations. Behavior should be maintained and should transfer because the individual is the source of behavioral control rather than an external agent associated with one situation. Although self-control procedures were detailed in the last chapter, it is important to refer to them here briefly insofar as they can be used to develop response maintenance and transfer of training.

Control of reinforcement contingencies can gradually be transferred to clients so that eventually they have virtually complete control over the program. Clients can implement various aspects of the contingencies such as evaluating their own behavior, setting the criteria for reinforcement, and determining the amount of reinforcers to which they are entitled (Felixbrod & O'Leary, 1973; Fixsen et al., 1973; Glynn, 1970; Kaufman & O'Leary, 1972;

Lovitt & Curtiss, 1969). Although self-control procedures are used increasingly, evidence pertaining to their effect on response maintenance and transfer of training is sparse.

In a recent study, the effect of self-reinforcement was evaluated on children's disruptive classroom behavior in ten elementary school classrooms (Bolstad & Johnson, 1972). After baseline, all children received points for nondisruptive behavior from an experimenter in the room. In a subsequent phase, some of the children continued to receive points from the experimenter on the basis of classroom performance. Other students, however, were instructed to record their own behavior. These students received points on the basis of how well (accurately) they had scored their own behavior during the observation period. Some of the children who self-recorded their own behavior lost points, if their observations differed dramatically from the experimenter's observations. Eventually, checks on the accuracy of self-observations were eliminated. In the last phase of the experiment, reinforcing consequences were withdrawn. The major issue is the degree to which behavior was maintained during extinction after students had exerted some control over the reinforcers.

As soon as reinforcement was withdrawn, disruptive classroom behavior increased. Those children who had observed their own behavior and thus determined how many points they were to receive tended to show slightly greater resistance to extinction than those who had no part in the contingency. However, the differences were very small. Moreover, since the extinction phase lasted only seven days, the long-term effects of self-reinforcement procedure could not be observed. Other reports (Johnson & Martin, 1972) suggest that there is little or no difference in response maintenance when an individual is reinforced by someone else or partially determines his own reinforcement.

Self-instruction training (Meichenbaum, 1973) has led to changes which are maintained once training is terminated. For example, impulsive children were trained to administer instructions to themselves to perform various tasks methodically (Meichenbaum & Goodman, 1971). Not only was the training program quite effective in improving their work, but also the gains made during training were maintained after one month. Similarly, when schizophrenic patients were trained to instruct themselves on verbal and motor tasks, their performance improved (Meichenbaum & Cameron, 1973). The behavior gains resulting from training were maintained at a three-week follow-up assessment. Moreover, the effects of self-instructional training transferred to tasks not included in training.

The effects of self-reinforcement and self-instructional training on long-term response maintenance and transfer of training have not been thoroughly assessed. Intuitively, self-control is a viable approach to achieve these goals. Since self-control procedures can alter behavior often as well as programs in which the consequences are controlled by others, these procedures should be explored extensively in future years.

Programming Response Maintenance and Transfer of Training: Summary. The procedures discussed above are not mutually exclusive. They can be used independently or in conjunction with each other. For example, programs in treatment facilities can begin to wean a client from a reinforcement program by providing increasingly intermittent reinforcement. Moreover, the reinforcement that is delivered can be increasingly delayed as the program continues. Additionally, parents or other individuals in the client's nontreatment or noneducational environment can be trained to continue the contingencies to ensure transfer of training to new settings. The client can have some input into the contingencies such as in a contract system. However, the client can be given more control over the terms of the contract so that he or she dictates the behavioral requirements as well as reinforcing and punishing consequences. To develop self-control procedures, the client can make a "self-contract" witnessed by others. The terms of the contract can specify the consequences that the client will administer to himself. Other maintenance and transfer procedures discussed earlier can be incorporated so that several techniques are used simultaneously.

In a recent program, a few of the above techniques were combined to develop response maintenance (Jones & Kazdin, 1975). In a special education classroom, four educably retarded children received token reinforcement for paying attention to their lesson. The effects of the token program were demonstrated on inappropriate motor behaviors (rocking in a chair, facing away from the lesson, engaging in repetitive body movements, sitting slumped in the chair) in a multiple-baseline design across time (morning and afternoon periods of the day). After it was clear that the program was responsible for change, a few of the procedures discussed above were implemented to maintain behavior.

First, a "natural" reinforcer (peer praise) was substituted for the tokens. If the children performed well throughout the day, they would come up individually at the end of the day and receive applause from their peers. A group contingency was also implemented so that desirable performance by all of the four children on a given day, earned an activity for the class as a whole at the end of the day. This procedure was used to increase the likelihood that peer reinforcement would be given for appropriate behavior after tokens were withdrawn.

Second, back-up reinforcement was delayed before being eliminated entirely. The delay was made between the delivery of tokens and their exchange for back-up reinforcers. Initially, tokens were exchanged for back-up reinforcers at the end of each day. However, before eliminating tokens, exchange of tokens for back-up reinforcers was shifted to every other day only. On days in which tokens could not be exchanged, they were simply collected by the teacher at the end of the day. Essentially, with this procedure the contingencies were gradually removed since the consequences (back-up reinforcers) for behavior were faded.

After the maintenance procedures had been in effect for less than two weeks, all contingencies (tokens, peer-group applause, group activity, delayed back-up reinforcers) were eliminated entirely. No specific program remained in effect. However, follow-up information was collected to determine whether inappropriate behavior was maintained at the low rate achieved during the token program. Behaviors were maintained at their low rate (and slightly lower than during the token program) up to nine school weeks after the program had been completely terminated. These results suggest that specific procedures can successfully maintain behavior. The results are preliminary because the procedures have not been evaluated extensively. In future projects, it will be especially important to conduct long-term follow-up studies to determine whether behavior changes are maintained over long periods such as one or two years. At the present time, a number of procedures appear useful in maintaining behavior. However, it is not clear what procedures or combination of procedures will be best suited to a given situation, behavior, or population of clients.

Conclusion

Two major concerns in the evaluation of behavior modification programs are the degree to which behaviors are maintained once the program has been withdrawn and the degree to which behaviors transfer to settings different from the one in which training has taken place. The concerns are referred to as response maintenance and transfer of training, respectively. Behaviors have been maintained after a program was withdrawn and have transferred to new settings in some investigations, although these are exceptions. Presently, it appears that response maintenance and transfer are not automatic by-products of a program. Rather, they have to be programmed directly by including specific procedures in the program.

Procedures designed to enhance response maintenance and transfer include: (1) substituting "naturally occurring" reinforcers in place of extraneous events which may have been used to change behavior initially, (2) training relatives or other individuals in the client's environment to carry out the contingencies, (3) gradually removing or fading the contingencies, (4) varying the conditions in which training takes place, (5) altering schedules of reinforcement, (6) increasing the delay of reinforcement, and 7) using self-control procedures. Many of these procedures have not been thoroughly evaluated since response maintenance and transfer of training have only recently begun to receive attention. Thus, definitive statements regarding their efficacy cannot be made. Nevertheless, preliminary work suggests the viability of the above techniques.

10

Ethical Considerations
and Future Directions

Behavior modification offers promise for treatment populations for whom traditional psychotherapeutic procedures have made only relatively minor advances. Yet, the techniques raise major concerns over the misuse and the ethics of the behavioral technology. The use of behavior modification to restructure institutional living of psychiatric or retarded residents and prison inmates stimulates concern for client rights and potential abuses associated with treatment (e.g., Lucero, Vail, & Scherber, 1968). Extrapolating behavioral principles to design society (Skinner, 1949; 1971) leads to additional objections and ethical concerns (Wheeler, 1973). People are concerned about the technology of behavioral control and rightly so. Even though behavioral research is only at an early stage of development, a sufficient technology already exists which could be misused against individuals or groups of individuals. Thus, discussion of the ethical and social implications of behavioral technology is not academic. Salient ethical concerns include the matter of behavioral control, the use of aversive techniques, and many issues derived from these concerns. It is important to discuss these issues because future directions in behavior modification point to increasingly widespread applications of behavioral techniques in society. The implications of misusing behavioral techniques in these broader applications are especially great. The present discussion will consider ethical issues and future directions of behavior modification.

Behavior Control

Behavior control refers to exerting power over people by manipulating environmental conditions to which individuals are exposed to achieve a definite end such as developing new behavior and maintaining or eliminating already existing behaviors (Ulrich, 1967). The concern over behavioral control is that behaviors, attitudes, thoughts, and feelings of individuals will be regulated, perhaps for despotic ends (London, 1969). The fear that advances in behavioral technology will lead to behavior control encompasses three related issues, namely, the *purpose* for which behavior is to be controlled, *who* will decide the ultimate purpose and exert control, and whether behavior control entails an abridgment of individual *freedom.*

Each concern has become increasingly salient as the technology of behavior change has developed (Miron, 1968). However, the concerns of behavior control are neither new nor peculiar to behavior modification (London, 1969; Skinner, 1953, 1974). In areas of science other than psychology, the ethics of behavior control also arise. For example, research in psychopharmacology has led to the use of drugs to control behavior. Drugs have had undeniable benefits in, for example, altering anxiety and hallucinations. Yet, there is a major concern with drug abuse in society at large and its potentially deleterious consequences. Similarly, work in genetics and biochemistry has sought means to detect physiological anomalies so that at least in some cases disorders can be controlled. Yet, the prospect of genetic manipulation and eugenics has become increasingly threatening in light of recent advances. Also, biochemically controlled behavior may be evident in warfare where entire cities are immobilized and made readily amenable to military invasion. Similarly, advances in electronics and brain research suggest techniques that can ameliorate intractable pain. Yet, electrical stimulation resulting from brain implantations can influence social interaction patterns and conceivably can be used to control society (London, 1969). Most of the problems of behavior control are similar among the various technologies (e.g., behavior modification, pharmacy, medicine).

Control of behavior is socially institutionalized in government and law, business, education, religion, psychotherapy, and the military. Each of these institutions explicitly attempts to alter behavior and supports specific procedures to achieve its ends. Indeed, some authors have commented upon the elaborate technology which uses systems of rewards and punishment already widely in evidence in government and organized crime (London, 1969). The behavior of everyone who interacts socially is controlled in some way. Controlling agents include parents, teachers, employers, peers, spouses, siblings, and so on. These agents by design or accident provide consequences or fail to provide consequences for behavior. As discussed earlier, presenting consequences (e.g., reinforcement or punishment) or failing to present them (extinction) influence behavior. Thus, behavior is always modified whether or not a particular behavioral program is specifically designed for this purpose.

The sources of behavioral control in everyday life often do not evoke major concern because they are part of the existing social structure and are considered essential for social functioning. Perhaps another reason there is little concern with many pervasive sources of behavioral control is that there is somewhat of a balance of influences and counterinfluences on behavior. The influences exerted on people conflict (Kanfer & Phillips, 1970). For example, cigarette smokers are enticed with advertisements of new brands of cigarettes and even receive token reinforcement (redeemable coupons) for smoking. The attempt of advertising to control behavior is obvious. However, there also are counterinfluences which discourage smoking such as warnings by the American Cancer Society. Analogously, advertisements display tempting vacation sights to entice the consumer. At the same time, banks and savings and loan associations provide incentives for investing and saving money for protracted periods. The attempts of behavior control in society are simplified here. There are not merely two opposing influences on behavior. Rather, there are diverse influences representing various positions with regard to the performance of a particular behavior. Each influence contributes to the final behavior. For example, sexual expression is influenced by biological determinants, the mass media, the clergy, parental training, peer influences, as well as other factors. Each influence is a source of control over behavior. Yet, the relative weight of each influence is different for each individual and even for the same individual at different points in time. Thus, the influences compete and exert "pull" in different directions. The final outcome is varied across individuals and contributes to vast differences in behavior patterns. All the influences attempt to control people. Each one attempts to do so in a fairly systematic fashion. Yet, because there are conflicting sources of control, the net effect varies across individuals. The control is no less behavior control because there are variations in the final success.

Any objection to a technology of behavior control ignores existing sources of control. As Skinner (1974) stated, "We cannot choose a way of life in which there is no control. We can only change the controlling conditions [p. 190]." The desirability of selecting certain controlling conditions which are to govern behavior is dictated in part by the efficiency with which alternative means of control achieve a desired end and the inadvertent or unintended effects (e.g., unhappiness) associated with different means of control (cf. Willems, 1974). Skinner (1953) suggests that many controlling features which are widely practiced are based upon aversive control rather than positive reinforcement and consequently may have undesirable side effects.

Control for What Purposes—by Whom? Behavioral technology as any other technology is ethically neutral. The potential for both use and misuse of technology is always present. The concern with behavioral control is not with the technology per se but rather with the purposes for which the technology is used and the individual(s) who will have the power to exert control. As Skinner (1971) noted, the technology can be used by a "villian or saint [p. 143]."

Behavior modification, in one sense, is purposeless. It only specifies how to attain goals (e.g., develop certain behaviors) and not what the goals or purposes should be. There is nothing inherent in a technology which dictates the values governing its use (Skinner, 1971). Setting goals for society represents value judgments for which scientific training does not prepare a professional. Indeed, philosophers have argued, without resolution, the doctrines by which societal goals should be selected. Social goals can be determined by the people themselves as expressed in their political choices. A scientist might well be able to predict where a preselected goal will lead, make recommendations to avert undesirable consequences, or investigate the actual effects of pursuing certain goals. Yet the initial selection of the goal is out of the scientist's hands.

The effective use of a behavioral technology to achieve social goals requires that these goals be clearly specified in advance. Yet agreeing upon goals in society and the implications of selecting certain courses of action is extremely difficult, to say the least. What the goals should be remains an issue which has not changed throughout the history of man and reduces to questions of the good life and human values. A concern that misdirected goals or purposes will be selected by society or a given leader is not raised by behavior modification. However, the problem of vague or misdirected purposes is aggravated by the potent technology. If there is no efficient means to achieve a goal, it is academic to debate the desirability of different goals. If such a means exists in a technology of social change, discussions about desirable ends become more meaningful and the hazards of selecting deleterious goals more treacherous.

In most applications of behavioral principles the issue of purpose or goal is not raised because the psychologist or psychiatrist who uses the techniques is employed in a setting where the goals have been determined in advance. Behavior modification programs in hospitals and institutions, schools, day-care treatment facilities, and prisons have established goals already endorsed by society, such as returning the individual to the community, accelerating academic performance, developing self-help, communication, and social and vocational skills, alleviating bizarre behaviors, and so on.

In outpatient therapy and counseling, the client comes to treatment with a goal, namely, to develop some adaptive skill or to alleviate a problem which interferes with effective living. The primary role of the behavior modifier is to provide a means to obtain the goal insofar as the goal is consistent with generally accepted social standards. In virtually all cases, the goals of a client are compatible with generally accepted social values. If an individual is free from some behavior which impedes his or her functioning, the community is either enhanced or is not deleteriously affected. Such functioning is consistent with the social value that, within limits, an individual should freely pursue his or her own objectives.

There are two ends of a continuum which reflect the type of behavior change a client may seek in outpatient treatment. At one end of the continuum is a client whose behavior, if changed, would clearly *help* society (e.g., alleviating anxiety in a government leader so he or she may effectively perform the duties of office). At the other end of the continuum is a client whose behavior, if changed, would clearly *hinder* society (e.g., alleviating anxiety which restrains an individual from committing criminal acts). In the first case, treatment of anxiety will contribute to social ends, whereas in the latter case treatment will contribute to antisocial ends. Virtually all cases in therapy are not at the ends of the continuum. In these cases, the therapist usually acts in accord with the client's wishes. Sometimes it is not clear to the client what the goal of therapy should be. For example, a homosexual client may come to therapy because of the anxiety and self-condemnation resulting from socially unaccepted sexual practices. Alleviation of the client's perceived problem may result from one of two courses of action. Either treatment can eliminate homosexual behavior or the self-condemnation which is associated with these sexual practices. In one case treated, the client chose to give up his strong religious beliefs which condemned homosexual behavior (London, 1964, p. 120).

The scientific study and practice of behavior change is *not* value free (Krasner, 1966; Rogers & Skinner, 1956; Szasz, 1960). There is no neutral or value-free position in implementing a technology of behavior change although the technology itself may not embrace a particular value position. Endorsing an individual client's goal, the goals of a treatment institution, or the "treatment" of particular "disorders" (e.g., sexual deviance) reflects a definite stance. Leaving the selection of goals to others such as a client or institution is an attempt to hide from the issue of values but still represents a definite position as to those behaviors which are change-worthy, deviant, or socially desirable. Thus, the position to which the therapist adheres with respect to desirable and undesirable behavior represents a definite value stance (London, 1964). The values of the individual therapist do influence the course of therapy and the values of the client (Rosenthal, 1955). While values enter into the process of behavior change, specialists in science and technology are not trained to dictate the social ends for which their specialties should be used. Indeed, it is unclear what training could serve as a basis for selecting the values of others.

An issue directly related to determining the purposes for which behavioral techniques are used is *who* shall be in control of society. The issue assumes that one individual or a small number of individuals (presumably psychologists) will be in charge of society and misuse behavioral techniques. Who should control society is not an issue raised by behavior modification or advances in technology. Countries differ philosophically in conceptions of how leaders should come to power. A behavioral technology is compatible with various philosophies. Indeed, the citizenry can be completely in charge of leadership and, in this sense, exert ultimate control. A behavioral technology can help the citizenry achieve goals (e.g., ameliorate social ills and improve education) with no actual change in who "controls" society. Society can determine the goals to be achieved relying on technological advances to obtain them.

Individual Freedom.   Another aspect of behavior control is the widespread concern that behavioral technology will necessarily mean an abridgment of individual freedom. Will the deliberate control of human behavior reduce an individual's ability to make choices and freely select his or her own goals? Whether or not an individual ever is free to behave counter to existing environmental forces has been actively discussed by philosophers, scientists, and theologians (Wheeler, 1973). However, a source of agreement among those who posit or disclaim the existence of freedom is that it is exceedingly important for individuals to feel they are free independently of whether in fact they are (Kanfer & Phillips, 1970; Krasner & Ullmann, 1973; London, 1964). In any case, the question is whether a behavioral technology will decrease the extent to which an individual can exert control over his or her environment or to which the individual can feel free to make his or her own choices.

The fear that behavioral technology threatens to eliminate or reduce freedom and choice ignores most of the applied work in behavior modification. Applied work usually is conducted with individuals whose behaviors have been identified as problematic or ineffective in some way. The responses may include deficits or behavior which are not under socially accepted stimulus control. Such clients ordinarily have a limited number of opportunities to obtain reinforcers in their life as a function of their deficient or "abnormal" behavior. Individuals who differ from those who normally function in society are *confined* by their behavioral deficit which delimits those areas of social functioning from which they might choose. An alcoholic or drug addict is not free to fulfill himself in a personally desired fashion because of a single but all encompassing behavioral obstacle. An alcoholic who goes untreated is "free" only in the weakest sense of the term.

Behavior modification is used to increase an individual's skills so that the number of response alternatives or options is increased. By overcoming debilitating or delimiting behaviors which restrict opportunities, the individual is freer to select from alternatives which were not previously available (Ball, 1968). For individuals whose behavior is considered "normal," and even for those who are gifted, behavioral techniques can increase performance or develop competencies beyond those achieved with current practices. As improved levels of performance are achieved, whether or not an individual initially was deficient in some way, response opportunities and choices increase. Thus, behavior modification, as typically applied, increases rather than stifles individual freedom.

Behavior Control: Summary. Even though behavioral techniques may increase individual freedom, in the sense discussed above, it may be possible for some individuals who gain political control to misuse the technology to decrease the choices of those governed. However, there are defenses against such a control. Initially, awareness of the people is a defense against coercive behavioral control and manipulation (Roe, 1959). Individuals who are unaware of those factors which control behavior are easily controlled by others. Thus, people need to be informed about factors controlling their behavior and the principles upon which such control is based. Awareness of controlling factors allows an individual to submit to or resist their influence. In this sense, knowledge and awareness of controlling factors are conditions for individual freedom (Ulrich, 1967).

Aside from awareness of controlling factors, there are defenses against behavior control which stem directly from the technology itself. While the behavioral technology provides would-be controllers with special powers, it also gives those individuals who are controlled greater power over their own behavior (London, 1969). As discussed earlier, individuals can use behavioral principles to achieve their own goals. Thus, self-control is a partial deterrent against control by others.

A final deterrent to control by others is the direct application of behavioral principles to the behavior of the controllers. Methods of control which can be used against the people can also be used for countercontrol against the controllers (Platt, 1973). It might well be possible to systematically train individuals to utilize the principles of behavior modification to control the behavior of the "controllers." Behavioral techniques need not only be imposed by those who ordinarily are in the role of controllers (e.g., legislators, therapists, and parents) to alter the behavior of the controllees (e.g., citizens, clients, and children).

In a recent project which made this point, junior high school students who were in a special class for problem children were trained to modify the behavior of their teachers (Gray, Graubard, & Rosenberg, 1974). Students received instruction and practice in behavior modification. The students returned to their regular classes part of the day to shape the teachers. The goal was to train teachers to engage in positive interactions with the students. Of course, since the students had a history of behavioral problems, it was unlikely that teachers would normally engage in a high rate of positive interactions with them. Prior to actually implementing behavior change techniques, the students gathered data on the teachers' use of positive and negative comments. Students were trained to identify teacher behavior by role-playing and studying videotapes. The teachers were unaware that data were gathered or that a systematic program was implemented to alter their behavior. After baseline observations, students reinforced positive comments. The students reinforced the teachers by smiling, making eye contact, sitting up straight and making comments such as, "I like to work in a room where the teacher is nice to kids." To discourage negative teacher comments, statements were made such as, "It's hard for me to do good work when you're cross with me." The results showed that positive teacher comments increased during the five weeks of the program but declined when student reinforcement was terminated. The teachers were enthusiastic when informed of the program. Interestingly, most teachers believed that the project primarily changed the children rather than themselves. Other investigations also have shown that alteration of student behavior improves both the quantity and quality of teacher responses to the students (Sherman & Cormier, 1974).

As illustrated by classroom investigations, behavior control techniques can be used by individuals who ordinarily play a relatively small role in designing a "system" (e.g., education) of which they are a part. Of course, the social implications of training individuals to influence others remain to be determined. An effective strategy to control the behavior of would-be controllers is to ensure that their desirable (benevolent) behavior is reinforced and undesirable behavior is extinguished or punished. Of course, modification of and control over behavior is reciprocal. The effectiveness of a leader, in part, depends upon the consequences which derive from his or her leadership. If a leader cannot satisfy the needs to be met in a given society, countermovements are likely to grow and remove the leader.

Admittedly, if the behavioral technology becomes increasingly sophisticated, awareness of controlling factors, self-control, and countercontrol may not be sufficient antidotes. Governments have access to control of strong reinforcers such as food, water, and money and effectively deliver aversive consequences such as execution and imprisonment. There is no counterpart that the individual has to overcome such control techniques. In the structure of virtually all governments are explicit means to handle individuals or groups whose purpose is to reduce or eliminate the government's control. Obviously, then, in the case of despotic governments the possibility of behavior control is a concern. The concern is seemingly aggravated by providing the despot with powerful behavioral control techniques. Yet, despots already use powerful control techniques (e.g., execution or imprisonment) to achieve their goals (London, 1969). The problem of a despotic government is certainly not introduced by a behavioral technology. The fear introduced by a behavioral technology is that an unreasonable leader will have even more power at his (or her) disposal to control the people. This remains an open question. Hopefully, the people will have greater means for self-control and countercontrol at their disposal to avert such control.

Use of Aversive Techniques

The therapeutic use of aversive methods to alter behavior almost always elicits strong emotional protests. These protests are at odds with society's reliance upon aversive control. Aversive techniques appear more deeply embedded in society than are techniques based upon positive reinforcement. As mentioned before, aversive techniques pervade education, government and law, and religion.

The concern over the use of aversive techniques in behavior modification revolves around two techniques, namely, the use of painful stimuli and deprivation. Prior to discussing these controversial techniques, it is important to reiterate that behavior modification *deemphasizes* the use of *aversive techniques* in applied settings. Most of the reasons for this deemphasis were presented in the discussion of punishment and negative reinforcement. Potential side effects and the ineffectiveness of mildly aversive events when not combined with positive reinforcement militate against the widespread application of punishment. The ethical concerns and emotional social reactions associated with aversive stimuli also have limited the use of punishment. Positive reinforcement and not aversive techniques constitute the major application of behavior modification. Nevertheless, the use of aversive events evokes concern and requires serious consideration of a number of issues.

Painful Stimuli. The concern with aversive techniques in behavior modification is raised when painful stimuli are used. Among studies using aversive techniques, painful stimuli are rarely employed. Yet the attention painful stimuli receive is so great, it is worth elaborating the rationale behind their use.

Initially, it is important to distinguish types of aversive techniques of behavior modification. Aversive events are not necessarily painful or demeaning. They do not require a violation of rights or deprivation of essential human needs. Many events which serve as punishing stimuli are not at all painful, such as withdrawing slips of paper with a child's name on it (Hall et al., 1971), taking brief pauses during a meal (Barton et al., 1970), pausing while listening to music (Barrett, 1962), or hearing one's voice played back immediately after speaking (Goldiamond, 1965), and numerous others reviewed earlier. As noted earlier, in some behavior therapy techniques, the aversive events (e.g., nausea) are *imagined* so that nothing is actually done to the client. Thus, the objection to aversive techniques rarely acknowledges that the majority of aversive events employed are not painful.

Painful aversive stimuli sometimes appear to be useful when the behavior to be changed is already under control of strong positive reinforcers. For example, sexual deviance, drug addiction, and alcohol consumption frequently are treated with aversive events such as shock or nausea-inducing drugs (Rachman & Teasdale, 1969). Aversive techniques in these contexts attempt to accomplish two related goals. First, an attempt is made to change the valence of a highly desirable stimulus (e.g., alcohol), through classical conditioning. A painful or intense aversive stimulus which elicits an anxiety and escape reflex sometimes is required. A strong aversive event is needed so that a reflex reaction is elicited. Eventually, by repeatedly pairing the desirable stimulus (e.g., alcohol) with the strong aversive event (e.g., shock), the escape reaction is elicited in the presence of the previously desirable stimulus alone. Thus, the previously desirable stimulus loses its attraction because of its association with an aversive event.

A second goal in treating behaviors which are maintained by strong positive reinforcers is to suppress approach responses to obtain the desired stimulus. A painful stimulus is needed to overcome the highly reinforcing properties of the attractive stimulus. Obviously, fining an individual ten cents for engaging in a sexually deviant behavior is not likely to be effective. A response maintained by a powerful reinforcer is less easily suppressed than one maintained by a weak reinforcer. The aversive event may need to be commensurate with the attraction of the positive reinforcer to suppress behavior. Thus, in cases where maladaptive behavior is maintained by strong reinforcers, strong and sometimes painful aversive events are used.

Painful stimuli, such as shock, have been used in a number of outpatient cases (Rachman & Teasdale, 1969). However, ethical concerns have not been strongly voiced for outpatient applications of aversive techniques. The client who seeks outpatient treatment gives his consent for the use of such procedures and usually may leave treatment at any time.

Deprivation. One aversive technique which evokes strong emotional responses is the use of deprivation. The main thrust of the objection is directed toward deprivation of primary reinforcers which are essential for human existence including food, water, shelter, and human contact. The argument against depriving an individual is that this is a violation of basic human rights and dignity. Aside from the deprivation of primary reinforcers, secondary reinforcers such as activities, privileges, and attention may also be withheld. If the objection to deprivation includes these secondary reinforcers, it has much wider application because an exceedingly small number of programs withhold food and shelter.

Deprivation, in a variety of forms, plays a major role in ordinary social existence. For example, normal social living requires deprivation in areas such as sexual expression and free speech. Moreover, different social groups (e.g., minorities) undergo diverse types of deprivation. Individuals who experience poverty are deprived of essential materials such as food and shelter. Finally, certain social institutions which actually serve or operate under the guise of treatment and rehabilitation (e.g., psychiatric hospitals and prisons), by their very design, deprive individuals of rights and privileges. The conditions which "justify" or require deprivation normally im-

posed in society are ambiguous at best, even without the advent of behavior modification in treatment settings.

In behavior modification programs the alternatives are rarely as simple
as deciding whether or not to deprive the client of something. The majority
of individuals for whom behavior modification techniques are used are
deprived in some significant way by virtue of their failure to perform certain
behaviors (Lucero et al., 1968). Institutionalized clients are deprived of
"normal" community living, friends, and freedom to choose where and how
they would like to live. Students in educational settings who are having
academic difficulties may at some point be deprived of access to employment, additional academic work, and economic opportunities as a function
of their behavior. Delinquents are deprived of some desirable features of
social living because of their antisocial acts.

For individuals who are functioning normally in society, a lack of
specific behaviors or the presence of mildly debilitating problems also
constitute a deprivation of some kind. For example, an individual may
decry his or her "shyness" because of the deprivation of social experiences
with which this may be associated. Children and adults with debilitating,
albeit circumscribed, problems are deprived of moving about in life freely
because of some behavior which presents obstacles.

The social deprivation that individuals normally experience as a function of their behavior problems or deficits has to be weighed against any
other deprivation temporarily resulting from treatment (Ball, 1968; Cahoon, 1968). The issue of deprivation versus no deprivation would be
relatively easy to decide. Yet, weighing the relative disadvantages of different types of deprivation and the duration of each type makes the issue
more complex (Baer, 1970).

Considerations for Justifying Use of Painful Stimuli or Deprivation

The decision to use painful stimuli, deprivation, or any other controversial technique requires consideration of at least four issues: the kind
of painful stimuli or deprivation, the duration of the program, availability
of alternative treatment strategies, and demonstrable benefits resulting
from their use. These issues determine, in part, whether use of the aversive
technique might be justified.

Kind of Painful Stimuli or Deprivation. Certainly, the aversiveness of
the stimulus or deprivation has to be carefully weighed. Cruel or unusual
events should not be employed for behavior change nor could their use be
readily justified. When painful events such as shock are used, the stimuli
are not immobilizing, usually have no after-effects, and are not permanently damaging (Tanner, 1973). For example, the pain associated with
shock typically is described as resembling an injection, a sting, or feeling
as if an unanesthetized tooth were being drilled (Lovaas & Simmons, 1969;

Miron, 1968). In some cases, such as outpatient treatment with alcoholics, the "painful" or rather uncomfortable aversive event is drug-induced nausea. Thus, it should be readily apparent that those relatively infrequent uses of painful stimuli bear no resemblance to torture, misery, and agony.

When deprivation is used, it is usually deprivation of secondary reinforcers such as activities or privileges rather than primary reinforcers. In virtually all programs basic needs are satisfied. Clients have access to shelter, suitable quarters, food, water, and care. Yet, they can earn reinforcers which add considerably to the desirability of their conditions. For example, in one token economy in a psychiatric hospital, patients could spend their tokens for private living-quarters, recreational events, trips to town, extra time (than was normally available) with a ward chaplain or nurse, listening to a live band, and other reinforcing events (Ayllon & Azrin, 1965). Since patients normally had access to many of these events, this might constitute deprivation. However, deprivation included those events not normally considered to be essential for existence. Moreover, at least some of the events provided as reinforcers normally were unavailable in the setting (e.g., extra religious services). Thus, deprivation of all activities or privileges was not required for the program. Many programs either provide previously unavailable reinforcers or increase the delivery of reinforcers already available in the setting. Programs employing this approach avoid deprivation, as usually conceived. Nevertheless, an objection sometimes voiced is that extra privileges or activities which are introduced as reinforcers should be given to all individuals noncontingently to improve their existence. Yet, if the goal of a program or treatment facility is therapeutic behavior change, the noncontingent delivery of all available reinforcers is not likely to advance this goal.

There are infrequent exceptions which report deprivation of basic needs. As mentioned earlier, in one program hospitalized patients were told they would not receive food unless they worked (Cotter, 1967). This kind of deprivation represents a misuse of behavior modification for a variety of reasons. Food was withdrawn without making any provisions for a client's basic needs or ensuring that less drastic procedures would achieve the same end.

Even when primary reinforcers such as food are used, an individual should not be completely deprived. For example, in a reinforcement program the clients may not respond to candy, tokens, praise, or activities. Deprivation may be used to increase the reinforcing value of food. Yet the deprivation can be mild such as temporarily reducing or eliminating dessert after a meal rather than omitting the meal itself. As mentioned earlier, small meals are sometimes used so that the client never is satiated and food will be reinforcing over a long period throughout the day (O'Brien et al., 1972). In programs where deprivation of complete meals is used as a last resort, patients are normally given a concentrated nutritive substance daily or are placed on a special diet to ensure that their survival is not in jeopardy. Even so, deprivation of meals certainly is objectionable and probably does not meet some other conditions (see below) which might justify the use of controversial techniques. In the actual practice of behavior modification in applied settings, the kind of aversive events employed, in part, dictates whether the program is justified. Of course, other conditions which might justify the use of aversive techniques are important to consider.

Duration of the Program. An important consideration in justifying the use of painful stimuli or deprivation is the duration of the program. The program should have reasonably well specified limits as to how long it can be in effect and the conditions which will lead to its termination or continuation. Most individuals in treatment facilities already undergo aversive conditions which stem directly from their behavioral deficits or socially censured responses. For example, retarded children are deprived of possibilities for a variety of reinforcers throughout their lives. To invoke further hardship such as subjecting them to any aversive event or further deprivation as part of a behavior modification program must be for a limited time only. Otherwise adverse conditions of the program are merely superimposed upon social deprivation that is constantly experienced. It might be better not to intervene unless the aversive consequences are scheduled for a relatively short period and promise to result in improved conditions.

The duration of the aversive techniques used as part of the program needs to be weighed against the aversive conditions resulting from the client's deficits or aberrant behaviors. Since punishment usually shows rapid effects, aversive consequences can be withdrawn in a relatively short period. For example, the elimination of self-injurious behavior in autistic and retarded children may take only a few sessions (Lovaas & Simmons, 1969). In many cases, self-destructive behavior has been ongoing for years. Thus, the duration of the program is exceedingly short relative to the length of time that self-imposed aversive conditions have been in effect. Independent of the history of the client's behavior, the duration of any punishment program should be limited. If the effects of punishment are not immediate, the program should be altered or discontinued whether or not painful stimuli or deprivation are employed.

Availability of Alternative Treatment Strategies. Perhaps the most important single consideration in selecting painful stimuli or deprivation is the lack of availability of other techniques to change behavior for a given individual. Generally, programs attempt to alter behavior using only reinforcement or reinforcement with a relatively limited amount of punishment. When positive reinforcement is used, mildly aversive events or nonpainful aversive consequences (e.g., time-out or fines) usually are effective in suppressing behavior. If these approaches fail, there may be some justification for turning to painful stimuli or deprivation. For example, in one case, shock was used to suppress chronic sneezing of a female high school student. Shock was used only after numerous other procedures (e.g., psychotherapy, hypnosis, hospitalization, medication) had been unsuccessful (Kushner, 1968). However, in most programs procedures which are less objectionable than painful stimuli and deprivation are readily available.

Sometimes other techniques are available but they are inefficient or have undesirable consequences. For example, withholding attention from individuals who perform self-destructive behavior effectively reduces the rate of such behavior (Lovaas & Simmons, 1969). Yet, as the slow process of extinction unfolds, there is danger that the individual will mutilate himself. Electric shock when used briefly can eliminate the behavior quickly. Institutions ordinarily may use physical restraint (e.g., straitjackets or tying residents to benches) to reduce self-destructive behavior or aggressive tantrums. Indeed, restraint may be continued for a period of months or even years (Lovaas et al., 1965; Miron, 1968). Brief punishment is seen as an alternative to a life of physical restraint. (This is an interesting example because physical restraint, which deprives an individual of interaction with the physical and social environment, can be obviated by briefly using painful stimuli to eliminate the behavior that led to restraint.)

Programs considering aversive techniques, particularly the use of painful stimuli or deprivation, need as one basis of justification some assurance that less objectionable techniques do not work. At least some attempt is needed to determine whether a reinforcement program using a variety of different reinforcers is sufficient to change behavior. Since the evidence is vast that reinforcement techniques will work across a variety of settings and treatment populations (Kazdin & Bootzin, 1972), only the unambiguous lack of their efficacy might justify relying on aversive events. Even when a reinforcement program has not altered client behavior sufficiently, a number of techniques are available to increase the effect of reinforcement rather than turning to aversive events (Kazdin, 1973e). Using aversive techniques such as shock or deprivation, without trying other procedures first, including mildly aversive events, is ethically objectionable.

Demonstrable Benefits of Aversive Techniques. A final consideration in determining whether the use of painful stimuli or deprivation is justified is whether there are clear benefits which result. Unfortunately, this is not the criterion for use of painful stimuli or deprivation in society. Deprivation and pain are inherent in many social institutions which are not clearly justified by their efficacy in changing behavior. For example, criminals are obviously deprived of individual rights when incarcerated. A rationale for this procedure is to protect society. Yet, such deprivation does not always appear to be in the best interest of the criminals (i.e., increase their subsequent noncriminal behavior) or society (i.e., prevent or reduce further crimes). Indeed, it is likely that the overall frequency of crimes is augmented by the "training" one receives while in prison. Capital punishment represents an extreme case of deprivation (one's life). Any beneficial effects obviously are not experienced by the individual himself. Moreover, capital punishment does not appear to benefit society, at least in terms of reducing the frequency of capital crimes (Bedau, 1967). If there are favorable effects resulting from deprivation and pain to which criminals are exposed, they are not clear and rarely carefully demonstrated.

Similarly, psychiatric patients represent a group for whom social deprivation has dubious demonstrable effects. Supposedly, individuals are hospitalized to protect them from endangering others or themselves. Unfortunately, rarely is there evidence that individuals are hospitalized because they present an actual danger (Scheff, 1966). Hospitalized patients are deprived of a variety of rights, varying across states and countries, which include the right to vote, to obtain a marriage or driver's license, to convey property, and to procreate children. Social deprivation might be justified, if clear beneficial effects are derived from its use. However, the benefits derived from hospitalization both for the patient himself and society have been seriously questioned. Indeed, evidence suggests that the patient becomes more bizarre and withdrawn after hospitalization (e.g., Wing, 1962).

The justification for deprivation in behavior modification depends upon effecting a demonstrable change in behavior, in addition to the other conditions discussed above. If behavior does not change or show a trend in the direction of change, continuation of deprivation, and indeed of *any* program, is not justified. The experimental stance of evaluating effectiveness of the techniques is particularly important when those techniques are a source of ethical concern.

Use of Aversive Techniques: Summary. The four considerations for using controversial aversive techniques to change behavior represent minimum requirements. They provide guidelines rather than definitive ethical imperatives. Yet it is not readily conceivable that a program would fail to meet these minimal requirements and still be justified. There are basic rights to which all individuals should be entitled. Certainly one of these rights is to not be deprived of those events which are required for existence. It is unclear precisely under what conditions deprivation of those things not essential to life would be justified. As mentioned earlier, social institutions invoke deprivation such as prison confinement. Yet the ethics of deprivation in society are not explicit. What is socially approved as suitable for "punishment" is not approved under the guise of "treatment."

Probably the ethically least undesirable use of deprivation of any kind is part of a self-control regimen or contingency contract system where the client selects the deprivation (e.g., of a privilege) as an appropriate means to achieve a self-selected or agreed upon outcome. In many cases in society, individuals voluntarily submit to aversive events to eradicate discomfort or portending problems such as when one attends a dentist to repair a tooth or a surgeon to perform an operation (Tanner, 1973). In these instances, as with outpatient treatment in aversion therapy, the individual consents to undergo some aversive condition to achieve a beneficial (self-selected) gain. In cases of consent, there is relatively little problem in invoking aversive conditions. Yet, sometimes consent cannot be given (e.g., because the client does not understand the alternatives) and the issue becomes complex. Of course, other individuals (e.g., parents or spouses) can give consent (e.g., for surgery) when the individual himself cannot. Yet, there are limitations in consent by others, particularly in the domain of "mental health." An individual may be judged as "mentally incompetent" and lose his or her right of consent. Consent can be vested in those whose interests might not benefit the client.

Future Directions

Initially, behavioral techniques were developed from investigations in laboratory settings conducted on a relatively narrow range of infrahuman species. Early laboratory work with humans assessed the extent to which the principles extended to human behavior in relatively restricted laboratory situations on simple responses (e.g., lever pulling). Thus, most early applications did not attempt to alter behavior for purposes of treatment, rehabilitation, and education. The principles established with infrahuman species were shown to apply to human behavior. Of course, humans introduced new complexities such as having much of their behavior governed by language and cognitions. Eventually, pioneering efforts were made to apply simple principles to humans in applied settings to change behaviors of social significance. The techniques have been extended successfully primarily to individuals whose behavior is regarded as "abnormal" or "deficient." The majority of behavior modification programs are conducted in institutions and hospitals, special education classrooms, facilities for delinquents, and in the homes of children who are considered to have "problems." The techniques are applied to individuals whose behavior is traditionally included in the domain of "mental health."

Since the applications have shown considerable promise in the domain of "problematic" behavior, recently the techniques have been extended to contemporary social problems usually not included as part of mental health. For example, behavioral techniques have been applied on a small scale to racial integration, ecological problems, community organization, unemployment, and military training. These investigations do not represent widespread programs which claim to resolve a particular social issue. Yet, the investigations focus upon important issues. Future directions in behavior modification will probably emphasize amelioration of social ills which threaten the existence of society. Recent work which may represent preliminary samples of these applications will be briefly reviewed.

Racial Integration. Racial integration represents a multifaceted issue. No attempt should be made to define a simple response as the sole target for social integration of groups which encounter discrimination. Procedures to facilitate racial integration usually are aimed at changing attitudes. Yet changes in racial attitudes do not necessarily result in corresponding changes in behavior (Mann, 1959). It is important to consider whether interracial social interaction at any level can be altered systematically with behavioral techniques.

A recent program focused on socially integrating five black children in a predominantly white first grade classroom (Hauserman, Waylen, & Behling, 1973). All students in the classroom were reinforced for sitting with "new friends" during lunch. "New friends" included interracial combinations of students although this was not specified to the children. Whenever the children were sitting with their "new friends," they received praise and a token. Tokens were redeemable after lunch for a cookie, candy, or another snack. Interracial interactions increased when reinforcement was delivered. Interestingly, interaction generalized to a free play period even though no reinforcement was provided for interracial socialization. Unfortunately, when the program was withdrawn, racial integration returned to baseline levels. No particular procedures were employed to ensure response maintenance or transfer of training. Nevertheless, as a preliminary inquiry into the area of integration, the results suggest that interracial social interaction can be readily programmed in naturalistic settings. Interaction has been focused upon in a number of studies (Bennett & Maley, 1973; Buell et al., 1968; Kale et al., 1968). Yet, racial interaction represents a relatively unexplored area of behavior modification.

Littering. Littering in public places represents a problem of increased concern. Cleaning litter is expensive in terms of tax dollars. Moreover, in recent years the cost has increased (Clark, Burgess, & Hendee, 1972). National campaigns such as "Keep America Beautiful" have attempted to reduce littering. Although campaigns may make individuals more sensitive to the problem and change attitudes toward littering, there appears to be no relationship between anti-litter attitudes and littering behavior (cf. Clark et al., 1972). Investigations have shown that merely instructing people not to litter or providing campaign materials do not result in consistent changes in littering (e.g., Burgess, Clark, & Hendee, 1971). Recently, the feasibility of using operant techniques to control littering has been explored. Programs have been conducted in national campgrounds, movie theaters, zoos, and school settings.

In one project, littering was controlled in a national campground during a summer weekend (Clark et al., 1972). The campground (over 100 acres) was divided into separate areas so that litter could be counted on foot. One weekend served as baseline to determine the amount of accumulated litter. Litter (bags, beverage cans, bottles) was planted in the campground to provide a consistent level for the weekends of baseline and the program. During the weekend of the program, seven families on the campground were contacted and told of the litter problem. The families were asked whether the children would help clean the grounds. The children were told they could earn any of various items (e.g., Smokey Bear shoulder patch, comic book, ranger badge, gum, and so on). Children were given a large plastic bag and told they had one day to earn the badge. The children were not told where to look for litter or how much litter had to be collected to earn the reward. The amount of litter was markedly reduced during the incentive program. The children collected between 150 and 200 pounds of litter. The rewards given to them cost approximately $3. To accomplish the clean-up using camp personnel would have cost approximately $50 to $60. These results show that a relatively inexpensive incentive system was associated with a dramatic reduction in littering. Of course, the results are preliminary but do suggest a viable solution to a practical problem.

Mass Transportation. Increasingly, major cities are developing mass transit systems in the hopes of decreasing reliance upon automobiles. The number of individuals who drive cars to work is overwhelming. Only recently has it been emphasized that the use of personal transportation is ecologically unsound. The use of mass transit in place of cars would conserve energy (fuel), decrease pollutants in the air, and reduce crowding and noise attributable to traffic. Moreover, the expense of law enforcement required for traffic control would be reduced considerably with mass transit. The issues of energy conservation and pollution are particularly salient.

Recently, operant techniques have been used to increase bus ridership. To demonstrate this on a relatively small scale, reinforcement was used to increase bus ridership on a large university campus (Everett, Hayward, & Meyers, 1974). Buses in the university traveled a number of routes within campus. To increase bus ridership, boarders received either 25 cents for riding the bus or tokens (slips of paper) which could be saved and spent either toward future bus rides or at various stores in town for items such as food, movies, cigarettes, beer, and other rewards. Throughout the program, riders continued to pay the usual 10 cents bus fee. However, the 25 cents or ticket was delivered to them immediately after boarding the bus. The program increased ridership during the reinforcement phase as shown in a reversal design. The influence of token reinforcement on bus ridership was especially pronounced with those individuals who walked rather than those who used a car. While the major concern with mass transit is to increase ridership of those who ordinarily use their cars, this initial project was conducted on a university campus where automobile transportation was already minimal. Nevertheless, the reliability of a reinforcement system in altering bus ridership was demonstrated.

Training Self-help of Welfare Recipients. Welfare recipients have mutual concerns in the community which might be expressed and resolved, given united action among community members. Self-help groups some-times develop to address community issues such as urban renewal, city government, and education. Yet, it is unlikely that individuals will con-sistently attend self-help group meetings. Lower socioeconomic class in-dividuals usually participate less than middle-class individuals in volunteer organizations (Berelson & Steiner, 1964). Moreover, long range goals of self-help programs may be too delayed to provide sufficient incentives to attend meetings.

One program attempted to increase attendance of welfare recipients to self-help meetings (Miller & Miller, 1970). During the initial phase of the project, the welfare counselor mailed notices to each self-help group mem-ber indicating when the next meeting was scheduled. During the rein-forcement phase, group members were informed that they could select two free Christmas toys for each of their children, if they attended the meeting. Toys were donated by "concerned middle-class citizens". In a reversal design, the effect of reinforcement on attendance to self-help group meetings was demonstrated. Moreover, while the reinforcement contingency was in effect, new members were attracted to the self-help group. Of course, developing attendance to self-help group meetings is far from resolving the community issues which face welfare recipients. Indeed, attendance alone is unlikely to ensure that the group will actually engage in socially significant activities. Nevertheless, it does suggest that an incentive program might be useful in initiating community action. The rewards for community action are usually delayed. A behavior modifica-tion program can provide interim incentives to initiate social action.

Obtaining Employment. A significant social concern is procuring jobs for the unemployed. Lack of employment is associated with a number of social ills including crime, "mental illness," alcoholism, racial discrimi-nation, medical neglect, and family desertion (see Jones & Azrin, 1973). Recent research (Jones & Azrin, 1973; Exp. I) suggests that a major portion of jobs are obtained through informal contacts regarding job opportunities which are not made public. Information about job openings often is made available to friends, acquaintances, and relatives by individuals who have early access to such information (e.g., employees). Thus, a major task in job procurement is disclosing existing job opportunities.

Working with a state agency, Jones and Azrin (1973; Exp. II) evaluated the effect of an incentive condition for obtaining information about jobs which actually resulted in employment. Using a reversal design, an initial phase evaluated the effect of placing a newspaper ad, under the auspices of the agency, noting several occupational categories for which individuals registered at the agency were qualified (e.g., truck drivers, sales clerk) and asked readers to phone in any positions which were known to be avail-able. After one week, an experimental ad was placed in the same newspaper. The ad was similar to the previous one but indicated that anyone who reported a job opening that led to employment would receive $100. After one week the experimental ad was removed and the initial ad was reinstated.

With the initial (no incentive) ad, two calls were received and only one of these led to employment of an individual registered at the agency. With the incentive ad, 14 calls were received which resulted in 8 instances of employment. With the reinstatement of the no incentive ad, no openings were reported and, of course, no individuals could be hired as a result. Thus, the incentive condition resulted in information about more openings and greater job procurement than did the no incentive condition.

Although the incentive condition may seem extravagant, from a cost-benefit analysis it was less expensive than was the no incentive condition. In the incentive condition, the average cost per successful placement was $130 (which included the cost of the ad and the reward to persons who called in the jobs). In the no incentive condition, the cost per successful placement was $470 (which included the cost of the ad). These preliminary results suggest that the manipulation of incentive conditions can benefit the procurement of employment.

Military Training.   Training individuals to function in the military is a task for virtually every government. Typically, initial training is intense and may lead to severe psychological distress. Although basic training is inherently physically demanding, investigators have questioned the necessity of placing men under severe psychological stress as part of training (Datel & Legters, 1970). Much of indoctrination into the military and techniques for behavior change are based upon aversive control. Arbitrary punishments and seemingly unnecessary penalties sometimes are levied for minor offenses. Moreover, individuals are required to submit and surrender to authority and suffer under seemingly unreasonable demands. Self-devaluation may result (Goffman, 1961). Some of the problems of morale may be a function of reliance upon aversive control. Undesirable side effects of aversive control, discussed earlier, such as emotional reactions and escape and avoidance may result.

An initial attempt to deemphasize aversive control in the military was reported at one training base (Datel & Legters, 1970). A merit system was devised where tokens could be earned. Thus, positive reinforcement for desirable behavior was emphasized rather than punishment for undesirable behavior. Tokens were earned for behaviors such as performance at daily inspections, training formations, proficiency in physical combat, marksmanship, written-test performance, and work. The tokens (punches on a card carried by the trainee) could be spent for a variety of back-up reinforcers highly valued by recruits such as attending a movie, taking an overnight pass off the base, or being considered for promotion. In order to apply reinforcement effectively, points were delivered immediately after

performance. Moreover, performance which surpassed minimal requirements on a task (e.g., drill sergeant's daily evaluation for barracks inspection)
achieved extra points. The purpose of the system was to increase the morale
of the recruits and minimize the aversive contingencies usually present.
Yet, no evidence was provided regarding the success of the program.
Nevertheless, the program represents an initial attempt in only one training camp to alter an institution which has relied heavily on aversive control.

Aside from the investigations sampled above, a number of other socially
relevant applications have been reported. Behavioral techniques have been
used to improve the punctuality of industrial workers (Hermann, de
Montes, Dominguez, Montes, & Hopkins, 1973), to increase job performance of Neighborhood Youth Corps workers (Pierce & Risley, 1974), to increase the consumption of "middle class" i.e., nutritionally balanced) meals
by rural Head Start children (Madsen, Madsen, & Thompson, 1974), and
to structure small community living conditions of students in a university
setting (Miller & Feallock, 1975).

Conclusion

The principles and their applications suggest that effective means may
be available for resolving significant human problems. The illustrations
of programs applied to social concerns represent the early stages of a
technology. Presently, behavior modification is applied primarily to the
individuals whose behavior has been identified as problematic. Thus,
throughout previous chapters, discussions focused upon psychiatric patients, retardates, delinquents, learning disabilities, and a host of individual cases with idiosyncratic aberrant behaviors. Yet, a technology devoted primarily to amelioration of problems is only in its germinal stage
of development. The analog in medicine would be *treating* diseases when
they occur rather than *preventing* them entirely. When behavioral programs are applied to prevent problems, the technological advances will
be more evident. For example, behavior modification is being used extensively in education to ameliorate academic deficiencies. It is very likely
that parents could execute procedures in the home to accelerate performance of their children to prevent problems in schools. Moreover, education could be structured to foster accelerated performance of all children in general rather than those who require a special program.

Along with the prevention of behavioral "problems," the behavioral
technology will be increasingly applied to social ills. Positive social implications of behavior modification have not yet been realized. Naturally,
people have misgivings regarding the implementation of a technology to
govern behavior. Yet, resolution of social problems is imperative and
immediate intervention in many cases is essential. The probable costs
of not using must be weighed against the possible costs of misusing the

available technology. This point was lucidly expressed by London (1969):

> Whatever the hypothetical dangers of an efficient behavior technology may be, the real social evils sustained by abstention from it are severe. There are problems of motivation and incentive, as with high school dropouts and unskilled workers; problems of social organization and responsibility, as with demonstrators, protesters, rioters, and police, with delinquents and criminals, with businessmen who destroy forests and pollute waterways, and with plain litterbugs; problems of attitude and prejudice as with enemies of Negro civil rights or with employers who reject Catholics and Jews. All these problems abound, and to be solved, they must finally be reduced to the level of changing individual behavior. Some of the needed solutions can of course, be legislated, and for those, the problem of changing individual behavior applies only to people who defy the law. But for many of these problems no direct legislation is possible, and other answers to them must be sought. Behavior-control technology offers one avenue of approach to this purpose [pp. 8–9].

Although many of the applications of the current technology are impressive, extrapolation to social problems will require extensive research beyond that presently available. While many of the basic principles which will be useful for change are known, practical problems derived from their extrapolation to social problems are not. As Skinner (1974) pointed out, "Knowing the basic principles without knowing the details of a practical problem is no closer to a solution than knowing the details without knowing the basic principles [p. 250]." The majority of behavioral interventions have been in applied settings in which relatively circumscribed responses are altered in fairly well controlled situations. As behavioral principles are extended to large-scale interventions in society, the consequences are less well known. Social problems are deeply enmeshed in an entire social system and with social institutions. Altering one behavior in society probably has far reaching consequences for the social system in general (Willems, 1974). For example, as alluded to earlier, advances in behavioral technology including curriculum design and reinforcement techniques could vastly accelerate education. Individuals might well be able to complete their college years long before what is now ordinarily the case. However, acceleration of education on a large scale may have intricate consequences. Releasing a large number of individuals from schools at an early age might affect employment, retirement, the expenditure of leisure time, crime, marriage, divorce, population control, and so on. Successfully altering one area (e.g., education) could bear diverse consequences. The application of technology to social problems requires considering what effects changes in one area of behavior have on other behaviors in society (Willems, 1974). At the current state of knowledge, a behavioral technology is available to effect significant social change. While existing knowledge calls for optimism regarding the potential solution for plaguing social problems, the lack of complete understanding requires caution.

Glossary

ABAB Design—See Reversal Design.

Alternate Response Training—A technique used in therapy (as desensitization) and as a self-control strategy in which the individual is trained to engage in a response (e.g., relaxation) which interferes with or replaces another response which is to be controlled or eliminated.

Aversive Event—A stimulus which suppresses a behavior it follows or in-increases a behavior which results in its termination.

Avoidance—Performance of a behavior which postpones or averts the presentation of an aversive event.

Back-up Reinforcer—An object, activity, or event (primary or secondary reinforcer) that can be purchased with tokens. Those reinforcers which "back up" the value of the tokens.

Baseline—The frequency that behavior is performed prior to initiating a behavior modification program. The rate of performance used to evaluate the effect of the program. Operant rate of behavior. Initial phase of reversal, multiple-baseline, and changing-criterion designs.

Behavior—Any observable and measurable response or act of an individual. (The terms "behavior" and "response" are used synonymously.)

Behavior Control—Exerting power or influence over others by altering the environmental contingencies to achieve a definite end.

Chain—A sequence of behaviors that occurs in a fixed order. Each behavior in the chain serves as a discriminative stimulus (S^D) for the next re-

251

sponse. Also each behavior in the chain (except the first behavior) serves as a conditioned reinforcer which reinforces the previous response.

Chaining—Developing a sequence of responses in a backward order. The terminal response in the chain is developed first. The next to the last response is trained second. Remaining responses are trained in the reverse order of their performance once the chain is finally performed. Developing a complex behavior by training individual components of the behavior in a backward fashion.

Changing-Criterion Design—An experimental design in which the effect of the program is evaluated by repeatedly altering the criterion for reinforcement or punishment. If behavior matches or tracks the criterion as the criterion is altered, this suggests that the contingency reinforcement or punishment. If the behavior matches or tracks the criterion is repeatedly changed follows preliminary baseline assessment.

Classical (or Respondent) Conditioning—A type of learning in which a neutral (conditioned) stimulus is paired with an unconditioned stimulus which automatically elicits a reflex response. After repeatedly following the conditioned stimulus with the unconditioned stimulus, the conditioned stimulus alone will elicit a reflex response. In classical conditioning new stimuli gain the power to elicit respondent behavior.

Conditioned Aversive Stimulus—An event which is initially neutral may acquire aversive properties by virtue of being paired with other aversive events or a signal that no reinforcement will be forthcoming.

Conditioned Reinforcer—See Secondary Reinforcer.

Conditioned Response—A reflex response elicited by a conditioned stimulus alone in the absence of the unconditioned stimulus. It resembles, but is not identical to, the unconditioned response. See Classical Conditioning.

Conditioned Stimulus—A previously neutral stimulus which through repeated associations with an unconditioned stimulus elicits a reflex response. See Classical Conditioning.

Contingency—The relationship between a behavior (the response to be changed) and the events (consequences) which follow behavior. Sometimes events which precede the behavior are also specified by a contingency.

Contingency Contracts—A behavior modification program in which an agreement or contract is made between individuals who wish behavior to change (e.g., parents) and those whose behavior is to be changed (e.g., their children). The contract specifies the relationship between behavior and the consequences which will follow.

Contingent Delivery of a Reinforcer—The delivery of a reinforcer only when a specified behavior has been performed. Contrast with Non-contingent Delivery of a Reinforcer.

Continuous Reinforcement—A schedule of reinforcement in which a response is reinforced each time it is performed.

Control Group Design—An experimental design in which the effect of the program is evaluated by comparing (at least) two groups, a group which receives the program and another group which does not receive the program.

Coverant—A private event such as a thought, fantasy, or image which is not "observable" to anyone other than the individual to whom it is occurring. Private events can be viewed as responses which can be altered by varying the consequences which follow them. "Coverant" is a contraction of "covert" and "operant."

Covert Event—A private event such as a thought, fantasy, or image. See Coverant.

Cue—See Discriminative Stimulus (S^D).

Delay of Reinforcement—The time interval between a response and delivery of the reinforcer.

Deprivation—Reducing the availability of or access to a reinforcer.

Differential Reinforcement—Reinforcing a response in the presence of one stimulus (S^D) and extinguishing the response in the presence of other stimuli (S^Δ). Eventually the response is consistently performed in the presence of the S^D but not in the presence of the S^Δ.

Differential Reinforcement of Other Behavior (DRO)—Delivery of a reinforcer after any response *except* the target response. The individual is reinforced only when he or she is not performing the target response. Behaviors other than the target response are reinforced. The effect of a DRO schedule is to decrease the target (unreinforced) response.

Discrimination—Responding differently in the presence of different cues or antecedent events. Control of behavior by discriminative stimuli. See Stimulus Control.

Discriminative Stimulus (S^D)—An antecedent event or stimulus which signals that a certain response will be reinforced. A response is reinforced in the presence of an S^D. After an event becomes an S^D by being paired with reinforcement, its presence can increase the probability that the response will occur.

Elicit—To automatically bring about a response. Respondent or reflex behaviors are elicited by unconditioned stimuli. Contrast with Emit and Operant Behavior. See Classical Conditioning.

Emit—To perform a response spontaneously. An emitted response is not automatically controlled by stimuli which precede it. Operant behaviors are emitted. They are controlled primarily by the consequences which follow them. Contrast with Elicit and Respondent. See Operant Conditioning.

Escape—Performance of a behavior which terminates an aversive event.

Experimental Design—The plan of the program which determines how the effect of the experimental contingency will be causally demonstrated. The plan to evaluate whether the behavior modification program rather than various extraneous factors was responsible for behavior change.

Extinction—A procedure in which the reinforcer is no longer delivered for a previously reinforced response.

Extinction Burst—An increase in the frequency and intensity of responding at the beginning of extinction.

Fading—The gradual removal of discriminative stimuli (S^D) including prompts such as instructions or physical guidance. Initially, developing behavior is often facilitated by prompts. Yet it is important in most situations to *fade* the prompt. Fading also can refer to the gradual removal of reinforcement as in the progressive thinning of a reinforcement schedule.

Fixed-interval Schedule—A schedule of administering reinforcement. In an FI schedule, the first occurrence of the target response after a fixed time interval elapses is reinforced.

Fixed-ratio Schedule—A schedule of administering reinforcement. In an FR schedule, an unvarying number of occurrences of the target response is required for reinforcement.

Functional Relationship—A relationship between the experimental condition or contingency and behavior. A functional relationship is demonstrated if behavior systematically changes when the contingency is applied, withdrawn, and reapplied.

Generalized Conditioned Reinforcer—A conditioned reinforcer that has acquired reinforcing value by being associated or paired with a variety of other reinforcers. Money is an example of a generalized conditioned reinforcer.

Group Contingencies—Contingencies in which the group participates. There are two major variations: (1) An individual's behavior can determine the consequences delivered to the group; (2) the behavior of a group as a whole determines the consequences that the group (each member) receives.

High Probability Behavior—A response which is performed with a relatively high frequency when the individual is given the opportunity to select among alternative behaviors. See Premack Principle.

Incompatible Behavior—Behavior that cannot be performed at the same time as or that interferes with another behavior.

Intermittent Reinforcement—A schedule of reinforcement in which a response is not reinforced every time it is performed. Only some occurrences of the response are reinforced.

Interval Schedule of Reinforcement—A schedule in which reinforcement is delivered on the basis of the amount of time that passes before a response can be reinforced. Contrast with Ratio Schedule of Reinforcement.

Medical Model—A view which specifies that psychological symptoms or maladaptive behavior are caused by underlying processes which are "diseased." The underlying psychological "disease" must be treated before overt behavior can be changed.

Modeling—See Observational Learning.

Multiple-Baseline Designs—Experimental designs which demonstrate the effect of a contingency by introducing the contingency across different behaviors, individuals, or situations at different points in time. The effect of the contingency is demonstrated without a reversal phase.

Multiple-Baseline Design Across Behaviors—An experimental design in which baseline data are gathered across two or more behaviors. The experimental contingency is applied to the first behavior while baseline conditions are continued for the other behaviors. After all behaviors have stabilized, the contingency is introduced for the second behavior. This is continued until the experimental contingency is applied to all target behaviors at different points in time. A causal relationship between the experimental contingency and behavior is demonstrated, if each behavior changes when and only when the contingency is introduced.

Multiple-Baseline Design Across Individuals—An experimental design in which baseline data are gathered across two or more individuals. The experimental contingency is applied to the first individual while baseline conditions are continued for the other individuals. After behavior has stabilized for all individuals, the contingency is introduced for the second individual. This is continued until the experimental contingency is applied to all individuals at different points in time. A causal relationship between the experimental contingency and behavior is demonstrated, if each individual's behavior changes when and only when the contingency is introduced.

Multiple-Baseline Design Across Situations—An experimental design in which baseline data are gathered across two or more situations. The experimental contingency is applied to behavior in the first situation while baseline conditions are continued for the behavior in the other situations. After behavior has stabilized in each situation, the contingency is introduced for behavior in the second situation. This is continued until the contingency is applied to all situations at different points in time. A causal relationship between the experimental contingency and behavior is demonstrated, if behavior in each situation changes when and only when the contingency is introduced.

"Naturally Occurring" Reinforcers—Those reinforcing events in the environment which are not contrived but are usually available as part of the setting. Attention, praise, completion of an activity, and mastery of a task are some events which are "naturally occurring" reinforcers.

Negative Reinforcement—An increase in the frequency of a response which is followed by termination or removal of a negative reinforcer. See Negative Reinforcer.

Negative Reinforcer—An aversive event or stimulus which when terminated increases the frequency of the preceding response. The increase in frequency of the response which terminates or removes the aversive event is called negative reinforcement.

Noncontingent Delivery of a Reinforcer—The delivery of a reinforcer independently of behavior. The reinforcer is delivered without reference to how the individual is behaving. Contrast with Contingent Delivery of a Reinforcer.

Observational Learning—Learning by observing another individual (a model) engage in a behavior. To learn from a model, the observer need not perform the behavior nor receive direct consequences for his performance.

Occasion—To increase the likelihood that a response is performed by presenting an S^D. Certain cues in the environment (e.g., music) occasion certain responses (e.g., singing).

Operant Behavior—Emitted behavior that is controlled by its consequences.

Operant Conditioning—A type of learning in which behaviors are altered primarily by regulating the consequences which follow them. The frequency of operant behaviors is altered by the consequences which they produce.

Operant Rate—See Baseline.

Overcorrection—A punishment procedure which consists of two components. First, the environmental consequences of the undesirable behavior must be corrected (e.g., cleaning up a mess). Second, correct forms of desirable behavior must be thoroughly rehearsed or practiced (e.g., cleaning up messes made by several other people).

Overt Behavior—Behavior that is publicly observable and measurable. Contrast with Covert Event.

Positive Reinforcement—An increase in the frequency of a response which is followed by a positive reinforcer. See Positive Reinforcer.

Positive Reinforcer—An event which, when presented, increases the probability of a response it follows.

Premack Principle—A principle that states that of any pair of responses or activities in which an individual freely engages, the more frequent one will reinforce the less frequent one.

Primary Reinforcer—A reinforcing event which does not depend on learning to achieve its reinforcing properties. Food, water, and sex are primary reinforcers. Contrast with Secondary Reinforcer.

Prompt—An antecedent event which helps initiate a response. A discriminative stimulus which occasions a response. Instructions, gestures, physical guidance, and modeling cues serve as prompts.

Psychodynamic View—An explanation of personality which accounts for behavior by positing underlying psychological forces. The behavior of an individual is traced to psychological drives, impulses, or personality dynamics.

Punishment—Presentation of an aversive event or removal of a positive reinforcer contingent upon a response which decreases the probability of that response.

Ratio Schedule of Reinforcement—A schedule in which reinforcement is delivered on the basis of the number of responses which are performed. Contrast with Interval Schedule of Reinforcement.

Reinforcement—An increase in the frequency of a response when the response is immediately followed by a particular consequence. The consequence can be either the presentation of a positive reinforcer or removal of a negative reinforcer.

Reinforcer Sampling—A case of response priming where the purpose is to develop or increase utilization of an event as a reinforcer. The client is provided with a sample or small portion of the event which increases the likelihood that the entire event can serve as a reinforcer.

Reliability of Assessment—The consistency with which different observers working independently score a target response. Reliability can be calculated with different methods depending upon the method used to assess behavior (i.e., frequency, interval, or duration methods). The calculation of reliability yields a percentage of agreement between observers.

Resistance to Extinction—The extent to which a response is maintained once reinforcement is no longer provided.

Respondent—Behavior that is elicited or automatically controlled by antecedent stimuli. Reflexes are respondents because their performance automatically follows certain stimuli. The connection between unconditioned respondents and antecedent events which control them is unlearned. Respondents may come under the control of otherwise neutral stimuli through classical conditioning.

Response Cost—A punishment procedure in which a positive reinforcer is lost or some penalty is invoked contingent upon behavior. Unlike time-out, there is no specified time limit to the withdrawal of the reinforcer. Fines represent a common form of response cost.

Response Generalization—Reinforcement of one response increases the probability of other responses which are similar to and resemble the target response. Contrast with Stimulus Generalization.

Response Priming—Any procedure which initiates early steps in a sequence of responses. Response priming increases the likelihood that the terminal behavior in a sequence of responses will be performed by initiating early responses in the sequence.

Reversal Design—An experimental design where the target behavior of a subject or group of subjects is assessed to determine baseline performance. After a stable rate of behavior is shown, the experimental condition is introduced until behavior changes. A reversal phase follows where the program is withdrawn. Finally, the experimental condition is reintroduced. A functional relationship is demonstrated if behavior changes in each phase in which the experimental condition is presented and reverts to baseline or near baseline levels when it is withdrawn. Also called an ABAB design.

Reversal Phase—A phase in the reversal design in which the program is withdrawn or altered to determine whether behavior reverts to baseline or near baseline levels. During a reversal phase one of three changes usually is made: (1) the program is withdrawn, (2) the consequences are delivered noncontingently, or (3) the consequences follow a DRO schedule.

Satiation—Providing an excessive amount of reinforcer. A loss of effectiveness that occurs after a large amount of the reinforcer has been delivered.

Schedule of Reinforcement—The rule denoting how many responses or which responses will be reinforced.

S^D—See Discriminative Stimulus.

S^Δ—An antecedent event or stimulus which signals that a certain response will not be reinforced.

Secondary (or Conditioned) Reinforcer—An event which becomes reinforcing through learning. An event becomes a secondary reinforcer by being paired with other events (primary or conditioned) which are already reinforcing. Praise and attention are examples of secondary reinforcers. Contrast with Primary Reinforcer.

Self-Administered Reinforcement—Refers to the client delivering the reinforcer to himself.

Self-Control—Refers to those behaviors an individual deliberately undertakes to achieve self-selected outcomes by manipulating antecedent and consequent events.

Self-Determined Reinforcement—Refers to the client specifying the criteria for reinforcement.

Self-Instruction—A self-control technique in which an individual prompts his or her own behavior by providing covert self-instructions or statements which direct and guide performance.

Self-Observation—Assessing or recording one's own behavior. Sometimes used as a self-control technique.

Self-Punishment—Providing oneself with punishing consequences contingent upon behavior.

Self-Reinforcement—Providing oneself with reinforcing consequences contingent upon behavior. To qualify as self-reinforcement, the client must be free to partake of the reinforcer at any time whether or not a particular response is performed.

Shaping—Developing a new behavior by reinforcing successive approximations toward the terminal response. See Successive Approximations.

Social Reinforcers—Reinforcers which result from interpersonal interaction such as attention, praise and approval, smiles, and physical contact.

Spontaneous Recovery—The temporary recurrence of a behavior during extinction. Even though the response has not been reinforced, it may suddenly reappear during the course of extinction. The magnitude of a response which temporarily recovers spontaneously is usually lower than its magnitude prior to extinction.

Stimulus—A measureable event that may have an effect upon the behavior of an individual.

Stimulus Control—The presence of a particular stimulus serves as an occasion for a particular response. A response is performed when in the presence of a particular stimulus but not in its absence. See Discriminative Stimulus.

Stimulus Generalization—Transfer of a trained response to situations or stimulus conditions other than those in which training has taken place. The behavior generalizes to other situations. Contrast with Response Generalization.

Successive Approximations—Responses which increasingly resemble the terminal behavior which is being shaped. See Shaping.

Symptom Substitution—The view stemming from the medical model that if maladaptive behavior is treated without focusing on the underlying psychological problem, a substitute symptom may develop in place of the one which was treated.

Target Behavior—The behavior to be altered or focused upon during a behavior modification program. The behavior assessed and to be changed.

Terminal Response—The final goal or behavior that is achieved at the end of shaping. See Shaping.

Time-Out from Reinforcement—A punishment procedure in which access to positive reinforcement is withdrawn for a certain period of time. The opportunity to receive reinforcement is removed contingent upon behavior. Isolation from a group exemplifies time-out from reinforcement.

Token—A tangible object which serves as a generalized conditioned reinforcer. It can be exchanged for back-up reinforcers from which it derives its value. Poker chips, coins, tickets, stars, points, and checkmarks are commonly used as tokens. See Token Economy.

Token Economy—A reinforcement system where tokens are earned for a variety of behaviors and purchase a variety of back-up reinforcers. A token economy represents a system analogous to a national economy where money serves as a medium of exchange, and can be earned and spent in several ways.

Traits—Patterns of behavior which are enduring over time and across situations.

Transfer of Training—The extent to which responses trained in one setting transfer to settings other than those in which training takes place. See Stimulus Generalization.

Unconditioned Response—A reflex response elicited by an unconditioned stimulus. See Classical Conditioning and Respondent.

Unconditioned Stimulus—A stimulus which elicits a reflex response. The response is automatically evoked by the unconditioned stimulus. See Classical Conditioning.

Variable-Interval Schedule—A schedule of administering reinforcement. In a VI schedule, the first occurrence of the target response after a given time interval has elapsed is reinforced. However, the time interval changes each time, that is, it is variable. The schedule is denoted by the average time which must elapse before a response can be reinforced.

Variable-Ratio Schedule—A schedule of administering reinforcement. In a VR schedule, a number of occurrences of the target response is required for reinforcement. The number of responses required varies each time reinforcement is delivered. The schedule is denoted by the average number of occurrences of the response required before reinforcement is delivered.

Vicarious Reinforcement—Reinforcement of one individual sometimes increases performance of the reinforced behavior in other individuals who are not directly reinforced. A spread of reinforcement effects to other individuals who are not themselves directly reinforced.

References

Adams, M. R., & Popelka, G. The influence of "time-out" on stutterers and their dysfluency. *Behavior Therapy,* 1971, **2**, 334–39.

Alford, G. S., Blanchard, E. B., & Buckley, T. M. Treatment of hysterical vomiting by modification of social contingencies: A case study. *Journal of Behavior Therapy and Experimental Psychiatry,* 1972, **3**, 209–12.

Allen, K. E., & Harris, F. R. Elimination of a child's excessive scratching by training the mother in reinforcement procedures. *Behaviour Research and Therapy,* 1966, **4**, 79–84.

Allen, K. E., Hart, B. M., Buell, J. S., Harris, F. R., & Wolf, M. M. Effects of social reinforcement on isolate behavior of a nursery school child. *Child Development,* 1964, **35**, 511–18.

Allen, K. E., Turner, K. D., & Everett, P. M. A behavior modification classroom for Head Start children with problem behaviors. *Exceptional Children,* 1970, **37**, 119–27.

Allerhand, M. E. Effectiveness of parents of Head Start children as administrators of psychological tests. *Journal of Consulting Psychology,* 1967, **31**, 286–90.

Aronfreed, J., & Reber, A. Internalized behavioral suppression and the timing of social punishment. *Journal of Personality and Social Psychology,* 1965, **1**, 3–16.

Arthur, A. Z. Diagnostic testing and the new alternatives. *Psychological Bulletin,* 1969, **72**, 183–92.

Atthowe, J. M., & Krasner, L. Preliminary report on the application of contingent reinforcement procedures (token economy) on a "chronic" psychiatric ward. *Journal of Abnormal Psychology,* 1968, **73**, 37–43.

Axelrod, S. Comparison of individual and group contingencies in two special classes. *Behavior Therapy,* 1973, **4**, 83–90.

Axelrod, S., Hall, R. V., & Maxwell, A. Use of peer attention to increase study behavior. *Behavior Therapy,* 1972, **3**, 349–51.

Axelrod, S., Hall, R. V., Weis, L., & Rohrer, S. Use of self-imposed contingencies to reduce the frequency of smoking behavior. In M. J. Mahoney & C. E. Thoresen (Eds.), *Self-Control: Power to the person.* Monterey, California: Brooks/Cole, 1974, pp. 77–85.

Ayllon, T. Intensive treatment of psychotic behavior by stimulus satiation and food reinforcement. *Behaviour*

Research and Therapy, 1963, **1**, 53–61.

Ayllon, T. Some behavioral problems associated with eating in chronic schizophrenic patients. In L. P. Ullmann & L. Krasner (Eds.), *Case studies in behavior modification.* New York: Holt, Rinehart & Winston, 1965, pp. 73–77.

Ayllon, T., & Azrin, N. H. Reinforcement and instructions with mental patients. *Journal of the Experimental Analysis of Behavior,* 1964, **7**, 327–31.

Ayllon, T., & Azrin, N. H. The measurement and reinforcement of behavior of psychotics. *Journal of the Experimental Analysis of Behavior,* 1965, **8**, 357–83.

Ayllon, T., & Azrin, N. H. Reinforcer sampling: A technique for increasing the behavior of mental patients. *Journal of Applied Behavior Analysis,* 1968, **1**, 13–20. (a)

Ayllon, T., & Azrin, N. H. *The token economy: A motivational system for therapy and rehabilitation.* New York: Appleton-Century-Crofts, 1968. (b)

Ayllon, T., & Haughton, E. Control of the behavior of schizophrenic patients by food. *Journal of the Experimental Analysis of Behavior,* 1962, **5**, 343–52.

Ayllon, T., & Haughton, E. Modification of symptomatic verbal behaviour of mental patients. *Behaviour Research and Therapy,* 1964, **2**, 87–97.

Ayllon, T., & Michael, J. The psychiatric nurse as a behavioral engineer. *Journal of the Experimental Analysis of Behavior,* 1959, **3**, 324–34.

Ayllon, T., & Roberts, M. D. Eliminating discipline problems by strengthening academic performance. *Journal of Applied Behavior Analysis,* 1974, **7**, 71–76.

Ayllon, T., & Wright, P. New roles for the paraprofessional. In S. W. Bijou & E. Ribes-Inesta (Eds.), *Behavior modification: Issues and extensions.* New York: Academic Press, 1972, pp. 116–25.

Azrin, N. H. Time-out from positive reinforcement. *Science,* 1961, **133**, 382–83.

Azrin, N. H., & Foxx, R. M. A rapid method of toilet training the institu-tionalized retarded. *Journal of Applied Behavior Analysis,* 1971, **4**, 89–99.

Azrin, N. H., & Holz, W. C. Punishment. In W. K. Honig (Ed.), *Operant behavior: Areas of research and application.* New York: Appleton-Century-Crofts, 1966, pp. 380–447.

Azrin, N. H. & Powell, J. Behavioral engineering: The use of response priming to improve prescribed self-medication. *Journal of Applied Behavior Analysis,* 1969, **2**, 39–42.

Baer, D. M. Laboratory control of thumbsucking by withdrawal and re-presentation of reinforcement. *Journal of the Experimental Analysis of Behavior,* 1962, **5**, 525–28.

Baer, D. M. A case for the selective reinforcement of punishment. In C. Neuringer & J. L. Michael (Eds.), *Behavior modification in clinical psychology.* New York: Appleton-Century-Crofts, 1970, pp. 243–49.

Baer, D. M., & Sherman, J. A. Reinforcement control of generalized imitation in young children. *Journal of Experimental Child Psychology,* 1964, **1**, 37–49.

Baer, D. M., Wolf, M. M., & Risley, T. R. Some current dimensions of applied behavior analysis. *Journal of Applied Behavior Analysis,* 1968, **1**, 91–97.

Bailey, J. S., Timbers, G. D., Phillips, E. L., & Wolf, M. M. Modification of articulation errors of pre-delinquents by their peers. *Journal of Applied Behavior Analysis,* 1971, 4, 265–81.

Ball, T. S. Issues and implications of operant conditioning: The re-establishment of social behavior. *Hospital and Commnity Psychiatry,* 1968, **19**, 230–32.

Bandura, A. Influence of models' reinforcement contingencies on the acquisition of imitative responses. *Journal of Personality and Social Psychology,* 1965, **1**, 589–95.

Bandura, A. *Principles of behavior modification.* New York: Holt, Rinehart & Winston, 1969.

Bandura, A. Psychotherapy based upon modeling principles. In A. E. Bergin & S. L. Garfield (Eds.), *Handbook of psychotherapy and behavior change: An empirical analysis.* New York:

John Wiley & Sons, 1971, pp. 653–708.

Bandura, A., Grusec, J., & Menlove, F. Some social determinants of self-monitoring reinforcement systems. *Journal of Personality and Social Psychology*, 1967, **5**, 449–55.

Bandura, A., & Kupers, C. J. Transmission of patterns of self-reinforcement through modeling. *Journal of Abnormal and Social Psychology*, 1964, **69**, 1–9.

Bandura, A., & Walters, R. H. *Adolescent aggression*. New York: Ronald Press, 1959.

Bandura, A., & Walters, R. H. *Social learning and personality development*. New York: Holt, Rinehart & Winston, 1963.

Barrett, B. H. Reduction in rate of multiple tics by free operant conditioning methods, *Journal of Nervous and Mental Disease*, 1962, **135**, 187–95.

Barton, E. S., Guess, D., Garcia, E., & Baer, D. M. Improvements of retardates' mealtime behaviors by timeout procedures using multiple-baseline techniques. *Journal of Applied Behavior Analysis*, 1970, **3**, 77–84.

Becker, W. C., Madsen, C. H., Arnold, C. R., & Thomas, D. R. The contingent use of teacher attention and praising in reducing classroom behavior problems. *Journal of Special Education*, 1967, **1**, 287–307.

Bedau, H. A. *The death penalty in America*. Garden City, New York: Anchor Books, 1967.

Bennett, P. S., & Maley, R. F. Modification of interactive behaviors in chronic mental patients. *Journal of Applied Behavior Analysis*, 1973, **6**, 609–20.

Berelson, B., & Steiner, G. A. *Human behavior*. New York: Harcourt, Brace, 1964.

Bergin, A. E. The evaluation of therapeutic outcomes. In A. E. Bergin, & S. L. Garfield (Eds.), *Handbook of psychotherapy and behavior change: An empirical analysis*. New York: John Wiley & Sons, 1971, pp. 217–70.

Bijou, S. W., Peterson, R. F., & Ault, M. H. A method to integrate descriptive and experimental field studies at the level of data and empirical concepts.

Journal of Applied Behavior Analysis, 1968, **1**, 175–91.

Bijou, S. W., Peterson, R. F., Harris, F. R., Allen, K. E., & Johnston, M. S. Methodology for experimental studies of young children in natural settings. *Psychological Record*, 1969, **19**, 177–210.

Birnbrauer, J. S. Generalization of punishment effects—A case study. *Journal of Applied Behavior Analysis*, 1968, **1**, 201–11.

Blanco, R. F. Fifty recommendations to aid exceptional children. *Psychology in the Schools*, 1970, **7**, 29–37.

Boe, E. E. Extinction as a function of intensity of punishment, amount of training, and reinforcement of a competing response. *Canadian Journal of Psychology*, 1964, **18**, 328–42.

Bolstad, O. D., & Johnson, S. M. Self-regulation in the modification of disruptive behavior. *Journal of Applied Behavior Analysis*, 1972, **5**, 443–54.

Bootzin, R. R. Stimulus control treatment for insomnia. *Proceedings of the 80th Annual Convention of the American Psychological Association*, 1972, **7**, 395–96.

Boren, J. J., & Colman, A. D. Some experiments on reinforcement principles within a psychiatric ward for delinquent soldiers. *Journal of Applied Behavior Analysis*, 1970, **3**, 29–37.

Bostow, D. E., & Bailey, J. B. Modification of severe disruptive and aggressive behavior using brief time-out and reinforcement procedures. *Journal of Applied Behavior Analysis*, 1969, **2**, 31–37.

Boudin, H. M. Contingency contracting as a therapeutic tool in the deceleration of amphetamine use. *Behavior Therapy*, 1972, **3**, 604–08.

Bricker, W. A., Morgan, D. G., & Grabowski, J. G. Development and maintenance of a behavior modification repertoire of cottage attendants through TV feedback. *American Journal of Mental Deficiency*, 1972, **77**, 128–36.

Brigham, T. A., Graubard, P. S., & Stans, A. Analysis of the effects of sequential reinforcement contingencies on aspects of composition. *Journal of Ap-*

plied Behavior Analysis, 1972, **5**, 421–29.

Bristol, M. M., & Sloane, H. N., Jr. Effects of contingency contracting on study rate and test performance. *Journal of Applied Behavior Analysis*, 1974, 7, 271–85.

Broden, M., Bruce, C., Mitchell, M. A., Carter, V., & Hall, R. V. Effects of teacher attention on attending behavior of two boys at adjacent desks. *Journal of Applied Behavior Analysis*, 1970, 3, 199–203.

Broden, M., Hall, R. V., & Mitts, B. The effect of self-recording on the classroom behavior of two eighth-grade students. *Journal of Applied Behavior Analysis*, 1971, 4, 191–99.

Bucher, B. Some ethical issues in the therapeutic use of punishment. In R. D. Rubin and C. M. Franks (Eds.), *Advances in behavior, 1968*. New York: Academic Press, 1969, pp. 59–72.

Bucher, B., & King, L. W. Generalization of punishment effects in the deviant behavior of a psychotic child. *Behavior Therapy*, 1971, 2, 68–77.

Bucher, B., & Lovaas, O. I. Use of aversive stimulation in behavior modification. In M. R. Jones (Ed.), *Miami symposium on the prediction of behavior: Aversive stimulation*. Coral Gables, Florida: University of Miami Press, 1968.

Buehler, R. E., Patterson, G. R., & Furniss, J. M. The reinforcement of behaviour in institutional settings. *Behaviour Research and Therapy*, 1966, 4, 157–67.

Buell, J., Stoddard, P., Harris, F., & Baer, D. M. Collateral social development accompanying reinforcement of outdoor play in a preschool child. *Journal of Applied Behavior Analysis*, 1968, 1, 167–73.

Burchard, J. D., & Barrera, F. An analysis of time-out and response cost in a programmed environment. *Journal of Applied Behavior Analysis*. 1972, 5, 271–82.

Burchard, J. D., & Tyler, V. O. The modification of delinquent behavior through operant conditioning. *Behaviour Research and Therapy*, 1965, 2, 245–50.

Burgess, R. L., Clark, R. N., & Hendee, J. C. An experimental analysis of antilitter procedures. *Journal of Applied Behavior Analysis*, 1971, 4, 71–75.

Bushell, D., Wrobel, P. A., & Michaelis, M. L. Applying "group" contingencies to the classroom study behavior of preschool children. *Journal of Applied Behavior Analysis*, 1968, 1, 55–61.

Cahoon, D. D. Issues and implications of operant conditioning: Balancing procedures against outcomes. *Hospital and Community Psychiatry*, 1968, **19**, 228–29.

Campbell, D. T., & Stanley, J. C. Experimental and quasi-experimental designs for research and teaching. In N. L. Gage (Ed.), *Handbook of research on teaching*. Chicago: Rand McNally, 1963, pp. 171–246.

Carlson, C. S., Arnold, C. R., Becker, W. C., & Madsen, C. H. The elimination of tantrum behavior of a child in an elementary classroom. *Behaviour Research and Therapy*, 1968, **6**, 117–19.

Cautela, J. R., A behavior therapy treatment of pervasive anxiety. *Behaviour Research and Therapy*, 1966, 4, 99–109.

Cautela, J. R. Covert sensitization. *Psychological Record*, 1967, **20**, 459–68.

Cautela, J. R. Behavior therapy and self-control: Techniques and implications. In *Behavior therapy: Appraisal and status*. New York: McGraw-Hill, 1969, pp. 323–40.

Cautela, J. R. Rationale and procedures for covert conditioning. In R. D. Rubin, H. Fensterheim, J. D. Henderson, & L. P. Ullmann (Eds.), *Advances in behavior therapy*. New York: Academic Press, 1972, pp. 85–96.

Chadwick, B. A., & Day, R. C. Systematic reinforcement: Academic performance of underachieving students. *Journal of Applied Behavior Analysis*, 1971, 4, 311–19.

Christopherson, E. R., Arnold, C. M., Hill, D. W., & Quilitch, H. R. The home point system: Token reinforcement procedures for application by parents of children with behavior problems. *Journal of Applied Behavior Analysis*, 1972, 5, 485–97.

Church, R. M. The varied effects of punishment on behavior. *Psychologi-*

cal Review, 1963, **70**, 369–402.

Clark, H. B., Rowbury, T., Baer, A. M., & Baer, D. M. Timeout as a punishing stimulus in continuous and intermittent schedules. *Journal of Applied Behavior Analysis,* 1973, **6**, 443–55.

Clark, R. N., Burgess, R. L., & Hendee, J. C. The development of anti-litter behavior in a forest campground. *Journal of Applied Behavior Analysis,* 1972, **5**, 1–5.

Colman, A. D., & Boren, J. J. An information system for measuring patient behavior and its use by staff. *Journal of Applied Behavior Analysis,* 1969, **2**, 207–14.

Cooper, M. L., Thomson, C. L., & Baer, D. M. The experimental modification of teacher attending behavior. *Journal of Applied Behavior Analysis,* 1970, 3, 153–57.

Cossairt, A., Hall, R. V., & Hopkins, B. L. The effects of experimenter's instructions, feedback, and praise on teacher praise and student attending behavior. *Journal of Applied Behavior Analysis,* 1973, **6**, 89–100.

Cotler, S. B., Applegate, G., King, L. W., & Kristal, S. Establishing a token economy program in a state hospital classroom: A lesson in training student and teacher. *Behavior Therapy,* 1972, 3, 209–22.

Cotter, L. H. Operant conditioning in a Vietnamese mental hospital. *American Journal of Psychiatry,* 1967, **124**, 23–28.

Coughlin, R. C. The aversive properties of withdrawing positive reinforcement: A review of the recent literature. *Psychological Record,* 1972, **22**, 333–54.

Cumming, E., & Cumming, J. *Closed ranks.* Cambridge, Mass.: Harvard University Press, 1957.

Datel, W. E., & Legters, L. J. The psychology of the army recruit. Paper presented at meeting of American Medical Association, Chicago, June 1970.

Davison, G. C. Elimination of a sadistic fantasy by a client-controlled counter-conditioning technique: A case study. *Journal of Abnormal and Social Psychology,* 1968, **73**, 84–90.

Dinoff, M., & Rickard, H. C. Learning that privileges entail responsibilities. In J. D. Krumboltz & C. E. Thoresen (Eds.), *Behavioral counseling: Cases and techniques.* New York: Holt, Rinehart & Winston, 1969, pp. 124–29.

Dittes, J. E. Galvanic skin response as a measure of patient's reaction to therapist's permissiveness. *Journal of Abnormal and Social Psychology,* 1957, **55**, 295–303.

Dollard, J., & Miller, N. E. *Personality and psychotherapy: An analysis in terms of learning, thinking, and culture.* New York: McGraw-Hill, 1950.

Dornbusch, S. M., Hastorf, A. H., Richardson, S. A., Muzzy, R. E., & Vreeland, R. S. The perceiver and the perceived: Their relative influence on the categories of interpersonal cognition. *Journal of Personality and Social Psychology,* 1965, **1**, 434–40.

Drabman, R. S., Spitalnik, R., & O'Leary, K. D. Teaching self-control to disruptive children. *Journal of Abnormal Psychology.* 1973, **82**, 10–16.

Dunn, L. M. Special education for the mildly retarded—Is much of it justifiable? In W. C. Becker (Ed.), *An empirical basis for change in education.* Chicago: Science Research Associates, 1971, pp. 41–59.

D'Zurilla, T. J. Reducing heterosexual anxiety. In J. D. Krumboltz & C. E. Thoresen (Eds.), *Behavioral counseling: Cases and techniques.* New York: Holt, Rinehart & Winston, 1969, pp. 442–54.

Etzel, B. C., & Gewirtz, J. L. Experimental modification of caretaker-maintained high-rate operant crying in a 6- and a 20-week-old infant (infans tyrannotearus): Extinction of crying with reinforcement of eye contact and smiling. *Journal of Experimental Child Psychology,* 1967, **5**, 303–17.

Everett, P. B., Hayward, S. C., & Meyers, A. W. The effects of a token reinforcement procedure on bus ridership. *Journal of Applied Behavior Analysis,* 1974, **7**, 1–9.

Eysenck, H. J. Learning theory and behaviour therapy. *Journal of Mental Science,* 1959, **105**, 61–75.

Eysenck, H. J. *The effects of psychother-*

apy. New York: International Science Press, 1966.

Fairweather, G. W., & Simon, R. A further follow-up of psychotherapeutic programs. *Journal of Consulting Psychology*, 1963, **27**, 186.

Feldman, M. P., & MacCulloch, M. J. The application of anticipatory avoidance learning to the treatment of homosexuality: I. Theory, technique and preliminary results. *Behaviour Research and Therapy*, 1965, **2**, 165–83.

Felixbrod, J. J., & O'Leary, K. D. Effects of reinforcement on children's academic behavior as a function of self-determined and externally imposed contingencies. *Journal of Applied Behavior Analysis*, 1973, **6**, 241–50.

Ferster, C. B. Positive reinforcement and behavioral deficits of autistic children. *Child Development*, 1961, **32**, 437–56.

Ferster, C. B., Nurnberger, J. I., & Levitt, E. B. The control of eating. *Journal of Mathetics*, 1962, **1**, 87–110.

Ferster, C. B., & Skinner, B. F. *Schedules of reinforcement*. New York: Appleton-Century-Crofts, 1957.

Fixsen, D. L., Phillips, E. L., & Wolf, M. M. Achievement Place: The reliability of self-reporting and peer-reporting and their effects on behavior. *Journal of Applied Behavior Analysis*, 1972, **5**, 19–30.

Fixsen, D. L., Phillips, E. L., & Wolf, M. M. Achievement place: Experiments in self-government with pre-delinquents. *Journal of Applied Behavior Analysis*, 1973, **6**, 31–47.

Flanagan, B., Goldiamond, I., & Azrin, N. H. Operant stuttering: The control of stuttering behavior through response-contingent consequences. *Journal of the Experimental Analysis of Behavior*, 1958, **1**, 173–77.

Fox, L. Effecting the use of efficient study habits. *Journal of Mathetics*, 1962, **1**, 75–86.

Foxx, R. M. & Azrin, N. H. Restitution: A method of eliminating aggressive-disruptive behavior of retarded and brain damaged patients. *Behaviour Research and Therapy*, 1972, **10**, 15–27.

Foxx, R. M., & Azrin, N. H. The elimination of autistic self-stimulatory behavior by overcorrection. *Journal of*

Applied Behavior Analysis, 1973, **6**, 1–14.

Gardner, J. M. Teaching behavior modification to nonprofessionals. *Journal of Applied Behavior Analysis*, 1972, **5**, 517–21.

Gates, J. J. Overspending (stealing) in a token economy. *Behavior Therapy*, 1972, **3**, 152–53.

Gewirtz, J. L., & Baer, D. M. Deprivation and satiation of social reinforcers as drive conditions. *Journal of Abnormal and Social Psychology*, 1958, **57**, 165–72.

Glynn, E. L. Classroom applications of self-determined reinforcement. *Journal of Applied Behavior Analysis*, 1970, **3**, 123–32.

Glynn, E. L., Thomas, J. D., & Shee, S. M. Behavioral self-control of on-task behavior in an elementary classroom. *Journal of Applied Behavior Analysis*, 1973, **6**, 105–13.

Goffman, E. *Asylums*. New York: Doubleday, 1961.

Goldfried, M. R., & Merbaum, M. (Eds.), *Behavior change through self-control*. New York: Holt, Rinehart & Winston, 1973.

Goldfried, M. R., & Pomeranz, D. M. Role of assessment in behavior modification, *Psychological Reports*, 1968, **23**, 75–87.

Goldiamond, I. Self-control procedures in personal behavior problems. *Psychological Reports*, 1965, **17**, 851–68.

Goocher, B. E., & Ebner, M. A behavior modification approach utilizing sequential response targets in multiple settings. Paper presented at a meeting of Midwestern Psychological Association, Chicago, May 1968.

Gray, F., Graubard, P. S., & Rosenberg, H. Little brother is changing you. *Psychology Today*, 1974, **7**, 42–46.

Greene, R. J., & Hoats, D. L. Reinforcing capabilities of television distortion. *Journal of Applied Behavior Analysis*, 1969, **2**, 139–41.

Guerney, B. G., Jr. (Ed.) *Psychotherapeutic agents: New roles for nonprofessionals, parents, and teachers*. New York: Holt, Rinehart & Winston, 1969.

Hall, C. S., & Lindzey, G. *Theories of personality*. New York: John Wiley & Sons, 1970.

Hall, R. V., Axelrod, S., Foundopoulos, M., Shellman, J., Campbell, R. A., & Cranston, S. S. The effective use of punishment to modify behavior in the classroom. *Educational Technology,* 1971, **11**, 24–26.

Hall, R. V., Axelrod, S., Tyler, L., Grief, E., Jones, F. C., & Robertson, R. Modification of behavior problems in the home with a parent as observer and experimenter. *Journal of Applied Behavior Analysis,* 1972, **5**, 53–64.

Hall, R. V., Cristler, C., Cranston, S. S., & Tucker, B. Teachers and parents as researchers using multiple-baseline designs. *Journal of Applied Behavior Analysis,* 1970, **3**, 247–55.

Hall, R. V., Fox, R., Willard, D., Goldsmith, L., Emerson, M., Owen, M. Davis, F., & Porcia, E. The teacher as observer and experimenter in the modification of disputing and talking-out behaviors. *Journal of Applied Behavior Analysis,* 1971, **4**, 141–49.

Hall, R. V., Lund, D., & Jackson, D. Effects of teacher attention on study behavior. *Journal of Applied Behavior Analysis,* 1968, **1**, 1–12.

Hamilton, J., & Allen, P. Ward programming for severely retarded institutionalized residents. *Mental Retardation,* 1967, **6**, 22–25.

Hamilton, J., Stephens, L. Y., & Allen, P. Controlling aggressive and destructive behavior in severely retarded institutionalized residents. *American Journal of Mental Deficiency,* 1967, **71**, 852–56.

Harris, M. B. Self-directed program for weight control: A pilot study. *Journal of Abnormal Psychology,* 1969, **74**, 263–70.

Hart, B. M., Allen, K. E., Buell, J. S., Harris, F. R., & Wolf, M. M. Effects of social reinforcement on operant crying. *Journal of Experimental Child Psychology,* 1964, **1**, 145–53.

Hart, B. M., Reynolds, N. J., Baer, D. M., Brawley, E. R., & Harris, F. R. Effect of contingent and non-contingent social reinforcement on the cooperative play of a preschool child. *Journal of Applied Behavior Analysis,* 1968, **1**, 73–76.

Hart, B. M., & Risley, T. R. Establishing use of descriptive adjectives in the spontaneous speech of disadvantaged preschool children. *Journal of Applied Behavior Analysis,* 1968, **1**, 109–20.

Hauserman, N., Waylen, S. R., & Behling, M. Reinforced racial integration in the first grade: A study in generalization. *Journal of Applied Behavior Analysis,* 1973, **6**, 193–200.

Heckel, R. B., Wiggins, S. L., & Salzberg, H. C. Conditioning against silences in group therapy. *Journal of Clinical Psychology,* 1962, **18**, 216–17.

Henderson, J. D., & Scoles, P. E. A community-based behavioral operant environment for psychotic men. *Behavior Therapy,* 1970, **1**, 245–51.

Henriksen, K., & Doughty, R. Decelerating undesired mealtime behavior in a group of profoundly retarded boys. *American Journal of Mental Deficiency,* 1967, **72**, 40–44.

Herbert, E. W., & Baer, D. M. Training parents as behavior modifiers: Self-recording of contingent attention. *Journal of Applied Behavior Analysis,* 1972, **5**, 139–49.

Hermann, J. A., de Montes, A. I., Dominguez, B., Montes, F., & Hopkins, B. L. Effects of bonuses for punctuality on the tardiness of industrial workers. *Journal of Applied Behavior Analysis.* 1973, **6**, 563–70.

Hersen, M., Eisler, R. M., Alford, G. S., & Agras, W. S. Effects of token economy on neurotic depression: An experimental analysis. *Behavior Therapy,* 1973, **4**, 392–97.

Hewett, F. M. *The emotionally disturbed child in the classroom.* Boston: Allyn & Bacon, 1968.

Hewett, F. M., Taylor, F. D., & Artuso, A. A. The Santa Monica Project: Evaluation of an engineered classroom design with emotionally disturbed children. *Exceptional Children,* 1969, **35**, 523–29.

Hoffman, M. L. Power assertion by the parent and its impact on the child. *Child Development,* 1960, **31**, 129–43.

Homme, L. E. Perspectives in psychology—XXIV Control of coverants: The operants of the mind. *Psychological Record,* 1965, **15**, 501–11.

Homme, L., Csanyi, A., Gonzales, M., & Rechs, J. *How to use contingency contracting in the classroom.* Champaign, Illinois: Research Press, 1969.

Homme, L. E., deBaca, P. C., Devine, J. V., Steinhorst, R., & Rickert, E. J. Use of the Premack Principle in controlling the behavior of nursery school children. *Journal of the Experimental Analysis of Behavior*, 1963, **6**, 544.

Hopkins, B. L. Effects of candy and social reinforcement, instructions, and reinforcement schedule learning on the modification and maintenance of smiling. *Journal of Applied Behavior Analysis*, 1968, **1**, 121–29.

Hunt, J. G., & Zimmerman, J. Stimulating productivity in a simulated sheltered workshop setting. *American Journal of Mental Deficiency*, 1969, **74**, 43–49.

Hutchinson, H. C. Reciprocal inhibition therapy as an alternative to psychotherapy in the treatment of certain neurotic conditions. Paper read at the meeting of the American Psychological Association, St. Louis, 1962.

Hutchinson, R. R., Azrin, N. H., & Hunt, G. M. Attack produced by intermittent reinforcement of a concurrent operant response. *Journal of the Experimental Analysis of Behavior*, 1968, **11**, 489–95.

Hutt, P. J. Rate of bar pressing as a function of quality and quantity of food reward. *Journal of Comparative and Physiological Psychology*, 1954, **47**, 235–39.

Isaacs, W., Thomas, J., & Goldiamond, I. Application of operant conditioning to reinstate verbal behavior in psychotics. *Journal of Speech and Hearing Disorders*, 1960, **25**, 8–12.

Jacobs, A., & Sachs, L. B. (Eds.), *The psychology of private events: Perspectives on covert response systems.* New York: Academic Press, 1971.

Jacobson, E. *Progressive relaxation.* Chicago: University of Chicago Press, 1938.

Jens, K. E., & Shores, R. E. Behavioral graphs as reinforcers for work behavior of mentally retarded adolescents. *Education and Training of the Mentally Retarded*, 1969, **4**, 21–28.

Johnson, S. M., & Martin, S. Developing self-evaluation as a conditioned reinforcer. In B. Ashem & E. G. Poser (Eds.), *Behavior modification with children.* New York: Pergamon, 1972.

Johnston, J. M. Punishment of human behavior. *American Psychologist*, 1972, **27**, 1033–54.

Jones, M. C. The elimination of children's fear. *Journal of Counseling Psychology*, 1924, **7**, 383–90.

Jones, R. J., & Azrin, N. H. An experimental application of a social reinforcement to the problem of job-finding. *Journal of Applied Behavior Analysis*, 1973, **6**, 345–53.

Jones, R. T., & Kazdin, A. E. Programming response maintenance after withdrawing token reinforcement. *Behavior Therapy*, 1975, in press.

Kale, R. J., Kaye, J. H., Whelan, P. A., & Hopkins, B. L. The effects of reinforcement on the modification, maintenance, and generalization of social responses of mental patients. *Journal of Applied Behavior Analysis*, 1968, **1**, 307–14.

Kanfer, F. H., & Goldfoot, D. A. Self-control and tolerance of noxious stimulation. *Psychological Reports*, 1966, **18**, 79–85.

Kanfer, F. H., & Karoly, P. Self-control: A behavioristic excursion into the lion's den. *Behavior Therapy*, 1972, **3**, 398–416.

Kanfer, F. H., & Marston, A. R. Conditioning of self-reinforcing responses: An analogue to self-confidence training. *Psychological Reports*, 1963, **13**, 63–70.

Kanfer, F. H., & Phillips, J. S. Behavior therapy: A panacea for all ills or a passing fancy? *Archives of General Psychiatry*, 1966, **15**, 114–28.

Kanfer, F. H., & Phillips, J. S. A survey of current behavior therapies and a proposal for classification. In C. M. Franks (Ed.), *Behavior therapy: Appraisal and status.* New York: McGraw-Hill, 1969, pp. 445–75.

Kanfer, F. H., & Phillips, J. S. *Learning foundations of behavior therapy.* New York: John Wiley & Sons, 1970.

Kanfer, F. H., & Saslow, G. Behavioral diagnosis. In C. M. Franks (Ed.), *Behavior therapy: Appraisal and status.* New York: McGraw-Hill, 1969, pp. 417–44.

Katz, R. C., Johnson, C. A., & Gelfand, S. Modifying the dispensing of reinforcers: Some implications for behavior modification with hospitalized patients. *Behavior Therapy,* 1972, **3,** 579–88.

Kaufman, K. F., & O'Leary, K. D. Reward, cost, and self-evaluation procedures for disruptive adolescents in a psychiatric hospital school. *Journal of Applied Behavior Analysis,* 1972, **5,** 293–309.

Kaufman, M. E. The effects of institutionalization on development of stereotyped and social behaviors in mental defectives. *American Journal of Mental Deficiency,* 1967, **71,** 581–85.

Kazdin, A. E. The effect of response cost in suppressing behavior in a pre-psychotic retardate. *Journal of Behavior Therapy and Experimental Psychiatry,* 1971, 2, 137–40. (a)

Kazdin, A. E. Toward a client administered token reinforcement program. *Education and Training of the Mentally Retarded,* 1971, **6,** 52–55. (b)

Kazdin, A. E. Response cost: The removal of conditioned reinforcers for therapeutic change. *Behavior Therapy,* 1972, **3,** 533–46. (a)

Kazdin, A. E. Nonresponsiveness of patients to token economies. *Behaviour Research and Therapy,* 1972, **10,** 417–18. (b)

Kazdin, A. E. Covert modeling and the reduction of avoidance behavior. *Journal of Abnormal Psychology,* 1973, **81,** 87–95. (a)

Kazdin, A. E. The effect of response cost and aversive stimulation in suppressing punished and nonpunished speech disfluencies. *Behavior Therapy,* 1973, **4,** 73–82. (b)

Kazdin, A. E. The effect of vicarious reinforcement on attentive behavior in the classroom. *Journal of Applied Behavior Analysis,* 1973, **6,** 71–78. (c)

Kazdin, A. E. The effect of vicarious reinforcement on performance in a rehabilitation setting. *Education and Training of the Mentally Retarded,* 1973, **8,** 4–11. (d)

Kazdin, A. E. The failure of some patients to respond to token programs. *Journal of Behavior Therapy and Experimental Psychiatry,* 1973, **4,** 7–14. (e)

Kazdin, A. E. Issues in behavior modifi-

cation with mentally retarded persons. *American Journal of Mental Deficiency,* 1973, **78,** 134–40. (f)

Kazdin, A. E. Methodological and assessment considerations in evaluating reinforcement programs in applied settings. *Journal of Applied Behavior Analysis,* 1973, **6,** 517–31. (g)

Kazdin, A. E. Role of instructions and reinforcement in behavior changes in token reinforcement programs. *Journal of Educational Psychology,* 1973, **64,** 63–71. (h)

Kazdin, A. E. Time out for some considerations on punishment. *American Psychologist,* 1973, **28,** 939–41. (i)

Kazdin, A. E. Covert modeling, model similarity, and reduction of avoidance behavior. *Behavior Therapy,* 1974, **5,** 325–40. (a)

Kazdin, A. E. Effects of covert modeling and model reinforcement on assertive behavior. *Journal of Abnormal Psychology,* 1974, **83,** 240–252. (b)

Kazdin, A. E. Self-monitoring and behavior change. In M. J. Mahoney & C. E. Thoresen (Eds.), *Self-control: Power to the person.* Monterey, California: Brooks/Cole, 1974, pp. 218–46. (c)

Kazdin, A. E. Recent advances in token economy research. In M. Hersen, R. M. Eisler, & P. M. Miller (Eds.), *Progress in behavior modification.* New York: Academic Press, 1975, in press.

Kazdin, A. E., & Bootzin, R. R. The token economy: An evaluative review. *Journal of Applied Behavior Analysis,* 1972, **5,** 343–72.

Kazdin, A. E., & Bootzin, R. R. The token economy: An examination of issues. In R. D. Rubin, J. P. Brady, & J. D. Henderson (Eds.), *Advances in behavior therapy. Vol. 4.* New York: Academic Press, 1973, pp. 159–76.

Kazdin, A. E., & Craighead, W. E. Behavior modification in special education. In L. Mann & D. A. Sabatino (Eds.), *The first review of special education, Volume 2.* Philadelphia: Buttonwood Farms, 1973, pp. 51–102.

Kazdin, A. E., & Klock, J. The effect of nonverbal teacher approval on student attentive behavior. *Journal of Applied Behavior Analysis,* 1973, **6,** 643–54.

Kazdin, A. E., & Moyer, W. Training teachers to use behavior modification. In S. Yen (Ed.), *Training behavior modifiers*, Kalamazoo, Michigan: Behaviordelia, 1975, in press.

Kazdin, A. E., & Polster, R. Intermittent token reinforcement and response maintenance in extinction. *Behavior Therapy*, 1973, **4**, 386–91.

Keirsey, D. W. Systematic exclusion: Eliminating chronic classroom disruptions. In J. D. Krumboltz and C. E. Thoresen (Eds.), *Behavioral counseling: Cases and techniques*. New York: Holt, Rinehart & Winston, 1969, pp. 89–113.

Kelley, K. M., & Henderson, J. D. A community-based operant learning environment II: Systems and procedures. In R. D. Rubin, H. Fensterheim, A. A. Lazarus, & C. M. Franks (Eds.), *Advances in behavior therapy*. New York: Academic Press, 1971, pp. 239–50.

Keutzer, C. S. Use of therapy time as a reinforcer: Application of operant conditioning techniques within a traditional psychotherapy context. *Behaviour Research and Therapy*, 1967, **5**, 367–70.

Kimble, G. A. *Hilgard and Marquis' conditioning and learning*. New York: Appleton-Century-Crofts, 1961.

Kimmel, H. D. Instrumental conditioning of autonomically mediated behavior. *Psychological Bulletin*, 1967, **67**, 337–45.

Kircher, A. S., Pear, J. J., & Martin, G. L. Shock as punishment in a picture-naming task with retarded children. *Journal of Applied Behavior Analysis*, 1971, **4**, 227–33.

Koegel, R. L., & Rincover, A. Treatment of psychotic children in a classroom environment: I. Learning in a large group. *Journal of Applied Behavior Analysis*, 1974, **7**, 45–59.

Kohlenberg, R. J. The punishment of persistent vomiting: A case study. *Journal of Applied Behavior Analysis*, 1970, **3**, 241–45.

Kondas, O., & Scetnicka, B. Systematic desensitization as a method of preparation for childbirth. *Journal of Behavior Therapy and Experimental Psychiatry*, 1972, **3**, 51–54.

Kounin, J. S. *Discipline and group management in classrooms*. New York: Holt, Rinehart & Winston, 1970.

Krasner, L. The behavioral scientist and social responsibility: No place to hide. *Journal of Social Issues*, 1966, **21**, 9–30.

Krasner, L., & Ullmann, L. P. *Behavior influence and personality: The social matrix of human action*. New York: Holt, Rinehart & Winston, 1973.

Kushner, M. The operant control of intractable sneezing. In C. D. Spielberger, R. Fox, & B. Masterson (Eds.), *Contributions to general psychology*. New York: Ronald Press, 1968, pp. 361–65.

Kushner, M. Faradic aversive controls in clinical practice. In C. Neuringer & J. L. Michael (Eds.), *Behavior modification in clinical psychology*. New York: Appleton-Century-Crofts, 1970, pp. 26–51.

Lahey, B. B. Modification of the frequency of descriptive adjectives in the speech of Head Start children through modeling without reinforcement. *Journal of Applied Behavior Analysis*, 1971, **4**, 19–22.

Lanyon, R. I., & Goodstein, L. D. *Personality assessment*. New York: John Wiley & Sons, 1971.

Lattal, K. A. Contingency management of toothbrushing behavior in a summer camp for children. *Journal of Applied Behavior Analysis*, 1969, **2**, 195–98.

Lawson, R. *Frustration*. New York: Macmillan, 1965.

Lazarus, A. A., Davison, G. C., & Polefka, D. A. Classical and operant factors in the treatment of a school phobia. *Journal of Abnormal Psychology*, 1965, **70**, 225–29.

Leitenberg, H. Is time-out from positive reinforcement an aversive event? A review of the experimental evidence. *Psychological Bulletin*, 1965, **64**, 428–41.

Leitenberg, H., Agras, W. S., Thompson, L. E. & Wright, D. E. Feedback in behavior modification: An experimental analysis in two phobic cases. *Journal of Applied Behavior Analysis*, 1968, **1**, 131–37.

Levin, G., & Simmons, J. Response to food and praise by emotionally disturbed boys. *Psychological Reports*, 1962, **2**, 539–46.

Levitt, E. E. Research on psychotherapy with children. In S. L. Garfield & A. E. Bergin, (Eds.), *Handbook of psychotherapy and behavior change: An empirical analysis*, New York: John Wiley & Sons, 1971, pp. 474–94.

Liberman, R. P. Community mental health and behavior modification: A skeleton in search of muscles that work. Paper presented as discussion of a panel, Community Psychology in Theory and Practice, Western Psychological Association, San Francisco, April 1971.

Liebert, R. M., & Allen, M. K. The effects of the rule structure and reward magnification on the acquisition and adoption of self-reward criteria. *Psychological Reports*, 1967, **21**, 445–52.

Lindsley, O. R. Direct measurement and prosthesis of retarded behavior. *Journal of Education*, 1964, **147**, 62–81.

Linscheid, T. R., Malosky, P., & Zimmerman, J. Discharge as the major consequence in a hospitalized patient's behavior management program: A case study. *Behavior Therapy*, 1974, **5**, 559–64.

Lipinski, D., & Nelson, R. Problems in the use of naturalistic observation as a means of behavioral assessment. *Behavior Therapy*, 1974, **5**, 341–51.

Locke, B. Verbal conditioning with retarded subjects: Establishment or reinstatement of effective reinforcing consequences. *American Journal of Mental Deficiency*, 1969, **73**, 621–26.

Locke, E. A., Cartledge, N., & Koeppel, J. Motivational effects of knowledge of results: A goal setting phenomenon? *Psychological Bulletin*, 1968, **70**, 474–85.

Loeber, R. Engineering the behavioral engineer. *Journal of Applied Behavior Analysis*, 1971, **4**, 321–26.

Logan, F. A. *Fundamentals of learning and motivation*. Dubuque, Iowa, William C. Brown, 1969.

London, P. *The modes and morals of psychotherapy*. New York: Holt, Rinehart & Winston, 1964.

London, P. *Behavior control*. New York: Harper & Row, 1969.

Lovaas, O. I. Some studies on the treatment of childhood schizophrenia. In J. M. Shlien (Ed.), *Research in psychotherapy*. Vol. 3. Washington, D.C.: American Psychological Association, 1968, pp. 103–21.

Lovaas, O. I., Koegel, R., Simmons, J. Q., & Long, J. S. Some generalization and follow-up measures on autistic children in behavior therapy. *Journal of Applied Behavior Analysis*, 1973, **6**, 131–66.

Lovaas, O. I., Schaeffer, B., & Simmons, J. Q. Building social behavior in autistic children by use of electric shock. *Journal of Experimental Research in Personality*, 1965, **1**, 99–109.

Lovaas, O. I., & Simmons, J. Q. Manipulation of self-destruction in three retarded children. *Journal of Applied Behavior Analysis*, 1969, **2**, 143–57.

Lovibond, S. H. *Conditioning and enuresis*. Oxford: Pergamon, 1964.

Lovitt, T. C., & Curtiss, K. A. Academic response rate as a function of teacher- and self-imposed contingencies. *Journal of Applied Behavior Analysis*, 1969, **2**, 49–53.

Lucero, R. J., Vail, D. J., & Scherber, J. Regulating operant-conditioning programs. *Hospital & Community Psychiatry*. 1968, **19**, 53–54.

Luria, A. *The role of normal and abnormal behavior*. New York: Liveright, 1961.

MacDonald, W. S., Gallimore, R., & MacDonald, G. Contingency counseling by school personnel: An economical model of intervention. *Journal of Applied Behavior Analysis*, 1970, **3**, 175–82.

Madsen, C. H., Becker, W. C., & Thomas, D. R. Rules, praise and ignoring: Elements of elementary classroom control. *Journal of Applied Behavior Analysis*, 1968, **1**, 139–50.

Madsen, C. H., Becker, W. C., Thomas, D. R., Koser, L., & Plager, E. An analysis of the reinforcing function of "sit down" commands. In R. K. Parker (Ed.), *Readings in educational psychology*. Boston: Allyn & Bacon, 1970, pp. 265–78.

Madsen, C. H., Jr., Madsen, C. K. & Thompson, F. Increasing rural Head Start children's consumption of middle-class meals. *Journal of Applied Behavior Analysis.* 1974, **7**, 257–62.

Mahoney, K., VanWagenen, R. K., & Meyerson, L. Toilet training of normal and retarded children. *Journal of Applied Behavior Analysis,* 1971, **4**, 173–81.

Mahoney, M. J. The self-management of covert behavior: A case study. *Behavior Therapy,* 1971, **2**, 575–78.

Mahoney, M. J., Kazdin, A. E., & Lesswing, N. J. Behavior modification: Delusion or deliverance. In C. M. Franks & G. T. Wilson (Eds.), *Annual review of behavior therapy theory and research.* Vol. 2. New York: Brunner/Mazel, 1974, pp. 11–40.

Mahoney, M. J., Moura, N. G. M., & Wade, T. C. Relative efficacy of self-reward, self-punishment, and self-monitoring techniques for weight loss. *Journal of Consulting and Clinical Psychology,* 1973, **40**, 404–07.

Maley, R. F., Feldman, G. L., & Ruskin, R. S. Evaluation of patient improvement in a token economy treatment program. *Journal of Abnormal Psychology,* 1973, **82**, 141–44.

Mann, J. H. The effect of inter-racial contact on sociometric choices and perceptions. *Journal of Social Psychology,* 1959, **50**, 143–52.

Mann, R. A. The behavior-therapeutic use of contingency contracting to control an adult behavior problem: Weight control. *Journal of Applied Behavior Analysis.* 1972, **5**, 99–109.

Masling, J. M. The influence of situational and interpersonal variables in projective testing. *Psychological Bulletin,* 1960, **57**, 65–85.

McGuire, R. J., & Vallance, M. Aversion therapy by electric shock: A simple technique. *British Medical Journal,* 1964, **1**, 151–53.

McNamara, J. R. Teacher and students as a source for behavior modification in the classroom. *Behavior Therapy,* 1971, **2**, 205–13.

McReynolds, W. T., & Church, A. Self-control, study skills development and counseling approaches to the improvement of study behavior. *Behaviour Research and Therapy,* 1973, **11**, 233–35.

Medland, M. B., & Stachnik, T. J. Good-behavior game: A replication and systematic analysis. *Journal of Applied Behavior Analysis,* 1972, **5**, 45–51.

Meehl, P. E. The cognitive activity of the clinician. *American Psychologist,* 1960, **15**, 19–27.

Meichenbaum, D. H. The effects of instruction and reinforcement on thinking and language behaviour of schizophrenics. *Behaviour Research and Therapy,* 1969, **7**, 101–14.

Meichenbaum, D. H. Examination of model characteristics in reducing avoidance behavior. *Journal of Personality and Social Psychology,* 1971, **17**, 298–307.

Meichenbaum, D. H. Cognitive factors in behavior modification: Modifying what clients say to themselves. In R. D. Rubin, J. P. Brady, and J. D. Henderson (Eds.), *Advances in behavior therapy.* Vol. 4. New York: Academic Press, 1973, pp. 21–36.

Meichenbaum, D. H., Bowers, K., & Ross, R. R. Modification of classroom behavior of institutionalized female adolescent offenders. *Behaviour Research and Therapy,* 1968, **6**, 343–53.

Meichenbaum, D. H., & Cameron, R. Training schizophrenics to talk to themselves: A means of developing attentional controls. *Behavior Therapy,* 1973, **4**, 515–34.

Meichenbaum, D. H., & Goodman, J. Training impulsive children to talk to themselves: A means of developing self-control. *Journal of Abnormal Psychology,* 1971, **77**, 115–26.

Migler, B., & Wolpe, J. Automated self-desensitization: A case report. *Behaviour Research and Therapy,* 1967, **5**, 133–35.

Milby, J. B. Modification of extreme social isolation by contingent social reinforcement. *Journal of Applied Behavior Analysis,* 1970, **3**, 149–52.

Miller, L. K., & Feallock, F. A behavioral system for group living. In E. Ramp & G. Semb (Eds.), *Behavioral analysis and education.* New York: Prentice-Hall, 1975, in press.

Miller, L. K., & Miller, O. L. Reinforcing self-help group activities of welfare recipients. *Journal of Applied Behavior Analysis,* 1970, **3**, 57–64.

Miller, N. E. Learning of visceral and glandular responses. *Science,* 1969, **163,** 434–45.

Miller, N. E., & Stevenson, S. S. Agitated behavior of rats during experimental extinction and a curve of spontaneous recovery. *Journal of Comparative and Physiological Psychology,* 1936, **21,** 205–31.

Miller, P. M. The use of behavioral contracting in the treatment of alcoholism: A case report. *Behavior Therapy,* 1972, **3,** 593–96.

Miller, P. M., & Drennen, W. T. Establishment of social reinforcement as an effective modifier of verbal behavior in chronic psychiatric patients. *Journal of Abnormal Psychology,* 1970, **76,** 392–95.

Miron, N. B. Issues and implications of operant conditioning: The primary ethical consideration. *Hospital & Community Psychiatry,* 1968, **19,** 226–28.

Mischel, W. *Personality and assessment.* New York: John Wiley & Sons, 1968.

Mischel, W. *Introduction to personality.* New York: Holt, Rinehart & Winston, 1971.

Mischel, W., & Ebbesen, E. Attention in delay of gratification. *Journal of Personality and Social Psychology,* 1970, **16,** 329–37.

Mischel, W., & Liebert, R. M. Effects of discrepancies between observed and imposed reward criteria on their acquisition and transmission. *Journal of Personality and Social Psychology,* 1966, **3,** 45–53.

Morgan, W. G., & Bass, B. A. Self-control through self-mediated rewards. In R. D. Rubin, J. P. Brady, & J. D. Henderson (Eds.), *Advances in behavior therapy. Vol. 4.* New York: Academic Press, 1973, pp. 117–26.

Mowrer, O. H., & Mowrer, W. A. Enuresis: A method for its study and treatment. *American Journal of Orthopsychiatry,* 1938, **8,** 436–47.

Nordquist, V. M. The modification of a child's enuresis: Some response-response relationships. *Journal of Applied Behavior Analysis,* 1971, **4,** 241–47.

Nunnally, J. C., Jr. *Popular conceptions of mental health.* New York: Holt, Rinehart & Winston, 1961.

O'Brien, F., & Azrin, N. H. Developing proper mealtime behaviors of the institutionalized retarded. *Journal of Applied Behavior Analysis,* 1972, **5,** 389–99. (a)

O'Brien, F., & Azrin, N. H. Symptom reduction by functional displacement in a token economy: A case study. *Journal of Behavior Therapy and Experimental Psychiatry,* 1972, **3,** 205–07. (b)

O'Brien, F., & Azrin, N. H. Interaction-priming: A method of reinstating patient-family relationships. *Behaviour Research and Therapy,* 1973, **11,** 133–36.

O'Brien, F., Azrin, N. H., & Bugle, C. Training profoundly retarded children to stop crawling. *Journal of Applied Behavior Analysis,* 1972, **5,** 131–37.

O'Brien, F., Azrin, N. H., & Henson, K. Increased communications of chronic mental patients by reinforcement and response priming. *Journal of Applied Behavior Analysis,* 1969, **2,** 23–29.

O'Brien, F., Bugle, C., & Azrin, N. H. Training and maintaining a retarded child's proper eating. *Journal of Applied Behavior Analysis,* 1972, **5,** 67–72.

O'Brien, J. S., Raynes, A. E., & Patch, V. D. An operant reinforcement system to improve ward behavior in in-patient drug addicts. *Journal of Behavior Therapy and Experimental Psychiatry,* 1971, **2,** 239–42.

O'Connor, R. Modification of social withdrawal through symbolic modeling. *Journal of Applied Behavior Analysis,* 1969, **2,** 15–22.

O'Leary, K. D. The effects of self-instruction on immoral behavior. *Journal of Experimental Child Psychology,* 1968, **6,** 297–301.

O'Leary, K. D., Becker, W. C., Evans, M. B., & Saudargas, R. A. A token reinforcement program in a public school: A replication and systematic analysis. *Journal of Applied Behavior Analysis,* 1969, **2,** 3–13.

O'Leary, K. D., & Drabman, R. Token reinforcement programs in the classroom: A review. *Psychological Bulletin,* 1971, **75,** 379–98.

O'Leary, K. D., Kaufman, K. F., Kass, R., & Drabman, R. The effects of loud and soft reprimands on the behavior of disruptive students. *Exceptional Children,* 1970, **37**, 145–55.

O'Leary, K. D., & Kent, R. N. Behavior modification for social action: Research tactics and problems. In L. A. Hamerlynk, P. O. Davidson, & L. E. Acker (Eds.), *Critical issues in research and practice.* Champaign, Ill.: Research Press, 1973, pp. 69–96.

O'Leary, K. D., O'Leary, S., & Becker, W. C. Modification of a deviant sibling interaction pattern in the home. *Behaviour Research and Therapy,* 1967, **5**, 113–20.

O'Leary, K. D., Poulos, R. W., & Devine, V. T. Tangible reinforcers: Bonuses or bribes? *Journal of Consulting and Clinical Psychology,* 1972, **38**, 1–8.

Olson, R. P., & Greenberg, D. J. Effects of contingency contracting and decision-making groups with chronic mental patients. *Journal of Consulting and Clinical Psychology,* 1972, **38**, 376-83.

Osborne, J. G. Free time as a reinforcer in the management of classroom behavior. *Journal of Applied Behavior Analysis,* 1969, **2**, 113–18.

Page, E. B. Teacher comment and student performance: A seventy-four classroom experiment in school motivation. *Journal of Educational Psychology,* 1958, **49**, 173–81.

Panyan, M., Boozer, H., & Morris, N. Feedback to attendants as a reinforcer for applying operant techniques. *Journal of Applied Behavior Analysis,* 1970, **3**, 1–4.

Patterson, G. R. A learning-theory approach to the treatment of the school phobic child. In L. P. Ullmann & L. Krasner (Eds.), *Case studies in behavior modification.* New York: Holt, Rinehart & Winston, 1965, pp. 279–84. (a)

Patterson, G. R. An application of conditioning techniques to the control of a hyperactive child. In L. P. Ullmann & L. Krasner (Eds.), *Case studies in behavior modification.* New York: Holt, Rinehart & Winston, 1965, pp. 370–75. (b)

Patterson, G. R., Cobb, J. A., & Ray, R. S. A social engineering technology for retraining aggressive boys. In H. Adams & L. Unikel (Eds.) *Issues and trends in behavior therapy.* Springfield, Illinois: Charles C. Thomas, 1973, pp. 139–224.

Patterson, G. R., & Reid, J. B. Reciprocity and coercion: Two facets of social systems. In C. Neuringer & J. L. Michael (Eds.), *Behavior modification in clinical psychology.* New York: Appleton-Century-Crofts, 1970, pp. 133–77.

Paul, G. L. *Insight vs. desensitization in psychotherapy: An experiment in anxiety reduction.* Stanford, Calif.: Stanford University Press, 1966.

Paul, G. L. Chronic mental patient: Current status—future directions. *Psychological Bulletin,* 1969, **71**, 81–94. (a)

Paul, G. L. Outcome of systematic desensitization II: Controlled investigations of individual treatment, technique variations, and current status. In C. M. Franks (Ed.), *Behavior therapy: Appraisal and status.* New York: McGraw-Hill, 1969, pp. 105–59. (b)

Pendergrass, V. E. Timeout from positive reinforcement following persistent, high-rate behavior in retardates. *Journal of Applied Behavior Analysis,* 1972, **5**, 85–91.

Peterson, D. R. *The clinical study of social behavior.* New York: Appleton-Century-Crofts, 1968.

Phillips, D. L. Rejection: A possible consequence of seeking help for mental disorders. *American Sociological Review,* 1963, **28**, 963–72.

Phillips, E. L. Achievement Place: Token reinforcement procedures in a home-style rehabilitation setting for "predelinquent" boys. *Journal of Applied Behavior Analysis,* 1968, **1**, 213–23.

Phillips, E. L., Phillips, E. A., Fixsen, D. L., & Wolf, M. M. Achievement Place: Modification of the behaviors of predelinquent boys within a token economy. *Journal of Applied Behavior Analysis,* 1971, **4**, 45–59.

Pierce, C. H., & Risley, T. R. Improving job performance of Neighborhood Youth Corps aides in an urban recreation program. *Journal of Applied Behavior Analysis,* 1974, **7**, 207–15.

Pierce, M. L. A behavior modification approach to facilitating a disturbed child's school re-entry by teaching time-out procedures to the child's classmates. *School Applications of Learning Theory,* 1971, **3**, 1–6.

Platt, J. R. The Skinnerian revolution. In H. Wheeler (Ed.), *Beyond the punitive society.* San Francisco, Calif.: W. H. Freeman and Co., 1973, pp. 22–56.

Poser, E. G. The effect of therapist's training on group therapeutic outcome. *Journal of Consulting Psychology,* 1966, **30**, 283–89.

Powell, J., & Azrin, N. The effects of shock as a punisher for cigarette smoking. *Journal of Applied Behavior Analysis,* 1968, **1**, 63–71.

Premack, D. Toward empirical behavior laws: I. Positive reinforcement. *Psychological Review,* 1959, **66**, 219–33.

Premack, D. Reinforcement theory. In D. Levine (Ed.), *Nebraska symposium on motivation.* Lincoln: University of Nebraska Press, 1965, pp. 123–80.

Rachman, S. Clinical applications of observational learning, imitation, and modeling. *Behavior Therapy,* 1972, **3**, 379–97.

Rachman, S., & Teasdale, J. *Aversion therapy and behaviour disorders.* Coral Gables, Fla.: University of Miami, 1969.

Random House dictionary of the English language. College Edition. New York: Random House, 1968.

Redd, W. H. Effects of mixed reinforcement contingencies on adults' control of children's behavior. *Journal of Applied Behavior Analysis,* 1969, **2**, 249–54.

Redd, W. H., & Birnbrauer, J. S. Adults as discriminative stimuli for different reinforcement contingencies with retarded children. *Journal of Experimental Child Psychology,* 1969, **7**, 440–47.

Rehm, L. P., & Marston, A. R. Reduction of social anxiety through modification of self-reinforcement: An instigation therapy technique. *Journal of Consulting and Clinical Psychology,* 1968, **32**, 565–74.

Reisinger, J. J. The treatment of "anxiety-depression" via positive reinforcement and response cost. *Journal of Applied Behavior Analysis,* 1972, **5**, 125–30.

Reynolds, G. S. *A primer of operant conditioning.* Glenview, Ill.: Scott, Foresman & Co., 1968.

Rickard, H. C., Dignam, P. J., & Horner, R. F. Verbal manipulation in a psychotherapeutic relationship. *Journal of Clinical Psychology,* 1960, **16**, 364–67.

Rickard, H. C., & Dinoff, M. A follow-up note on "Verbal manipulation in a psychotherapeutic relationship." *Psychological Reports,* 1962, **11**, 506.

Rioch, M. J., Elkes, E., Flint, A. A., Usdansky, B. C., Newman, R. G., & Silber, E. National Institute of Mental Health pilot study in training mental health counselors. *American Journal of Orthopsychiatry,* 1963, **33**, 678–89.

Risley, T. R. The effects and side effects of punishing the autistic behaviors of a deviant child. *Journal of Applied Behavior Analysis,* 1968, **1**, 21–34.

Risley, T. R. Behavior modification: An experimental-therapeutic endeavor. In L. A. Hammerlynck, P. O. Davidson, & L. E. Acker (Eds.), *Behavior modification and ideal mental health services.* Calgary, Canada: University of Calgary Press, 1970, pp. 103–27.

Risley, T. R., & Wolf, M. Establishing functional speech in echolalic children. In H. N. Sloane, Jr., & B. D. Mac Aulay (Eds.), *Operant procedures in remedial speech and language training.* Boston: Houghton Mifflin, 1968, pp. 157–84.

Roe, A. Man's forgotten weapon. *American Psychologist,* 1959, **14**, 261–66.

Rogers, C. R. *Client-centered therapy.* Boston: Houghton Mifflin, 1951.

Rogers, C. R., & Skinner, B. F. Some issues concerning the control of human behavior: A symposium. *Science,* 1956, **124**, 1057–66.

Rosenthal, D. Changes in some moral values following psychotherapy. *Journal of Consulting Psychology,* 1955, **19**, 431–36.

Ross, A. O. Behavior therapy. In H. C. Quay & J. S. Werry (Eds.), *Psychopathological disorders of childhood.* New York: John Wiley & Sons, 1972, pp. 273–315.

Ross, J. A., & O'Driscoll, J. Long-term retention after use of a free-time contingency to increase spelling accuracy. *Behaviour Research and Therapy,* 1972, **10,** 75.

Ryan, T. A., & Krumboltz, J. D. Effect of planned reinforcement counseling on client decision-making behavior. *Journal of Counseling Psychology,* 1964, **11,** 315–23.

Sailor, W., Guess, D., Rutherford, G., & Baer, D. M. Control of tantrum behavior by operant techniques during experimental verbal training. *Journal of Applied Behavior Analysis,* 1968, **1,** 237–43.

Sajwaj, T., Twardosz, S., & Burke, M. Side effects of extinction procedures in a remedial preschool. *Journal of Applied Behavior Analysis,* 1972, **5,** 163–75.

Salzberg, B. H., Wheeler, A. A., Devar, L. T., & Hopkins, B. L. The effect of intermittent feedback and intermittent contingent access to play on printing of kindergarten children. *Journal of Applied Behavior Analysis,* 1971, **4,** 163–71.

Sanders, R. M. A timeout procedure for the modification of speech content—A case study. *Journal of Behavior Therapy and Experimental Psychiatry,* 1971, **2,** 173–79.

Santogrossi, D. A., O'Leary, K. D., Romanczyk, R. G., & Kaufman, K. F. Self-evaluation by adolescents in a psychiatric hospital school token program. *Journal of Applied Behavior Analysis,* 1973, **6,** 277–87.

Sarason, I. G., & Ganzer, V. J. Developing appropriate social behaviors of juvenile delinquents. In J. D. Krumboltz & C. E. Thoresen (Eds.), *Behavioral counseling: Cases and techniques.* New York: Holt, Rinehart & Winston, 1969, pp. 178–93.

Schachter, S. Some extraordinary facts about obese humans and rats. *American Psychologist,* 1971, **26,** 129–44.

Schaefer, H. H., & Martin, P. L. Behavioral therapy for "apathy" of hospitalized schizophrenics. *Psychological Reports,* 1966, **19,** 1147–58.

Scheff, T. J. *Being mentally ill: A sociological theory.* Chicago: Aldine, 1966.

Schmidt, G. W., & Ulrich, R. E. Effects of group contingent events upon classroom noise. *Journal of Applied Behavior Analysis,* 1969, **2,** 171–79.

Schmidt, H. O., & Fonda, C. P. The reliability of psychiatric diagnosis: A new look. *Journal of Abnormal and Social Psychology,* 1956, **52,** 262–67.

Schnelle, J. F. A brief report on invalidity of parent evaluations of behavior change. *Journal of Applied Behavior Analysis,* 1974, **7,** 341–43.

Schultz, J. H., & Luthe, W. *Autogenic training.* New York: Grune & Stratton, 1959.

Schwartz, A. N., & Hawkins, H. L. Patient models and affect statements in group therapy. *Proceedings of the 73rd Annual Convention of the American Psychological Association,* 1965, pp. 265–66.

Sherman, J. A. Use of reinforcement and imitation to reinstate verbal behavior in mute psychotics. *Journal of Abnormal Psychology,* 1965, **70,** 155–64.

Sherman, J. A., & Baer, D. M. Appraisal of operant therapy techniques with children and adults. In C. M. Franks (Ed.), *Behavior therapy: Appraisal and status.* New York: McGraw-Hill, 1969, pp. 192–219.

Sherman, T. M., & Cormier, W. H. An investigation of the influence of student behavior on teacher behavior. *Journal of Applied Behavior Analysis,* 1974, **7,** 11–21.

Shier, D. A. Applying systematic exclusion to a case of bizarre behavior. In J. D. Krumboltz & C. E. Thoresen (Eds.), *Behavioral counseling: Cases and techniques.* New York: Holt, Rinehart & Winston, 1969, pp. 114–23.

Sidman, M. *Tactics of scientific research.* New York: Basic Books, 1960.

Skinner, B. F. *Walden two.* New York: Macmillan, 1948.

Skinner, B. F. *Science and human behavior.* New York: Free Press, 1953.

Skinner, B. F. Operant behavior. In W. K. Honig (Ed.), *Operant behavior: Areas of research and application.* New York: Appleton-Century-Crofts, 1966, pp. 12–32. (a)

Skinner, B. F. What is the experimental analysis of behavior? *Journal of the*

Experimental Analysis of Behavior, 1966, **9**, 213–18. (b)

Skinner, B. F. *Beyond freedom and dignity.* New York: Knopf, 1971.

Skinner, B. F. Answers for my critics. In H. Wheeler (Ed.), *Beyond the punitive society.* San Francisco, Calif.: W. H. Freeman, 1973, pp. 256–66.

Skinner, B. F. *About behaviorism.* New York: Knopf, 1974.

Slamecka, N. J. Tests of the discrimination hypothesis. *Journal of General Psychology,* 1960, **63**, 63–68.

Sobell, L. C., Schaefer, H. H., Sobell, M. B., & Kremer, M. E. Food priming: A therapeutic tool to increase the percentage of meals bought by chronic mental patients. *Behaviour Research and Therapy.* 1970, **8**, 339–45.

Sobey, F. *The nonprofessional revolution in mental health.* New York: Columbia University Press, 1970.

Solomon, R. L., Kamin, L. J., & Wynne, L. C. Traumatic avoidance learning: The outcomes of several extinction procedures with dogs. *Journal of Abnormal and Social Psychology,* 1953, **48**, 291–302.

Staats, A. W., & Staats, C. K. *Complex human behaviors: A systematic extension of learning principles.* New York: Holt, Rinehart & Winston, 1963.

Staats, A. W., Staats, C. K., Schultz, R. E., & Wolf, M. The conditioning of textual responses using "extrinsic" reinforcers. *Journal of the Experimental Analysis of Behavior,* 1962, **5**, 33–40.

Steeves, J. M., Martin, G. L., & Pear, J. J. Self-imposed time-out by autistic children during an operant training program. *Behavior Therapy,* 1970, **1**, 371–81.

Stuart, R. B. Operant-interpersonal treatment for marital discord. *Journal of Consulting and Clinical Psychology,* 1969, **33**, 675–82.

Stuart, R. B. *Trick or treatment: How and when psychotherapy fails.* Champaign, Ill.: Research Press, 1970.

Stuart, R. B. Behavioral contracting with the families of delinquents. *Journal of Behavior Therapy and Experimental Psychiatry,* 1971, **2**, 1–11.

Stuart, R. B. Situational versus self-control. In R. D. Rubin, H. Fensterheim,

J. D. Henderson, & L. P. Ullmann (Eds.), *Advances in behavior therapy.* New York: Academic Press, 1972, pp. 129–46.

Stuart, R. B., & Lott, L. A., Jr. Behavioral contracting with delinquents: A cautionary note. *Journal of Behavior Therapy and Experimental Psychiatry,* 1972, **3**, 161–69.

Surratt, P. R., Ulrich, R. E., & Hawkins, R. P. An elementary student as a behavioral engineer. *Journal of Applied Behavior Analysis,* 1969, **2**, 85–92.

Szasz, T. S. The myth of mental illness. *American Psychologist,* 1960, **15**, 113–18.

Tanner, B. A. Aversive shock issues: Physical danger, emotional harm, effectiveness and "dehumanization." *Journal of Behavior Therapy and Experimental Psychiatry,* 1973, **4**, 113–15.

Tate, B. G., & Baroff, G. S. Aversive control of self-injurious behaviour in a psychotic boy. *Behaviour Research and Therapy,* 1966, **4**, 281–87.

Tharp, R. G., & Wetzel, R. J. *Behavior modification in the natural environment.* New York: Academic Press, 1969.

Thoresen, C. E., & Mahoney, M. J. *Behavioral self-control.* New York: Holt, Rinehart & Winston, 1974.

Thorndike, E. L. *The fundamentals of learning.* New York: Teachers College, 1932.

Traux, C. B. The use of supportive personnel in rehabilitation counseling: Process and outcome. In G. R. Leslie (Ed.), *Supportive personnel in rehabilitation centers: Current practices and future needs.* Washington, D.C.: Association of Rehabilitation Centers, 1967, pp. 123–54.

Ullmann, L. P., & Krasner, L. (Eds.), *Case studies in behavior modification.* New York: Holt, Rinehart & Winston, 1965.

Ullmann, L. P., & Krasner, L. *A psychological approach to abnormal behavior.* Englewood Cliffs, N.J.: Prentice-Hall, 1969.

Ulrich, R. Behavior control and public concern. *Psychological Record,* 1967, **17**, 229–34.

Upper, D. A "ticket" system for reducing ward rule violations on a token economy program. *Journal of Behavior Therapy and Experimental Psychiatry*, 1973, 4, 137–40.

Vukelich, R., & Hake, D. F. Reduction of dangerously aggressive behavior in a severely retarded resident through a combination of positive reinforcement procedures. *Journal of Applied Behavior Analysis*, 1971, 4, 215–25.

Wahler, R. G. Behavior therapy for oppositional children: Love is not enough. Paper read at Eastern Psychological Association, Washington, D.C., April 1968.

Wahler, R. G. Setting generality: Some specific and general effects of child behavior therapy. *Journal of Applied Behavior Analysis*, 1969, 2, 239–46.

Wahler, R. G. Some ecological problems in child behavior modification. In S. W. Bijou & E. Ribes-Inesta (Eds.), *Behavior modification: Issues and extensions.* New York: Academic Press, 1972, pp. 8–18.

Wahler, R. G., Winkel, G. H., Peterson, R. F., & Morrison, D. C. Mothers as behavior therapists for their own children. *Behaviour Research and Therapy*, 1965, 3, 113–24.

Walker, H. M., & Buckley, N. K. Programming generalization and maintenance of treatment effects across time and across settings. *Journal of Applied Behavior Analysis*, 1972, 5, 209–24.

Walker, H. M., Mattson, R. H., & Buckley, N. K. The functional analysis of behavior within an experimental class setting. In W. C. Becker (Ed.), *An empirical basis for change in education.* Chicago: Science Research Associates, 1971, pp. 236–63.

Walton, D. The application of learning theory to the treatment of a case of neurodermatitis. In H. J. Eysenck (Ed.), *Behavior therapy and the neuroses.* London: Pergamon, 1960.

Watson, D. L., & Tharp, R. G. *Self-directed behavior: Self-modification for personal adjustment.* Monterey, California: Brooks/Cole, 1972.

Watson, D. L., Tharp, R. G., & Krisberg, J. Case study in self-modification: Suppression of inflammatory scratching while awake and asleep. *Journal of Behavior Therapy and Experimental Psychiatry*, 1972, 3, 213–15.

Watson, J. B., & Raynor, R. Conditioned emotional reactions. *Journal of Experimental Psychology*, 1920, 3, 1–14.

Weil, G., & Goldfried, M. R. Treatment of insomnia in an eleven-year-old child through self-relaxation. *Behavior Therapy*, 1973, 4, 282–84.

Weiner, H. Some effects of response cost upon human operant behavior. *Journal of the Experimental Analysis of Behavior*, 1962, 5, 201–08.

Weisberg, P., & Waldrop, P. B. Fixed-interval work habits of Congress. *Journal of Applied Behavior Analysis*, 1972, 5, 93–97.

Werry, J. The diagnosis, etiology, and treatment of hyperactivity in children. In J. Hellmuth (Ed.), *Learning disorders.* Seattle: Special Child Publications, 1967.

Whaley, D. L., & Tough, J. Treatment of a self-injuring mongoloid with shock-induced suppression and avoidance. *Michigan Department of Mental Health,* 1968, 4.

Wheeler, H. (Ed.), Operant conditioning: Social and political aspects. *Beyond the punitive society.* San Francisco, Calif.: W. H. Freeman and Co., 1973.

White, G. D., Nielsen, G., & Johnson, S. M. Timeout duration and the suppression of deviant behavior in children. *Journal of Applied Behavior Analysis,* 1972, 5, 111–20.

Whitman, T. L., Mercurio, J. R., & Caponigri, V. Development of social responses in two severely retarded children. *Journal of Applied Behavior Analysis,* 1970, 3, 133–38.

Willems, E. P. Behavioral technology and behavioral ecology. *Journal of Applied Behavior Analysis,* 1974, 7, 151–65.

Williams, C. D. The elimination of tantrum behavior by extinction procedures. *Journal of Abnormal and Social Psychology,* 1959, 59, 269.

Wing, J. K. Institutionalism in mental hospitals. *British Journal of Social and Clinical Psychology,* 1962, 1, 38–51.

Winkler, R. C. Reinforcement schedules

for individual patients in a token economy. *Behavior Therapy,* 1971, **2,** 534–37. (a)

Winkler, R. C. The relevance of economic theory and technology of token reinforcement systems. *Behaviour Research and Therapy,* 1971, **9,** 81–88. (b)

Wolf, M. M., Birnbrauer, J. S., Williams, T., & Lawler, J. A note on apparent extinction of the vomiting behavior of a retarded child. In L. P. Ullmann & L. Krasner (Eds.), *Case studies in behavior modification.* New York: Holt, Rinehart & Winston, 1965, pp. 364–66.

Wolf, M. M., Giles, D. K., & Hall, R. V. Experiments with token reinforcement in a remedial classroom. *Behaviour Research and Therapy,* 1968, **6,** 51–64.

Wolf, M. M., Hanley, E. L., King, L. A., Lachowicz, J., & Giles, D. K. The timer-game: A variable interval contingency for the management of out-of-seat behavior. *Exceptional Children,* 1970, **37,** 113–17.

Wolpe, J. *Psychotherapy by reciprocal inhibition.* Stanford, Calif.: Stanford University Press, 1958.

Wolpe, J. Conditioned inhibition of craving in drug addiction: A pilot experiment. *Behaviour Research and Therapy,* 1965, **2,** 285–88.

Wolpe, J. *The practice of behavior therapy,* New York: Pergamon, 1969.

Yates, A. J. *Behavior therapy.* New York: John Wiley & Sons, 1970.

Zeilberger, J., Sampen, S. E., & Sloane, H. N., Jr. Modification of a child's problem behaviors in the home with the mother as therapist. *Journal of Applied Behavior Analysis,* 1968, **1,** 47–53.

Zeisset, R. M. Desensitization and relaxation in the modification of psychiatric patients' interview behavior. *Journal of Abnormal Psychology,* 1968, **73,** 18–24.

Zigler, E., & Phillips, L. Psychiatric diagnosis and symptomatology. *Journal of Abnormal and Social Psychology,* 1961, **63,** 69–75.

Zimmerman, J., Overpeck, C., Eisenberg, H. & Garlick, B. Operant conditioning in a sheltered workshop, *Rehabilitation Literature,* 1969, **30,** 326–34.

Zimmerman, J., Stuckey, T. E., Garlick, B. J. & Miller, M. Effects of token reinforcement on productivity in multiply handicapped clients in a sheltered workshop. *Rehabilitation Literature,* 1969, **30,** 34–41.

Author Index

Nielsen, G., 154, 156
Nordquist, V. M., 15, 98
Nunnally, J. C., 11
Nurnberger, J. I., 195, 201

O

O'Brien, F., 116, 121, 135, 136, 143, 159, 216, 240
O'Brien, J. S., 121, 122
O'Connor, R., 17, 72
O'Driscoll, J., 120
O'Leary, K. D., 27, 49, 58, 79, 82, 90n, 128, 134, 148, 163, 185, 201, 203, 207, 208, 209, 210, 215, 216, 217, 219, 225
O'Leary, S., 219
Olson, R. P., 58, 140
Osborne, J. G., 91, 120, 122
Owen, M., 184
Overpeck, C., 169, 214

P

Page, E. B., 125
Panyan, M., 215
Patch, V. D., 121, 122
Patterson, G. R., 21, 31, 140, 158, 174, 179, 181, 215
Paul, G. L., 7, 174, 205
Pavlov, I., 13
Pear, J. J., 155, 159
Pendergrass, V. E., 151, 163, 164
Peterson, R. F., 6, 7, 18, 68, 70, 72, 76, 81, 87, 158, 166, 186, 214
Phillips, D. L., 20
Phillips, E. A., 148, 165, 166, 220, 224
Phillips, E. L., 17, 58, 66, 70, 74, 126, 128, 134, 141, 148, 152, 156, 165, 166, 210, 215, 220, 224, 225
Phillips, J. S., 7, 15, 33, 173, 174, 190, 192, 193, 194, 197, 231, 234
Pierce, C. H., 249
Pierce, M. L., 179
Plager, E., 27, 148
Platt, J. R., 235
Polefka, D. A., 174
Polster, R., 53, 90, 110, 216, 223
Pomeranz, D. M., 7
Popelka, G., 147, 151
Porcia, E., 184
Poser, E. G., 10
Poulos, R. W., 49, 58
Powell, J., 136, 162, 203
Premack, D., 29, 109

Q–R

Quilitch, H. R., 67, 85, 128
Rachman, S., 14, 16, 33, 139, 150, 170, 237, 238

Ray, R. S., 215
Raynes, A. E., 121, 122
Raynor, R., 13
Reber, A., 158
Rechs, J., 55, 131, 133
Redd, W. H., 5, 44, 74, 83, 189, 215
Rehm, L. P., 201, 207
Reid, J. B., 21, 31, 181
Reisinger, J. J., 217, 219
Reynolds, G. S., 16, 33, 38, 111, 135, 176
Reynolds, N. J., 117
Richardson, S. A., 5
Rickard, H. C., 118, 132, 133
Rickert, E. J., 30
Rincover, A., 222
Rioch, M. J., 10
Risley, T. R., 23, 87, 88, 101, 103, 115, 116, 117, 121, 149, 154, 159, 163, 164, 214, 215, 249
Roberts, M. D., 143
Robertson, R., 15, 34, 124
Roe, A., 235
Rogers, C. R., 7, 233
Rohrer, S., 98, 99, 203, 209
Romanczyk, R. G., 201, 208, 210
Rosenberg, H., 235
Rosenthal, D., 233
Ross, A. O., 14
Ross, J. A., 120
Ross, R. R., 51, 163, 216
Rowbury, T., 157
Ruskin, R. S., 98
Rutherford, G., 70
Ryan, T. A., 119

S

Sachs, D. A., 22
Sailor, W., 70
Sajwaj, T., 48
Salzberg, B. H., 120, 123, 125
Salzberg, H. C., 169
Sampen, S. E., 69, 158
Sanders, R. M., 152, 169
Santogrossi, D. A., 201, 208, 210
Sarason, I. G., 17
Saudargras, R. A., 90n, 128, 134, 185, 216, 217
Scetnicka, B., 205
Schachter, S., 195
Schaefer, H. H., 77, 100, 102, 138
Schaeffer, B., 31, 32, 65, 70, 168, 242
Scheff, T. J., 8, 11, 12, 243
Scherber, J., 229, 239
Schmidt, G. W., 141, 142, 152
Schmidt, H. O., 7
Schnelle, J. F., 67
Schultz, R. E., 129
Schwartz, A. N., 17

Subject Index